Studies in the Legal History of the South

Edited by Paul Finkelman and Kermit L. Hall

This series explores the ways in which law has affected the development of the southern United States and in turn the ways the history of the South has affected the development of American law. Volumes in the series focus on a specific aspect of the law, such as slave law or civil rights legislation, or on a broader topic of historical significance to the development of the legal system in the region, such as issues of constitutional history and of law and society, comparative analyses with other legal systems, and biographical studies of influential southern jurists and lawyers.

The Southern Judicial Tradition

The Southern Judicial Tradition

State Judges and
Sectional Distinctiveness,
1790–1890

TIMOTHY S. HUEBNER

The University of Georgia Press
Athens & London

© 1999 by the University of Georgia Press
Athens, Georgia 30602
All rights reserved
Designed by Walton Harris
Set in 10/13 Sabon by G & S Typesetters, Inc.
Printed and bound by Maple-Vail

The paper in this book meets the guidelines for
permanence and durability of the Committee on
Production Guidelines for Book Longevity of the
Council on Library Resources.

Printed in the United States of America
99 00 01 02 03 C 5 4 3 2 1

Library of Congress Cataloging in Publication Data

Huebner, Timothy S., 1966–
The southern judicial tradition : state judges and
sectional distinctiveness, 1790–1890 / Timothy S.
Huebner.
p.   cm. — (Studies in the legal history of the
South)
Includes bibliographical references and index.
ISBN 0-8203-2101-X (alk. paper)
1. Judges—Southern States—
Biography.   2. Judges—Southern States—
History.   3. Justice, Administration of—Southern
States—History.   4. Southern States—
History.   I. Title.   II. Series.
KF367.H84   1999
347.75′014′0922—dc21
[b]   98-47279

British Library Cataloging in Publication Data available

Dedicated to the memory of Alberta Sloan Wadsworth

CONTENTS

PREFACE

This book concerns the relationship between sectionalism and the southern judiciary. Apart from the law of slavery, about which there has been a vast outpouring of scholarship over the past several years, historians and legal scholars know little about the effects of regional peculiarities and attitudes on legal development. Despite being some of the most influential men in the nineteenth-century South, the state appellate judges examined in this work have largely escaped the notice of scholars. While this is neither an exhaustive study of the hundreds of men who made up the nineteenth-century southern judiciary nor a comprehensive discussion of the legal doctrines they formulated, this examination of six specific judges seeks to address this gap in the literature of both southern history and American legal history. By doing so, I hope to contribute to the ongoing debate over the nature of southern distinctiveness as well as to scholars' understanding of American legal culture.

Much of this study relies on the published reports of nineteenth-century state supreme court cases. A gold mine for historians, these sources are easily available yet seldom used. Appellate reports offer insights into the myriad issues with which dealt the southern legal system dealt—into the relationships between buyers and sellers, rich and poor, criminals and their victims, trial judges and juries, and masters and slaves. Social, cultural, and political historians can learn much from these sources traditionally regarded as the exclusive domain of legal history. In addition to these reports, I utilize judges' personal letters and manuscripts as well as those of their colleagues, friends, and family. Newspapers, statutes, legal treatises, and other contemporary works also inform this work. My use of both legal, public sources and private, personal documents brings out one of the central assumptions of this book: that historians cannot understand judicial behavior apart from the political activities and personal beliefs of those whom they study. Thus, this book examines southern judges both on and off the bench—as formulators of legal doctrine and as prominent citizens whose lives were deeply imbedded in the contemporary social values and political debates of the nineteenth-century South.

All scholarship, of course, is truly a collective effort, and I have accumulated many debts over the past several years. Librarians, archivists, and staff members at the following institutions have provided crucial research support: Alabama State Archives, Alabama Supreme Court Library, Birmingham Public Library, Burrow Library at Rhodes College, Duke University Libraries, Emory University Libraries, Florida International University Library, University of Florida Libraries, University of Georgia Libraries, University of Memphis Libraries, Memphis Public Library, University of Miami Libraries, University of North Carolina Libraries, North Carolina State Archives, Pennsylvania State Archives, University of South Carolina Libraries, Tennessee State Library and Archives, University of Tennessee Libraries, Virginia Historical Society, and College of William and Mary Libraries. I especially wish to thank H. G. Jones of the North Caroliniana Society for providing me with an Archie K. Davis Fellowship, Nelson Lankford at the Virginia Historical Society for awarding me an Andrew Mellon Fellowship, and the Faculty Development Committee at Rhodes College for giving me a Faculty Development Endowment Grant, all of which helped to fund my travels. I thank the *Virginia Magazine of History and Biography* and *Western Legal History* for granting permission to republish portions of chapters 1 and 4, respectively. Also, I acknowledge the Library of Virginia; Tennessee Historical Society; Georgia Department of Archives and History; Tarlton Law Library, University of Texas at Austin; North Carolina State Archives; and Alabama Supreme Court and State Law Library for allowing me to reproduce the images and photographs contained in this book.

My graduate advisors, Kermit L. Hall and Bertram Wyatt-Brown, contributed greatly to this project in its initial stages. The time I spent studying with them has proven invaluable in terms of my own professional development, and to these two fine teachers and scholars I will always be grateful. Professors Robert Zieger and the late Darrett and Anita Rutman played a particularly important role in developing my skills as a writer, while Professors Eldon Turner, Charles Sidman, John Sommerville, and Charles Thomas provided intellectual support and criticism during my graduate career. Fellow students—now historians—Michael Justus, Anders Lewis, Eric Rise, Daniel Stowell, and Lou Falkner Williams have offered continued moral support and lasting friendship over the years.

Fellow legal historians James Paulsen, John P. Reid, E. Lee Shepard, and Mike Widener each read parts of the manuscript and offered important insights and useful criticisms, while Paul Finkelman and Daniel Stowell read the entire manuscript and provided invaluable advice about how to turn the dissertation into a book and how to make my prose mean exactly what I wanted it to mean. Friends and students Mike Andrew, John Feild, James Manley, Thomas Muther, Charles D. Norris, Aldo J. Regalado, and Christopher Schneck ably assisted me along the way with various research tasks.

Kimberly Perry and the history department office staff at Rhodes, especially Jennifer Lunsford, proved particularly helpful in the final stages of the manuscript's preparation.

My academic colleagues have served as an enormous source of support. I am especially grateful to each of my department chairs, Donald Spivey at the University of Miami, Mark Szuchman at Florida International University, and Michael Drompp at Rhodes College, as well as to Deans Marshall McMahon and John Planchon at Rhodes, for providing the type of atmosphere that encouraged and enabled me to engage in research and writing. My undergraduate mentor, Whittington B. Johnson, inspired me long ago with his love of history, and today he continues to offer unfailing support and loyal friendship. Fellow academicians and friends at Rhodes, especially Dee Garceau, Stephen Haynes, Mike LaRosa, James Lanier, Frank Mora, Gail Murray, Michael Nelson, and Russell Wigginton have continually offered wisdom, humor, and inspiration over the past few years. I am also grateful to Patrick and Shelley Donahue for the encouragement and advice they provided over countless Sunday lunches at "Cancun's."

Finally—special thanks to some very special people: My Aunt JoAnne and Uncle Scotty served me many meals while I was in graduate school, and I thank them for helping sustain me through the early days of my academic career. My parents and brothers, John and Jeff, and sister, Allison, have always provided love, friendship, and support, and I thank them for continuing to believe in me. Kristin Lensch, whom I met as I was completing this manuscript, helped make the race toward the finish line all the more enjoyable, and I thank her for her commitment to me and to my work. Now I am proud to call her my wife. Finally, I dedicate this book to Alberta Sloan Wadsworth, who, had she lived to see its publication, would have been very proud of her grandson.

All of these people have made this a better book, but any errors or shortcomings remain my own.

The Southern Judicial Tradition

Southerners, Judges, and Southern Judges

The public lives of southern state appellate judges, including both their conception of the judicial role and the substance of their decisions, mirrored the simultaneous growth of sectionalism and nationalism in the nineteenth-century United States. As southerners, their careers reflected the influences of the region's political culture, especially the nineteenth-century South's emphasis on decentralized authority, white supremacy, and sectional identity. As appellate judges, they operated within an increasingly integrated American legal community in which judges asserted their independence, drew on common sources of authority, and developed a professional consciousness. The evolving relationship between these two larger developments—between political sectionalism and legal nationalism—lay at the heart of the formation and evolution of the nineteenth-century southern judicial tradition.

This book explores the association between sectionalism and nationalism through the lives of six of the South's leading state judges. These individuals—Spencer Roane, John Catron, Joseph Lumpkin, John Hemphill, Thomas Ruffin, and George Stone—all played significant roles in formulating legal doctrine in their home states. All served for lengthy periods of time (ranging from twelve to twenty-seven years), all wrote a large number of opinions, and all served as chief justices of their respective tribunals. In addition, by informally influencing the opinions of their colleagues and frequently engaging in the training of young lawyers, all exhibited the elusive qualities of judicial leadership.

These particular judges, moreover, represented the diversity among the southern judiciary in two respects. First, they embodied the regional and geographical divergence within the South: they came from six different states, from both the eastern seaboard and the southwestern frontier, from both the Lower and the Upper South. (The border slave states, as well as the civil-law state of Louisiana are not represented here.) Second, these judges personified the range of economic and educational backgrounds on the southern bench, from the Princeton-educated elite to those with modest backgrounds who attended only "common schools." Both types of jurists could be found among the ranks of the nineteenth-century southern appellate judiciary; both types emerged among its leadership. To be sure, the life experiences and judicial behavior of these particular individuals do not explain the entire range of attitudes and actions evident among the southern judiciary. But the stories of these six white southern judges, because of their representativeness and diversity, do provide a vehicle for understanding the southern legal system within the American context.[1]

The Judge and the Judiciary in the South

On one level, this book examines southern judges' conception of the judicial role. Like their counterparts on the U.S. Supreme Court and in northern state courts, southern jurists asserted the power of judicial review early in their history. Two of the earliest decisions in America establishing the practice of judicial review included *Commonwealth v. Caton* (1782), a Virginia case involving the legislative branch's attempt to grant a pardon, and *Bayard v. Singleton* (1787), a North Carolina case involving a statute pertaining to the jurisdiction of state courts. During the late eighteenth century, state judges—both North and South—carved out a unique place for themselves within their respective constitutional orders. Viewing themselves as both the guardians of constitutional principles and the preservers of popular sovereignty, appeals court judges challenged legislative supremacy. Throughout the rest of the nineteenth century, southern judges did not hesitate to overturn legislative enactments they believed were contrary to constitutional ideals.[2]

Consistent with national judicial thinking, southern jurists viewed the law as an instrument of social policy. Legal scholars and historians have described the first half of the nineteenth century as the "formative era," the "golden age," or the "age of discovery" in American legal history.[3] As Morton J. Horwitz argues, American jurists during this period moved from understanding the law as a set of fixed moral principles to adopting a creative and purposeful conception of judicial decision making. By demonstrating a willingness to overturn ancient doctrines and craft new innovations, nineteenth-century southern judges exemplified this trend in American legal history. While southern jurists certainly did not believe they were free to ignore or alter legislative enactments or common-law traditions, they usually did not hesitate to interpret legislative acts and judicial precedent to accommodate changing social and political demands. The Texas Supreme Court's liberal interpretation of the state's homestead exemption laws, which protected a debtor's homestead from seizure by creditors, proved one of the most significant examples of nineteenth-century judicial policy making. While Horwitz and others argue that the post–Civil War period marked the rise of a more "formalistic" mode of legal reasoning in which judges mechanically adhered to established precedents, an "instrumental conception of law" in many ways continued to dominate judicial thinking in the South until 1890.[4]

Despite the innovation and energy emanating from the bench, societal opposition to judicial power plagued the southern judiciary through much of the century. The South's political order placed a high value on decentralized authority, and many citizens expressed a visceral distrust of appellate courts that seemed removed from the public. Conflicts between southern states and the U.S. Supreme Court, evident in such landmark cases as *Chisholm v. Georgia* (1793), *Martin v. Hunter's Lessee* (1816), *Cohens v. Virginia* (1821), and the *Cherokee Cases* (1831–32), exacerbated opposition to a powerful judiciary.[5] Particularly during the early part of the century, southern state judges struggled to preserve their independence—as well as the existence of their tribunals—by fending off the insistent incursions of the legislative branch. In 1831, for example, the Tennessee legislature seriously debated abolishing its supreme court, while Georgia, although it passed legislation providing for the establishment of a supreme court in 1835, did not actually create a high court until a decade later. The national trend toward an elected judiciary also found expression in the South. In 1832, Mississippi became the first state in the nation to elect its appellate judges, a trend that during the 1850s swept through Alabama, Florida, Tennessee, Texas, and Virginia. Other southern states later joined the ranks, although some rescinded judicial election before later readopting the policy. Popular opposition to and distrust of a powerful judicial branch thus stood in the way of immediate acceptance of judges' authority.[6]

Still, in the long term southern appellate courts won legislative and public approval. In Georgia, where the state's tardiness in creating a supreme court made the triumph especially significant, the legislature in 1859 conferred upon the court's unanimous decisions all the authority of statutory law.[7] The leaders of the southern bench deserved much of the credit for such accomplishments. Usually crafting their opinions with the public good at the forefront of their minds, jurists often looked beyond provincial interests and attitudes. Their status as gentlemen and their connections within the community—their ties to the South's churches, agricultural organizations, literary societies, and universities—augmented their positions within society. Despite opposition to judicial authority in the early nineteenth century, over time southern appellate judges assumed an increasingly important public

role. As William Wiethoff argues, jurists viewed themselves as models of propriety and gentility—as examples for a younger generation of gentlemen
lawyers. Through the ritual practices of the courtroom, where judges skilled
in oratory delivered eloquent opinions to huge audiences, southern judges
helped to break down much of the societal opposition to legal authority. The
bold announcement of Judge George W. Stone's death in 1894 on the front
page of the *Birmingham Age Herald* with the headline "One of Alabama's
Purest and Most Eminent Citizens, Gone to His Reward" typified the South's
end-of-the-century reverence for its judicial leaders.[8] Over the course of the
nineteenth century, southern judges gradually succeeded in solidifying their
place within both polity and society.

The Substance of Judicial Opinions

On another level, this book examines the substantive law created by appellate judges. In this respect, four general issues lie at the center of this work:
the definition of homicide and self-defense, the course of economic development, the nature of the federal Union, and the status of African Americans.
All these questions confronted the southern judiciary and proved critical to
regional and national legal and constitutional development. How southern
judges interpreted these matters of private and public law has significant implications for the debate over the distinctiveness of the South, for historians
have argued that the region in some way distinguished itself from the North
with respect to each of these questions.[9] While southern judges certainly encountered other matters of prime importance, this study confines itself to
these issues.

Homicide pervaded the social and cultural landscape of the nineteenth-
century South. Many historians have described the region's propensity toward
violent conflict resolution, especially during the antebellum period. Both the
duel between gentlemen and the brawl between backwoodsmen emanated
from a larger culture of honor and masculinity that also sacralized drinking,
gambling, cockfighting, and other community rituals.[10] After the Civil War,
excessive violence and epidemic killing continued to haunt the region. In
1880 H. V. Redfield, a social commentator and researcher, compiled *Homicide, North and South,* an exhaustive comparison of the frequency of murder
in the two sections. Examining newspaper evidence, Redfield asserted that
"more men have fallen in personal combat in the South since 1840 than were
killed in battle on both sides in the rebellion." While the unavailability and
unreliability of nineteenth-century crime statistics make it impossible to support or refute such a claim, Redfield believed this phenomenon lay at the

heart of sectional distinctiveness. "There is nothing that so distinguishes the Southern civilization from the Northern as this one matter of homicide," he wrote.[11]

If the incidence of homicide formed part of the basis of sectional distinctiveness, the treatment of convicted murderers in appellate courts revealed unity within the national legal community. In general, southern jurists neither "blatantly expanded the common law doctrine of self-defense" nor "gave judicial approval to street-fight killing."[12] On the contrary, southern judges continually fought their region's tendency toward violent and murderous behavior. They emphatically condemned the practice of dueling (although they themselves in some instances engaged in the practice), consistently held that malice (the legal requirement to prove homicide) could be inferred from the actions of the accused, routinely sustained convictions despite the technical insufficiencies of indictments, and generally adhered to a strict definition of self-defense that required an individual to "retreat to the wall" before slaying an assailant. By upholding such convictions and by adhering to Blackstone and leading American authorities, southern jurists demonstrated their commitment to the Anglo-American rule of law rather than to the southern code of honor.

Economic growth and development, another significant matter confronted by the judiciary, came slowly to the South. To many antebellum southerners, the region's plantation economy, which rested on the cultivation of cash crops and the labor of black slaves, did not seem compatible with large-scale industrial development. Those who did champion the building of cotton mills and the funding of internal improvements gained little headway within the planter-dominated South.[13] The North, of course, far outpaced the South in terms of economic diversification and development, and legal historians have given much of the credit for northern economic expansion to judges and legislators who formulated doctrines and policies that facilitated such changes. While historians acknowledge that southern judges in some respects followed national trends favoring economic progress, some scholars, like David Bodenhamer and James Ely Jr., speculate about "whether the southern legal system, at least until the Civil War, did not operate to retard such development."[14]

Throughout the nineteenth century, the principle of community interest informed southern judicial thinking about law and the economy. Ensuring that the law did not promote or protect special interests, southern judges believed, effectively promoted the public good. Virginia's Spencer Roane, for example, noted in *Currie's Administrators v. Mutual Assurance Society* (1809) that if the object of a corporation was "merely private or selfish, if it is detrimental to, or not promotive of, the public good," then the corporation had no valid claim to exist.[15] Such a position did not mean that southern jurists opposed the development of a market economy or a competitive capitalist order. On the contrary, for much of the nineteenth century this commitment to the public welfare manifested itself in what Howard Gillman calls a "police powers jurisprudence" that opposed economic privilege and upheld regulatory measures that promoted the public interest. Southern judges adhered to a flexible, dynamic conception of property that included reserving new lands for pioneer settlers instead of speculators, overturning implied exclusive rights for the building of bridges, and taking private property for the construction of railroads. Interested less in promoting ventures—and even less in protecting holdings—southern jurists sought to create an ideal, well-ordered society in which the public good stood above private interest or special privilege.[16] As the century wore on, however, this opposition to privilege evolved into an increasing judicial willingness to invalidate regulatory measures. Decrying regulation of corporations as unjust "class legislation," during the 1870s and 1880s southern judges such as George W. Stone began to join their northern counterparts in protecting corporate interests in the name of promoting public welfare.[17]

Federalism, the third issue treated here, emerged as the central constitutional question in the nineteenth-century United States. Politicians at both the national and state levels continually debated the nature of the federal relationship, and as the sectional rift widened the issue assumed even greater significance. Of course, both sections, at different points in the history of the early republic, utilized states' rights claims to protect their interests, but southerners constructed a more elaborate state-centered constitutional theory to preserve the institution of slavery. John Taylor of Caroline and John C. Calhoun, probably the South's most articulate constitutional spokesmen, held that the people of the states—rather than the people of the United States as a whole—had come together to create the Constitution and the Union. As sovereign entities, states thus preserved the power to nullify federal acts or even withdraw from the compact if they so chose. Although historian Arthur Bestor demonstrated that secession was not the planned outcome of antebellum southern proslavery constitutional theory, southerners—unlike northerners—repeatedly expressed a willingness to secede.[18]

While appellate judges had few occasions in their judicial opinions to address directly this issue of the nature of the federal Union, many did so in their extrajudicial political writings. Moreover, the attitudes of southern judges during the nullification and secession crises and during the Civil War offer clues as to judicial thinking on this matter. Like politicians, whose views of state power often reflected popular attitudes in the midst of specific crises, southern appellate judges' beliefs about the nature of the Union shifted depending on the political universe. Few southern judges, in other words, held up state sovereignty as a constitutional article of faith; instead, judicial attitudes and behavior varied depending on the political and social context: the degree of sectional partisanship in specific states at specific times, the extent of the political costs associated with taking one side or the other, personal commitment to slavery. Georgia's Joseph H. Lumpkin, for example, championed national unity during the nullification crisis but later advocated secession in 1850 and in 1861. Other southern jurists, such as North Carolina's William Gaston, Texas's James H. Bell, and South Carolina's John Belton O'Neall, never embraced the disunionist cause. When the secession crisis arose, many southern judges turned to state sovereignty in the form of secession to defend slavery, just as northern judges during the 1850s utilized the theory to protect fugitives. Such arguments constituted part of the larger matrix of constitutional debate during the nineteenth century, but southern judges proved no more willing to embrace state-sovereignty theory than did their northern counterparts.[19]

Slavery and race, unlike federalism, consistently preoccupied southern jurists. Although cases involving slaves and African Americans made up a minor portion of the total number of opinions written by southern judges, historians have devoted considerable attention to judicial behavior in this area. Most of the scholarship on slavery focuses on appellate outcomes—on the ways in which judges weighed "considerations of humanity and interest," exhibited "fairness and formalism," or considered the "rights" of slaves.[20] The variety and inconsistency of outcomes in slave cases, though generating fierce scholarly debate, do not preclude the existence of general patterns in southern judicial thought about slavery and race.

Sectional politics and the ideology of paternalism defined southern judicial thinking on slavery and racial issues. Specific events and political episodes like the Missouri Crisis, the publication of David Walker's *Appeal*, the Nat Turner Rebellion, and the debate over the Wilmot Proviso prompted southern judges to strengthen their commitment to the legal position of the peculiar institution. In a broad sense, moreover, the breakdown of national political parties and the sectionalization of the American polity during the 1840s and 1850s profoundly affected judicial attitudes. While this change did not always manifest itself in harsh legal ramifications for slaves, it did foster the development of a paternalistic proslavery position among the southern judiciary. Developing alongside the South's religious proslavery argument, this paternalistic conception of race relations emphasized the supposed improvidence of blacks, the need for white protection, and the "civilizing" and Christianizing benefits of bondage. Paternalism sometimes manifested itself in the recognition of slave humanity and the protection of slaves from cruel masters. At other times, paternalism sanctioned strict laws regarding manumission and the necessity of slaves' obedience. In other words, southern judges argued that most of their decisions regarding slavery promoted peaceful race relations, the happiness of slaves, and the public good. As William Wiethoff contends, southern judges spoke from their own experiences as slaveholders and articulated a defense of slavery based on their ideal of a harmonious, hierarchical social order.[21] After the war, southerners clung to antebellum notions of paternalism and white supremacy. They joined the U.S. Supreme Court and northern state courts in narrowly defining the constitutional guarantees of civil rights won during Reconstruction. Moreover, in their continued devotion to the Democratic Party and the ideals of the Lost Cause, southern state judges adhered to southern orthodoxy on racial issues.[22]

Southerners and Judges

Through both their conception of the judicial role and the substance of their opinions, the lives of nineteenth-century southern judges revealed the tensions between their involvement in the southern political order and their connection to the American legal community. Operating within a society where the existence and authority of formal legal institutions seemed more tenuous than in the North, southern judges felt the pressures of a political order that continually demanded judicial accountability. On the most important of issues to white southerners—the question of race—southern judges faithfully expressed the values of their region. Here and only here did the record of the southern judiciary differ substantially from that of northern judges, who, as Paul Finkelman observes, provided important legal protections for blacks at least during the antebellum era.[23] On other matters—homicide, economic development, federalism—southern judges remained more open to broad trends in American legal and constitutional thought than to exclusively sectional principles.

Southern judges were thus in some respects caught between two worlds. On one side was the South, where the issues of slavery and racial control dominated the political arena both before and after the war. On the other side was the domain of the American appellate judge, a realm of discourse that increasingly promoted a national professional consciousness through the publication of law reports, magazines, journals, and treatises. Tensions arose out of these dual loyalties, but to nineteenth-century southern jurists these divisions were not as stark as they may appear more than a century later. In some instances, southern judges did not conceive of their connections and commonalities with the northern legal community as necessarily conflict ridden or even unusual. As David Potter argued many years ago, nationalism and southernism were not mutually exclusive and, in fact, existed alongside each other. "Copious evidence shows," he concluded, "that national as well as local loyalties prevailed in both the North and the South." [24]

Southern state appellate judges were both sectionalists and nationalists, political figures and legal expositors, southerners and Americans. As such, a study of their public lives offers insights into both the nature of southern distinctiveness and the development of American legal culture. [25]

CHAPTER ONE

Spencer Roane,
Virginia Legal Culture, and the
Rise of a Southern Judiciary

Let us cherish, also, the western people. They have an identity of interests with us. . . . If driven to it, we can yet form with them a great nation. The influence of a southern sun has given to them a justice and generosity of character, which we look for in vain among the northern Yankies. — SPENCER ROANE TO JAMES MONROE, FEBRUARY 16, 1820

Spencer Roane's judicial career lay within a peculiar middle period in American history. Appointed to the bench in 1789 and serving until his death in 1822, Roane's term of service fell between two important demarcations in American history: he served after the American Revolution and the establishment of the Constitution and before the Market Revolution and the explosion of sectional tensions. In his day public officials viewed their world through the lens of the war for independence, and the eighteenth-century idea of the struggle between liberty and power remained in the forefront of their minds. The full force of the rising market economy and heated debates over sectionalism and slavery remained over the horizon.

Roane's judicial and political universe clearly differed from that of his successors. During his day, appellate judges North and South were only begin-ning to assert the power of judicial review, and Roane joined his contempo-raries in advocating a powerful and independent judiciary. American courts had only just begun to publish reported opinions, and most of what Roane knew and wrote about the law had its roots in English tradition. Many southern intellectuals and political leaders spoke disapprovingly of slavery, and Roane too seemed a bit embarrassed by an institution that apparently clashed with revolutionary principles. Judges in all jurisdictions and at all levels placed the highest premium on protecting vested rights, and Roane himself viewed property rights as the most sacred of American liberties. In the wake of a war for independence and a sharp struggle over the ratifica-tion of a new constitution, the issue that still vexed many early-nineteenth-century Americans was the exact nature of the federal Union—the proper constitutional relationship between the national government and the states. Roane made his name on this last issue.

The Revolution and Virginia Legal Culture

Born in 1762 in Essex County, Virginia, the second son of William Roane Jr. and Elizabeth Ball Roane, Spencer Roane came from a wealthy, respectable Tidewater family of Scottish origin and grew up in Virginia's tobacco cul-ture.[1] Although William Roane Jr., owner of plantations in both Essex and a neighboring county, had succeeded in making a comfortable life for his fam-ily, by the 1760s the fortunes of the Tidewater gentry were deteriorating. A century of tobacco farming in Essex County had adversely affected the fer-tility of the soil, and fresh lands to the west and south began producing a better leaf for a more competitive price. Planters, whose lives had centered on tobacco for generations, found themselves faced with having to find new staple crops like cotton, wheat, and corn. Moreover, growing indebtedness to English merchant houses foreshadowed trouble with Great Britain. As in-ternational economic tensions rose, British creditors called in long-standing debts, causing Virginia's gentry to feel betrayed and dishonored.[2] When the American Revolution came, Spencer Roane was only fourteen years old, but the war left indelible memories. Though he did not fight, in later years he recalled mustering with a company of militia in his native county while wear-ing a hunting shirt emblazoned with the words "Liberty or Death."[3]

In the midst of economic uncertainty and revolutionary upheaval, William Roane Jr. sought to ensure a successful future for his young son by providing the best education available. After an emphasis on classical learning under the guidance of private tutors, Spencer entered the College of William and

Mary in 1779.[4] At that time, the college was undergoing a change in curriculum. As governor and a member of the board of trustees, Thomas Jefferson had abolished some of the college's traditional disciplines in favor of professorships in "law and police," medicine, and modern languages; of these, the law professorship, under the leadership of Jefferson's mentor, George Wythe, proved the most successful. Jefferson's educational reforms were an integral part of a larger goal, shared by Wythe, of reforming the commonwealth's legal system. Both men believed that to secure a legal culture compatible with the ideals of the Revolution, Virginia required a professionally trained bench and bar composed of men both technically skilled and liberally educated.[5] At William and Mary, Roane began his study of the law, thus initiating a lifelong membership in the commonwealth's legal community.

As a teacher and mentor, Wythe played a key role in Roane's professional development. Born on a Virginia plantation in 1726, Wythe had risen rapidly at the bar and figured prominently in revolutionary politics. Before assuming his position at William and Mary, he had signed the Declaration of Independence, served as speaker of the House of Delegates, and been one of three judges of the newly established High Court of Chancery. In an attempt to adjust Virginia to its new status as an independent state, during the late 1770s, Wythe had joined Edmund Pendleton and Jefferson in undertaking a comprehensive review and revision of the laws of the commonwealth.[6] Having brought a wealth of legal knowledge and experience to his position as a law professor, Wythe succeeded brilliantly with his students. He lectured twice a week, held moot court once or twice a month, and presided weekly over a mock legislature.[7]

Under Wythe, Roane received an outstanding—and thoroughly English—legal education. Aside from studying Blackstone and the laws of Virginia, Roane delved deeply into all the major English legal treatises, including the writings of Littleton and Coke and the decisions of Hale and Holt. "Coke was unquestionably [Roane's] favorite author," according to a close friend's account. Roane "not only read over and again [Coke's] commentary on Littleton, but the whole of his reports were perfectly familiar to him." Roane even committed many of Coke's Latin maxims to memory. In 1780 Roane graduated from William and Mary and, along with classmates John Marshall and Bushrod Washington, earned membership in the original Phi Beta Kappa Society. Roane continued his study of the law over the next few years, first at a legal society in Philadelphia and then as a student of lawyer John Warden in Richmond.[8]

Soon after receiving his license to practice law, however, Roane, like many young attorneys of the day, turned to politics.[9] In 1783 he won election to the House of Delegates from Essex County, and over the next two years his legislative record demonstrated a hostility toward any connection with the English. He voted for the disestablishment of the Anglican Church in Virginia and against a bill to repeal all state laws preventing compliance with the provisions of the peace treaty with England.[10] But his most openly anti-English action occurred outside the legislative sphere. In the spring of 1783, an angry mob tarred and feathered a Tory merchant who returned to post-revolutionary Essex County. While the citizens of the county enjoyed this public display, the governor and other state officials expressed their outrage at the unruly behavior. When the governor brought charges against many in the mob, the accused turned to Essex County's young legislator. In their defense, Roane presented a petition, signed by 185 of the county's citizens, calling for a dismissal of the charges, and Roane lobbied the House of Delegates to nullify the prosecution.[11] Key to the prospects for passage of the proposal was the attitude of Patrick Henry, at the time the most influential man in Virginia politics. Although Henry viewed Roane's measure as an intrusion of the legislature into the realm of law enforcement, he nevertheless informed Roane that "he admired the Whig spirit that actuated" Roane and agreed not to oppose him on the matter. Henry's neutral position resulted in the dismissal of all charges against the Essex mob and a victory for Roane.[12]

Roane went on to form a strong political and personal relationship with Henry. After working on committees with him in the House of Delegates, Roane served during 1783–84 on the Privy Council, an eight-member executive advisory body, while Henry was governor. In 1786, Roane's marriage to Henry's daughter, Anne, further cemented his ties to the famed revolutionary orator.[13] Thereafter the two men maintained a close and politically useful connection. Henry described Roane as "a man of honor, of talents, and of an open, generous disposition," while Roane expressed equal admiration for Henry's skills as a speaker and a lawyer.[14]

Roane imbibed the principles espoused by Henry—his revolutionary ardor and fierce opposition to central authority—but by the end of the 1780s the political passions of many Virginians had subsided. Roane thus invited embarrassment when he again led a public fight against a loyalist—this time, Robert Beverley, a wealthy Tidewater planter. When members of the Court of Essex County, to which Beverley had belonged before the outbreak of hostilities, asked Beverley to rejoin their ranks, Roane went on the offensive. Writing to Governor Edmund Randolph in 1787, Roane enumerated his grievances against the Tory: Beverley had "associated only with men of sentiments notoriously inimical to the cause of America" and had "refused toasting Gen'l Washington and the American army during the war."[15] The governor initially suspended Beverley's nomination, but when the members of the court claimed that Roane's letter contained "illiberal insinuations, and in some instances erroneous reflections on the Court," the governor was convinced and Beverley was reinstated.[16] Roane's partisanship also put him on the wrong side of the debate over the ratification of the Constitution. Roane publicly opposed the document and described Virginia's 1788 decision to ratify as "distressing and awful to great numbers." Like Henry, Roane feared that delegating great power to a central government invited the same tyranny from which Americans had recently freed themselves.[17] In keeping with this fierce opposition to central authority, in 1794 Roane even refused to pay the federal carriage tax on the grounds that it was a direct tax that had to be apportioned among the states. (In 1796 the U.S. Supreme Court rejected this argument in *Hylton v. United States*.)[18]

Still, Roane's public defeats adversely affected neither his social rank nor his political fortunes. During the early nineteenth century, he became one of the leading planters of the Virginia Tidewater. In 1782, after his father's remarriage, Roane received some land in the parish of South Farnham and fifteen slaves, and in 1785, at the death of his father, Roane inherited the family's lands in Essex County as well as other property in King and Queen County. In 1801, after the death of his wife, Anne, Roane left Essex County and purchased new lands in Hanover County. This estate, known as Spring Garden, contained 620 acres southeast of the Hanover courthouse on the Pamunky River. Over the next several years, Roane added substantially to his landholdings, particularly when he purchased over a thousand acres near Newcastle, an important tobacco shipping point. Between 1802 and 1822, Roane increased the number of slaves he owned from sixteen to forty. The continued land purchases, accumulation of personal property and slaves, and construction of new buildings on his lands revealed Roane's success as a planter.[19]

Roane's political fortunes were also on the rise. He served two sessions in the state senate, during 1788 and 1789, and during the latter year he received an appointment to the General Court, which was at the time the commonwealth's highest tribunal in criminal matters and the intermediate appeals court in civil cases. Membership on the General Court required judges to ride circuit and preside over district courts throughout the state, a practice that allowed Roane to become acquainted with most of Virginia's lawyers. Five years later, in December 1794, the General Assembly elected Roane to the Court of Appeals, the highest appellate court concerning matters of equity, admiralty law, and civil law. Every member of the General Court had been nominated for the opening on the Court of Appeals, but the thirty-two-year-old Roane defeated all his competitors on the first ballot. The following spring, he took his seat on the state's highest court, a position he would occupy for the next twenty-seven years.[20]

The Judicial Role

Roane believed in a strong, independent judiciary, and over the course of his career he advocated judicial review and unanimity in decision making to further the legitimacy and authority of the court. He rejected the idea of legislative supremacy as he repeatedly asserted the power of the judiciary to declare acts of the legislature unconstitutional. Yet, unlike judges of the mid–nineteenth century, who often freely fashioned the law to fit the changing needs of antebellum society and conceived of themselves as performing a legislative function, Roane tempered his belief in an active judiciary with an equally strong commitment to English common law. Roane thus represented the transition between the old eighteenth-century view of judging that stressed fidelity to precedent and the new style of the early and mid–nineteenth century.[21]

By the end of the eighteenth century, many southern appellate judges began to assert the power of judicial review, and through more than three decades of judicial service, Roane played a key role in this expansion of judicial power in his own state. During the decade before his first judicial appointment in 1789, the Virginia Court of Appeals first began to expand its role in the state's new government by asserting the power to review legislative acts. In *Commonwealth v. Caton* (1782), a case involving an extralegal attempt by the House of Delegates to pardon three prisoners condemned for treason, Wythe asserted what was at that time an unprecedented degree of judicial power. "If the whole legislature . . . should attempt to overleap the bounds, prescribed to them by the people," he wrote, "I, in administering the public justice of the country, will meet the united powers at my seat in this tribunal; and, pointing to the constitution, will say to them, here is the limit of your authority; and hither shall you go, but no further."[22] In at least two more cases, the Virginia Court of Appeals again asserted the power to review acts of the legislature.[23] At about the same time, the supreme courts of North Carolina and South Carolina claimed this right, while northern state courts in New York, Rhode Island, Massachusetts, Pennsylvania, and New Hampshire did the same.[24]

At a time of confusion over the exact relationship of the courts to the legislative branch, Roane vigorously championed judicial review. While a member of the General Court, Roane delivered an important opinion in

Kamper v. Hawkins (1793), a case involving a 1792 law that eliminated some of the important distinctions between courts of law and equity. The act allowed district court judges to grant injunctions to stay proceedings on any judgment obtained in a district court and declared that district courts might proceed to the final hearing of all suits commenced by injunction—powers previously reserved to the state's High Court of Chancery. While Roane and Judge St. George Tucker were sitting at the Dumfries District Court, Peter Kamper petitioned under the new law for an injunction to stay the proceeding on a judgment Mary Hawkins had previously obtained against him. When Tucker declined to hear the motion on jurisdictional grounds, Roane, not wanting to decide this important matter by himself, adjourned the case to the General Court because of the subject's "novelty and difficulty." [25]

When a five-member General Court convened to decide the case, Roane and Tucker took similarly strong stands in favor of judicial review. Born in Bermuda in 1752, Tucker had arrived in Virginia in 1770 and, like Roane, studied law under Wythe. Tucker later succeeded his mentor as professor of law at William and Mary, where he prepared and published a multivolume annotated edition of Blackstone's *Commentaries*. Already regarded among the leaders of the Virginia legal community, Tucker's learned and lengthy opinion in *Kamper* further contributed to his reputation. Drawing on the accumulated wisdom of William Blackstone, Thomas Paine, and Alexander Hamilton, among others, Tucker eloquently argued for constitutional supremacy and judicial review. The commonwealth's constitution, he believed, stood above acts of the legislature, and, because it was a written constitution, all branches of the government were clearly subject to its dictates. Moreover, Tucker contended, "the duty of expounding" the constitution "must be exclusively vested in the judiciary." "The judiciary are bound to take notice of the constitution, as the first law of the land," he summarized, "and that whatsoever is contradictory thereto, is not the law of the land." [26]

Equal to Tucker's opinion in its substantive support for judicial review, the style of Roane's decision was less doctrinal and more practical. Roane reversed his position from when the case had first come before him in the district court; at that time he had doubted whether the judiciary possessed the power to prevent the execution of an act passed by the legislature. "My opinion, on more mature considerations," he wrote in *Kamper*, "is changed in this respect." Roane's turnaround was dramatic, for he supported judicial review in more explicit language than did any of his fellow judges, including Tucker. "I now think that the judiciary may and ought not only to refuse to execute a law expressly repugnant to the Constitution," he wrote, "but also one which is, by a plain and natural construction, in opposition to the fundamental principles thereof."[27] While Tucker described the judiciary in defensive terms—as "a barrier against the possible usurpation or abuse of power in other departments"—Roane portrayed the courts as active agents of review, as the branch of government that "may and ought to adjudge a law unconstitutional and void."[28]

Roane, like Tucker, argued that the constitution—not legislative action— was the expression of the people's sovereign will and that the judiciary alone could determine a law's constitutionality. In his view, by severing ties with England, the Revolution had created a unique set of circumstances for Virginians. The commonwealth's constitutional convention, because it neither served nor derived any power under the former government, constituted "a spontaneous assemblage of the people of Virginia." Moreover, according to Roane, the decisions of the courts and even the proclamations of the legislature had continually upheld the idea that the constitution, as the product of the people's work, was superior to any legislative act.[29] Constitutional interpretation, Roane concluded, was the domain of the judiciary. Because the courts examined all laws dealing with a particular subject when deciding a case, Roane reasoned that it was also within the bounds of judicial responsibility to assess a law within the context of the constitution. "In expounding laws," he argued, "the judiciary considers every law which relates to the subject: would you have them to shut their eyes against that law which is of the highest authority of any, or against a part of that law, which either by its words of by its spirit, denies to any but the people the power to change it?"[30] On the issue of judicial review, Roane's opinion in *Kamper v. Hawkins* was decisive.

Roane then declared the law unconstitutional. Because the legislation in question transferred important powers from the chancery courts to the district courts—from constitutionally created tribunals to legislatively created tribunals—Roane viewed the act as an unlawful expansion of legislative authority. The act not only violated the theory of separation of powers but also threatened the independence and power of the judiciary, especially the principle of judicial review. "If the legislature can transfer from constitutional to legislative courts all judicial powers," Roane argued, "these dependent tribunals being the creatures of the legislature itself, will not dare to oppose an unconstitutional law, and the principle I set out upon, viz. that such laws ought to be opposed, would become a dead letter, or in other words, this would pave the way to an uncontrolled power in the legislature." In Roane's view, judicial review and judicial independence were inseparable. Because the 1792 law seemed to violate both of these principles, Roane deemed the act unconstitutional.[31]

Throughout his later career as a member of the Court of Appeals, Roane continued to operate within the spirit of *Kamper* by asserting the power of judicial review. Although, like the U.S. Supreme Court, the Virginia Court of Appeals actually overruled few legislative acts before the Civil War, Roane did not hesitate to argue that the legislature had to act within the bounds of the constitutions of Virginia and the United States as well as in accordance with the dictates of natural law.[32] In *Jones v. Commonwealth* (1799), for example, Roane overruled a lower-court decision that imposed a joint fine against three defendants found guilty of assault as antithetical to both "principles of natural justice" and the Bill of Rights's prohibition on excessive fines. Even if the legislature were to pass an act codifying the lower court's decision, Roane argued, the imposition of a joint fine was "so unjust and contrary to the spirit of the Bill of Rights" that he would certainly declare such a law void.[33] In *Currie's Administrators v. Mutual Assurance Society* (1809), Roane drew specific limits around the legislature's ability to alter corporate charters. When counsel argued that the legislature possessed unlimited powers, Roane responded, "What is this, but to lay prostrate, at the footstool of the legislature, all our rights of person and of property, and abandon those great objects, for the protection of which, alone, all free governments have been instituted?" Although Roane decided in this case that the legislature had not overstepped its bounds, he affirmed the idea articulated in *Kamper* that the legislature was bound "by the principles and provisions of the constitution and bill of rights, and by those great rights and principles, for the preservation of which all just governments are founded."[34]

The court's decision in *Kamper v. Hawkins,* as well as Roane's and his successors' continued assertions of judicial power, firmly established the practice of judicial review in Virginia. Drawing on the ideas of Wythe and Tucker, Roane explicitly described the judiciary as the agent of review when legislative acts violated either the letter or the "fundamental principles" of the constitution. Because of his directness on the issue, Roane earned a reputation as one of the progenitors of judicial review in Virginia.[35]

In addition to advancing the concept of judicial review, Roane sought to strengthen the Court of Appeals by promoting the practice of issuing unanimous opinions. At Roane's arrival on the Court of Appeals in 1795, unanimity prevailed among the judges, all of whom were advanced in years and conservative in outlook. Their president, Judge Edmund Pendleton, had effectively guided the five-member tribunal through its early history and had assiduously labored to establish the court's reputation within the state and the nation. A longtime leader within Virginia's conservative party, Pendleton had reluctantly advocated independence from England and had consistently opposed the more radical politics of Patrick Henry and others. Pendleton's conservatism made his support crucial to the revolutionary cause; he served in the first Continental Congress and chaired the Committee of Safety. Already a giant within Virginia's legal community, Pendleton's appointment as president of the newly created Court of Appeals in 1779 made him the undisputed leader of the state's judiciary. From his position on the Court of Appeals, Pendleton exercised the final say over decisions rendered in the state's lower courts—a fact that renewed an old rivalry with Wythe, who served as head of the state's High Court of Chancery. Pendleton's antagonisms, however, did not affect his relationship with Roane. Although the son-in-law of Pendleton's political enemy and the protégé of his judicial adversary, Roane immediately earned Pendleton's respect and confidence. In the same way, the elder jurist became a source of wisdom and an example of mature judicial leadership for Roane.[36]

Pendleton's death in 1803 cast the Court of Appeals into a period of conflict and disarray. A series of structural changes in the first few years of the nineteenth century left the institution with only three judges by 1807: President William Fleming, Tucker, and Roane. Tucker, as the eldest and most respected legal thinker of the three, no doubt viewed himself as the heir to Pendleton. When an alliance quickly developed between Tucker and Fleming, Roane often found himself forced to dissent from the opinions of his colleagues. Fleming seemed content to yield to Tucker and allowed him to prepare the court's opinions before conferences—a practice that rendered Roane powerless and conferences unimportant. Not only was this situation threatening to Roane's personal position as a member of the court, but the division among the judges also undermined the body's unanimity and authority.[37]

In 1808 Roane attempted to return the court to the position it had maintained under Pendleton's leadership by introducing a set of resolutions establishing formal rules and procedures for the court's operation. He suggested that judges refrain from excusing themselves from cases unless they were closely related to the parties involved; that judges confer about their decisions and, if differences existed, exchange opinions before delivering them in open court; that they avoid rendering seriatim opinions (the practice of each judge issuing a separate opinion in a case); that they keep a written record of witnesses' testimony and seek power from the legislature to refer cases involving witnesses of questionable credibility to juries; and that they prescribe the legal conduct of all other judges in the state. When Fleming and Tucker refused to accept these measures, Roane withdrew the resolutions from consideration during the following term.[38]

But Roane remained unsatisfied. His opposition to Tucker's preconference opinion writing and de facto dominance of the court led to a three-year feud between the two judges, a conflict that erupted first in conference and eventually in open court. During one conference in 1809, for example, while Tucker was reading an opinion, Roane accosted Tucker, grabbed the decision from his hands, threw it to the floor, and told Tucker that he could not bear to listen to another "long, tedious, and ridiculous" opinion. After a similar incident occurred the next day, an unbridgeable rift developed between Roane and Tucker. Deeply offended, Tucker lamented to Fleming the "unprovoked injuries" he had suffered at Roane's hands and refused to meet with Roane in conference.[39] With the disappearance of the conference as a viable forum for the discussion of legal issues, Roane carried his differences with Tucker into open court. Again turning to a sympathetic Fleming, Tucker continued to complain about the "denunciation[s] . . . made against" him and to refuse, despite the efforts of Roane and others, to meet in conference.[40] Although as members of the General Court Roane and Tucker had labored together to ensure the independence and power of the Virginia judiciary, by 1809 the cooperation that had characterized their early personal and professional association had disappeared.

The Tucker-Roane conflict represented a showdown not only between two impetuous, uncompromising personalities but also between two distinct views of the judicial role. Roane envisioned a return to Pendleton's style of judicial decision making, in which the judges met privately to work out differences before delivering a unanimous opinion. Although lacking Pendleton's judicial statesmanship and consensus-building skills, Roane sought to implement a decision-making process that would maintain the prestige of the institution and strengthen the force of its opinions. Tucker, conversely, wanted to preserve the practice of rendering seriatim opinions. Eventually, Roane came to view Tucker's departure as the only chance for the court to adopt procedures that would encourage unanimity.

Roane's persistence ultimately yielded dividends in terms of both his view of judicial decision making and his own position on the court. Tucker resigned in 1811, stunned by Roane's continuing opposition and offended by a new judicial reorganization act that expanded both the size of the court and the duties of its members. In a lengthy letter explaining his departure, Tucker expressed his opposition to the restructuring of the courts and his unwillingness to comply with the expanded duties imposed on the judges. Yet he was the only one of the judges to express resistance to the measure, and his sudden resignation makes little sense apart from his three-year struggle with Roane. Having found a valid reason to retire, Tucker finally chose to end the

bitter dispute with his judicial colleague.[41] In effect, the "irascible, independent" Roane had forced Tucker from the bench.[42]

The results of Tucker's exit, from Roane's perspective, were immediate
and impressive. While the new judges never specifically adopted Roane's
proposed reforms for the court's operation, they nonetheless acceded to his
judicial leadership. During the rest of Roane's tenure as a judge, the court
issued short, unanimous opinions in an overwhelming majority of its cases.
Although he never served as the court's president, Roane assumed a commanding presence among his colleagues, especially after an illness dictated
Fleming's frequent absence. Of the 609 opinions issued during the eleven-
year period from Tucker's departure to Roane's death, 556 (91 percent)
were unanimous decisions of the court. Of these, Roane authored almost
half.[43] During the same period, he delivered only forty-eight separate opinions. Tucker's departure enabled Roane to fashion the Court of Appeals in
his own image.

Roane's commitment to a strong and authoritative judiciary, freely asserting the power of judicial review and usually speaking with one voice, had
limitations. He clearly did not perceive of the court or the law as a means of
shaping society, and he repeatedly expressed his devotion to precedent. Particularly in the first decade of the century, Roane often decided cases based
on precedents even when such rulings ran counter to his personal opinions.
For example, in *Young v. Gregorie* (1803), a case involving an attempted
prosecution that failed to aver the want of probable cause, Roane upheld the
letter of the law despite his own convictions. "In this case I am compelled to
yield my impressions, relative to the real justice of the appellant's cause," he
wrote, "to the established principles of the law, as settled by successive and
long existing decisions." Similarly, in *Ballard v. Leavell* (1805), another case
involving an incorrectly constructed charge, Roane again looked to the established principle as the basis for his decision. "It gives me pain to reverse
judgments upon grounds which appear to be technical, and do not entirely
accord with the general understanding of men," he admitted. "But I hold
myself bound by well-established precedents, and disclaim a power to change
the law." And in *Johnson v. Johnson's Widow* (1810), a case involving the
conveyance of property under a will, Roane again set aside his own opinions
on the matter "in deference to" a previous decision of the court.[44]

English precedents and principles held a place of particular importance
in Roane's decisions. Although a zealous revolutionary and ardent Jeffersonian, he did not view independence from England as severing the bonds of
law and tradition between the two nations. Tucker once noted that "no decision in England since our independence commenced has any authority in

this court."[45] In contrast, in areas of the common law that remained unaffected by the revolutionary transfer of sovereignty from England to America, Roane did not hesitate to draw on the writing of both ancient and contemporary English legal thinkers. "I shall certainly not be accused of partiality towards the government of Great-Britain," he wrote in *Baring v. Reeder* (1806), "but I wish not, without necessity, to sound the tocsin against that nation; to indulge my prejudices against her to an unreasonable length; nor to shut out from our eyes that light, which, while it conduces to truth, will certainly not contaminate our political institutions." In view of the lack of an established legal tradition in Virginia and America as a whole, Roane believed that English authorities retained significant influence in the United States and offered solutions to the young nation's most important legal questions. In this way, Roane followed in the footsteps of his Virginia predecessors Wythe and Pendleton and paralleled the work of contemporary northerners like James Kent and Joseph Story, who relied heavily on English authorities. "I do not see why," Roane summarized in *Baring*, "the testimony of Lord Mansfield delivered in 1777, is not of equal weight with his testimony delivered in 1775."[46]

In Roane's view, English authorities stood on equal footing with decisions of Virginia courts. Confronted with these two different types of precedents in *Claiborne v. Henderson* (1809), a case involving a widow's relationship to her deceased husband's estate, Roane abided by the principles established by the line of English decisions rather than by an opinion from his own state's General Court. "Undoubtedly, would such a series of decisions by [English] Courts overrule a single decision . . . made by a coequal Court in this country, whatever may be the case of single and recent decisions, which have neither been long acquiesced in, nor grown into rules of property." Hearkening back to the great tradition of English legal scholarship, Roane cited Blackstone and others in support of adherence to such long-established precedents. "These are a few of the innumerable instances to be found in the books, of a reverence for decisions, and rules of property which have been established by the concurrent decisions of successive Judges, and acted under, for a long series of time," he wrote. "They ought to be adhered to as the sine qua non of all certainty and stability in the law, the private opinion of any single Judge to the contrary notwithstanding."[47] While Roane did not view English legal sources as "binding authority," he considered the opinions of such "eminent judges" invaluable in arriving at his own decisions.[48]

Roane's conception of the judicial role combined a belief in a strong, independent, authoritative judiciary with a devotion to the wisdom of the ages as expressed through the common law. In his devotion to judicial review and unanimous decision making, Roane set the tone for the future of his court. By 1837 Judge Henry St. George Tucker, the son of Roane's early judicial rival, observed that the power of reviewing a law's constitutionality was "too firmly settled to be now questioned." Moreover, despite a few instances of seriatim opinion writing in the first half of the nineteenth century, the judges of the court continued Roane's practice of drafting short majority opinions.[49] But future jurists were less inclined to adhere to Roane's strict ideas of precedent. Roane thus stood in the middle of an ongoing transition in the role of appellate judging during the early nineteenth century. While state courts increasingly assumed a lawmaking function by declaring legislative acts unconstitutional and imposing the judicial will on society, Roane only embraced half of this formula. He advocated judicial review but often deferred to common-law tradition.

Slavery and Property

Just as Roane's conception of the judicial role represented the transitions and tensions of his day, so too did his attitudes toward slavery and property. As an ardent advocate of revolutionary principles, Roane championed the ideals of liberty and, like many of his Virginia contemporaries, expressed some uneasiness about the institution of slavery. Yet Roane's Spring Garden plantation, which yielded an abundance of tobacco, corn, and wheat, depended on the labor of dozens of slaves.[50] In property cases not involving slaves, Roane upheld the rights of established owners with all the zeal of a revolutionary patriot opposed to unfair taxation, yet these deeply held principles collided with his desire for economic expansion and development. In short, as a judge Roane discovered that the beliefs formed during the revolutionary era did not always suit the demands of early-nineteenth-century Virginia society.

Slavery presented a peculiar problem for southerners of the revolutionary generation. As legal historian William Wiecek observes, southern jurists from the Revolution to the 1830s often elevated principles of liberty and natural law above the rights of slaveholders. In many instances, these judges "went out of their way" to uphold the free status of onetime slaves who had since been taken by their masters to free jurisdictions and then returned to slave states. In Virginia, for example, Judge Wythe declared in 1806 that "freedom is the birth-right of every human being, which sentiment is strongly inculcated by the first article of our 'political catechism,' the bill of rights." The Kentucky Court of Appeals went even further in 1820 and held that "freedom is the natural right of man" and that slavery was "without foundation in the law of nature, or the unwritten and common law." In Louisiana in an 1824 case, the high court similarly held that a slave freed anywhere, no matter how brief a period of time, could never be reenslaved.[51] Such overtly antislavery sentiments infused the writings of judges all over the South well into the 1820s.

Roane's judicial opinions too displayed the revolutionary generation's preoccupation with liberty. *Pleasants v. Pleasants* (1800), his first and most studied slavery opinion, perhaps best exemplified Roane's early willingness—almost eagerness—to emancipate.[52] The case involved the will of John Pleasants, head of the state's "leading Quaker family" and a large slaveholder. Pleasants's will stated that all of his slaves "shall be free if they chuse it when they arrive to the age of thirty years, and the laws of the land will admit them to be set free without their being transported out of the country." Pleasants's will continued, "I say all my slaves now born or hereafter to be born, whilst their mothers are in the service of me or my heirs, to be free at the age of thirty years . . . to be adjudged of by my trustees their age." The will was executed and probated at a time when the state did not permit manumission, but in the midst of the Revolution, in 1782, the legislature passed a law allowing emancipation under certain conditions. Several years later, Pleasants's son and executor, Robert Pleasants, brought the suit into court when the devisees refused to emancipate Pleasants's slaves. The case gave the court its first opportunity to interpret the 1782 legislation. Because the will had been executed prior to the emancipation legislation, the document could not legally free Pleasants's slaves. Only if the judges construed the will as creating a trust with the legatees to carry out the testator's intentions would any slaves gain their freedom. The court's ruling would demonstrate whether the Virginia judiciary would merely "tolerate" or would "favor" manumission.[53]

Revealing his enthusiasm for emancipation, Roane rendered an expansive interpretation of the testator's aims. First, he upheld the terms of the will as creating a trust and ruled that all the slaves in question were entitled to their freedom at age thirty. Then, Roane ruled that children would be freed when their mothers reached thirty. "Such children are not the children of slaves," he wrote. "They never were the property of the testator or legatees, and he, or they, can no more restrain their right to freedom, than they can that of other persons born free." Roane eloquently championed the liberty of such children: "The power of the testator, in this respect, has yielded to the great principle of natural law, which, is also a principle of our municipal law, that the children of a free mother are themselves also free."[54] Thus, he voided the provisions of the will that might have been interpreted to keep such children as slaves until they themselves reached the age of thirty, and he ruled instead that all of the children in question would remain slaves only until their mothers reached that age. On this point, Roane's two judicial colleagues disagreed with and thus overruled him: Judges Paul Carrington and Pendleton thought Roane's grant of freedom to the children went well beyond the testator's original intention.[55]

The substance and the tone of Roane's decision in *Pleasants* revealed him to be an eager emancipator. He began his opinion by noting that he would treat the case as one involving "the rules of the common law relative to ordinary cases of limitations of personal chattels." But "if their claim will be sustained on this foundation, and by analogy to ordinary remainders of chattels," Roane declared, "every argument will hold, with increased force, when the case is considered in its true point of view, as one, which involves human liberty."[56] To Roane, liberty was the issue at hand. He described the state's policy of "authorizing or encouraging emancipation" as a practice that "must always be dear to every friend of liberty and the human race." Finally, he concluded, "I rejoice to be an humble organ of the law in decreeing liberty to the numerous appellees now before the court." Because this ruling stood on the grounds of "strict legal right," he argued, the emancipation would not "agitate and convulse the Commonwealth to its centre."[57] Roane thus placed the ideal of liberty above whatever adverse public policy implications his opinion might have generated.

In his other, less well-known opinions, Roane revealed a similar preference for liberty. *Charles v. Hunnicut* (1804) involved a Quaker testator who had bequeathed his slaves to the monthly meeting, "to be manumitted by such members of the said meeting, as the meeting shall appoint." Here Roane joined his colleagues in approving the manumission.[58] Unlike *Pleasants*, where the testator directed emancipation when the law should allow, the will in *Hunnicut* provided for the freeing of the slaves on a specific date, which happened to be just prior to the effective date of the 1782 law permitting manumission. The court looked past the specifics of the will to the underlying principles and wishes of the testator. "Being proved a Quaker," Roane wrote, "I believe that this court might, to make the case stronger, take official notice of the principles of that society, holding slavery in abhorrence." With clear evidence of the testator's desire for his slaves to gain their freedom, the court ruled accordingly. "It appears to be the intention of the testator, on the will itself," Roane wrote, "that these negroes should be manumitted, and that they should enjoy their freedom; he was certainly far from meaning to throw them into a more grievous state of bondage."[59] In *Wilson v. Isbell* (1805), by rendering a broad construction of the state's 1778 act to prevent the importation of slaves, Roane and his colleagues again sided with a slave seeking her freedom. Isbell, who had been born in Virginia and carried to Maryland, was sold in her new state of residence before being brought back to Virginia as a slave. The court ruled that returning her to the state constituted an "importation" of a slave, and the judges pronounced her a free woman.[60]

Yet Roane's sentiments favoring liberty clashed with the realities of slave society. When forced to choose between the principles of liberty and the claims of a creditor, Roane sided with the latter. In *Woodley v. Abbey* (1805), Roane began his opinion by making known the tension present in his own thinking. "In considering this case, I cannot, for a moment forget, (whatever my sentiments may be on the abstract questions discussed before us) that slaves are a species of property recognized and guaranteed by our laws," he wrote. "The most that this court can do, in the case, is to extend to the appellees all the consideration and favour which is compatible with the rights of property." In 1792 the legislature had amended its 1782 emancipation law to declare that manumitted slaves were subject to the owner's debts contracted prior to the emancipation. Roane upheld this provision, conceding that "justice and vested rights" needed to be protected.[61] A few years later, Roane reiterated this holding in *Patty v. Colin* (1807), a similar case involving the debts of a testatrix who had directed the manumission of her slaves. However much he championed the policy "in favour of human rights" embodied in the 1782 emancipation statute, Roane believed that creditors' interests needed to be protected.[62]

Moreover, Roane never advocated anything even remotely resembling the abolition of slavery. Although he often saw eye to eye with his colleague St. George Tucker in emancipation cases, Roane did not endorse Tucker's 1796 proposal for gradual abolition. Even this conservative plan, which would have transformed slavery "into a kind of serfdom," as Edmund Morgan put it, proved too radical for Roane, who shared the racist assumptions of his society and of his society's laws.[63] "In the case of a person visibly appearing to be a negro," Roane succinctly stated in one case, "the presumption is, in this country, that he is a slave, and it is incumbent on him to make out his right to freedom."[64] Thus although Roane proved an avid emancipator in many instances, he held tightly to the racial assumptions of Virginia slave law. When forced to choose, Roane ultimately pushed revolutionary-era abstractions about human liberty aside and embraced the notion of slaves as property, subject to the financial transactions of whites.

Apart from slavery, the rights of property held a place of preeminence in Roane's thinking. During the early nineteenth century, the Virginia legislature played a limited role in the promotion of internal improvements, as enterprises remained "organized, financed, and directed principally by private citizens." Because Virginia relied primarily on private investment to promote growth and development, according to Bruce A. Campbell, "the legislature scrupulously respected chartered rights."[65] The Court of Appeals followed the legislature's lead and strictly upheld the principle of vested rights. In a few instances, the court even kept the conservative legislature from straying from the sacred protection of these rights. In a 1792 case, for example, Pendleton protected vested rights by ruling that an amendment to an existing statute did not apply retrospectively to previous contractual relationships. "Changing titles founded upon existing statutes, would be subject to every objection which lies to ex post facto laws," Pendleton wrote, "as it would destroy rights already acquired under the former statute, by one made subsequent to the time when they became vested."[66]

Roane followed both the legislature and Pendleton in his devotion to vested rights. In *Elliott's Executor v. Lyell* (1802), like Pendleton, Roane confronted the issue of whether an action of debt was governed by the common law in effect when the contract was made in 1782 or whether a 1786 legislative alteration of the common law governed the transaction. Roane authoritatively stated his opinion on the matter: "I stand upon this broad principle, that men, in regulating their contracts, shall have the benefit of existing laws, and not have them overturned or affected by future laws, which they certainly could not foresee or provide against." Quoting Lord Mansfield of England, Roane concluded, "here is a right vested; and it is not to be imagined that the Legislature could, by general words, mean to take it away from the person in whom it was so legally vested."[67] Moreover, in *Turpin v. Lockett* (1804), a case involving the state's confiscation of lands belonging to the disestablished Episcopal Church of Virginia, Roane reiterated in dicta his commitment to the inviolate rights associated with private property. "I shall not be among those, who assert a right in the government, or even in the people," he asserted, "to violate private rights, and perpetrate injustice. The just end and object of all governments, and all revolutions, reprobate this idea."[68]

Roane's most complete statement about the relationship between the legislature and property rights came in *Currie's Administrators v. Mutual Assurance Society* (1809). The case involved the Mutual Assurance Society, an insurance company originally chartered by the legislature in 1794. Under the charter, every member of the society became the insurer for every other member, but in 1805 the legislature, under pressure from a majority of the membership, separated the subscribers into two groups: town subscribers and country subscribers. Rural members favored this distinction because

they had discovered that the danger of fire was greater in the town than in
the country, and country subscribers felt they were paying unduly high rates.
Currie, a town dweller, brought suit against the society, claiming that the
1805 act violated the society's original charter by increasing his rates without
his consent. The case presented the issue of whether the legislature had the
power to alter the charter of the corporation, a matter with serious implications for the relationship between law and the economy.[69]

Roane laid down two principles in his opinion. He first reaffirmed the
sacredness of vested rights and the injustice of legislative interference with
such rights. "When any legislative act is to be questioned," he argued, "on
the ground of conflicting with the superior acts of the people, or of invading
the vested rights of individuals, the case ought to be palpable and clear . . .
that the immediate representatives of the people, representing as well the justice as the wisdom of the nation, have forgotten the great injunctions under
which they are called to act." Roane then described the conditions under
which the legislature issued corporate charters. Following the rule under English common law, the Virginia constitution provided that the state granted
corporate charters only "in consideration of public services." Citing Blackstone, Roane reaffirmed this principle. "It may be often convenient for a set
of associated individuals to have the privileges of a corporation bestowed
upon them, but if their object is merely private or selfish, if it is detrimental
to, or not promotive of, the public good, they have no adequate claim upon
the legislature for the privilege." Thus, in Roane's opinion, the legislature
could not violate vested rights, and all corporate charters needed to serve the
public interest.[70]

The key to Roane's opinion was his interpretation of the nature of a corporate charter. Unlike John Marshall, who in the famous *Dartmouth College
v. Woodward* (1819) decision later ruled that the Dartmouth College charter
was a contract, Roane did not view the Mutual Assurance Society's charter
as such. These charters, Roane believed, were neither sacred nor inviolate,
and the legislature retained the power to alter them for the sake of the public
interest. Coincidentally, in light of Marshall's ruling in the Dartmouth College case, Roane used the College of William and Mary as an example of the
public nature of corporate charters in general. The college's founding document had provided for a divinity school associated with the Church of England and a seminary for the instruction of Indians in the arts and sciences.
But changing circumstances—the disestablishment of the church as well as
changing relations with Native Americans—spelled the discontinuation of
both of these functions. Roane believed, therefore, that the legislature retained the power to adjust corporate charters to meet changing social de-

mands. "As it is not expected that corporations shall exist for ever, when the reason for granting them shall have passed away, and no public utility can ensue from their continuance, this right of surrender must incontrovertibly exist, even in derogation of the fundamental laws and principles."[71] Applying this reasoning to the facts of the case, Roane upheld the 1805 act altering the charter of the Mutual Assurance Society. The corporation possessed the power to alter its "ordinary regulations," he argued, especially when the powers and purposes under the charter no longer proved useful or expedient.[72]

Roane and Marshall thus disagreed over the extent to which states ought to be able to regulate property rights. Writing to a friend after Marshall's *Dartmouth College* decision, Roane reiterated his belief that the legislature had the power to "get rid of oppressive charters." Referring to his opinion in *Currie's Administrators,* Roane wrote, "That principle it is now all-important to adhere to. It affords the only check against the rapid strides which are everywhere making to multiply charters said to be irrepealable. Certain I am that all our checks and restrictions must be put in requisition to preserve the rights of the people from the ever active and increasing encroachment of those in power." Cognizant of the economic implications of Marshall's opinion, Roane feared that Marshall was establishing a precedent by which federal courts could attempt to protect property from state regulation.

Roane's opinion in *Currie's Administrators* demonstrated a moderate approach toward the power of law to effect economic change. On the one hand, Roane reaffirmed his commitment to the vested rights of property and the sacred nature of contracts, and such a view prevailed among the leading judges of the day. Chancellor James Kent of New York, for example, perhaps best exemplified this early-nineteenth-century judicial devotion to vested rights. Over the course of his career, Kent ruled that a legislative grant of a steamboat monopoly prevented lawmakers from granting a steamboat license to another entrepreneur, that a franchise to a bridge company prohibited another from building a competing bridge, and that a contract granting the rights of the public to fish along the banks of an individual's waterfront property did not give the fishermen the right to take any wood, grass, or even seaweed from along the shore. "The slow increase and its usefulness as a manure and as a protection to the bank," Kent wrote of the seaweed, "will upon every just and equitable principle vest the property of the weed in the owner of the land."[73] While Roane never issued a similarly extreme declaration, the general tone of his judicial decisions demonstrated a clear commitment to vested rights.

On the other hand, Roane's opinion in *Currie's Administrators* allowed the legislature flexibility in altering charters based on changing social needs, and in this way Roane foreshadowed the course of nineteenth-century American legal development. Like Justice Joseph Story in his *Dartmouth College* concurrence, Roane based his opinion on the pragmatic notion that legislatures might need to alter corporate charters. The two judges' means of attaining this end were different: Story argued that legislatures could reserve the power to amend corporate charters within the charters themselves, while Roane viewed the corporation as serving an exclusively public purpose, thereby allowing legislative interference. The end result of both formulas was the same, for each allowed the legislature the power to direct economic change as it saw fit. As the nation underwent a transition from the eighteenth-century idea of property that emphasized the vested rights of owners to the nineteenth-century conception that stressed "the release of energy," Roane's opinions reflected the changing legal environment.

Still, Roane, Kent, Story, and even Marshall belonged to an older generation of jurists, born during the revolutionary era, that valued the rights of "established landowners" over "aspiring entrepreneurs and property holders." [74] Not until later, especially after Chief Justice Roger B. Taney of the U.S. Supreme Court took the side of entrepreneurial expansion in the Charles River Bridge case, did state judges begin to conceive of the public good apart from the interests of established property owners. Roane's opinion in *Currie's Administrators* may have foreshadowed the future, but in many respects he still belonged to an older generation that stressed the sacredness of all contractual relationships.

Roane's record on slavery and property demonstrated the subtle shifts in his thinking during the early nineteenth century. Initially, Roane looked at both issues through the lens of an eighteenth-century jurist—he decided such cases based on fixed principles regarding the sacredness of liberty or the inviolability of property rights. When cases involving individual emancipation of slaves first came before Roane, he delighted in acting as a "humble organ of the law decreeing liberty." [75] Yet Roane became increasingly aware of the larger policy implications of this stand, and over time he proved more cautious in his attitudes toward emancipation. Similarly, when it came to the issue of vested rights, Roane initially expressed his commitment to preserving the sacred rights of property and warned against legislative interference with such liberties. Yet, as with the slavery issue, Roane gained an awareness that other considerations might dictate a less-than-absolute devotion to protecting property owners—the public interest might require that the court favor the granting of new charters or legislative alteration of existing agreements.

Roane's commitment to liberty in slave cases and vested rights in property cases thus underwent a slow transformation over time, and his flexibility on such issues mirrored the fluidity of society in the early republic. But on an issue of greater importance to Roane—the nature of the federal Union and the jurisdiction of state courts—he stood his ideological ground.

State Power

Roane is best known not for his judicial labors but for his political writings championing state power in opposition to the U.S. Supreme Court.[76] Although long characterized by historians as the leader of the "Richmond Junto," Roane did not wield the political influence usually attributed to him. As F. Thornton Miller argues, there is "precious little" evidence that the junto, a supposedly secret and powerful political organization that dominated Virginia's public life, even existed.[77] True, Roane was no stranger to politics. Active as a Democratic-Republican Party official at the state level and visible on the national political scene after the first of his battles with the U.S. Supreme Court, Roane even emerged as a possible candidate for the presidency in the 1820s. But, in Miller's words, Roane "was not a political boss and there is no evidence that he tried to play that kind of role."[78]

Most historians who have examined Roane's political writings have done so with an eye toward the ultimate expression of state sovereignty in the South—secession. Imposing the values of the fire-eating disunionists of 1861 onto Roane, some writers have labeled him the "original secessionist" and have attempted to understand his early-nineteenth-century commitment to state power as part of a narrowly sectional, proslavery, agrarian agenda.[79] Yet Roane was obviously neither a proslavery partisan nor a reactionary agrarian. In terms of his ideas about the judicial role, about slavery, and about property, Roane was a typical American state judge at the turn of the nineteenth century. His early opposition to the U.S. Supreme Court developed not out of a longing to defend slavery, to hinder economic advancement, or to champion a southern set of values. Instead, Roane's early opposition to Marshall grew out of the revolutionary ideals he had held back to the days of his opposition to the Constitution and his association with Patrick Henry. Quite simply, Roane worried that a consolidated national government, in the form of a powerful U.S. Supreme Court, threatened to undermine the power of both state legislatures and state courts. As Roane once wrote to James Monroe, "The only fear is, that carried away by the Vortex of Power—feeling power and forgetting right—the safeguard for our liberties by the virtue of our fathers, will be demolished."[80] Rather than a precursor to mid-nineteenth-century secessionists, Roane was more the heir to late-eighteenth-century patriots in his defense of states. Only after the Missouri Crisis made slavery a national issue did Roane's rhetoric take on a more strident and sectional tone.

Roane began his crusade against the Supreme Court with his opinion in *Hunter v. Martin* (1814), a case involving Virginia's postrevolutionary confiscation of Tory lands. After the U.S. Supreme Court voided the state's confiscation act in *Fairfax's Devisee v. Hunter's Lessee* (1813) on the grounds that the law violated the Treaty of 1794 with England, Roane led the way both in declaring Section 25 of the Judiciary Act of 1789 unconstitutional and in refusing to obey the mandate of the Supreme Court. Roane viewed the dispute as a judicial clash, involving the independence, power, and jurisdiction of two distinct court systems, one of which was trying to overrun the other. His lengthy opinion in *Hunter v. Martin,* reprinted in the *Richmond Enquirer,* earned the Virginia judge a national reputation as the Supreme Court's chief foe and initiated a crusade against the Court that ended only with Roane's death.[81]

Roane attacked Section 25 of the 1789 act, which allowed for appeals from state courts to the federal judiciary, as inconsistent with the U.S. Constitution's provisions regarding judicial power and jurisdiction. Roane believed that unless stated otherwise, all of the Constitution's provisions regarding the jurisdiction of courts applied only to the federal judiciary. "Naturally the jurisdiction granted to a government is confined to the courts of that government," Roane claimed. "It does not, naturally, run into and affect the courts of another and distinct government."[82] With the exception of Article 6, which specifically referred to state judges, Roane found no constitutional provisions regulating state courts. Section 2 of Article 3, for example, which provided for trial by jury in the state in which the crime was committed, applied only to federal courts. Such was also the case with the Seventh Amendment's establishment of the right of trial by jury in civil cases. "It will not be contended that it relates to the jurisdiction of the state courts," Roane wrote, "as most of the state constitutions had already provided for the inviolability of jury trial." And in Roane's view, when the Eighth Amendment afforded the right of speedy trial in the state in which the crime was committed, the reference again was undoubtedly to the federal courts. To Roane, in short, Section 25 of the Judiciary Act of 1789, by intruding into the jurisdiction of state courts, was inconsistent with the Constitution's exclusive concern with federal court jurisdiction.[83] Because the Constitution did not subordinate the state judiciary to the federal, the two court systems stood on equal footing, with neither holding power over the other. Therefore, the Virginia Court of Appeals, as a coequal judicial body, had legitimate grounds on which to oppose the Supreme Court's decision.

To defend further his belief in the distinct and equal character of the state and federal judiciaries, Roane turned in *Hunter* to the theory of state sovereignty as articulated in a Pennsylvania Supreme Court case. In *Commonwealth v. Cobbett* (1799), the Pennsylvania court unanimously refused to permit the defendant to remove a cause from the state courts into the federal courts.[84] According to Roane, the court concluded that the federal government derived its authority to rule from the states, which had originally come together to form a new union through the Constitution. Under this scheme, because the states retained all powers except those granted to the government of the United States, the national government through its judiciary possessed no authority to coerce state courts. With precedent on his side, Roane believed that the Virginia Court of Appeals stood on solid ground in its battle with the Supreme Court. "I consider this decision by the Supreme Court of Pennsylvania as a complete and solemn authority to show," he wrote, "that in case of a difference of opinion between the governments as to the extent of the powers vested by the Constitution, while neither party is competent to bind the other, the courts of each have power to act upon the subject."[85] State sovereignty, then, expressed through judicial precedent, became a key means by which Roane attempted to defend the power of the Virginia Court of Appeals against the intrusion of the Supreme Court.

In subsequent political writings, state sovereignty emerged as the centerpiece of Roane's challenge to Marshall. In advancing this argument, Roane drew upon the Antifederalist tradition of the 1780s as well as the Kentucky and Virginia Resolutions of 1798–99. Roane's attachment to Jefferson, the author of the Kentucky Resolution, accelerated Roane's devotion to the doctrine of state sovereignty.[86] In 1815 Roane sought Jefferson's view of the decision in *Hunter v. Martin*, initiating an important political friendship that continued until Roane's death. When Jefferson said that he agreed with Roane's opinion in *Hunter v. Martin*, Roane expressed a renewed sense of confidence about the ruling. "The opinion here seem pretty general in favour of the decision," he wrote to James Barbour, one of Virginia's U.S. senators. "If we have erred, we have erred with Plato & Socrates—for Mr. Jefferson is with us." Roane's deep respect for Jefferson, coupled with the former president's long-standing commitment to state sovereignty, help to explain Roane's fervent adoption of the theory and his renewed sense of determination on the matter.[87] With Jefferson on his side, Roane made it known that

future Supreme Court decisions of a like nature would meet with similar defiance. "The 25th Section of the judicial act," he asserted to Barbour, "can
never be enforced in Virginia."[88]

Backed by Jefferson, Roane continued his campaign against the Supreme
Court. Marshall's vigorous endorsement of national supremacy and implied
powers in *McCulloch v. Maryland* (1819) provoked a series of essays by
Roane in the *Richmond Enquirer.*[89] *McCulloch* involved the constitutionality of the national bank and the ability of the state of Maryland to tax a
branch of that institution. Roane supported the national bank. In at least two
instances, he affirmed the necessity of the bank, once observing that "a great
a general distress would pervade all classes" were the bank to disappear. He
even purchased fifty shares of stock in the bank for his son, William.[90] In
response to the *McCulloch* decision, therefore, Roane did not write as an
opponent of the national bank itself. Even though the Virginia Court of Appeals was not involved in *McCulloch*, Roane viewed Marshall's decision as a
flagrant perversion of the Supreme Court's proper role and a threat to the
sovereignty of the states.

As in *Hunter v. Martin*, Roane used state sovereignty to attack the Supreme Court's jurisdiction in particular and the national government's power
in general. "It is not competent to the general government to usurp rights
reserved to the states, nor for its courts to adjudicate them away. . . . Our
government is a federal and not a consolidated government." This distinction
was important. If the nation were truly federal in character, the Supreme
Court would have no jurisdiction over a state matter, as such issues would
remain the domain of the states' legislators and judges. By augmenting the
Supreme Court's jurisdiction to permit review of state laws, Roane believed,
Marshall threatened to replace the federal system with a consolidated scheme
in which the national government was superior. To combat this idea, Roane
turned again to state sovereignty. "The Constitution of the United States was
not adopted by the people of the United States, as one people," he wrote,
countering the Court's popular sovereignty and national supremacy argument. "It was adopted by the several states, in their highest sovereign character, that is, by the people of the said states, respectively; such people being
competent, and they only competent, to alter the preexisting governments
operating in the said states."[91] Under this theory of sovereignty, the Supreme
Court, as an agent of the national government, possessed no jurisdiction over
state laws, whether judicial decisions or statutes.

While Roane employed state sovereignty to make the jurisdictional argument, he drew on the common-law tradition to undermine Marshall's notion
of the implied powers of Congress. Roane contended that the Necessary and

Proper Clause in no way extended the powers that the Constitution specifically granted to the legislative branch. Instead, the words of the clause, he
wrote, were "tautologous and redundant, though harmless." In other words,
the Necessary and Proper Clause, in Roane's view, was a mere truism that
had no meaning in and of itself and certainly did not augment the enumerated powers of the national government.[92] Citing the works of Littleton,
Coke, and Blackstone, Roane contended that grants of power included only
those accessory powers that were "fairly incident" to the enumerated powers.
Roane thus disagreed with Marshall's liberal interpretation of the Necessary
and Proper Clause as out of line with established principles of the common
law.[93] Again, Roane did not attack the specific act of Congress establishing
the national bank. Rather, he condemned Marshall's broad grant of authority to Congress seemingly to assume whatever powers it wished at the expense of the states. "I principally make war against the declaratory decision
of the Supreme Court," Roane wrote, "giving Congress power to 'bind us in
all cases whatsoever.'" [94]

Finally, Roane assailed Marshall for his expansive view of judicial power.
Marshall's broad attempt to establish national supremacy and to expand the
central government's implied powers struck Roane as a flagrant perversion
of the Supreme Court's role. In a case that dealt with specific issues regarding the national bank, Marshall's sweeping pronouncements on the scope
of congressional power and the nature of the Union appeared to Roane to
be "entirely extrajudicial and without authority." Moreover, Roane saw the
Court assuming the form of a legislative body. The Supreme Court "often
puts its veto upon the acts of the immediate representatives of the people,"
he charged. "It in fact assumes legislative powers by repealing laws which the
legislature have enacted." [95]

When taken within the context of Roane's own spirited assertions of judicial review of legislation at the state level, these statements in support of
legislative supremacy seem out of character or at least ironic. However, one
of the key issues in this debate for Roane was that of defending his position
as a state judge. If the Supreme Court under Marshall were allowed to continue unabated its dramatic expansion of national judicial power and jurisdiction, what would become of the Virginia Court of Appeals and other
state courts? Prodded by Jefferson, Roane argued that Marshall's decision in
McCulloch was another step in the creation of a consolidated national judiciary that presented a looming threat to state judicial power. "While I would
consent to . . . support the federal judiciary within the states, in all its legitimate objects," Roane wrote in 1819, "I would not set up without necessity a
batch of courts strong enough to withdraw from the state courts their proper

powers."[96] In Roane's view, the Supreme Court's continued attempts to further its power threatened to render state courts—including his own Court of Appeals—weak and ineffective.

The Rise of a Southern Judiciary

In the years after *McCulloch,* Roane's attitudes assumed a more stridently sectional tone. With the emergence of the slavery issue within the context of Missouri's admission to the Union, Roane had another reason to cling to the doctrine of state power and to oppose the Supreme Court's rapid assumption of power. Many northern congressmen advocated the Tallmadge Amendment, a proposal to ban the further importation of slaves into Missouri and provide for the gradual emancipation of slaves already there. This 1819 proposal ignited a firestorm in Congress over the national government's relationship to slavery. While Roane initially regarded the Missouri question as relatively inconsequential compared to his ideological battles with Marshall, by the early months of 1820 Roane's feelings on the issue of the future of slavery ran deep.[97] "If any thing could add to the calamitous condition of our country," he wrote to President James Monroe, "it would be that the principles of 1799 are trodden under foot, and our slaves are incited to insurrection." Roane vented his hostility toward those who proposed territorial limits on the institution of slavery, labeling them "Eastern intriguers" driven by "their lust of dominion and power." He suggested that the issue of slavery would tear apart the Union, and he even referred to forming an alliance against northeasterners. "Let us cherish, also, the western people. They have an identity of interests with us, and they also hold the Keys of the Mississippi. If driven to it, we can yet form with them a great nation," he wrote. "The influence of a southern sun has given to them a justice and generosity of character, which we look for in vain among the northern Yankies."[98]

By 1820, the Missouri Crisis had profoundly altered Roane's attitudes toward slavery. The eager emancipator in a series of slave manumission cases in the early years of the century had become an ardent defender of slaveholders' rights. Roane's attitudes toward the Supreme Court and the national government thereafter took on a sharper tone. His eagerness to oppose concentrated national power rooted in his revolutionary principles and his desire to defend the jurisdiction of state courts based on his own judicial experience now converged with a defense of slavery. In the aftermath of the Missouri Crisis, Roane thus stepped up his attacks on the Court.[99]

The Supreme Court's decision in *Cohens v. Virginia* (1821) provided the context for Roane's final showdown with Marshall. As he had in *McCulloch,*

Marshall used his opinion in the case, which dealt with whether the Supreme Court possessed jurisdiction in an appeal from a borough court in Virginia, to enunciate broad constitutional principles relating to the nature of the Union and the power of the Supreme Court within the federal system. In granting jurisdiction under Section 25 of the Judiciary Act of 1789, Marshall again invited criticism from Roane.[100]

Roane's offensive again centered on the Supreme Court's lack of jurisdiction and drew support from the theory of state sovereignty. "It is an anomaly in the science of government, that the courts of one independent government are to control and reverse the judgments of the courts of another," he contended. The facts of the case made this claim particularly outstanding, for *Cohens* did not involve an appeal from Virginia's highest court. Rather, the Cohen brothers, convicted of selling lottery tickets in violation of a Virginia law, appealed their case directly from the Norfolk borough court to the Supreme Court. This unusual situation—with the state of Virginia defending the decision of one of its lower courts—considerably weakened Roane's argument about the coequal nature of the state and federal judiciaries. Here Roane's position appeared untenable and his arguments forced. Unlike in *Fairfax's Devisee v. Hunter's Lessee* and *Martin v. Hunter's Lessee*, which involved Supreme Court challenges to the Virginia Court of Appeals, in *Cohens* Roane found himself arguing that the lowly Norfolk Borough Court, as a member of the Virginia court system, did not have to adhere to a decision of the U.S. Supreme Court.[101]

Beyond the jurisdictional argument, Roane subtly injected the slavery debate into his discussion by contending that the Supreme Court's consolidationist tendencies presented a threat to the entire scope of liberties enjoyed by the American people. The division of powers inherent in federalism, coupled with the system of checks and balances at both the state and national levels, Roane believed, were critical to the preservation of rights—including, no doubt, southerners' license to hold slaves. "This division and limitation of the granted powers, and the checks necessarily resulting therefrom," he reasoned, "forms the only security for our liberties." By usurping authority from the states, the Court undermined this structure and removed all obstacles to its continued acquisition of power. While other departments of the government were subject to restraint by means of the elective franchise, the Supreme Court could continue unchecked on a course toward despotic rule. "There is but one higher grade in this climax of arrogance and absurdity," Roane noted, "and that is, to claim to hold its powers by divine authority, and in utter contempt of the sovereign power of the people."[102]

Roane continued his struggle against the Supreme Court until his death.

To end what he perceived as the Court's destructive designs, he supported an amendment to the Constitution, proposed in the December 1821 session of Congress, that would have made the U.S. Senate, instead of the Court, the forum for review of state court decisions involving constitutional questions. The proposed amendment went nowhere, however, and most of Virginia's aging leaders did not even offer their support—a fact that bothered Roane. "Jefferson and Madison hang back too much in this great crisis," he confided to a friend. Roane had reached the pinnacle of his extremism at the end of his life. In the spring of 1822, at age sixty, he became ill, and he died on September 4 of that year.[103]

Spencer Roane's life spanned six decades of dramatic change in the history of Virginia and the early republic. Born into the hopeful yet uncertain setting of the prerevolutionary Tidewater, Roane came of age in the formative era of his state's and the nation's constitutional and legal development. Especially during the later years of his judicial career, Roane began to witness the rise of powerful state judiciaries, the creation of legal doctrines designed to facilitate economic expansion, and the beginnings of constitutional conflict over slavery. A product of revolutionary America, Roane often found the ideals of the late eighteenth century in conflict with those of the new American legal order that he saw emerging before his eyes. Tensions about the judicial role, slavery, and property all marked Roane's judicial tenure. But he remained true to his Antifederalist roots when it came to the issue of federalism. When Marshall's Supreme Court expanded its jurisdiction at the expense of the power of states, especially state courts, Roane struck back. The threat subsequently posed during the Missouri Crisis only deepened Roane's commitment to state sovereignty, slavery, and the South.

Roane was a Virginian through and through. Over the course of his lifetime, he learned significant lessons about law and politics from the leading members of his state's legal community—from George Wythe, St. George Tucker, Patrick Henry, Edmund Pendleton, and Thomas Jefferson. Through his unique experiences with each of these individuals, Roane drew on his state's rich heritage. In his career as a judge and a political writer, Roane combined the legal learning of Wythe and Tucker, the prideful partisanship of Henry, the judicial leadership of Pendleton, and the constitutional vision of Jefferson. In many ways, Roane became the embodiment of early-nineteenth-century Virginia legal culture (an ironic twist, since Roane battled another native of the Old Dominion who had imbibed a different set of principles). Through most of his life, though, Roane had no difficulty perceiving himself as both a Virginian and an American. He was, after all, throughout most of his career, the leading judge of the highest court in the most significant and populous state in the Union.

By the end of Roane's career, however, his position and that of his state were on the wane. Virginians anticipated the end of their White House dynasty and looked on in horror as the Missouri debate divided the nation. As Virginia's perspective and voice became less American and more southern, so did Roane's. By the time of his death, his outspoken positions on state sovereignty, slavery, and sectionalism had transformed him from a leading American judge into a passionate southern partisan, from a statesman into a firebrand. Like a "firebell in the night," the Missouri Crisis and the slavery issue had initiated the rise of a southern judicial tradition.[104]

CHAPTER TWO

John Catron,
Jacksonian Jurisprudence, and
the Expansion of the South

The interests of the Eastern Capitalists and the Southern and Western people come so directly in conflict that unanimity is not to be expected. —JOHN CATRON TO ANDREW JACKSON DONELSON, DECEMBER 31, 1829

Judge John Catron's state judicial career coincided with the territorial growth of the republic and the continued rise of sectional tensions. As Americans moved westward during the early nineteenth century, many carried their slaves with them, thus confirming the lesson of the Missouri Crisis: expansion had profound political and legal ramifications for the issue of slavery. But more than slaves, new settlers brought with them their customs, habits, and values—their ideas about government, law, and honor as well as their dreams about land, opportunity, and prosperity. Expansion therefore affected not only the questions surrounding slavery but also issues of social control and the distribution of resources on the frontier. Catron's Tennessee certainly witnessed these social transformations. Home of Andrew Jackson, whose election to the White House in 1828 symbolized the rise of the "common man" and the expansion of the nation, the state teemed with ambitious homesteaders and rough frontierspeople attempting to carve out new lives for themselves.

Catron emerged as a judicial leader in the state during the 1820s and eventually received an appointment from Jackson to the U.S. Supreme Court. Although some of Catron's Supreme Court opinions are well known, his years as a state judge during the 1820s and 1830s have gone unnoticed.[1] During these years, Catron fought the rough-and-tumble culture of dueling and violence, paved the way for economic opportunity in a frontier society, displaced Native Americans who stood in the way of white settlement, and upheld the legal rights of slaveholders. Along the way, Catron developed a fierce devotion to the Union that manifested itself both in the nullification crisis and again during the Civil War. In short, Catron demonstrated throughout his state judicial career a thorough devotion to Jacksonian principles.

Mountain Lawyer to State Judge

The world of John Catron could not have been more different from the realm of the Tidewater gentry from which Spencer Roane had emerged. Born in 1786 in Grayson County, Virginia, Catron's humble origins made him an unlikely candidate for juristic renown. His father Peter Catron, a native of Germany who had migrated to Pennsylvania, fought in the American Revolution and moved his family to Virginia a few years after the war's end. In 1804, like so many other Americans of their generation, the Catrons journeyed west to Kentucky, settling in Wayne County.[2] "Of poor but honest parentage," the young Catron struggled to gain whatever education he could in the rustic environs of the backcountry. He attended common schools in western Virginia and Kentucky and, probably because his father spoke little English, Catron insisted on studying English rather than Latin grammar, much to the dissatisfaction of his classically inclined tutor. Catron read anything and everything he could find, including the writings of Paine, Hume, and Gibbon as well as Blackstone and the Bible.[3]

Catron married Matilda Childress of Nashville in 1807, and they moved to Tennessee in 1812, settling in the tiny village of Sparta in the Cumberland Mountains. There he drove cattle and groomed his father's racehorse while studying law with George W. Gibbs. Soon afterward, when Creek Indians attacked the garrison at nearby Fort Mims, Catron joined other Tennesseans in a military campaign of retribution. Volunteering in the Second Tennessee Regiment, he marched to Alabama under the command of young Andrew Jackson and participated in the expeditions against the Creeks along the Coosa River and around Talladega and Fort Strother in the central portion of the state. Having "brought home some army popularity," as he later put it, and having earned admission to the bar in Overton County, Tennessee, Catron's legal career commenced. He established a friendship with Isaac Thomas, attorney general for the Third Judicial Circuit of middle Tennessee, and when Thomas won election to Congress in 1815, Catron assumed much of Thomas's law practice. Despite Catron's obvious lack of experience, the state legislature subsequently elected him to a two-year term as attorney general for the Third Circuit, which encompassed seven counties.[4] This much sought-after position allowed Catron to expand his circle of acquaintances and gain practical experience with the law. "The courts were full of indictments for crimes from murder down," Catron later wrote of his circuit experience. "Here I had to fight the battle single and alone and to work day and night."[5]

In 1818, after two years in the position, Catron moved to Nashville, where he began to establish ties within the community. As his wife was the great-niece of General James Robertson, one of the city's founders, the Catrons had little difficulty establishing themselves among Nashville's elite. Catron joined the Masonic Lodge on his arrival and in 1822 became a trustee of the University of Nashville. In the meantime, General Jackson, who had recommended the move to Nashville, assumed the role of patron for the young mountain lawyer. Jackson's assistance, as well as Catron's practical experience with the state's legal community, apparently helped Catron to overcome the handicap of his poor education and indelicate manners. Having made his home in the political and commercial capital of the state, he developed a successful law practice, in part because of his "unwearied industry [and] physical and mental ability." Economic circumstances also assisted Catron's rise, as the Panic of 1819 created countless opportunities for lawyers. "The town and country were overwhelmed with misfortunes in trade, and a general bankruptcy, not known before or since in that country," Catron later recounted. "By the end of that year, the courts had two thousand causes in them at the least, and I had more business than I could do in the town itself."[6] Many of these cases involved conflicting land titles, and Catron became somewhat of an expert on the law of real property. Although a success as a lawyer by any reckoning, he never excelled as an orator and always lacked the social grace and conviviality required of a gentleman. Democratic editor Samuel H. Laughlin described Catron as "exceedingly uncouth," with "no capacity for public speaking." Yet according to Laughlin, Catron also displayed a "wise, mysterious knowing manner," as if attempting to beguile the public, and avoided "all social intercourse with common people." This aristocrat-like aloofness, Catron's critic jealously observed, only "added to his reputation for knowledge."[7]

Despite such criticism, Catron's fortunes continued to rise, and after six years of successful practice in Nashville, the legislature elected him judge of the Supreme Court of Errors and Appeals in 1824. In contrast to Roane, heir to a well established Virginia judicial tradition, Catron joined a court with a brief and undistinguished history. Formed in 1809 by an act of the Tennessee legislature, the court originally had only two members and possessed limited jurisdiction until a series of measures added a judge and ultimately granted the tribunal appellate jurisdiction in all cases of law and equity.[8]

By the time of Catron's accession to the bench, the court consisted of three other members, all of whom were competent and well educated but not especially distinguished. Judge John Haywood, a North Carolinian by birth and former member of the supreme court of North Carolina, was by far the most highly regarded of the group. In 1801 Haywood had published *A Manual of the Laws of North Carolina,* and he later edited reports of the opinions of the Superior Court of North Carolina. In 1816 he moved to Tennessee, where he settled in Nashville. Immediately elected to the Tennessee Supreme Court, Haywood wrote *The Civil and Political History of the State of Tennessee* and served on the court until his death in 1826. Intelligent and dedicated, Haywood gained a reputation in North Carolina as one of the greatest judges in the state's early history, though his contributions to Tennessee proved less substantial. Catron's other colleagues were solid but unspectacular. Judge Robert Whyte, a Scotsman and a linguist, taught at the College of William and Mary and practiced law in North Carolina before coming to Tennessee; Judge Jacob Peck, a Virginian, was perhaps better known for his dabbling in the natural sciences than his work as a jurist. Haywood and Catron served together for only a few years, but both Whyte and Peck sat with Catron for nearly his entire tenure on the state court. Judge Nathan Green, among the most distinguished of all nineteenth-century Tennessee jurists, served alongside Catron for a few years at the end of Catron's Tennessee career.[9]

Catron's service on the supreme court coincided with intense legislative debate over questions of judicial accountability and independence. During this period, the members of the court rode circuit across the state and conducted business in six different places. The heavy burden of circuit riding and large volume of cases caused innumerable delays in the administration of justice. In 1831, the Judiciary Committee of the state House of Representatives inquired specifically into the causes of delay in the court's completion of its business. Judge Catron's response to these inquiries only aroused further suspicion of the judiciary. He contended that it was "impossible" under the existing system to conduct all the business of the court. "I feel very safe in saying," Catron wrote to the committee, "that were not another cause placed on the docket, except such as were left undecided at the last term, it would take the court three years to do the business on it, and that it would be badly done at that." Even if the court were to conduct all its business in one place, he contended, the judges still would not be able to cover the entire docket within a reasonable length of time. In particular, Catron criticized the fact that state law authorized appeals and writs of error in all cases. Under this system, Catron insisted, the court could not continue to operate. After sending this frank appraisal of the judicial system to the legislature, Catron tendered his resignation from the bench.[10]

Catron's report and resignation sparked three months of debate in the legislature over the future of the state supreme court. Legislators discussed whether to reform the court or to abolish the institution altogether. In debating reform, lawmakers considered various proposals for making the judiciary more accountable and more efficient, including abolishing tenure during good behavior, publishing the court's written opinions, alleviating the circuit-riding duties, and creating the position of chief justice. After consideration of such issues, in December 1831 the legislature passed a compromise measure. The statute added a fourth member to the court, the chief justice; fined judges twelve dollars for each day absent from the court; required each judge to file an affidavit certifying how many days he had been absent; and held that if the four members of the court were equally divided in opinion, the inferior court's ruling stood. The law also created the position of supreme court reporter, who was to furnish the public printer with a manuscript copy of the court's decisions.[11] Lawmakers thus satisfied those calling for more accountability from the state judiciary but obviously did not accede to those who favored the abolition of the court. Catron, whose candor about the judiciary's failings had initiated the whole debate, won the praise of legislators for his "patriotism and virtue." In December 1831 lawmakers elected him Tennessee's first chief justice.[12]

A product of frontier Tennessee and the political culture of Jacksonian America, Catron as a judge emphasized the experience of everyday life over legal expertise. He once described a lawyer without common sense as "a sheer pedant in his profession." "But force a young lawyer to battle his way up on the circuit," he continued, "to go and see the land surveyed, and the corner trees blocked before he tries his ejectment; to go into the workshop, or steamboat, or countinghouse, and see how the thing is done his client is lawing about, and he will beat a dozen of his equals in capacity, crammed with law to the throat." Catron's beliefs, representative of his meager educational background and modest social standing, translated into a distaste for overreliance on precedent and excessive citation of legal authorities. He objected, as he put it, "to piles of references and figures, formidable as a treasury report, gathered from the index, and having no value in the particular case; and which parade of authorities is notoriously an address of vanity to ignorance and pedantry." In contrast to Spencer Roane's revolutionary Virginia, where judges still labored under the shadow of the great English barristers, Catron's Tennessee of the early nineteenth century lent itself to a new style of judging as linked to lived experience as to Anglo tradition.[13]

During the early nineteenth century, as Americans moved westward into new states, appellate courts like Catron's grappled with the legal ramifications of expanding frontier settlement. Tennessee confronted the legal issues surrounding the persistence of violent cultural habits, the changes associated with economic growth and the opening of western lands, the existence of a large Cherokee Indian population in the eastern portion of the state, and an expanding slave population in the western half. In one form or another, all of these potential social and political tensions evolved into legal controversies that came before the Tennessee Supreme Court.

Dueling and Self-Defense

Two of Catron's most significant state opinions involved the South's cultural predisposition to violence. Historians of the region have long noted that southerners tended to resolve their disputes in violent ways. The practice of dueling, the epitome of this cultural trait, involved an elaborate set of rituals whereby gentlemen could resolve disputes and maintain their honor.[14] Frontier lawyers seemed particularly prone to such behavior. When describing his early duties as the attorney general for Tennessee's Third Circuit, Catron himself noted that most attorneys who traveled the circuit carried with them "pistols and holsters." "The pistols were carried, not to shoot thieves and robbers," he wrote, "but to fight each other, if by any chance a quarrel was hatched up, furnishing occasion for a duel." (Catron too packed a set of dueling pistols, although, according to his autobiographical account, he "managed to keep from fighting.")[15] To combat the practice, most southern states passed antidueling legislation during the early nineteenth century, and many of these measures prohibited duelists from holding public office or practicing law, medicine, or the ministry. Tennessee passed a few such laws, one in 1801 that declared killing in a duel to be murder and another in 1809 that barred duelists from holding office, testifying in court, or serving as jurors. In addition, the state required its attorneys to be morally and mentally fit to practice their profession.[16]

The case of *Smith v. State* (1829) raised the question of whether the Tennessee Supreme Court would rule that a lawyer's participation in a duel violated these statutes. Antidueling laws existed all across the South at the same time that distinguished gentlemen challenged each other to combat. The question of judicial attitudes toward and actual enforcement of antidueling laws was thus of primary importance. Would the court be influenced by the South's code of honor to the extent that the judges would turn a blind eye toward the practice? In Tennessee, the case of Calvin Smith would provide the answer. Smith, an attorney, had accepted a challenge, crossed the border into Kentucky, and killed his opponent on the field of honor. Indicted for murder in Kentucky, a Tennessee circuit court had moved to strike him from the roll of attorneys before the court, whereupon Smith appealed to the Tennessee Supreme Court.[17]

Catron seized the opportunity to denounce not only Smith's actions but the entire culture of honor and violence that so pervaded the state. He held that an attorney could be stricken from the roll "for good cause," provided a judge deemed the charges against the lawyer sufficient to warrant removal. Believing that the charges against Smith clearly sanctioned his disbarment, Catron entered into a lengthy discussion of the meaning and the motivation of dueling. He put those who fought duels into three categories. "Many men of strong minds have equally strong passions, which are ill controlled," he wrote. These "men of worth" who fought duels were, in Catron's words, no "less wicked than others we will name, but their standing renders it more difficult to punish them." Here the judge probably remembered his own patron, Andrew Jackson, who had, of course, developed quite a reputation as a duelist during his days in Tennessee politics and had killed a man in an 1806 fray.[18] "Another set of men fight duels (or more generally make a show toward it)," Catron continued, "to gratify their vanity, by drawing upon themselves a little temporary notice, which their personal worth or good conduct cannot procure." Catron came down hard on this class of duelists, whom he labeled "pretenders to bravery and gentlemanship" and "absolute cowards."[19] A third group accepted and issued challenges to fight out of a desire to attain "true courage." According to Catron, these weak-minded individuals lacked the "moral and independent firmness" to stand up to their neighbors. "The pride, weak nerves, and morbid sensibility of such a man," the judge wrote, "forces him to the pistol's mouth of a ruthless and unprincipled antagonist as feeble, trembling and unresisting as the lamb to the shambles, and with almost an equal certainty of destruction, because he still more fears the detraction of the malicious and the gossip of the giddy."[20]

Regardless of the category to which they belonged, Catron believed that all men who fought duels clung to an outmoded and false code of honor. He attacked the idea that combat was often "the only redress" for injury. "This is not the precept that our Saviour taught, our religion inculcates, and our laws enjoin," he wrote. "Malice, vengeance, and crime, have no place but in the catalogue of iniquity." Elevating Christian principles over cultural norms and practices, Catron advised men who were insulted to wait, calm their passions, and "in a firm, serious, and just temper" attempt to reason with the offending party. Pessimistic about the effect of his admonitions, Catron admitted that the course of action he recommended required "more moral courage and fearless firmness than most men are masters of." Yet he insisted that dueling was a destructive practice that needed to be eliminated by the strict adherence to statutes. Law—not honor—was to govern southern society. "We are told this is only a kind of honorable homicide!" he sternly concluded. "The law knows it as a wicked and wilful murder, and it is our duty to treat it as such. We are placed here firmly and fearlessly to execute the laws of the land, not visionary codes of honor, framed to subserve the purposes of destruction."[21]

Catron's opinion in *Smith* demonstrated his unwillingness to bend to community opinion or cultural norms on the issue of violence. The response of the state's lawyers to Catron's ruling proved harsh, but Catron stood by the decision. As the judge himself noted, "I was scorched with many a racy sarcasm; such as, that a sinner who had carried blank challenges in the crown of his hat, and slept with his pistols under his head, was a very proper man to turn saint and lecturer, to put down a vice he so well understood in all its bearings." Indeed, one contemporary described Catron as a "fighting lawyer" who carried a pair of pistols "in his saddlebags with his clean shirts." Though he no doubt understood the practice of dueling, Catron certainly did not condone it from the bench. Referring with pride to the *Smith* decision, he noted in an 1853 autobiographical letter that, among the legal community, "we have not had a duel since."[22]

In another famous opinion, Catron adhered to established common-law rules regarding the legal definition of homicide in self-defense. *Grainger v. State* (1830) involved a conflict between Grainger and a man named Broach, who had been drinking with Grainger at a tavern. The two left the tavern and parted seemingly on good terms, but while they were riding home on their horses, Broach overtook Grainger and "struck him a violent blow on the breast." Broach continued to harass Grainger while chasing him. The frightened Grainger continued to ride until he came to a neighbor's house, where he dismounted and sought asylum. Broach too left his horse and went after Grainger. Shouting for help to the neighbor, Grainger came toward the house, "standing two or three yards from the wall, Broach advancing upon him." A hunter, Grainger carried a rifle, and he threatened to shoot the unarmed Broach if he came any closer. When Broach continued to advance, Grainger fired and killed his assailant.[23] Tried and convicted for murder, Grainger was sentenced to hang.

Catron's opinion in the "timid hunter case," as it came to be called, excused Grainger's actions because of the circumstances surrounding the killing. "Grainger used all the means in his power to escape from an overbearing bully," the judge wrote, shooting "only to protect his person from threatened violence." Reviewing common-law precedents, Catron concluded that no malice accompanied Grainger's actions. Instead, Catron argued, Grainger "behaved like a timid, cowardly man; was much alarmed, in imminent danger of a violent and instant assault and battery, and was cut off from the chances of probable assistance." For these reasons, Catron ruled that the homicide was excusable, and he overruled the conviction. As one scholar later described it, Catron's opinion "was avowedly based on standard common law authority, and not intended to change the settled doctrines of the law of self-defense."[24]

Yet Catron unwisely or perhaps carelessly omitted an important phrase from the holding in the case. "If the jury had believed that Grainger was in danger of great bodily harm from Broach, or thought himself so," Catron concluded, "then the killing would have been in self-defense." Had Catron included the words "upon sufficient grounds" after "thought himself so," the opinion would never have stirred the controversy that surrounded its subsequent interpretation. In Grainger's case, the grounds for his fears were clearly sufficient, which probably explained why Judge Catron omitted this language.[25] Nevertheless, not until later decisions—in 1846 and 1856—did the court clarify Catron's holding. In the latter case, for example, the Tennessee Supreme Court upheld a trial judge's restatement of the *Grainger* rule to a jury, where he charged that "the proof ought to show that his (the prisoner's) fears were founded on some reasonable ground; that the law would not excuse the criminal act of the defendant, though under the influence of fear, if his fears were baseless, and the phantoms of the imagination." The court in this instance thus held that the judge's instructions and the *Grainger* rule were "in accordance with the well-established doctrine of the common law."[26] According to the Tennessee Supreme Court, the *Grainger* ruling clearly did not mean that any person fearing great bodily harm could kill his assailant without proving that the grounds for those fears were sufficient.

While the Tennessee Supreme Court worked to clarify Catron's *Grainger* opinion, lawyers and legal authorities literally interpreted the decision and ignored the court's subsequent interpretation of the case. In 1849, while reviewing a series of homicide decisions, the New York Court of Appeals wrote disapprovingly of the *Grainger* ruling: "The Supreme Court of Tennessee has gone still further and held that one who kills another, believing himself in danger of great bodily harm, will be justified, although he acted from cowardice, and without any sufficient ground, in the appearance, for the killing." Francis Wharton's famous *Treatise on the Law of Homicide,* published in 1855, similarly portrayed the Tennessee ruling as extreme. Lawyers arguing cases in Tennessee, and perhaps in other states as well, apparently also took the ruling to mean that legal excuse lay within the reach of killers who merely believed themselves in danger. One authority noted that *Grainger* "became notorious as a bulwark of defense and was not uncommonly supposed to have introduced new doctrines into the law of homicide in self-defense, whereby a man, especially if a coward, could justify himself in killing his unarmed assailant with a deadly weapon." [27]

Catron and the judges who followed him intended to formulate no such new doctrine. Nearly three decades after *Grainger,* the Tennessee Supreme Court definitively declared this literal interpretation of the case to be a corruption of the original intent of the opinion. In *Rippy v. State* (1858), Judge Robert Caruthers wrote of *Grainger,*

> No case has been more perverted and misapplied by advocates and juries. We have had one case before us in the last few years, in which the broad proposition [that mere apprehension of danger excused homicide] was charged as law. But for this, and the indication that it has obtained to some limited extent in the legal profession, it would scarcely be deemed necessary to notice it. There is not authority for such a position. It would be monstrous. No court should for a moment entertain or countenance it. The criminal code of no country ever has, nor, as we presume, ever will, give place to so bloody a principle.

To remove all doubt about where the court stood on this issue, the judge concluded with a succinct restatement of the rule of self-defense in Tennessee. "To excuse a homicide, the danger of life, or great bodily injury, must either be real, or honestly believed to be so at the time, and upon sufficient grounds. It must be apparent and imminent." [28]

Both the *Smith* and *Grainger* decisions demonstrated Catron's commitment to combating southern violence and upholding common-law principles. Historians of southern law and violence have slightly distorted Catron's record on this issue by focusing almost exclusively on the *Grainger* opinion. One historian wrote, for example, that the *Grainger* rule "swept through the South," when in fact it hardly swept through Tennessee before the state supreme court attempted to halt the influence of this misunderstood opinion.[29] When read in conjunction with the *Smith* case, it becomes clear that Catron never intended to expand the common-law doctrine of self-defense to allow a supposed fear of bodily harm to excuse murder. On the contrary, Catron and his colleagues worked actively to end the widespread mayhem and violence that enveloped the state.

Liberty, Economy, and the Public Interest

Catron's state judicial career paralleled a period of economic expansion the likes of which the state had never seen. The Market Revolution of the antebellum era penetrated even Tennessee: ironworks and other industry began to dot the landscape during the early nineteenth century, while steamboats regularly transported tobacco, cotton, iron, and other products down the state's rivers by the 1820s. Catron himself engaged in speculative enterprises soon after his appointment to the court. In 1827 he invested in an ironworks on the Natchez Trace along the Buffalo River, south of Nashville. After entering into a partnership with his brother and another investor, Catron and his partners obtained cheap land from the state under a recently passed law that encouraged the establishment of new industry. The Buffalo Iron Works, as it was called, acquired extensive landholdings, but the business operated just a single forge, probably indicating that only small amounts of iron were ever produced there. In 1833 Catron—by that time the sole owner—sold the fledgling business.[30]

This fleeting experience as an entrepreneur, combined with Catron's common origins, profoundly affected his outlook on the economic issues before the American public during the 1820s and 1830s. Like Jackson, himself an "enterpriser of middling success," Catron sympathized with the average American eager for social and economic advancement—the master mechanic who hoped to open his own shop, the small farmer who purchased new lands, or the struggling shopkeeper who dreamed of becoming a prominent merchant. Catron could relate to the hopes and aspirations of these "expectant capitalists," and he became a public spokesman for the interests of such small producers. Catron sought to use the law to uphold the public interest and to oppose the conferring of special privileges.[31]

Catron's earliest and most forceful statement on political economy came in his attack on the national bank. Well before President Jackson's famous campaign against the bank during the 1830s, Catron and other Tennesseans charged that the bank, by virtue of its many wealthy eastern and European shareholders, harmed the economic interests of average citizens and endangered the cause of liberty. In particular, in a pair of 1829 essays in the *Knoxville Register* addressed to "the cultivators of the soil and the laboring people in Tennessee," Judge Catron argued that Tennesseans paid $170,000 in interest to the national bank each year on loans made within the state. Noting that no one in the state owned stock in the bank, Catron saw this interest payment as a "positive tax by foreigners" on the people of Tennessee. "Who pays it?" he asked. "The people at large; the merchant who borrows to buy goods, groceries, &c. lays the seven per cent, (bank interest) on the goods, and makes you pay it; on every article of dry goods and groceries, you pay part of this tax; it is drawn from you silently by shillings without your knowledge." Catron believed that this interest paid by Tennesseans constituted taxation without representation.[32]

In typical Jacksonian fashion, Catron thus linked economic interests to political liberty. Sharply distinguishing between the interests of Tennesseans and those of the investors in the bank, he portrayed the latter as a villainous monied elite, disinterested in the welfare of average Americans. "Do the wealthy stockholders as individuals pay part of our taxes, aid in the promotion of education and religion, assist the friendless in want, contribute to the improvement of the country?" Catron asked. "No, they reside in Europe, and the eastern states, know little of our condition as a people and care nothing for our wants, or oppressions; the money is upon us, like a cloud of Egyptian locusts to eat up our substance and be withdrawn."[33] This "monied aristocracy," as Catron once referred to it, concentrated "real power in the hands of a few individuals." Comparing the power of the bank's investors to that of the English monarchy during the revolutionary era, Catron exhorted Tennesseans to assist in the abolition, or at least the reform, of the bank. Indeed, he even suggested a more democratic alternative: directors appointed by the president and Congress, branches established by the petitions of state legislatures, and branch directors appointed by state legislative action. Something had to be done, he believed, "to save the Constitution." "Are the people of Tennessee prepared to deposit their liberties with a few strangers partly subjects of European Monarchs," he asked, "or will they retain them in their own keeping?" In Catron's mind, economic opportunity and political liberty were thus inseparable.[34]

Catron's 1829 indictment of the bank presaged Jackson's famous veto message three years later. Both statements emphasized the threat to American liberty posed by concentrated capital and foreign stockholders, and both questioned the constitutionality of the bank itself. Moreover, like Jackson, who criticized the institution's eastern stockholders, Catron viewed the issues surrounding the bank in sectional terms. "On the subject of the U.S. Bank, the interests of the Eastern Capitalists and the Southern and Western people come so directly in conflict that unanimity is not to be expected," he wrote in 1829 to Andrew Jackson Donelson, the president's nephew. "It is our business to wrench from the group of the Eastern Merchants, a monopoly of the circulating medium of the whole union, to crush an aristocracy controlled by a few individuals for their own benefit, at the expense of the mass everywhere." Like Roane, who in the midst of the Missouri Crisis had envisioned an alliance of the South and West against "Eastern intriguers," Catron viewed suspiciously the concentration of economic and political power in northeastern cities.[35] Even after the demise of the national bank in the late 1830s, Catron continued to express his resentment of the monied aristocracy epitomized by the bank's president, Nicholas Biddle. Writing to fellow Tennessean James Polk in 1837, Catron derided these merchants for "think[ing] of money and little else" and compared the aristocratic Biddle to the Pope.[36]

This antagonism toward special privilege and the desire to protect the public interest emerged from Catron's judicial opinions as well as his political writings. During his years as a lawyer, he acquired a reputation as a specialist in suits involving land claims, and some of his most influential judicial opinions involved the question of the rights of landholders. At the time of his appointment, a long-running dispute involving land titles had paralyzed the state's fledgling legal system. Speculators and settlers clashed over whether a title from the state was necessary for ownership of land when the occupant had maintained seven years' continuous possession of land under the appearance of holding title. When the original holders of land grants or their heirs sold property in the early days of the state's history, little attention had been given to the preservation or registration of deeds or to the tracing of land titles. Consequently, many settlers could not trace the title to their lands back to the original land grants. To make matters more complicated, the state of North Carolina continued to issue land grants in Tennessee, even after Tennessee gained statehood and North Carolina lacked any claim on Tennessee lands. The question of legal titles in Tennessee was thus exceedingly murky.

To resolve the situation, a 1797 Tennessee statute of limitations stated that "no person who shall have any right or title to lands, shall thereunto enter or make claim, but within seven years after his right or title accrued; and in default thereof shall be forever barred." Yet conflicting judicial interpreta-

tions of this statute, coupled with inadequate case reporting, allowed speculators and others to take advantage of the uncertain situation. According to
one source, for example, a man named Patrick Darby "made champertous
contracts with grantees and their heirs to institute suits all over Middle Tennessee against the parties in possession" until "nearly half the landed estate
in Tennessee was being involved in litigation."[37]

For its part, the legislature clearly favored the interests of the settlers who
occupied the land. In 1819 lawmakers passed an act guaranteeing land to
those who possessed it, but this measure could not apply retrospectively and
thus did not resolve the trouble. Catron, who had argued many cases against
the devious Darby, shared the legislature's prosettler view on this matter.
When a seat opened on the court in 1824, legislators elected Catron to the
position largely because of his views on this important issue.

As expected, Catron proceeded to decide cases in favor of pioneer settlers.
The first and most important of these decisions came in *Hickman's Lessee v.
Gaither and Frost* (1828). In this case, Catron strictly adhered to the language of the 1797 statute of limitations and rebuked those who claimed that
the seven-year limitation did not begin until a claimant initiated a suit against
a landholder. "The great object of the statute of 1797 was the quiet of settlers," he wrote. Surveyors, Catron argued, particularly opposed the passage
of this legislation, as they knew of the best lands and hoped to gain the property for themselves. Catron observed how, before the law was enacted, surveyors could survey "a 5000 acre entry, calling to include a notorious object," so that the lot included that object in any part of the surveyed area. In
other words, surveyors could essentially choose to include any five thousand
acres they wanted in the plot of land as long as it included the "notorious
object" mentioned in the land claim. Such "floating claims," according to
Catron, threatened to hold "in terror and dismay almost half a county of
population." The 1797 act, he argued, had been designed to protect occu-
piers of land from surveyors and speculators claiming the right to survey and
claim the disputed land.[38] "By the act of 1797," Catron summarized, "it is
provided, that if any one has seven years' peaceable possession of land, . . .
then the person holding possession shall be entitled, in preference to all
claimants, to the quantity of land covered by said grant, or deed." The oc-
cupiers rather than the claimants would keep the land.[39]

In subsequent decisions, Catron continued to interpret the legislation of
1797 in the interests of settlers. *Love v. Love's Lessee* (1829) involved property originally owned by John Love. At Love's death, Seymour Catching had
purchased the land at sheriff's sale, and James Love later purchased it from
Catching. Ultimately, Anne Love, James Love's mother, took possession of

the land after her son's death, and she occupied the land for more than the seven years required under the statute of limitations. A representative of John Love's estate brought suit and claimed that "James Love, in his lifetime, had said that he did not believe he had a good title to the land, and that if John Love sued for it, he would recover."[40] Based on this evidence, a circuit court judge had charged jurors that if they believed James Love knew that he was not acquiring a good title when he purchased the land from Catching, they should find for John Love's lessee. The jury subsequently did so, thus taking the land from Anne Love. On consideration by the Tennessee Supreme Court, Catron reversed the lower court's ruling and found the circuit judge's charge in error.

Catron again held to the letter of the 1797 statute of limitations. "The statue having made no exceptions against one purchasing and holding possession, with the knowledge he was not acquiring a good title at the time he obtained the conveyance under which he seeks protection," he reasoned, "the courts have no power to make any; to do so would be legislating." Despite the circumstances of this particular case, Catron took the side of the resident owner of the land. "Has the land been granted? Has the defendant a deed, executed in fact, for the land? and has he, coupled with these, had seven years' peaceable possession, holden by virtue thereof, adverse in character? If so, the bar is formed beyond the reach of the courts of justice."[41]

Catron asserted this position a third time in *Guion's Lessee v. Bradley Academy* (1833), another case where litigants attempted to gain an exception to the seven-year statute of limitations. In this instance, the judge offered obiter dicta that helped explain his firm devotion to pioneer settlers and their claims. Commenting on the original 1715 act passed by the North Carolina assembly to settle land claims in what later became Tennessee, Catron argued that "a leading object of the act was to cut off the expectancies of heirs." Although "the temptations to pursue and attend to the claims were few in 1715," he reasoned, eventually the rapid settlement and increasing value of these lands made disputes more common. Under these circumstances, Catron believed, there was only one way to resolve such conflicts. "Common justice at the hands of the great proprietors required that the settler who was subjected to the hardships of commencing agriculture in a wilderness, to which he had emigrated, perhaps from Europe, and where he had to contend with the savage foe," he wrote, "should enjoy his farm in fee, to him, and to his children."[42] In other words, those who struggled to tame the wilderness ought to reap the rewards of their efforts.

In this and all of his opinions favoring established settlers, Catron revealed his sympathies for the frontier folk of the southwest—the rough-hewn men and women of sturdy stock around whom he lived for most of his life. He was, as he once put it, "a Western man," raised in the hills of Tennessee and possessed of, as another put it, a "gruff, blunt, and plain-spoken" manner. Catron's decisions in favor of settlers reportedly drove Patrick Darby, the land speculator who initiated many of these suits, out of the state and "gave repose to the people and the country."[43]

Throughout his career, Catron stood against special privilege and promoted what he believed to be the public good. Like Roane, who in *Currie's Administrator v. Mutual Assurance Society* (1809) had warned against the use of state power to create corporate charters for "merely private or selfish" purposes, Catron opposed a national bank dominated by wealthy interests and foreign investors, and he stood against speculators' attempts to capitalize on legal ambiguities regarding the state's land titles. In a broad sense, Catron and other Jacksonians opposed the use of state power to facilitate the aggregation of private wealth through monopolies, charters, licenses, land grants, and other forms of privilege. Catron believed that the state could not play favorites and that every rule of law needed to apply to the entire body politic. "Were this otherwise," he wrote in *Vanzant v. Waddel* (1829), "odious individuals and corporate bodies would be governed by one rule, and the mass of the community who made the law, by another. The idea of a people through their representatives making laws whereby are swept away the life, liberty and property of one or a few citizens by which neither the representatives nor their other constituents are willing to be bound, is too odious to be tolerated in any government where freedom has a name." A desire to promote the public interest rather than special privilege thus characterized Catron's political economy.[44] Later, other southern state judges would develop further this idea of state regulation in the public interest.

Native Americans and Slaves

Catron had not always proven completely sympathetic to the claims of pioneer settlers. Even though in *Guion's Lessee* he had exalted the rugged frontierspeople who cleared the wilderness and "had to contend with the savage foe," in a series of decisions before that 1833 ruling Catron had expressed an apparently strong commitment to the land claims and rights of Native Americans. In particular, Catron repeatedly upheld the validity of treaties negotiated with Tennessee's Cherokee Indian population and contended that these agreements prevented white Tennesseans from seizing Cherokee property.

Over time, however, Catron's principled defense of Cherokee rights fell victim to a political environment that encouraged southern fears about the sovereignty of states and the constitutional rights of slaveholders. By 1835 Catron stoutly defended Jackson's aggressive Indian removal policy and linked the issue of state power over Indians to the question of state control over slavery.

As the number of free white settlers and their slaves in Tennessee exploded during the early nineteenth century, the potential for conflict with the Cherokee accelerated. A series of treaties worked out between 1791 and 1819 cleared all of Tennessee of Indian land claims except those of the Cherokee in the southeastern corner of the state. Most Cherokee lived in Georgia, which ultimately took the most aggressive steps to expel its Indian population, but a sizable number of Cherokee remained on several hundred thousand acres in the mountains of Tennessee. During the late eighteenth and early nineteenth centuries, as U.S. Indian policy vacillated between acculturation and removal, the Cherokee leadership increasingly settled on a policy of coexistence and "controlled acculturation." Despite the Cherokee's incorporation of many white cultural norms into their society, during the late 1820s Georgia began a determined policy of harassment and removal that culminated in 1828 with legislation declaring all Cherokee laws and customs void by June 1, 1830. Following suit, Alabama and Mississippi passed similar measures in 1829 and 1830, respectively.[45]

In the meantime, Catron and the Tennessee Supreme Court emerged as ardent defenders of Cherokee rights. Early in his judicial career and prior to Georgia's initiation of a removal policy, Catron upheld Cherokee land claims. When deciding whether a white settler's claim under an 1800 North Carolina grant or that of a Cherokee under an 1819 treaty was a better legal title, Catron sided with the Cherokee. In *Cornet v. Winton's Lessee* (1826), he praised the Cherokee people for their apparent willingness to adopt certain elements of white culture. They were, he wrote, "far removed from the mere wandering and wild savage who depends upon hunting and game for the means of subsistence, and makes war a livelihood." Instead, he continued, they "had much use for their soil; and that they had the right to use and occupy it within their own territorial limits, unmolested by our citizens, has not been controverted for many years."[46] Catron proceeded to explain how a series of treaties with the Cherokee brought them "under the tutelage" of the U.S. government and how agents protected and partially governed these Native Americans. The treaties of which Catron spoke granted to the Cherokee the legal rights to specific lands, and states could not issue land grants including this territory because it was not the states' land to give. "The rights of the Indians are in practice protected with as much fidelity through our Indian agent, and governor in fact of the nation, as are the rights of American citizens," Catron proudly noted, "and are as much protected by our laws where by treaty we have solemnly pledged ourselves to do so." Remarkably, the judge concluded by describing those who had for years carelessly trampled on the rights of American Indians as "at this day deemed by the people of the United States more savage and cruel than those they despoiled."[47]

Following Jackson's election as president in 1828, the assault on Indian lands proceeded at a rapid pace. In December 1829 Jackson, near the end of his first year in office, announced to Congress his hope of removing completely all Indian tribes to the trans-Mississippi West. Old Hickory also made known his support for Georgia's attempts to extend its legal jurisdiction over all its territory, including Indian lands. Congress responded favorably to the president's initiative, and in May 1830 Jackson signed the Indian Removal Act. The law authorized the president to create an Indian territory west of the Mississippi, to establish the Indians' legal title to the land in exchange for their current landholdings, and to initiate the process of removal.[48]

A few months after the passage of the removal act, Catron was still supporting Cherokee land claims. In *Blair and Johnson v. Pathkiller's Lessee* (1830), he confronted the conflict between state sovereignty and the treaty-making power of the national government. In this particular case, the U.S. government had in an 1806 treaty ceded certain territory to the state of Tennessee. Where Cherokee still resided on some portions of these lands, the treaty provided that such individuals retain their homesteads, encircled by a square mile of territory, including "residence and improvements, in the centre, as near as may be." Subsequent treaties in 1817 and 1819 upheld the rights of Cherokee homesteaders to maintain these reserves, but in this case plaintiffs claimed that the state of Tennessee could dispose of such lands in any way that it desired. Catron strongly reaffirmed the binding authority of all treaties negotiated by the U.S. government. "What rights to the possession of these lands Tennessee has acquired are by and through the treaty, and she is compelled to conform to its terms in the disposition of such possession," he wrote. "The treaty is an entire instrument, and it does not lie in the mouth of Tennessee more than that of the government of the United States to say, we will adopt all those parts of the treaty beneficial to us, and reject such parts as are prejudicial."[49]

Despite Catron's stand in favor of Indian claims, the Tennessee legislature increasingly threatened to violate those treaty provisions that allowed Cherokee settlers to maintain possession of lands. During their 1829 session, lawmakers had even adopted resolutions questioning the reasoning and correctness of Catron's decision in *Cornet v. Winton.* Twice in *Blair* Catron alluded to the legislature's attempt to undermine established law to distribute lands to white settlers. Reviewing a series of previous legislative acts that had complied with treaties, Catron referred to the "good faith which we hope Tennessee will ever observe in the performance of her contracts with neighboring powers, be they civilized or savage." Moreover, he assailed legislative statements that undermined his *Cornet* opinion. "That the resolutions were intended to dictate to this court the course of future decision we will not suppose," he wryly noted, "as this would be an attack upon the independence of the judiciary."[50] Just to make clear to the court's legislative adversaries that he meant to stand by his decision, Catron reiterated this position in another decision. His brief opinion in *M'Connell and Mayfield v. Mousepaine's Lessee* (1830) reaffirmed a Cherokee man's right to his homestead under treaty provisions despite his being driven from his lands "by threatening force."[51] By 1830, legislative protests notwithstanding, Catron still firmly believed that Cherokee Indians possessed rights to lands under treaties negotiated by the U.S. government.

But a changing political environment ultimately undermined Catron's pro-Cherokee position. During the early 1830s, the attacks simultaneously leveled against Jackson by his Whig political opponents and by South Carolina nullifiers made Judge Catron's personal devotion to his mentor all the more important. Whigs assailed the president for his vetoes of the Maysville Road Bill and the national bank's recharter, while Jackson's personal falling-out with Vice President John C. Calhoun and the continuing showdown with South Carolina over nullification of the federal tariff only compounded the president's political troubles. When *Cherokee Nation v. Georgia* (1831) and *Worcester v. Georgia* (1832) came before the U.S. Supreme Court in the midst of this turmoil, Jackson's opponents gleefully seized the opportunity to embarrass the chief executive. Whig leaders Daniel Webster and Henry Clay supported the rights of the Cherokee as much out of opposition to Jackson as commitment to Indian sovereignty. Clay's run against Jackson in the 1832 presidential campaign, along with Chief Justice John Marshall's decision in *Worcester* favoring Cherokee rights, pushed Catron even closer to his mentor.

The Tennessee judge, who on behalf of the president had helped lead Tennessee's opposition to nullification, would ultimately prove equally willing to implement Jackson's Indian removal policy in the state. As Catron wrote to Jackson a few years later, "Of living men, your health and happiness is perhaps nearest my affection: daily intercourse convinces me how much my onward course has been dependent on the few and how much real friends should be cherished."[52] Knowing that Jackson needed him, Catron abandoned his support for the Cherokee. In the end, Catron's loyalty to Jackson proved much stronger than his support for the rights of Native Americans.

In 1835 Catron delivered an opinion that provided the legal justification for Jackson's removal policy. Following the lead of its sister southern states, in 1833 the Tennessee legislature had extended the state's legal jurisdiction over its Cherokee population. A case subsequently arose involving the alleged murder of John Walker, a Cherokee, by another Cherokee man, James Foreman. Indicted in a county court for murder, Foreman claimed that the alleged offense occurred outside the jurisdiction of the courts of Tennessee and within the Cherokee nation. Foreman thus challenged the constitutionality of the 1833 act.[53]

In *State v. Foreman* (1835), Catron upheld Tennessee's extension of jurisdiction over the Cherokee nation. Writing in the midst of the removal and after Chief Justice Marshall's ruling in favor of Cherokee sovereignty in *Worcester,* Catron's opinion offered an extensive legal argument against the sovereign claims of any Indian tribe. As Catron later put it in a letter to Vice President Martin Van Buren, the *Foreman* opinion "attempted to disencumber this cause of the authority of that of *Worcester.*" Directly contradicting much of the reasoning and conclusions evident in his earlier decisions, Catron delivered a lengthy opinion (covering eighty pages of Yerger's reports) that drew on contemporary historical and legal theories regarding the relationship between Native Americans and European "discoverers." This "discovery doctrine," long a convention of European diplomacy, had traditionally kept rival nations from making overlapping land claims; Chief Justice Marshall had applied the notion to Native American–European relations in a few previous U.S. Supreme Court rulings. But while in *Worcester* Marshall abandoned this doctrine that gave seemingly unlimited sanction to European settlers to seize Indian lands, Catron willingly embraced the idea.[54]

The underlying assumption of the discovery doctrine, as enunciated by Catron, was that all Native Americans were heathen "savages" who possessed inferior customs and culture. Tracing the origins of this notion back to the crusades, the Tennessee judge compared those expeditions to Columbus's voyage to America. Both were efforts toward "propagating [the] faith and extending the dominion of the church." Because Native Americans possessed an inferior culture, Catron reasoned, they held no claims to the land after the arrival of Europeans. "We maintain," he asserted, "that the principles declared in the fifteenth century as the law of Christendom—that discovery gave title to assume sovereignty over, and to govern, the unconverted natives of Africa, Asia, and North and South America—has been recognized as a part of the national law for nearly four centuries, and that it is now so recognized by every Christian power." Although Catron expressed apparent doubts about the morality of such a position, he nevertheless asserted that law and experience validated European dominance. "The claim may be denounced by the moralist," he wrote. "We answer, it is the law of the land. Without its assertion and vigorous execution this continent never could have been inhabited by our ancestors. To abandon the principle now is to assert that they were unjust usurpers, and that we, succeeding to their usurped authority and void claims . . . should in honesty abandon it, return to Europe, and let the subdued parts again become a wilderness and hunting ground." [55] Despite some moral misgivings, Catron firmly positioned the court on the side of settlers of European origin rather than of the land's native inhabitants.

While Catron's loyalty to Jackson partially accounted for the judge's change of heart on Cherokee rights, ultimately the issues of slavery and state power also exerted a deciding influence. Just as the Missouri Crisis had prompted Roane to add proslavery arguments to his already well developed state-sovereignty position during the early 1820s, so the tense political atmosphere a decade later led Catron to reconsider his stand on Cherokee lands and the treaty-making power of the national government. "The principle that the monarch of the first Christian discoverer of a heathen land was the sovereign lord of that land, and that all unconverted savages found there were . . . subject to the jurisdiction of the country of the discoverer, comes in conflict with our religion and with our best convictions of a refined and sound morality," Catron bluntly admitted in *Foreman.* But, he forthrightly continued, "our individual titles to lands from the Atlantic to the western Missouri line depend upon its firm and unquailing support. . . . The title of every slave in America, North and South, rests on no better or different foundation." In *Foreman,* Catron thus made the connection between the right of European discoverers to conquer the land and the authority of white southerners to own slaves. [56]

By the early 1830s Tennessee was moving toward an increasingly restrictive position regarding its African-American population. For many years the state had one of the most liberal and humane emancipation policies in the South. In *Fields v. State* (1829), for example, Judge Whyte had held that common-law rules could apply in the case of the murder of a slave by a third party, a ruling subsequently followed only by the Texas Supreme Court. But after Nat Turner's revolt, Tennessee lawmakers took a different tack. Fearful of "the insurrectionary spirit of the times," legislators prohibited the immigration of free blacks into Tennessee, banned emancipation without removal from the state, and disfranchised free blacks in the 1834 constitution.

Catron's defensiveness about slavery reflected the attitudes of most Tennesseans during this time.[57]

While Catron reconsidered his stance on the rights of the Cherokee, the judge pronounced strict legal rules regarding emancipation. In his most famous opinion in a slave case, *Fisher's Negroes v. Dabbs* (1834), Catron made clear his desire to go even further than the legislature in prohibiting manumission. Fisher had freed all of his slaves in his will as well as given them land, livestock, and farming equipment. While the 1831 act had provided only that slaves be manumitted outside the state of Tennessee, Catron expressed his belief that they should have to be removed outside the United States. Describing free blacks as "a very dangerous and most objectionable population where slaves are numerous," Catron warned against forcing Tennessee's free black population on the other states of the South. "To treat our neighbors unjustly and cruelly," he reasoned, "and thereby make them our enemies, is bad policy and contrary to our interest. . . . How can we then as honest men, thrust our freed Negroes on our neighbors of the South?" Moreover, Catron argued, the unwillingness of some northern states to accept free African Americans within their borders further demonstrated the need for colonization outside the United States. In this case, Catron upheld the manumission under Fisher's will but did so only on the condition of transportation to Liberia.[58]

Catron's views regarding emancipation rested on a paternalistic conception of race relations. "The slave who receives the protection and care of a tolerable master holds a condition here superior to the Negro who is freed from domestic slavery," Catron wrote in *Dabbs*. Free blacks in the North, Catron believed, were no better off than their southern counterparts. In both sections of the country, free African Americans lived as "degraded outcast[s]." In short, he believed, "society suffers and the Negro suffers by manumission." Catron reiterated this perspective in *Loftin v. Espy* (1833), a case involving the attempted seizure of a slave for recovery of debt. There he refused to offer a remedy to the creditor because the judge believed that "the slave and the master should never be separated when affection exists between them." Catron thought that such a policy, as well as the practice of keeping slave families intact in such instances, would promote harmonious relations between masters and slaves. The alternative, he believed, was "domestic strife, the slave acting from fear for good, and through revenge for evil; the master protecting himself as well as he may by violence, but too often brutal."[59] Two years after the Nat Turner Rebellion, that seminal event in the history of slavery remained very much in the forefront of the judge's mind.

More generally for Catron, paternalistic relationships offered the best means of protecting and preserving the institution of slavery. Such a conception of race relations included both rules prohibiting emancipation and legal protections of the master-slave relationship where "affections" between the two existed. Catron's own relationship with his many slaves rested on the paternalistic ideal, as the judge provided well for all his bondspeople at his death, especially his personal house servant. Such generosity proved typical of many of his class but also of southern judges in particular, as jurists often advocated benevolent treatment as the key to maintaining social order and racial control. Catron's paternalistic logic foreshadowed the more overt "positive good" proslavery argument made by southern jurists during subsequent decades.[60]

During the early 1830s, political circumstances and legal disputes coalesced in such a way as to bring together in Catron's mind the issues of Indian lands, slave property, and state power. The tense political environment regarding slavery helped push Catron and the Tennessee Supreme Court toward a Native American policy that ignored Indian rights under federal treaties and supported Jackson's removal plan. Catron began to see the question of white control over Indian lands as similar to the issue of white power over African slaves. The national government—in the form of treaties with Indians or potentially restrictive legislation regarding the expansion of slavery—posed a potential threat to southern control over both of these populations. Thus, in *State v. Foreman,* where Catron explicated the discovery doctrine, he also turned to the theory of state sovereignty. Referring to the federal treaty power, Catron wrote, "It cannot, in times of peace, cede away to a people independent of the state a part of its territory and sovereignty. . . . The states are emphatically the basis of the Union and federal Constitution; to extinguish them is to extinguish the Constitution—to leave it nothing to operate upon."[61] Even though Catron opposed both nullification and later secession and had never before expressed his support for the idea that states retained their sovereignty within the Union, during the 1830s he realized the potential utility of asserting this doctrine when it came to controlling Indian lands and slave property.

Catron's assertion of state prerogative in *Foreman* signaled his gradual adoption of a sectional consciousness. In the same way that Spencer Roane began to assume a southern perspective on constitutional issues in the midst of the Missouri Crisis, so Indian Removal and slavery prompted Catron to refer in the mid-1830s to Tennessee's "sister states" and "neighbors of the South." Again, the issue of white southerners' authority to maintain racial control, prompted by Nat Turner's revolt and Tennessee's restrictive legisla-

tion regarding African Americans, lay behind the development of this southern way of thinking. Although the Tennessee Supreme Court during the
1830s–50s would go on to develop one of the most humanitarian reputations
of any antebellum state court in slavery cases, in the midst of a specific political crisis like that of the early 1830s, Catron insisted on policies that upheld
the established racial order.[62]

Politics, the U.S. Supreme Court, and Secession

Despite the influence of politics on his slavery decisions, Catron never
achieved the degree of popular acclaim that characterized the careers of so
many nineteenth-century southern state judges. His temperament and judicial opinions were partly to blame for his poor standing with the public.
As a lawyer, Catron admitted that he argued cases "with an arrogance that
would have done credit to Castlereagh," Britain's famous early-nineteenth-
century foreign minister. Catron's judicial record also failed to win him many
supporters. "With the floating masses I had nothing in common," he wrote
in his autobiographical sketch. "I punished many of them for crimes, and
always severely. They feared and disliked me. Among the great mass of
property-owners, thousands have been alienated by decisions adverse to their
interests." The losing parties in such property disputes, Catron thought, took
a natural dislike to the judge who decided against them, while the winners
frequently pronounced "that no judge, not corrupt, or a dunce, could have
decided otherwise." In his autobiographical essay, Catron concluded that
any jurist who did his duty would in some way alienate the public: "A judge
may have great cogency and influence with very many of the most intelligent
class; but if he be a stern and unquailing official, it is not in human natures
that he should be a popular man." Although respected within legal circles,
Catron never earned widespread public approval. Indeed, one observer later
described him as "one of the best hated men of his day."[63]

More than his personality or his judicial rulings, Catron's partisan activities ultimately undermined his state judicial career. An outspoken leader
in the political arena for decades, Catron had enthusiastically supported
Andrew Jackson throughout his public career. Most notably, in 1828, when
Jackson's opponents charged his wife, Rachel, with being an adulterous
woman (she had married him after believing incorrectly that she had obtained a legal divorce from her first husband), Catron and a group of prominent Nashville citizens united to refute the charges.[64] In light of Catron's lifelong devotion to Jackson, the judge's decision to support Jackson's chosen
successor in the 1836 presidential campaign proved unsurprising. Yet despite

the president's continued popularity in his home state, Tennesseans did not react favorably to his attempt to make Martin Van Buren the next occupant of the White House. As Catron succinctly put it, "It is declared every day and by the leaders that to Mr. Van B.'s personal character they do not object, but their great objection is to President Jackson nominating his successor. That he is not authorized to indicate openly his preference." Most in the state supported favorite son Hugh Lawson White, a former member of the state supreme court and a U.S. senator. Catron's intense loyalty to Jackson made him one of the state's leading champions of Van Buren's candidacy; this decision spelled Catron's political demise in Tennessee.[65]

By the end of 1835, Catron had made known throughout the state that he supported Van Buren. The previous year, Tennessee had written a new constitution that provided for a three-member supreme court whose members were to be elected by the legislature.[66] When lawmakers met to elect a court in 1835, the already "very unpopular" chief justice suffered the consequences of his political preference. Legislators strongly supported the candidacy of White, and in October of that year, the state House of Representatives even passed a resolution favoring White's nomination for president. Two months later, the legislature defeated Catron by a vote of seventy-one to twenty-seven, and Nathan Green, a member of the court since 1831, replaced the chief justice.[67] Just as partisanship had helped Catron land a seat on the court, a political dispute ended his state judicial career.

Stripped of the post that he had held for twelve years, Catron devoted his efforts to directing Van Buren's Tennessee campaign. Joined by other prominent Jackson loyalists, including James K. Polk and Felix Grundy, Catron worked tirelessly to elect Jackson's vice president. The former chief justice wrote a series of newspaper essays in 1836, and he even took over the job of editing the state's major Democratic newspaper, the *Nashville Union,* when its alcoholic editor Samuel Laughlin failed to keep up with his editorial duties.[68] Still, Van Buren's candidacy proved a losing cause in Tennessee, as White defeated the New Yorker by an overwhelming margin. In his home state at least, Catron remained persona non grata.

But in the nation's capital, Catron's loyalty to Jackson and Van Buren's national victory paid dividends for the former Tennessee judge. Early in 1837 Congress passed a judiciary act that created two new federal circuits and added two seats to the U.S. Supreme Court. Just before leaving office, President Jackson nominated Catron and John McKinley of Alabama to fill these associate justiceships. Writing to the president, fellow Tennessean and Speaker of the U.S. House Polk approvingly noted that the appointments would give the Court "a decided democratic bias." Though apocryphal stories abound of how Matilda Catron personally drove her reluctant husband from Tennessee to Washington and urged his nomination on a surprised president, Jackson's decision to appoint Catron did not issue from a whim. Rather, the choice of an old friend and valued political supporter was a calculated move by the outgoing executive to ensure the Court's continued shift toward the Democrats. Catron, moreover, had nicely positioned himself for the appointment through his years of devotion to Jackson, and the need for a westerner to ride the new circuit encompassing Tennessee, Kentucky, and Missouri made him a logical candidate. The *Nashville Union* viewed the selection as the perfect postscript to Catron's removal from the state bench. His ouster had occurred "because he would not abandon his old principles and become an humble supporter of Judge White," the paper claimed. Catron, the *Union* happily concluded, had "received the just reward of [his] independence and integrity." Without controversy, the Senate confirmed his appointment by a vote of twenty-eight to fifteen.[69]

For the next twenty-eight years, until his death in 1865, Catron served on the U.S. Supreme Court. At first he was "met with a cool reception" by his fellow justices. Like all nineteenth-century members of the Court, Catron spent the majority of his time riding the circuit, and some within his jurisdiction initially believed, he confided to Polk, that Catron "wanted legal skill." Catron thought it especially ironic that others complained that he "wanted lawyership in Kentucky, where the most important causes are heard & decided without reference to a single book!" Despite these early criticisms of his qualifications, Catron went on to earn the respect of the justices. Fellow Jacksonian Roger B. Taney affirmed to Old Hickory in 1838, "The more I have seen of him the more I have been impressed with the strength of his judgment, legal knowledge and his integrity of character. He is a valuable acquisition to the bench of the Supreme Court."[70]

Catron on the U.S. Supreme Court acted much like he had on the Tennessee Supreme Court. He tended to favor state control over commerce, but he also recognized the need for national uniformity of regulation in some areas. In the *License Cases* (1847), for example, Catron upheld state laws restricting the importation of liquor and affirmed the idea of state police power, but he accepted the doctrine of the "selective exclusiveness" of national regulatory power under the Commerce Clause in *Cooley v. Board of Wardens* (1852). Expressing a distrust of concentrated economic power as he had at the state level, in cases involving business corporations he feared the adverse consequences of giving corporations more power than "the state government creating them." He thus repeatedly argued against allowing stockholders to assume the legal status of a "citizen."[71] He also joined other southern justices in support of slavery. In *Dred Scott v. Sandford* (1857), the Tennessean agreed with Taney in holding the Missouri Compromise unconstitutional, though he differed with the chief justice in his reasoning. In a separate opinion, Catron upheld the right of masters to take slaves into Louisiana territory on the grounds that the treaty ratified for the purchase of Louisiana had guaranteed settlers the right to property. This treaty, he believed, restricted Congress's power to legislate on the matter. Unlike Taney, Catron did not address the issue of the citizenship rights of free blacks.[72] Unlike Taney, who was "an angry southern gentleman," according to Don E. Fehrenbacher, Catron's opinion was characterized more by sound legal reasoning than by partisan sectional rhetoric. Although some scholars have deemed Justice Catron a staunch defender of states' rights and slavery, the former Tennessee judge certainly steered a more moderate course as a member of the Supreme Court than his colleague the chief justice.[73]

This moderation became most evident during the secession crisis, when, ever true to his Jacksonian principles, Catron took a firm stand in favor of the Union. Early in the sequence of events that would lead to secession, just after Abraham Lincoln's election, Catron expressed to an acquaintance his belief that the excitement raging throughout the South would prove temporary and uneventful. "He insisted that if proper vigilance and energy should be used by the government in Washington City—such as Jackson had brought into exercise in 1832—the people of the South would be found as true supporters of the Union as they had been in former days," wrote Henry S. Foote. Catron's prediction proved no more than wishful thinking. By the time the Supreme Court adjourned its session on March 14, 1861, seven states had already seceded. Unlike his Supreme Court colleague from Alabama, John A. Campbell, Catron refused to resign his position and return home. Instead, he continued with his judicial duties in hopes of preserving federal authority throughout his southwestern circuit, where Union and Confederate sympathizers battled for control.[74]

As the storm clouds of war gathered during the spring of 1861, Catron began to ride circuit through the border states. As Kentucky and Missouri held their circuit terms during the same month, he headed to Kentucky and left his duties in St. Louis to judicial colleagues. After attending to business in Kentucky, Catron returned home to Nashville in an attempt to hold his home state in the Union. At that time, Tennessee had already held a secession referendum, and the initial vote had gone in favor of the Union. Despite the efforts of Catron and other Unionists, a subsequent June 1861 vote on secession—after the initiation of hostilities, Lincoln's call for troops, and the secession of Virginia—reversed the earlier result. Thus unsuccessful, Catron found himself behind enemy lines. Meanwhile, the Missouri governor's disunionist statements and a tense situation in St. Louis demanded Catron's presence in that city. The justice left Tennessee and hurried to hold court in St. Louis, where he and his circuit colleagues issued a forceful charge to a grand jury proclaiming that support for the rebellion constituted treason. The charge, subsequently published in newspapers across the country, also proclaimed that obstructing the operation of a U.S. court was included among treasonous activities.[75]

After completing the court's business there, Catron returned to Tennessee, where he hoped to defy the Confederacy by holding circuit in his hometown. But on reaching the outskirts of Nashville, a "committee" led by the federal marshal "urg[ed] him to go away at once." Aware of Catron's public proclamations on behalf of the Union, they informed Catron that, if he elected to stay and proceed with his plans to keep the courts of the United States in operation, his life was in danger. The committee advised him either to resign his seat on the Court or to leave the city within twenty-four hours. As the marshal refused to offer assistance, Catron reportedly fled "in terror and despair." [76]

As the tide of war turned in Tennessee, however, Catron returned to his home state. By the spring of 1862, the Union army had won important victories at Forts Henry and Donelson and at Shiloh; these triumphs eventually placed most of the state under Union control. In June 1862, less than a year after being asked to leave, Catron called to order the U.S. Circuit Court in Nashville, this time under the protection of federal troops.[77]

The war devastated Catron, who longed for the Unionism of Jackson among his fellow Tennesseans. "In old age he found himself in alienation from nearly all in whom he had most confided," noted a judicial colleague. Catron did not completely condone Lincoln's policies during the war. He dissented in the *Prize Cases* (1863), for example, where the Court upheld Lincoln's unprecedented order for a naval blockade of the South. Nevertheless, Catron cast his lot firmly with the Union, and in most cases involving the federal government's wartime powers Catron affirmed the actions of the Lincoln administration. As the war continued, the justice's health deteriorated, and he missed the 1864–65 Supreme Court term because of illness. He died at home in Nashville on May 30, 1865, only a little more than a month after the downfall of the Confederacy.[78]

Catron and the Expansion of the South

The old Southwest in which Catron began his judicial career bore little re-
semblance to Spencer Roane's Virginia. A product of the Tennessee frontier,
Catron lacked the education, manners, and social refinement that characterized Roane and the Tidewater gentry.[79] Unlike his counterpart from the Old
Dominion, Catron assumed a seat on a judicial tribunal still struggling to
distinguish itself during the 1820s. Instead of emulating prominent judicial
mentors like Edmund Pendleton and George Wythe, Catron's career developed alongside that of the ambitious frontier politician Andrew Jackson.
Catron assisted Jackson in some way along every step in Old Hickory's climb
to national prominence, and Catron reaped the benefits of his loyalty. Just as
Catron's background and early career clearly set him apart from Roane, so
did the issues that confronted Catron's Tennessee Supreme Court. Catron
and his colleagues had to deal with the problems associated with a still unsettled country—dueling and violence (even among members of the legal
profession), disputed land claims, and the removal of Native Americans. In
many respects, therefore, Catron's experience differed from that of Roane.

Yet as early-nineteenth-century state appellate judges, Roane and Catron
shared a regional identity developing among the southern judiciary. In particular, the issues of the national bank and the removal of the Cherokee
prompted Catron to think about law and constitutionalism in distinctively
southern ways. Like his mentor, when Catron considered the operation of
the bank, he saw a sinister plot on the part of eastern (and foreign) capitalist interests to line their own pockets at the expense of the hardworking men
and women of the South and the West. To Catron, the workings of the bank
resembled a plot against liberty as sinister as any in the short history of
America. Further, the question of Cherokee removal and its convergence
with Nat Turner's revolt forced Catron to rethink his stand in favor of Indian
rights and to adopt the perspective of most southerners. In Catron's mind,
the legal right to force Indians to the West became of a piece with masters'
legal rights to hold sway over slave property.

Concerns about slavery lay at the center of this developing sectional perspective among the southern judiciary. Catron's loyalty to Jacksonian principles and his subsequent service on the U.S. Supreme Court steered him
toward Unionism rather than secession, but he proved unswerving in his
commitment to slavery. Even though cases involving slaves and slavery constituted a small number of the total opinions rendered by Catron and other
state appellate judges, their commitment to preserving the peculiar institution became increasingly apparent during specific crises—the admission of

Missouri to the Union and the supposed threat of widespread insurrection after Nat Turner's revolt. Catron, like most southern appellate judges, responded to these external developments because of his intimate connection to the political system.

Certainly Catron's career—from the 1831 attempts to abolish the Tennessee Supreme Court to his 1835 defeat because of his stand in the 1836 presidential election—showed that southern appellate judges lived and worked within the unpredictable realm of partisan politics. The Tennessean proved keenly aware of the importance of slavery and race-related issues throughout his career. At about the time that he left the state supreme court, Catron expressed his vigorous support for the annexation of Texas and the subsequent expansion of slavery to new territories, and he candidly advised Jackson and Van Buren against the nomination of Kentuckian Richard Johnson as vice president in 1836. The candidacy of Johnson, who had a mulatto mistress and two mulatto daughters, the judge correctly warned, would prove "affirmatively odious" in Tennessee. Catron clearly understood the political world and the growing importance of slavery within that realm. By the end of his twelve-year state judicial career, Catron had adopted a southern perspective on law and constitutionalism.[80]

Joseph Henry Lumpkin
and the Vision of
an Independent South

The noble men who have fallen in this wicked struggle would have made a nation for numbers, and the most glorious nation yet known for worth of every kind. —JOSEPH HENRY LUMPKIN, 1864

While John Catron's career developed alongside that of Andrew Jackson, Joseph Henry Lumpkin's life and work paralleled that of early-nineteenth-century social reformers. Although most scholars have viewed the North as the only realm of reform, southern Whigs like Lumpkin embraced their own vision of social progress. Lumpkin devoted as much of his life to reform activities as he did to his judicial labors, and he came to view these dual roles as inseparable. Prior to his appointment to the Georgia Supreme Court in 1846, Lumpkin's career consisted of two parallel paths: he emerged as one of the leading legal professionals in his state at the same time that he championed various forms of social improvement.

Lumpkin's ascension to the supreme court marked the convergence of these two roads, and he frequently revealed this reformer's zeal in the pages of the *Georgia Reports.* "I rejoice to see edifices built . . . and covered with the moss of many generations," he once wrote, "swaying beneath the sturdy blows so unsparingly applied by the hand of reform. Why should the spirit of progress which is abroad in the world, and which is heaving and agitating the public mind in respect to the arts, sciences, politics and religion, halt upon the vestibule of our temples of justice."[1] Lumpkin's answer to this rhetorical question, of course, was that the law could not be separated from the early-nineteenth-century "spirit of progress." Over the course of a twenty-one-year judicial career, a reform ideology constituted the basis of much of Lumpkin's work as a legal craftsman.

Lawyer and Reformer

Lumpkin's early life portended future success in his chosen profession. Born in 1799 in what later became Oglethorpe County, Georgia, Lumpkin attended the newly established University of Georgia before completing his studies at the College of New Jersey (later Princeton University), where he graduated with honors in 1819. After returning to Oglethorpe County, where he read law under Judge Thomas W. Cobb, Lumpkin began his law practice in his hometown of Lexington in 1820 and married Scottish-born Callendar Cunningham Grieve in 1821.[2] The young lawyer quickly became known for his careful examination, close reasoning, and oratorical powers, "under whose magic spell," according to his memorial in the *Georgia Reports*, "jurors, oblivious of the stern authority of the Bench, have at time sprung from their seats electrified, and at others have uttered audible response to his stirring appeals." Lumpkin exhibited a "warm, often passionate interest" in the causes of his clients, a quality that won him the admiration of both fellow lawyers and potential patrons across the state. "There was not an important case tried in any part of his circuit," a contemporary observed, "in which he was not employed either for the prosecution or the defense, whilst his services were frequently brought into requisition in remote parts of the state."[3]

While Lumpkin's fame might have assisted him in pursuing a career in politics, he instead chose to devote himself to the law. After a two-year stint as a member of the General Assembly in the mid-1820s, Lumpkin shunned political office to engage in the teaching and training of Georgia lawyers. Invariably, he would place a copy of *Blackstone's Commentaries* in the hands of a new student and thereafter, on a weekly basis, would question the pupil about the text and explain the principles it contained. After these lessons, Lumpkin frequently entertained his students with lengthy tales of his most recent experiences in court, during which students came to learn all about the habits and practices of the most important judges and lawyers in the state. By 1833 Lumpkin's reputation as an advocate and educator helped

earn him a position, along with two of the state's other most respected lawyers, on the state committee to reform the penal code. Lumpkin had emerged
as one of the leading figures in the state's legal community.[4]

Over the next decade, while Lumpkin's reputation continued to climb,
Georgia debated whether to establish a supreme court. For many years the
state was unique as the only one in the Union without a high court for the
correction of errors. Its constitution of 1798 not only forbade the creation of
such a tribunal but also expressly denied the right of any court, other than
the superior court in the county of the original trial, to grant a new trial.
Many Georgians believed that a supreme court would not provide the same
degree of popular access as the locally based court system, while others noted
the delay and expense associated with the appeals process. By 1835, however, the press and the legal community within the state strongly urged the
creation of a supreme court, and in that year the General Assembly amended
the constitution to provide for the court's establishment.[5] Not until ten years
later, however, after much legislative wrangling, did the state's lawmakers
actually create the supreme court by legislative act, and the legislation provided that the members of the new tribunal would ride circuit throughout the
state. In this way the assembly accommodated those who wanted to retain
elements of the existing system of local review.[6]

Lumpkin eventually emerged as the unanimous choice to preside over the
new court. When the most obvious candidate for the position, John Mac-
Pherson Berrien, Andrew Jackson's attorney general and "the acknowledged
head of the Bar of Georgia," declined the offer because of the circuit-riding
duties, the General Assembly turned to Lumpkin. Though he possessed no
judicial experience and knew the hardships the job would entail, he accepted
the position as head of this new judicial body. The legislature did not grant
him the formal title of chief justice until 1863, but Lumpkin's initial appointment to a six-year term, as opposed to the shorter terms of his colleagues,
implicitly granted him command of the three-man tribunal.[7] For the next two
decades, Lumpkin remained the dominant presence on one of the South's
most prestigious judicial bodies.

Concurrent with his rapid rise within the legal profession, Lumpkin
emerged as one of the leading evangelical social reformers in his state. While
attending a Methodist camp meeting in the early 1820s, Lumpkin heard a
sermon on sin that prompted his conversion. The evangelist's message, according to a contemporary's account, "found such a lodgement in the heart
of the young lawyer that he could not extinguish the impression." Eventually,
Lumpkin "exercised the faith of his heart in the atonement of God's Son"
and "a spring of joy was unsealed within."[8]

Lumpkin's newfound evangelical faith merged typical southern gentility with Yankee-like zeal for social improvement. Described as "a temperate Christian gentleman, and one of the old school in manners and conversation" by Charles Colcock Jones Jr., son of the famous Georgia minister, Lumpkin impressed his contemporaries with his intelligence, character, and conviviality.[9] Active and respected within Oglethorpe County as well as his later home, Clarke County, Lumpkin's piety and civility assured his status among Georgia's elite. He took an active role in the affairs of the University of Georgia in Athens and in 1825 founded the Phi Kappa Society, a literary and oratorical organization. In 1846 the trustees offered him an appointment to the chair of oratory and rhetoric at the university as well as the chancellorship of the institution, both of which he declined because of his duties as a justice.[10] Lumpkin was thus a well-connected southern gentleman who stood within the top ranks of Georgia society.

Lumpkin's elite social status, however, did not hinder his reformist zeal. In addition to his civic involvement, he took part in a number of reform movements, most notably the temperance crusade. After taking a pledge of total abstinence from alcohol in 1828 and becoming president of the Oglethorpe County Temperance Society the following year, Lumpkin actively campaigned against the evils of strong drink for the next quarter century. Many southerners drank excessively, and, in Lumpkin's mind, such behavior led to a host of social and moral evils that stood in the way of the type of society that he envisioned and desired.[11] Lumpkin thus wholeheartedly devoted himself to the temperance cause. During the 1830s he represented Georgia at the first National Temperance Convention and led a statewide petition campaign to repeal the state's liquor licensing laws and end the sale of intoxicating drink. Later, while active in affairs at the University of Georgia, he frequently urged students to cease carousing and form temperance societies, and during the 1840s and 1850s he served for ten years as president of the Georgia Temperance Convention. Throughout his reform career, he wrote essays and made speeches across his state and the nation on behalf of the cause.[12] Lumpkin's involvement in the temperance movement epitomized his visionary commitment to a new social order based on evangelical moral standards.

In addition to temperance, Lumpkin championed economic diversification through development. Like many northerners, he stressed the values of industry, thrift, and sobriety. This set of assumptions emphasized the inevitability of progress and the interconnectedness of its social, moral, and economic components.[13] In frequent speeches at commercial conventions, Lumpkin urged the construction of cotton mills in the South to halt excessive exports to England and the North.[14] "Why, then, should we continue to ship our raw cotton abroad, to be spun and wove and brought back to us to be worn, at an expense four times as great as it would cost to do the same thing at home?" Lumpkin inquired before a meeting of southern industrialists. "The very idea," he claimed, was "preposterous!" In addition to helping achieve economic independence, according to Lumpkin, manufacturing fostered "the various branches of trade and business, in producing comfort, refinement and intelligence, and in stimulating the growth and populousness of the surrounding country."[15] Lumpkin, in short, saw diversification of enterprise as the remedy for the South's economic woes.

In Lumpkin's view, economic improvement served as the foundation for all forms of progress, including social, political, moral, and religious advancement. Responding to charges that industry would lead to crime and corruption of morals, for example, Lumpkin noted the advantages of industrious employment for the lower orders of society. "I am by no means ready to concede that our poor, degraded, half-fed, half-clothed, and ignorant population, without Sabbath-schools, or any other kind of instruction—mental or moral—or without any just appreciation of the value of character, will be injured by giving them employment," he wrote. "After all, the most powerful motives to good conduct is to give suitable encouragement to labor and bestow proper rewards upon meritorious industry." Lumpkin thus connected the economic advantages of industrialization with its broader social and moral benefits. Because the development of manufacturing provided employment for the poor and idle, Lumpkin viewed it as a means of moral regeneration. He believed that improvements in industry, communication, and transportation facilitated peace among nations and contributed to the spread of the gospel.[16]

Lumpkin even expressed opposition to slavery during his early career. His work on behalf of temperance and industrialization frequently drew him into northern evangelical circles, and in 1833, when speaking at a gathering of reformers in Boston, the young Lumpkin enthusiastically addressed his audience about the future welfare of slaves in his native South. According to the *Boston Courier,* Lumpkin stated that "the most violent abolitionist of the North could not more seriously desire the dissolution of the ties between the master and the slave, than himself." Lumpkin "truly believed," the paper reported, "that the interests of the owners, and the slave, were alike identified with emancipation, and the time was rapidly coming on when the principle would be abandoned and the only difference of opinion would be—How can the thing be done in the best manner?"[17] Such statements arose out of both

Lumpkin's personal moral questioning of slavery and the broader political climate of the time. Lumpkin was one of a rapidly disappearing breed of southern evangelicals who, as late as the 1830s, continued to express gnawing doubts about the morality of slaveholding. In addition, his words revealed a desire to reunite the nation after the sectionally disruptive nullification crisis. Following the showdown between South Carolina and the federal government, Lumpkin indicated his willingness to sacrifice the institution of slavery for the sake of national unity.[18]

Thus, Lumpkin the reformer exhibited all of the qualities of a southern gentleman at the same time that he embraced ideas often associated with the culture of northern Evangelicalism. Lumpkin was much admired in his home state—as a leader in his community, an elder in the Presbyterian Church, and a mentor to young lawyers. He undoubtedly stood within the top ranks of antebellum southern society. Yet his Princeton education, as well as his membership in such nationwide organizations as the National Temperance Convention, the American Bible Society, and the American Colonization Society, connected him to many in the North. Lumpkin, as Scots-Irish churchman Thomas Smyth once described him, was a man of both "distinguished piety" and "great zeal," both a member of the South's respectable churchgoing elite and a zealous reformer with strong ties north of the Mason-Dixon line. Lumpkin was a curious product of both northern and southern society—a "gentleman reformer" who, though a part of the elite, looked forward to a reformed southern social order.[19]

When in 1846 Lumpkin became his state's first chief justice, the lawyer and reformer did not disguise his intention to reshape the law to accommodate a changing society. Four years after his appointment, he submitted to the state legislature a detailed report on legal reform in which he observed that the legal process included "not only inherent defects . . . but principles and rules of practice . . . which by lapse of time and change of circumstances require repeal or modification." Lumpkin made it clear that he favored no "revolution" in the law, but he expressed his design to "lop off its excrescences, to winnow away the rottenness which the mildew of time has produced, and engraft on the main stock such new provisions as will accommodate the whole to the present state of society and of the world." Lumpkin thus declared that he in no way intended to separate his social-reform efforts from his judicial career. "The law cannot claim exemption any more than . . . government," he bluntly stated, "from the spirit of change, so strikingly characteristic of the present age."[20]

In general, Lumpkin believed that the law needed to be simplified and made understandable to laypersons. To this end, Lumpkin favored merging law and equity jurisdictions, increasing the power placed in the hands of juries, and codifying the state's laws. Codification in particular revealed Lumpkin's passion for the democratization of the legal system and his devotion to, as one scholar put it, "the great Beccarian notion of certainty." "Every man should be able to read and understand the law for himself," Lumpkin argued in his report on legal reform, "and for this purpose it should be divested of all technicality and intricacy as far as it is possible to do it, and accommodated to a plain, practical people, who desire to have justice dispensed to them in an intelligible manner." Lumpkin challenged the legislature or the governor to take immediate steps to consolidate the state's entire criminal and civil code into "a single volume of convenient size." "The sooner [the law] is emancipated from the appendages of the scholastic and feudal ages, the better," he claimed.[21]

In keeping with his interest in disseminating legal knowledge, the establishment of a law school became another of Lumpkin's goals as chief justice. In 1843, three years before his appointment, officials at the University of Georgia had created a law professorship for Lumpkin, who had for years trained law students from his Athens office.[22] Lumpkin, however, could not execute the demanding duties of being the university's only law professor, especially after he gained the chief justiceship. Not until 1859 did Lumpkin and the university again join forces to create a law school, this time with the help of Lumpkin's son-in-law, Thomas R. R. Cobb, and William Hope Hull, a former law partner of Howell Cobb's. University trustees voted to organize a school of law, and that fall the three men began to teach courses in international, constitutional, and common law. Owing to his judicial duties, Lumpkin devoted less time to the school than did his two associates, who were to be "regular in their attendance" there. In December 1859 the General Assembly incorporated this new institution as the Lumpkin Law School.[23]

The style and substance of Lumpkin's supreme court opinions provide further evidence of the convergence of the roles of lawyer and reformer. Replete with references to Blackstone and the Bible, Lumpkin's opinions, especially those regarding the most pressing issues of the day, at times read more like moral philosophy than legal argument. Lumpkin frequently elevated the discussion beyond the two litigants involved in the dispute to address the higher social or ethical considerations of a case. Through these philosophical explorations, Lumpkin articulated a broad vision for Georgia society and eventually, as the secession crisis loomed, the entire South.

But Lumpkin was no provincial southern apologist. To the contrary, his extensive contact with northern reformers and a yearlong stay in England

and Scotland in the mid-1840s made him keenly aware of the South's failings, and Lumpkin developed a critique of the South and a vision for the region's future based on these experiences outside his native land.[24] Cases involving homicide and violence, economic opportunity, and slavery particularly provided Lumpkin with chances to engraft his moral vision on the legal and social order. Aware of the best and the worst aspects of northern, southern, and English society, Lumpkin sought to create the optimal social order in his native South, to build "the most glorious nation yet known for worth of every kind."[25] It was a task that perfectly reflected his lifelong pursuits as a lawyer and reformer.

Combatting Violence

In the area of criminal law, Lumpkin labored vigilantly to stem the tide of vengeance and violence that characterized southern life. The institution of slavery, the code of honor, the predominance of patriarchy, and the rural nature of southern society—combined with southerners' attachments to firearms, hard liquor, and gaming—have all received part of the blame for the region's tendency toward contentiousness and conflict.[26] In contrast to this dominant ethic, Lumpkin represented the "civilizing" influence of evangelical Christianity. With the advent of the Second Great Awakening in the South, religion began to compete with the local community for control of individual values and behavior. Evangelical morality stressed the sanctity of human life and the perniciousness of vengeance and violence.[27] Influenced by evangelical thinking and common-law principles, Lumpkin's opinions in homicide cases revealed a general unwillingness to mitigate homicide convictions to manslaughter as well as a refusal to expand the bounds of justifiable homicide. He repeatedly upheld murder convictions on appeal and used his opinions as a forum from which to denounce society's disregard for human life. Thus, contrary to some historians, who have claimed that southern appellate courts gave sanction to community opinion by condoning the region's culture of violence, Lumpkin—even more than Catron before him—proved quite intolerant of such behavior.[28]

In many instances Lumpkin argued that malice, the necessary requirement for a homicide conviction, could be implied from the actions of the accused. The existence of this malicious intent negated whatever claim to manslaughter or justifiable homicide the defendant might have made. In *Hudgins v. State* (1847), for example, Lumpkin took up the case of Josiah Hudgins, who claimed that he shot and killed John Anderson in self-defense. After earlier threatening to beat Hudgins "into the earth," Anderson approached

Hudgins's house, "slackening his gait as he drew near." Hudgins, gun in hand, warned his unarmed assailant to stand back, but when Anderson continued his approach, Hudgins shot the other man. Citing English precedents and the Georgia penal code, Lumpkin flatly rejected Hudgins's claim of self-defense. "The law presumes every homicide to be felonious," Lumpkin asserted, "until the contrary appears, from circumstances of alleviation, of excuse, or justification; and it is incumbent on the prisoner to make out such circumstances to the satisfaction of the jury, unless they arise out of the evidence produced against him." At the trial level, jurors had decided that the defendant had not proven his actions justifiable, and Lumpkin agreed.[29]

The jury had the right to infer malice from the circumstances surrounding the killing, according to Lumpkin, and all indications in this case were that Hudgins's behavior sprang from "an abandoned and malignant heart" rather than the impulse of self-preservation. "After shooting his unarmed and defenceless foe," Lumpkin explained, Hudgins "struck him a blow sufficiently hard to break the barrel of his gun, . . . and from the print on the ground of the butt of the gun near the head of Anderson, it is not unlikely that the blow was given, or repeated even, after his unhappy victim fell. What provocation was there to justify this cowardly and demoniac conduct? Does this look like self-defense, or like savage assassination?"[30] Not satisfied simply to uphold the conviction, Lumpkin clearly noted his disapproval of such wanton acts of violence.

Lumpkin took a similar stand in *Hawkins v. State* (1858), another case where he believed malicious intent was apparent. Hawkins argued that his victim, Scott, had provoked the killing and that the conviction ought to be mitigated to manslaughter. According to testimony, the two men were gambling when an argument began and a fight ensued. Hawkins threw stones at Scott, punched him in the ribs, and then went home. When Hawkins later returned with two pistols in his hands, "Scott remarked that Hawkins was too mean to live and that he intended to kill him." Hawkins reacted by firing and killing Scott. Rejecting Hawkins's claim, Lumpkin held that "provocation by threats will not be sufficient to free the slayer from the guilt of murder." Because Hawkins had returned home to retrieve his weapons, his malicious intent was apparent—he had already decided to kill Scott. This was a case of "deliberate revenge," according to Lumpkin, "and punished as murder."[31]

Looking beyond the case at hand, Lumpkin again used the occasion to reprimand strongly a society that failed to exercise sufficient respect for life. "Human life is sacrificed at this day, throughout the land, with more indifference than the life of a dog, especially if it be a good dog," Lumpkin observed. "Scott may not have been a good citizen, still he was a human creature, under the protection of the laws of the State. . . . Cain was the first murderer, but who is the last, is known only to those who have read the morning papers. If this crime goes unpunished, let our skirts, at least, be free from the stain of bloodguiltiness." [32]

Malice could also be implied, according to Lumpkin, even if no personal ill will obviously existed between two individuals. In *Revel v. State* (1858), Lumpkin examined a confrontation at a grocery among four men who apparently had political differences. One of the men, named Hammack, had insulted another, Revel. Hammack subsequently apologized, and Revel accepted the apology. Even though the situation seemed to have been diffused, Revel apparently continued to seethe with anger, and he later walked out of the store with a revolver in his hand. When a few of the men followed him, hoping to calm him down, Revel shot and killed Hammack. Revel's attorney contended that the state could prove no malice on the part of his client and that the evidence regarding Revel's tempestuous behavior after the confrontation with Hammack should not have been admitted at the trial. [33]

Lumpkin sharply disagreed with this view and again contended that jurors could infer malice from the circumstances surrounding the victim's death. "It is argued that the malice which constitutes murder," Lumpkin wrote, "must be felt toward the individual killed. Is this true? Where a gun is fired at random into a crowd, and life is taken, malice, says the law, shall be implied; and so too shall it be, declares the Code, where no considerable provocation is given, and where the circumstances of the killing denote an abandoned and malignant heart." Moreover, Lumpkin made clear that such evidence about the suspect's intentions was perfectly admissible. Revel, he argued, "was determined to wash out the insult with the blood of the deceased," and "these contemporaneous acts were, we repeat, rightly let in to characterize the motives of the prisoner." [34]

Lumpkin's evangelical moral sense, combined with his admiration for strict English common-law rules regarding homicide, underlay his eagerness to uphold homicide convictions when defendants argued for a mitigated charge. "Human life, the most sacred of God's gifts," he succinctly stated, "must be protected." [35] Sharing Blackstone's fear that "the right to defend might be mistaken for the right to kill," Lumpkin believed that malice could be implied and that all killing was presumed felonious until the defendant could prove the charge should be mitigated or the actions deemed justifiable. Lumpkin, in other words, looked for ways to uphold homicide convictions rather than to give "judicial approval to street-fight killing," in the words of one scholar. [36]

The converse of Lumpkin's critique of violence and vengeance was equally important. Lumpkin just as surely believed that individuals needed to take responsibility for their own actions. His evangelical assumptions included the idea that all people were accountable to God for their behavior, and Lumpkin saw excuses—especially for taking human life—as immediately suspect. When a defendant, for example, argued that he had killed a man to prevent a potentially murderous confrontation between his victim and another, Lumpkin would have none of it. In *Mitchell v. State* (1857), Mitchell claimed the he shot Cole to prevent Cole's murder of another man, Thompson. Several months before the killing, Mitchell had heard Cole threaten to kill Thompson on seeing him again, because Thompson had supposedly committed adultery with Cole's wife. When Cole and Thompson eventually confronted each other at a grocery, Mitchell shot Cole in the back, allegedly to prevent Thompson's murder. Although he conceded the justifiability of homicide under common law for "the prevention of any forcible and atrocious crime," Lumpkin affirmed the conviction.[37] "[M]ust there not be an apparent necessity on the part of the slayer—yea, an absolute necessity for the act—to make the killing justifiable?" he asked. "And must it not have been done, bona fide, to save life, and not wantonly or wickedly to destroy it?" Lumpkin placed the burden of proof on Mitchell to show that he was without fault, "that he killed to prevent murder." Unsatisfied with Mitchell's rationale, Lumpkin held that the defendant had "aided and assisted in bringing about the fatal rencounter."[38]

Because Lumpkin believed strongly in the need for individuals to be morally responsible for their actions, he also rejected the notion that drunkenness arose from a mental disorder and thus constituted a legal excuse for homicide. In *Choice v. State* (1860), Lumpkin heard testimony from a physician who claimed that Choice, the defendant, suffered from "monomania or dipsomania" caused by "'elision' in the brain" resulting from a severe blow to the head many years earlier. "This disease of the brain," observed the physician, "is liable to relapse by causes over which the patient has no control. An act done in a relapse state is the act and deed of an insane man, and not of a drunken man."[39] Drinking spirits, according to the physician, led directly to such relapses. Although Lumpkin acknowledged insanity as a valid excuse for criminal activity, he steadfastly held that "if [one] has legal memory and discretion when sober, and voluntarily deprives himself of reason, he is responsible for his acts while in that condition." In contrast, an insane person, Lumpkin reasoned, lacked responsibility whether drunk or sober. Paying little attention to the claims of the physicians who testified on behalf of the defendant, Lumpkin dismissed the contention that Choice's insanity caused him to drink—and commit murder—as "a theory not yet satisfactorily established."[40]

In the same case, Lumpkin also lambasted the idea of "moral insanity," an alleged disorder that adversely affected people's ability to do right rather than their capacity to reason. According to legal historian Lawrence Friedman, carried to its logical extreme, the acceptance of the idea of moral insanity by the national legal establishment during the nineteenth century "would have eroded the conventional basis of criminal responsibility."[41] In rejecting the moral-insanity doctrine, Lumpkin, the career-long temperance advocate, blamed Choice's deviant behavior on his abuse of alcohol and held the defendant responsible for his actions.

Lumpkin's opinions in homicide cases clearly demonstrate the force of his moral beliefs and the breadth of his vision for society. An eagerness to uphold convictions, to criticize the violent ways of his countrymen, and to hold individuals accountable for their criminal behavior characterized Lumpkin's homicide opinions. In only a few instances did Lumpkin concede the justifiability of killing, once in the case of a husband who killed a man who was attempting the "seduction" of the first man's wife and again when a man refused to retreat from his own property while being violently assaulted.[42] In the latter case, even though he upheld a killing as justifiable, Lumpkin reiterated the thinking that lay behind all his other homicide opinions: "The slayer, himself, must be faultless; he must owe no duty to the deceased; be under no obligation of law to make his own safety a secondary object; otherwise, he is answerable to the law of the land, without any immunity under the shield of necessity." In the moral order envisioned by Lumpkin, all would conduct themselves responsibly, with prudence and temperance. Those who did not would have to answer "to the law of the land."[43]

Encouraging Development

In addition to waging warfare against the South's violent traditions, Lumpkin also challenged the region's dependence on agricultural production and its economic dependence on the North. "Our Southern people must to a certain extent," he noted in an 1850 article in *DeBow's Review*, "abandon their accustomed paths and devise new plans for future prosperity." According to Lumpkin, southerners needed to create an economic environment favorable to investment, progress, and development—a liberal economic order in which roads, canals, railroads, bridges, and cotton mills would stimulate the creation of manufacturing and markets. "Let us, then, cease to talk, and begin to act in earnest," he urged in the same article, "by resorting to those measures that will not only induce our population and property to remain at home, but which will encourage mechanics and capitalists to settle among us."[44] Lumpkin, himself a stockholder in the Georgia Railroad and Banking Company, had a deep faith in the redemptive powers of economic development, a theme he expressed most clearly in his speeches and writings as well as in decisions involving contracts.[45]

In such cases, Lumpkin emphasized a dynamic view of property, an unqualified faith in competitive practices, and a deep concern for the public interest. Like most antebellum American judges, Lumpkin conceived of the marketplace as the supreme regulator of economic activity. He put little stock in such traditional ideas as restricting the public use of property to "natural" (agricultural) purposes or negating contractual agreements based on the failure of one of the parties to establish a "just price." "The value of any commodity is its marketable price," he plainly stated in an 1849 decision, "which is, and always must be, forever changing."[46] Only the market, Lumpkin believed, should determine the value of a good or product, and only an open, competitive economic arena could ensure growth and progress.

This belief in market principles had important implications, both for figuring damages arising out of unfulfilled agreements and for assessing compensation for property taken by eminent domain. In *Bryant v. Hambrick* (1850), for example, Lumpkin applied this market ideology to a dispute over the value of land. In the case, Thomas Bryant brought an action of debt on a bond issued to him by Harrison Hambrick. The bond, carrying a penalty of five hundred dollars, would be satisfied when Hambrick "made good and sufficient titles" to Bryant for a specific piece of property. In the meantime, Bryant made several hundred dollars' worth of improvements to the property, thereby increasing its value. When the case came up in the trial court, the presiding judge charged the jury, "that the measure of damages in this case was the purchase money, with interest from the time the notes given for the land became due, and that they could not take into consideration the value of the land nor the improvements." Lumpkin, however, overruled this portion of the trial court's decision. "Such a rule would tempt the vendor," he observed, "in any case where the property increased in value, to violate his contract. The proper criterion is the value of the land at the time when the title should have been made."[47] Lumpkin arrived at a similar conclusion in *Harrison v. Young* (1851), an eminent-domain case in which he held that the value of land taken for public use must be measured in terms of "all purposes to which [the land] may be appropriated" rather than only its agricultural or productive qualities. "The value of land or anything else," he concluded, "is its price in the market."[48] In short, Lumpkin recognized the various uses of property and allowed the invisible hand of the market to determine the value of a particular commodity.

Lumpkin's belief that the competitive marketplace best served the public good was most evident in his opinion in *Shorter v. Smith and the Justices of the Inferior Court of Floyd County* (1851).[49] In the case, bridge operator Alfred Shorter sought an injunction to restrain William R. Smith from building a bridge across the Etowah River at the northern end of the town of Rome, Georgia, a mile down the river from Shorter's bridge. Although an order of the Inferior Court of Floyd County had authorized the construction of the new bridge, Shorter claimed that he had entered into a "solemn contract" with the county to erect "safe and durable" toll bridges across the river in exchange for exclusive rights of franchise. In his view, Smith's attempt to establish new roads and to construct the bridge threatened to divert considerable traffic from the original bridge because Smith promised residents of the county free use of his new bridge. The franchise that had been granted to Shorter contained no express clause of exclusive rights or privileges. Still, Shorter claimed that this original agreement prevented the establishment of a rival charter that might lessen profits or take away customers. The dispute presented a set of circumstances remarkably similar to those in *Charles River Bridge v. Warren Bridge* (1837), the landmark U.S. Supreme Court case in which Chief Justice Roger B. Taney had allowed the construction of a new bridge.[50]

Lumpkin's opinion demonstrated all at once his commitment to a dynamic view of property, his belief in unfettered competition, and his emphasis on the public interest over vested rights. In contrast to northern counterparts Chancellor James Kent of New York and U.S. Supreme Court Justice Joseph Story of Massachusetts, who for years bemoaned the *Charles River Bridge* decision as destined to destroy the obligation of contracts and to undercut, in Kent's words, the entire "moral sense of the community," Lumpkin wholly embraced Taney's opinion and flatly rejected the claim to monopoly rights.[51] "Notwithstanding the profound regrets expressed by Chancellor Kent at its overthrow," Lumpkin wryly noted, "I must be permitted to say, that [the doctrine of implied exclusive rights], in my opinion, is at war with the universally recognized principles of American constitutional law."[52] Citing *Charles River Bridge*, Lumpkin held that the chartering of a public road, bridge, or ferry conferred only the right to construct the improvement and to receive the specified toll rate. Unless expressly stated, monopoly privileges were not included in such charters.

In Lumpkin's mind, a static notion of property or vested rights would only hinder the South's technological advancement, retard its economic development, and harm the community interest. Whereas Kent and Story viewed the sacred obligation of contracts as central to maintaining social cohesion— as the glue that connected the moral sense of the community to the law— Lumpkin held a vastly different yet equally compelling conception of the public interest. "It is better that individuals should be at the mercy of the public," he wrote, "than that the public should be dependent on individuals." In Lumpkin's view, only a system of "free and unrestricted competition," a marketplace that protected ventures rather than holdings, would ultimately benefit the public.[53]

Lumpkin's decision in *Shorter,* more dramatically than his homicide opinions, also showed his willingness to exert judicial power and carry out legal reform. While he had endorsed strict common-law principles in his homicide opinions, Lumpkin rejected the English notion of implied exclusive rights. According to Lumpkin, this doctrine was incompatible with the U.S. Supreme Court's precedent as well as "totally inapplicable to our local situation and change of circumstances."[54] To apply the rules of English jurisprudence to an expanding economic order in mid-nineteenth-century Georgia seemed ludicrous to Lumpkin, and he aggressively asserted his court's authority to modify such long-standing doctrines. "While we have adopted the English system of jurisprudence . . . it is left to the courts to determine, whether there be anything in our local situation, or in the nature of our political institutions, which would render any portion of it inapplicable," he wrote. "Would it not be strange for the courts of this country at this day, to enforce a doctrine which had its origin in the feudal system?"[55] Although the common law served Lumpkin well in his interpretation of criminal and homicidal behavior, English principles did not suffice as a guide for economic expansion.

From Lumpkin's practical standpoint, by 1850 the legal implications of prohibiting the construction of the new bridge were unthinkable. If such charters granted monopoly rights, Lumpkin observed, the state of Georgia would have yielded "the most abundant crop of litigation, ever garnered in this or any other country." The rapid pace of economic growth and development experienced by the state during the antebellum period had brought innumerable changes. If Lumpkin decided for Shorter, nearly all of these advances could subsequently have been considered violations of charters granting exclusive rights. "Whole towns are frequently broken up," Lumpkin explained, "and all the property in them rendered worthless by the establishment of a new road, which diverts the business to some other point. . . . [I]t must be conceded, that in the march of empire and civilization, these vicissitudes are inevitable."[56] Put another way, risk and uncertainty were the natural, even beneficial, results of the reign of the competitive marketplace, and Lumpkin was not about to stand in the way of such progress. In the *Shorter* case, Lumpkin adapted the law to a society in need of economic growth and development by actively transforming the ancient notion of exclusive rights to accommodate technological advancement.

Contrary to the claims of some historians, Lumpkin's rejection of exclusive rights was by no means unique among southern jurists of his day. Lumpkin was neither the first nor the only southern appellate judge to favor competition over monopoly. As early as 1829 the Tennessee Supreme Court ruled against a ferry monopoly and trumpeted the "free and liberal spirit of laudable competition" within the state.[57] Moreover, three years after *Charles River Bridge,* the Virginia Court of Appeals led the way in applying the Supreme Court's decision to competition between canals and railroads. As Chief Justice Taney had anticipated, canal companies like the Tuckahoe in Virginia sought to restrain by injunction the chartering of railroads that allegedly impeded the operation of their waterways. Judge Henry St. George Tucker, however, rejected such claims by canal owners and in *Tuckahoe Canal Co. v. Tuckahoe and James River Railroad Co.* (1840) held that the canal charter did not grant an exclusive right-of-way. Noting that "monopoly is very ingenious in extending its rights and enlarging its pretension," Tucker concluded that the legislature had the power to grant railroad charters even if they impaired existing charters.[58] Though some historians have attempted to portray southern judges as champions of monopolistic practices, usually by citing various state court decisions favoring exclusive rights prior to 1837, few state courts, North or South, embraced the principles of "creative destruction" before Taney's landmark decision.[59] By the same token, once Taney announced the *Charles River Bridge* opinion, southern jurists were certainly no less inclined to follow the decision than its most famous critics, northerners Kent and Story.[60]

In short, Lumpkin's conception of law and the economy was dynamic. His adherence to market principles in determining the use and value of property promoted development, while his Taney-like repudiation of exclusive rights upheld the interest of the community and furthered technological progress. Underlying Lumpkin's decisions were deeply held values: a firm belief in the moral advantages of economic advancement and a confident assurance that only a competitive environment would serve the public interest. While Lumpkin's Whiggish enthusiasm for the marketplace set him apart from John Catron, the two nevertheless shared an aversion to special privilege and concentrated economic power. Both Lumpkin and Catron thus sought to encourage opportunity and undermine monopolies and charters that hindered

the public good. In Lumpkin's mind, finally, the marketplace became a positive means to both moral and sectional ends—the advancement of the southern people and their eventual emancipation from economic subservience to
the North.

Reforming Slavery

While Lumpkin's record on law and the economy may have come closer to
resembling the prodevelopment doctrines of northern judges than historians have acknowledged, on issues pertaining to slavery and race, Lumpkin
undoubtedly personified orthodox opinion within his home region. Unlike
many northerners, who believed that slavery degraded the value of the white
man's labor and impeded economic growth and social mobility, Lumpkin
came to view the peculiar institution as divinely ordained for eternity and
fully compatible with the South's ongoing economic development. Much of
Lumpkin's reasoning in slavery cases came not from legal arguments about
the protection of property but from southern Evangelicals' defense of slavery
as a positive good for both races.[61]

The rise of a highly vocal and well-organized movement for the abolition
of slavery in the late 1830s and 1840s, as well as national political debates
over slavery's extension after the introduction of the Wilmot Proviso, caused
Lumpkin to abandon the antislavery sentiments he had espoused earlier in
his career. The attacks of northern evangelical abolitionists of this period,
which focused on the "sin of slaveholding rather than on the system's institutional character," hit Lumpkin especially hard.[62] After cooperating with
northern evangelical reformers through a number of voluntary associations
during the early 1830s, Lumpkin had to face the accusations of immorality
and ungodliness leveled against him, and all southerners, by his evangelical
brethren.[63] "Had the abolitionists let us alone," Lumpkin later wrote, "we
should have been guilty, I verily believe, of political and social suicide by
emancipating the African race, a measure fatal to them, to ourselves, and to
the best interest of this Confederacy and of the whole world. The violent
assaults of these fiends have compelled us in self defence to investigate this
momentous subject in all of its bearings."[64]

The end result of this soul-searching was Lumpkin's conclusion that slavery had both divine origins and biblical justification. Though still an Evangelical, a temperance man, and an industrial advocate, by 1850 Lumpkin
had completely reversed the position he had announced at the 1833 Boston
reform meeting, where he had foreseen an end to the peculiar institution.
Speaking in the midst of heated sectional debate over the Wilmot Proviso and

the extension of slavery, Lumpkin exuded confidence and certainty on the slavery issue. "The conscience of the whole South," he concluded, "has become thoroughly satisfied that this institution . . . is of God. That being recognized and regulated by the Decalogue, it will, we have every reason to believe, be of perpetual duration. That it subserves the best interests of both races, and that we will preserve and defend it at any and all hazards." [65]

Lumpkin founded his belief in slavery's divine origins and the superiority of the white race on a dominant cultural myth of the South—the story of Shem, Ham, and Japheth, the sons of Noah.[66] In a letter written just before issuing an 1853 court decision, Lumpkin expressed his personal acceptance of this biblical story by praising the work of a contemporary proslavery author, Josiah Priest. Priest's book "should be in the house and hands of every southern slaveholder," Lumpkin wrote to his daughter. "It agrees with and fully confirms all of my previous notions as to the Bible doctrine of slavery. Which in short are neither more nor less than this—that the tribe of Ham are cursed. That they are judicially condemned to perpetual bondage. Did you ever suspect that Jezebel was a Negro wench with a black skin and wooly head? And that Nimrod was a big Negro fellow? Priest proves this incontestably." [67] Lumpkin's religious outlook gave him ample reason to believe that slavery, as a divinely ordained institution, would endure forever. He no doubt concurred with the views of his son-in-law, T. R. R. Cobb, a noted writer of legal treatises, who interpreted references to slaves in the Book of Revelation as evidence for slavery's perpetual existence.[68]

More important, Lumpkin's religiously rooted racism manifested itself in a paternalistic conception of race relations. Because God had willed slavery to exist perpetually, in Lumpkin's mind, whites had an enormous burden and responsibility to black slaves. The permanence of slavery mandated that masters do all in their power to reform and improve the institution. This society-wide process of reform began with individual slaveholders' treatment of their own slaves, and Lumpkin reportedly lived up his own standards. Anna Parkes, one of the many slaves owned by the Lumpkin family in Athens, later recalled her masters with fondness. "Ain't nobody, nowhar, as good to dey Negroes as my white fokses wuz," she proudly recounted. "Ole Marster never whipped none of his Negroes, not dat I ever heared of." Moreover, according to Parkes, Lumpkin even tried to instill in his slaves a sense of dignity by teaching them to enunciate distinctly the word *Negroes*. "He 'splained dat us wuz not to be 'shamed of our race," Parkes continued. "He said us warn't no 'niggers'; he said us wuz 'Negroes,' and he 'spected his negroes to be de best Negroes in de whole land." Another of Lumpkin's slaves, William Finch, who went on to become an officeholder and Atlanta civic leader after the Civil War, ascribed much of his success to conversations with his master.[69] The judge himself offered clues about his feelings toward and experiences with slaves when he noted that "fidelity, association, mutual struggles and benefits, and many other causes, often produce warm attachments between master and slave."[70] In the paternalistic order envisioned by Lumpkin, all masters would treat their slaves with Christian love and humanity while attempting to instill proper ethics and virtues.

Like another Georgia Presbyterian, Charles Colcock Jones, Lumpkin was among the state's earliest leading advocates of slave education and Christianization. Lumpkin considered slaves "rational and intelligent beings . . . far above the level of the brute," yet still inferior to the white race. For this reason, he believed, it was the duty of whites to take care of childlike blacks, whom he believed needed protection from their own improvidence.[71] Lumpkin thus frequently praised the institution of slavery for its civilizing and Christianizing influence on Africans. "The spectacle of three hundred thousand barbarians, emerging, under the mild and humane treatment of their owners, into near four millions of civilized Christians, is not only without a parallel in the history of the African race, but of the whole world," he boldly asserted in 1850. In Lumpkin's mind, slavery became a positive good for both races and abolitionism, in contrast, nothing more than a "false philanthropy." By espousing paternalism, Lumpkin thus mounted a challenge to northern reformers by interpreting the demand for emancipation as a call for unchristian irresponsibility toward blacks.[72]

Lumpkin's judicial record reflected his paternalistic attitude toward African Americans and his concern with reforming the institution of slavery. Because his paternalism and moral certainty about the institution ran deep, Lumpkin wrote an inordinate number of the court's opinions on the subject. During the fifteen years before the Civil War, Lumpkin penned the opinion of the court in twenty-eight of the fifty-four cases involving slaves. Thus he wrote more than half the court's opinions in this area, compared to his handling of roughly a third of the court's overall caseload.[73]

Lumpkin's paternalistic concern for the slave was especially evident in slave-hiring cases, where the chief justice ruled that hirers needed to assume full responsibility for their rented bondspersons. Lumpkin thus rejected the fellow-servant rule, the idea that a "master," or employer, could not be held responsible for the civil wrongs of his employees. Under this doctrine, made famous by Massachusetts Chief Justice Lemuel Shaw's opinion in *Farwell v. Boston and Worcester Railroad Corporation* (1842), a worker who incurred injury at the hands of a "fellow servant," or employee, could not sue the employer. In the North, *Farwell* spurred economic development by assuring risk-taking capitalists that they would not be fettered by excessive liability for their actions.[74] A few years after Shaw's decision, in *Scudder v. Woodbridge* (1846), a case involving a hired slave who drowned while caught in a steamboat's waterwheel, Lumpkin ruled that this doctrine could never apply in slave society. Hired slaves were not, as presumed under *Farwell,* independent agents with the ability to "see that every other person employed in the same service does his duty with the utmost care and vigilance." To the contrary, Lumpkin observed, slaves "dare not interfere with the business of others. They would be instantly chastised for their impertinence." Because slaves were bound by fidelity to their masters or hirers, it was inconceivable to Lumpkin that they assume the character of independent white workers, who could either complain about unsafe working conditions or quit their jobs.[75]

The unique status of slaves therefore required that hirers do all in their power to protect the slaves. Lumpkin believed that rejection of the fellow-servant rule was "indispensable to the welfare of the slave." Most types of enterprises hired a number of slaves or free blacks, many of whom were, in Lumpkin's words, "destitute of principle and bankrupt in fortune." Surely the welfare of slaves, not to mention that of the masters who owned them, could not be entrusted to these improvident "fellow servants." "Let it be understood and settled that the employer is not liable, but that the owner must look for compensation to the co-servant who occasioned the mischief," Lumpkin speculated, "and I hesitate not to affirm, that the life of no hired slave would be safe." Slaves, Lumpkin later observed in a similar case, were "incapable of self-preservation, either in danger or in disease."[76] Therefore, if hirers did not assume responsibility for the safety and protection of their rented slaves, then these temporary masters would have no incentive to protect or defend the slaves from injury or illness, which Lumpkin would not tolerate.

Aside from rejecting the fellow-servant rule, Lumpkin took further steps to hold hirers responsible for slaves' health and safety. In *Lennard v. Boynton* (1852), for example, Lumpkin held that a hirer could not have a portion of his rent returned to him if the hired slave died before completing his term of service. Although aware that the precedents of many slave states contradicted this position based on the principle that an "act of God falls on the owner, on whom it must have fallen if the slave had not been hired," Lumpkin persisted in holding hirers to the highest standard of responsibility. If the court were to allow a hirer to get away with paying a reduced rent to the owner following a slave's death, what would prevent the hirer from ignoring the health or imperiling the safety of the hired bondsperson? "Humanity to this dependant and subordinate class of our population requires," Lumpkin asserted, "that we should remove from the hirer or temporary owner, all temptation to neglect them in sickness, or to expose them to situations of unusual peril and jeopardy. . . . Let us not increase their danger, by making it the interest of the hirer to get rid of his contract, when it proves to be unprofitable." The following year, Lumpkin reiterated this ruling in *Latimer v. Alexander* (1853), holding that a hirer "is bound to use ordinary diligence in regard to the health of the slave." Further, Lumpkin held, if the hirer failed to fulfill this responsibility, not only would he be liable to the slave owner for any injury resulting from this neglect, but the owner himself could supply the aid necessary for the health of the slave and seek compensation from the hirer.[77]

Lumpkin's paternalistic outlook toward slaves, rather than an economic interest in assisting the slaveholding class, formed the basis for these decisions. To Lumpkin, the improvidence of black people mandated that whites, whether hirers or owners, take proper care of their inferiors. Lumpkin believed that as temporary masters, hirers assumed responsibility for slaves' physical well-being, and any effort by the court to lessen the seriousness of this duty only gave incentive for hirers to neglect slaves. At the same time, if for some reason hirers were unable to live up to these responsibilities, Lumpkin did not hesitate to cast the burden back on the slave owner. "The bare fact that the Negro had been hired to another," he wrote in *Latimer,* "does not necessarily and under all circumstances, absolve the owner from the duty which he owes, both to the slave and the community, to afford him protection, and provide for his wants in sickness and in old age." Thus, in instances where the hirer was insolvent or the slave absent from the hirer for some reason, Lumpkin stated that he "would not hesitate to hold the master bound" to make compensation to anyone who might come to the aid of a slave in need.[78]

Lumpkin no doubt believed that he had the interests of slaves, not masters, in mind in such cases. As he himself was not a large slave owner, Lumpkin probably did not hire out any of his slaves, and he stated as much when claiming in another case that he had "no interest in this class of contracts, either individually or collectively."[79] Lumpkin believed that slavery, as a divinely ordained institution, involved reciprocal obligations between masters and slaves. The law needed to elucidate these responsibilities on the part of slave owners so that slavery could be the sort of humane institution that he believed God had ordained. "Every safeguard, consistent with the stability of the institution of slavery, should be thrown around the lives of these people," he wrote. "For myself, I verily believe that the best security for the permanence of slavery, is adequate and ample protection to the slave, at our own hands." Thus, humanity on the part of hirers and masters harmonized with the divine plan and guaranteed the future existence of the peculiar institution.[80]

At the same time that he sought to reform the relationship between masters and slaves along paternalistic lines, Lumpkin continually affirmed the perpetual nature of this relationship. Indeed, Lumpkin believed, only within the institution of slavery could blacks live under the proper tutelage of whites. Postmortem manumission cases presented numerous opportunities for Lumpkin to express his thoughts on the need for slavery's continued existence, and Lumpkin vigorously restricted the possibilities for black freedom in most cases. When legislation opposed his evangelical proslavery views, however, Lumpkin treaded more cautiously. Like northern judges, who often encountered a tension between their personal antislavery beliefs and their duty to uphold the law, particularly in regard to fugitive slaves, at times Lumpkin's moral values encouraged a stricter policy toward slavery than the letter of the law allowed.[81] Although during the late 1840s and early 1850s Lumpkin's proslavery attitudes had not developed to the point to produce this "moral-formal" dilemma, by the mid-1850s, as the level of his proslavery fervor and racist rhetoric heightened, Lumpkin encouraged tighter controls over the black population than statutory regulations permitted.[82]

As Lumpkin came to accept the idea that slavery was divinely ordained, he attempted to narrow the possibilities for slaves to attain their freedom. In *Adams v. Bass* (1855), for example, the testator of a will had requested that his slaves be removed to a plot of land, "either in the State of Indiana or Illinois," be given the appropriate tools for farming, and be supplied with a year's provisions for subsistence purposes. The will could not be carried out, however, because both Indiana and Illinois had legally prohibited the admission of blacks. In such instances—when circumstances prevented the execution of a will—British and American judges had formulated the "Cy-pres doctrine" by which the courts would construct another will for the testator, in accordance with his intentions.[83] Applying this doctrine, Lumpkin reconstructed the will of the deceased and concluded that the testator's primary aim was to have his slaves settled in Indiana or Illinois. "Liberty, of course," he wrote, "would be the necessary terms of this disposition; and such, unquestionably, was contemplated by the testator. But to hold that he would have conferred the same boon, taking all the risks and disadvantages attendant on the change, anywhere else, is to assume what is incapable of proof."[84] Holding that the slaves could not be removed, Lumpkin ruled that they would be distributed to the testator's legal heirs.

Paternalism again entered into Lumpkin's argument against emancipa-

tion. The chief justice argued that slaves were better off in the South—under
the dominion of whites, who provided the necessary care and supervision for
them—than in the North. "What friend of the African or humanity," Lumpkin asked, "would desire to see these children of the sun, who luxuriate in
a tropical climate and perish with cold in higher latitudes, brought in close
contact and competition with the hardy and industrious population, which
teem in the territory northwest of the Ohio and who loathe Negroes as they
would so many lepers?" Again noting the "thriftlessness" of blacks, "when
not controlled by superior intelligence and forethought," Lumpkin concluded
that emancipation in the North could only be detrimental to slaves.[85]

Colonization was an equally frightful possibility, in Lumpkin's mind, and
when statutory barriers were not insurmountable, Lumpkin attempted to restrict that type of emancipation as well. In *American Colonization Society
v. Gartrell* (1857), Lumpkin deftly avoided a potentially onerous legislative
measure by narrowly interpreting the meaning of a charter. The constitution
of the American Colonization Society authorized the organization to receive
and dispose of property at its discretion, "for the purpose of colonizing, with
their own consent, in Africa, the free people of color residing in the United
States, and for no other purpose whatever." The will of Francis Gideon, conversely, bequeathed to the society "for the purpose of sending them to Liberia . . . all his slaves." Upholding the decision of a lower court, Lumpkin
quickly seized on the discrepancy between the society's charter and the testator's request: "The Negroes . . . are given as slaves, and not as free persons
of color, to be sent, not with, but with or without their consent, to Liberia. . . . Indeed, the testator could only give them as slaves. For, had their
status been changed by the will, from slavery to freedom, before the gift attached, the will itself would have been void by the statutes of 1801 and
1818." Therefore, Lumpkin held that the society could not take or hold
property inconsistent with the terms of its charter.[86] By so doing, he dealt
a severe blow to the cause of colonization in Georgia. The society could
no longer accept slave property; at the same time, statutory law prohibited
slaves from attaining their freedom within the state before being colonized.

Although a supporter of the colonization movement earlier in his career,
by the late 1850s Lumpkin's evangelical perspective on slavery made any
commitment to colonization untenable. Colonization, he thought, was a
"failure" because it contradicted his belief that blacks needed white guidance
as well as his conviction that God had ordained the peculiar institution.
Lumpkin thus eagerly criticized colonization and defended slavery. "To in-
culcate care and industry upon the descendants of Ham, is to preach to the

idle winds," he wrote. "To be the 'servant of servants' is the judicial curse pronounced upon their race. . . . Under the superior race and nowhere else, do they attain to the highest degree of civilization; and any experiment, whether made in the British West India Islands, the coast of Africa, or elsewhere, will demonstrate that it is a vain thing . . . to fight against the Almighty. His ways are higher than ours." [87]

Lumpkin's efforts to eliminate postmortem manumission, however, were not always as easily accomplished. In *Cleland v. Waters* (1855), the chief justice faced the tension between law and sentiment that characterized his judicial behavior into the late 1850s. In this case, the court had to decide the validity of specific provisions of George M. Waters's will, which authorized the domestic emancipation of a slave, along with "the future issue and increase of all the females mentioned in this item of [the] will." "If [manumission] is incompatible with the humanity, &c. of the authorities of the State of Georgia," the will read, "I direct my . . . executors to send the said slaves out of the State of Georgia, to such a place as they may select . . . and that the whole of this proceeding be conducted according to the laws and decisions of the State of Georgia." After a lower court upheld the manumission outside the state, Lumpkin reluctantly affirmed the ruling. Existing law, he explained, prohibited only emancipation within the state of Georgia.[88] "The state did not expect her judicial process to reach to Liberia or New York, and arrest, by warrant, liberated slaves, with a view to again reduce them to servitude," he conceded.

Yet Lumpkin let it be known that the decision ran counter to his personal convictions. "I take this occasion to state emphatically, however," he wrote, "that I am fully persuaded that the best interests of the slave, as well as a stern public policy, resulting from the framework of our social system, imperatively demand that all post mortem manumission of slaves should be absolutely and entirely prohibited." Lumpkin, moreover, chastised slave owners who made provisions in their wills for the foreign emancipation of their slaves. Specifically, he criticized such masters for ignoring "the scriptural basis upon which the institution of slavery rests" and for disregarding "the peace and welfare of the community." [89] Lumpkin even used the *Cleland* decision as a forum for transmitting his views to the legislature by actively encouraging the body to review the question. "I have earnestly solicited the immediate attention of the present Legislature, (1855–'6) through the Chairman of the Judiciary Committee of the Senate to the subject," he wrote. Despite such strong feelings on the subject, Lumpkin could not bring himself to simply overrule what he thought was the clear will of the legislature. Based on statutes passed in 1801 and 1818, masters could still emancipate their slaves outside the state.[90]

Lumpkin encountered a similar tension in *Sanders v. Ward* (1858), where he again reluctantly yielded to the intent of the legislators who passed the 1818 act. The chief justice made clear his dissatisfaction with the law. "During the session of the Legislature before the last," he wrote, "I addressed a communication to the eminent counsel who argues so earnestly against the validity of this will, and who was at that time chairman of the Senate's Judiciary Committee, calling his attention to this subject, and suggesting the propriety of passing a law forbidding all post-mortem manumission. Were I a legislator, I should vote for such a bill."[91] The legislature, however, after considering the proposed legislation as well as the chief justice's recommendations, rejected the bill by an overwhelming margin. Lumpkin, therefore, was again left with the moral-formal dilemma that confronted him in *Cleland*.

Demonstrating his dissatisfaction with the legislature and perhaps sensing the public's desire for a tougher manumission law, Lumpkin emphatically restated his own position on the issue: "For myself, I repeat, I have no partiality for foreign any more than domestic emancipation. I believe that policy, as well as humanity for the Negro, forbid both. Especially do I object to the colonization of our Negroes upon our northwestern frontier. They facilitate the escape of our fugitive slaves. In case of civil war, they would become an element of strength to the enemy, as well as of annoyance to ourselves." But Lumpkin refused to take it on himself—and his fellow justices—to prohibit all acts of emancipation. "Shall I therefore undertake, by my individual opinion, to dictate to more than a half a million of my fellow-citizens, what shall be the law, by wresting these ancient statutes from what I believe their true and only meaning? A construction adhered to without variableness or a shadow of turning for a quarter of a century? Such is not my understanding of my duty or privilege."[92] No doubt admiring Lumpkin's restraint and perhaps heeding his advice, the legislature a year later passed a law forbidding all manumissions.[93] Thus, although Lumpkin hesitated to use his judicial power to alter the legislatively created rules regarding postmortem manumission, his continued admonitions of the legislature ultimately achieved the desired aim.

An evangelically based paternalism, whether in the form of urging hirers to take care of slaves or interpreting wills to limit the possibilities for emancipation, thus marked Lumpkin's opinions on the subject of slavery and race relations. This outlook helped Lumpkin resolve the apparent contradiction inherent in the slaves' dual status as person and property. Southern evangelical thinking supported both sides of this incongruity: it commanded recognition of the slaves' moral and spiritual nature because of their need to be converted yet condemned African Americans to bondage because of the curse of Ham and the color of their skin. Once Lumpkin fully embraced this formula in the 1850s, there was no longer any doubt in his mind about the relationship between slaves and masters. Slavery's divine origins meant that emancipation ceased to be an acceptable legal option. At the same time, masters possessed a Christian obligation to treat their bondspersons with paternal kindness to provide moral uplift.[94] Slaves, in this paternalistic evangelical understanding, were to be owned as property yet treated as persons.

An Independent South

By the eve of the Civil War, after fifteen years on the Georgia Supreme Court, Joseph Henry Lumpkin had articulated a unified vision for the future of his state. An end to rampant violence, the establishment of a diversified competitive economy, and the perpetuation of a paternalistic slave system stood at the center of this vision. As a reformer, Lumpkin's judicial opinions had continually reflected his concern with social and philosophical—rather than merely legal—issues. His preoccupation with social improvement and the creation of an ideal society often overshadowed his devotion to legal niceties. In search of justice and progress, Lumpkin drew intellectual sustenance from divergent sources, including the Bible, English common law, and northern example. Still, Lumpkin was not such a reformer and freewheeling judicial activist that he merely cast aside legal precedent or ignored legislative mandates. His respect for the legislature was most apparent in slave-manumission cases, where, although pleading for statutory changes, he avoided overruling such measures. At the same time, Lumpkin's eagerness to look beyond the litigants and the case at hand in search of the larger social significance of his opinions revealed a breadth of vision common among many antebellum jurists.[95]

Indeed, the scope of Lumpkin's vision stretched beyond the boundaries of his state and included the entire South. One of the few truly fervent advocates of secession among the southern judiciary, Lumpkin envisioned, as he frequently described to his law students at the University of Georgia, a "Glorious South, cut loose from the North, with King Cotton and Free Trade." Lumpkin welcomed this promising future—a future he believed would be characterized by economic diversification and moral progress. "Let then, the cotton mill and the cotton field," he wrote, "and that most formidable of all trios, and most holy of all alliances, 'the plough, the loom, and the anvil,' be brought together." [96] On the eve of the Civil War, Lumpkin foresaw an ideal society—a vital, independent South, freed from economic reliance on the North and committed to both the preservation of slavery and the humane treatment of blacks.

Lumpkin's beliefs on secession and state sovereignty, however, did not manifest themselves in the form of bold public statements. In this regard, Judge Henry L. Benning, Lumpkin's colleague on the court, proved much more willing to discuss the nature of the relationship between the states and the national government. Known for his lengthy opinion in *Padelford v. Savannah* (1854), in which he described the Georgia Supreme Court as "co-equal and co-ordinate with the Supreme Court of the United States," Benning served as a delegate to the Nashville Convention of 1850 and later as one of the chairs of the Georgia Secession Convention. [97] Lumpkin never participated in such political proceedings, yet he undoubtedly envisioned an independent southern nation in his speeches and letters.

The Civil War, of course, shattered Lumpkin's vision. As President Abraham Lincoln began to wage, in Lumpkin's words, "an unnatural and unconstitutional war upon a portion of the States," the Georgia judge and reformer witnessed his plan to remake southern society on the pillars of Evangelicalism, industrialization, and slavery crumble to the ground. With the South locked in a "death-struggle, in which our people are engaged to save themselves and their posterity from subjugation by the abolition vandals of the North," Lumpkin's optimism began to wane. [98] He lost his son-in-law, Thomas R. R. Cobb, a famous writer of treatises on slavery and architect of secession in Georgia, at the Battle of Fredericksburg in 1862, and by the following spring Lumpkin expressed a painful awareness of the war's high costs. "The noble men who have fallen in this wicked struggle would have made a nation for numbers, and the most glorious nation yet known for worth of every kind," Lumpkin mused. "And then the genius of such a posterity as they would have left to bless and elevate the whole people for all time to come; all lost, and lost forever." [99] Instead of laying the legal foundation for the future, during the 1860s the chief justice and his colleagues were preoccupied with issues arising out of wartime—the constitutionality of the impressment of soldiers and the taking of property, the legal nature of Georgia's changing relationship with other states and with the federal Union, and the new status of blacks brought on by Confederate defeat and emancipation. [100] To be sure, the South was undergoing a transformation, but it was certainly not along the lines that Lumpkin had hoped. In the short term, Lumpkin's hopes for the future South lay in the ash heap of Confederate defeat: economic development fell victim to the destructive force of the Union army, while slavery succumbed to the euphoria of emancipation.

Still, toward the end of his career, it was clear that Lumpkin had made his mark on Georgia's legal culture and had earned the respect of those beyond his own state. Before the war, President Franklin Pierce had offered Lumpkin a seat on the newly created federal court of claims. Although he seriously considered accepting the offer to go to Washington, D.C., Lumpkin declined the position after careful consideration and advice from friends and colleagues. Many thought that his departure would have been a severe setback to the institutional prestige and authority of the Georgia Supreme Court. Judge Eugene Nisbet, one of Lumpkin's colleagues, commended him for his decision to remain in Georgia. "You have done right," he wrote. "Your resignation and a bad appointment to fill your vacancy would have killed the court." [101] Lumpkin's presence on the tribunal was crucial to its survival. The court's steady record of achievement, as well as the chief justice's personal popularity, prompted the Georgia General Assembly in 1859 to confer the power of statutes on the court's unanimous decisions. In just twelve years, the Georgia Supreme Court had changed from a much-debated, oft-maligned institution into a respected judicial body whose decisions carried all the force of legislative enactments.[102] Lumpkin died in 1867, but his legacy would endure: in the substance of more than two thousand written opinions, in a robust supreme court, and in the lives and minds of a new generation of Georgia lawyers.

In a larger sense, Joseph Henry Lumpkin's life and work during the years leading up to the Civil War demonstrated the continuing development of a sectional perspective among southern state judges. Though Spencer Roane and John Catron had confronted the slavery issue during specific crises in the nation's history and had expressed sectional sentiments in the midst of these conflicts, as state judges they did not have to grapple with the intensified sectionalization of politics that occurred in the late 1840s and 1850s. (Catron was already on the U.S. Supreme Court by this time.) As slavery came to dominate national political debate, state judges like Lumpkin invested greater time and effort in deciding cases involving slaves because the jurists realized the deep social and political implications of their opinions. Lumpkin's adjudication of such cases involving slaves constituted a public defense of the benevolence of the peculiar institution in the face of northern criticism and sectional conflict.

Because of the collision of his social-reform principles with the ongoing development of sectional tensions, Lumpkin constructed a more coherent social, moral, and judicial philosophy as a southerner than had either Roane or Catron. Lumpkin's evangelical moral sense caused him to view the issues of slaveholding and southern independence in stark, uncompromising terms. Ultimately convinced of the social benefits of slavery, Lumpkin viewed an independent southern nation as a morally superior civilization blessed by God. As a judge and reformer, Lumpkin did his best to make this vision a reality.

CHAPTER FOUR

John Hemphill,
the Texas Supreme Court, and
the "Taming" of the Frontier

What was the object of the colonization of this country? What kind of people did the Mexicans invite here? . . . [I]t was their intention to invite agriculturalists, every one of whom should be a warrior, to tame the wilderness, and to destroy, not only the wild beast, but the wild men of Texas. —JOHN HEMPHILL, 1845

While the 1840s and 1850s witnessed the emergence of social reformers like Lumpkin, the period also saw the continued expansion of the nation's boundaries. Texas and the American Southwest, in particular, captured national attention during this era as American political leaders focused their gaze on the future status of slavery in new lands. White settlers in Texas, meanwhile, who had already established a slaveholding republic, faced the task of transplanting American institutions to the former frontier of Mexico. Typical of these Texas transplants—who were mostly young, male, southern, and slaveholding—John Hemphill labored to bring "civilization" and stability to Texas during his eighteen years as the state's chief justice. A South Carolina gentleman known for his studious habits and fervent political beliefs, Hemphill arrived in Texas in 1838 and spent the next two decades in judicial service to the state before being elected to the U.S. Senate on the eve of the Civil War.

Hemphill and his judicial colleagues faced great obstacles that hindered their work: grueling circuit riding in a sparsely settled land; sporadic violence among Native Americans, Mexicans, and Anglo-American settlers; a lack of law books. Yet under Hemphill's leadership, the Texas Supreme Court crafted a legal order that fostered increasing Anglo-American settlement, created new agricultural and commercial opportunities for these settlers, condemned widespread violence among them, and encouraged the humane treatment of slaves. Although the results were devastating for Mexicans and Native Americans, Hemphill and his colleagues perceived themselves as bringing the blessings of liberty and law to an untamed frontier.

From South Carolina to Texas

Born in 1803 in Chester District in the South Carolina up-country, Hemphill was the fifth child of the Reverend John Hemphill and his wife, Jane Lind Hemphill. A native of northern Ireland, the Reverend Hemphill had come to America after the Revolution, studied in Pennsylvania, and migrated to South Carolina in 1795 to accept the call to preach at a small Presbyterian church. Jane Lind, herself the daughter of a pastor and theology professor, shared her husband's religious faith, and the two raised their six children in accordance with such principles. Mrs. Hemphill's death in 1806 left her son for a time to be reared by his father and older siblings, assisted by a local schoolmaster, until the Reverend Hemphill remarried in 1811.[1]

Young John Hemphill distinguished himself early in life by his exceptional educational achievement. After receiving his primary education in the "old field schools" in and around Chester District, Hemphill enrolled at Jefferson College (now Washington and Jefferson College) in Pennsylvania, where he became known for his "superior scholarship" and his talents as a linguist and orator.[2] In 1825 he graduated second in his class. Though under some pressure from his father to enter the ministry, Hemphill had other plans. He returned to South Carolina to teach in various classical academies, but the task turned out to be not all that Hemphill had hoped. The drudgery of working with beginning pupils left his mind "stationary," and after a few years, Hemphill undertook the study of law. In 1828 he entered the Columbia law office of D. J. McCord, the most prominent compiler and codifier of his state's statutes. Hemphill soon became certified to practice in the courts of common pleas, and in 1829 the two established their own law practice in Sumterville in the Sumter District of South Carolina. Two years later, Hemphill earned the right to practice in courts of equity.[3]

But just as Hemphill had left teaching for lawyering, a new interest—politics—soon drew his attention away from the law. In 1831 he had begun to write essays for the *Sumter Gazette,* and within a year's time had become a prominent proslavery, pronullification voice in the community.[4] When the Virginia legislature engaged in a debate over the slavery issue in 1832, the respected editor of the *Richmond Enquirer,* Thomas Ritchie, angered many in the South by publishing the whole of the debates in his newspaper. Many, especially in South Carolina, feared the consequences of such open discussion. Writing in the *Gazette,* Hemphill urged slave patrols to be on the alert and condemned Ritchie as "the apostate traitor, the recreant and faithless sentinel, the cringing parasite, the hollow-hearted, hypocritical advocate of Southern interests . . . who has scattered the firebrands of destruction everywhere in the South."[5]

When editor Maynard Richardson of the Sumterville *Southern Whig* challenged the tacit ban on debate over slavery in South Carolina and opposed the state's drift toward nullification, a two-month-long feud with Hemphill ensued. Richardson invited discussion of the slavery issue in the *Whig* and accused Hemphill of "sickly sensitiveness and ridiculous squeamishness" about addressing the subject. After a few months of trading barbs in the press over this issue as well as the merits of nullification, Hemphill and Richardson brawled on an April day in front of the Sumter courthouse. After the fight began, residents swarmed into the street and turned the contest into a riot. Hemphill, according to his brother, "was stabbed three times but not very much hurt."[6] A few months after the incident, in an Independence Day oration from the steps of the same courthouse, Hemphill vigorously advocated nullification and state sovereignty as defenses against economic ruin, political tyranny, and the abolition of slavery.[7]

Hemphill's partisan activities only intensified during the next few years. After becoming editor of the *Gazette* in September 1832, Hemphill took the oath of nullification and pressed the nullifiers' agenda through the newspaper.[8] Although the famous Clay-Calhoun compromise subsequently ended the showdown between South Carolina and the federal government, Hemphill continued to find himself in the thick of controversy. By the summer of 1833, for example, he had embroiled himself in another dispute involving his honor, this time with a merchant in nearby Camden who had taken offense at one of Hemphill's newspaper articles. Mordecai Levy and Hemphill dueled with smoothbore pistols, and Levy's bullet hit his opponent squarely on the shooting hand. Afterwards, the two settled on an "adjustment honorable to both parties," and Hemphill wore a scar from the incident for the rest of his life. Although his conduct as a gentleman was deemed "irreproachable," the young Hemphill often had a difficult time keeping his violent passions in check.[9]

A few years later, Hemphill's sense of duty and honor—as well as his passions—drew him to battle. In 1835, when U.S. forces became embroiled in a second war with Florida's Seminole Indians, Hemphill attempted to raise a local militia company. His recruiting efforts met with little success, however, and he joined a company from Columbia, which embarked by steamboat for St. Augustine, Florida. During the campaign, Hemphill contracted a serious illness, probably malaria or hepatitis. In the spring of 1836, General Winfield Scott signed Hemphill's honorable discharge for disabilities arising out of what was described as a "sequela to measles." On his release, Hemphill spent some time at the hot springs of Virginia recovering from his ailments before returning to South Carolina to practice law.[10]

Soon, however, Hemphill was again on the move. In 1838 he left the South Carolina up-country for the Texas frontier. Hemphill's reasons for departing South Carolina are unclear, but economic and political considerations were probably an important part of his decision. Financial opportunities for lawyers were diminishing in his home state, and Hemphill's partisanship might have seemed excessive to his political seniors. Like Louis Wigfall, another South Carolina firebrand with an uncertain future in the Palmetto State, Hemphill apparently envisioned new opportunities in the Republic of Texas.[11]

With its abundance of land and shortage of lawyers, Texas seemed the perfect destination for an ambitious young lawyer. Anglo-Americans, most of them born in the South, had been steadily flocking to Texas since the early 1820s, while it was still a Mexican territory. The Panic of 1819, which prompted the U.S. government to halt the issuing of general land grants on credit, provoked the initial burst of settlers, while the even more severe economic collapse of 1837 further encouraged migration. Cheap prices for land and independence for the republic made Texas all the more attractive to potential residents, many of whom were debtors seeking to escape their obligations and start anew.[12] Lawyers found the republic particularly alluring, as the insecurity of land claims arising out of the war for independence promised plenty of litigation. Many of these new members of the Texas bar, most of whom were young and inexperienced, envisioned attaining great heights of prestige and power in their new homeland. As a contemporary observer remarked, "Such men easily worked themselves up to the belief that in this new country in a very short time, they could become generals or statesmen."[13]

Hemphill too hoped to begin anew. In 1838, after arriving at a settlement called Washington, along the Brazos River, Hemphill received a license to practice and opened his law office. Afterwards, according to Texas tradition, he immediately went into seclusion to learn the Spanish language and Spanish civil law, which was at that time still in effect throughout the republic. Described by his brother as "always a student," Hemphill's devotion paid immediate dividends. In January 1840, although Hemphill had only resided in the republic for two years, President Mirabeau B. Lamar appointed him a district judge. At that time, the republic's supreme court consisted of its seven district judges, headed by a chief justice, so Hemphill's appointment placed him among the leading jurists in Texas.[14]

During his brief tenure as district judge, Hemphill impressed his fellow Texans both with his legal talents and his martial prowess. Soon after his appointment, Hemphill earned a somewhat heroic reputation as an Indian fighter for his role in the "Council House Fight." While Hemphill served as an observer to negotiations between whites and Comanche at a San Antonio courthouse, a bloody riot erupted, and an Indian "assailed" and "slightly wounded" the judge. Hemphill struck back with his bowie knife and "reluctantly" disemboweled the Comanche. When the fighting had ceased, thirty-three Comanche, six Texans, and one Mexican had lost their lives. After the incident, angry Texans, including Hemphill, banded together to chase the Comanche away from white settlements. In a political culture defined by military glory, where citizen-soldiers earned the highest honors and won the most prized political positions, Hemphill's exploits complemented his legal career.[15] Eleven months after his appointment as a district judge, upon the resignation of Chief Justice Thomas J. Rusk, Hemphill ascended to the chief justiceship of the Texas Supreme Court.

Hemphill's work as chief justice, and the role of the Supreme Court in general during the republic period, proved insignificant in comparison to the era of statehood. The court faced persistent difficulties that interfered with its judicial tasks. White Texans continued to struggle against periodic Mexican invasions, and beginning in early 1842 the court held no sessions for nearly a year and half. In fact, Hemphill joined General Alexander Somervell's military expedition to the Rio Grande and did not return to hold court again until the June 1843 term. Politics also drew Hemphill's attention away from judicial matters. He was considered as a candidate for president of the republic in both 1843 and 1844, although both times he declined to run. By 1845 annexation became the most pressing political issue in Texas, and Hemphill served as a delegate to the convention charged with taking action on annexation and drawing up a constitution. An advocate of annexation, he chaired the convention's judiciary committee, which recommended the establishment of a three-member supreme court and a system of district courts as well as the merging of the separate courts of law and equity. The convention approved all the recommendations, and the governor of the new state subsequently appointed Hemphill to the chief justiceship.[16]

The "Old Court"

Along with his judicial colleagues, Abner S. Lipscomb and Royall T. Wheeler, Hemphill became a member of what came to be known in Texas legal lore as the "Old Court." (The term distinguished the three from the new judges who ascended to the bench just before the Civil War.) For the next eleven years—until Lipscomb's death in 1856—these three men shaped Texas law and earned a reputation as the greatest assemblage of judicial talent in state history.

Lipscomb, like Hemphill, was a native of South Carolina. Born in 1789, Lipscomb studied law with John C. Calhoun and in 1811 moved to Alabama to begin his practice. He joined briefly in the military effort to subdue Native Americans along the nation's southern frontier during the War of 1812, and when the state of Alabama was organized in 1819 he became a member of the new state's supreme court. In 1823 he began an eleven-year tenure as chief justice of Alabama before resigning to practice law in Mobile. After serving briefly in the state legislature, in 1839 he moved to Texas, where "his fame as a lawyer and jurist had preceded him, and he immediately commanded a large practice." Again entering public life, he served as secretary of state of the republic, in which position he strongly advocated annexation, and served as a member of the constitutional convention of 1845.[17]

Wheeler, born in 1810 in Vermont, grew up in Ohio and in 1837 moved to Fayetteville, Arkansas. He practiced there briefly with William S. Oldham before moving again in 1839 to Nacogdoches, Texas. A teetotaler and a "young man of great purity of character," one contemporary observed, "the whole order of his mind very much unfitted him for the rude state of society" on the frontier. After establishing a law partnership with Kendreth L. Anderson, vice president of the republic, in 1842 Wheeler became district attorney, gaining valuable experience in criminal practice. Two years later he received an appointment as district judge, thus serving as a member of the supreme court of the republic. He subsequently joined Hemphill and Lipscomb on the state supreme court.[18]

The legislature, the public, and the press apparently held all three judges in high esteem. Both Hemphill and Lipscomb had served as delegates to the

1845 convention, and both were mentioned as candidates for the presidency of the republic and for the U.S. Senate at various points in their careers. Moreover, all easily won reelection to their judicial seats in 1851 and 1856 and earned consistent praise from the press and legal community. "It has rarely occurred that all the judges of the Supreme Court of any state have so completely commanded the confidence of the people upon whose rights they are requested to adjudicate," noted a typical contemporary newspaper editorial.[19]

The three justices tended to specialize in particular legal issues. Hemphill, nicknamed the "first Spanish civilian of Texas," earned a reputation as an expert in the civil law of Spain and Mexico, and he wrote many opinions in those areas of the law in which the Spanish influence was greatest: women's rights, community property, and real estate. Wheeler specialized in criminal matters and wrote the opinion in well over half of the criminal cases heard by the court. Wheeler wrote slightly more opinions than Lipscomb, while Hemphill wrote the fewest of the three—only about a quarter of the court's total reported decisions during this period. Hemphill's opinions, however, averaged about a third longer than those of his colleagues. As chief justice, he might have chosen to write opinions in the court's most difficult cases, or perhaps his expertise in Spanish matters forced him to do so. Hemphill also devoted more attention to the "literary excellence" of his opinions than did the others, an unsurprising fact given that he had been a classical schoolmaster.[20]

Despite the tendency toward specialization, differences periodically arose among the judges. When a disagreement did occur, it was usually between Wheeler and Lipscomb, who were, according to a later chief justice, Oran Roberts, "very different in their habits of thought on legal questions and in their mental organization." Wheeler once privately criticized Lipscomb's opinions as "crude, superficial, partial, and totally defective in legal accuracy and precision and habitually so." Differences between the two, according to Roberts, "often called into requisition the conciliatory influence of the chief justice." Yet whatever divisions arose did not interfere with the ultimate achievement of unanimity. Of all the reported opinions from 1846 to 1857, only seventy-one, or 3 percent, generated either a concurrence or dissent.[21]

In the frontier environment of antebellum Texas, hardships abounded for the bench and bar. Supreme court judges wearily traversed the vast circuit— from Austin to Tyler to Galveston—dispensing justice in the tiny wooden structures that served as courthouses across the sparsely settled landscape. Apparently never sure whether they would be paid on time or in full for their labors, these jurists carried out their duties in the midst of the threat of violence that often erupted between Anglo-American settlers and Native Americans or Mexicans. Moreover, the young bench and bar lacked extensive collections of law books, a fact that at times interfered with legal education, appellate advocacy, and opinion writing.[22] Hemphill's personal library at Washington-on-the-Brazos, reportedly the largest in the state, contained some 2,400 volumes, but the justices could not transport these materials around the circuit and had to make the best of a bad situation. Rutherford B. Hayes captured the conditions under which the members of the Texas Supreme Court lived and worked when he visited Austin in 1849. "Called at the room of an old law student of Delaware [Ohio], Royall T. Wheeler, now a judge of the Supreme Court," Hayes wrote in his diary. "His office as judge, 'den' as he called it, being a log cabin about fourteen feet square, with a bed, table, five chairs, a washstand, and a 'whole raft' of books and papers."[23]

The legal culture of the frontier, along with the presence of the Spanish tradition, created a setting amenable to judicial experimentation. Although Anglo-American lawyers, steeped in common-law tradition, dominated the legal landscape of Texas, New Orleans supplied the state and the rest of the Southwest with a sizable collection of written sources as well as lawyers knowledgeable in the Spanish law. In 1820 an English translation of the *Partidas* (a source of Spanish law governing the colonies) appeared, and in 1839 Joseph White, a lawyer and U.S. congressman, published his *New Collection of Laws, Charters, and Local Ordinances of the Governments of Great Britain, France, and Spain*. White's volume made available to Texas lawyers a summary of the entire body of Spanish private law, and the book became the principal source of Spanish law in Texas.[24] When the Texas republic gained independence in 1836, its constitution called for the Congress of the republic to enact legislation to "introduce the common law of England, with such modifications as our circumstances, in their judgment, may require," and in 1840 the Congress complied with this mandate. Over the next two decades, the members of the Supreme Court drew on a mix of Spanish civil law, English common law, and American decisions in formulating their opinions. Many times they ignored precedent altogether. As Wheeler once stated, "We have not the same reason to adhere to any particular course of decisions, which has constrained the English Courts to apply to their decisions the maxim, stare decisis."[25]

No matter the source of their opinions, the members of the Texas Supreme Court, especially Hemphill, viewed themselves as the carriers of civilization to a vast, uncultivated land. All of these men romantically perceived themselves as bringing liberty and law to this outpost of America. Like most white Texans, Hemphill frequently wrote and spoke admiringly of the cause of

Texas independence. Securing autonomy had not been a battle "for mere glory" or "for aggrandisement," he asserted. "This was a struggle by freemen who were born free, for their country, for their homes—for liberties secured to them by the most sacred guarantees, and which, without fault on their part, were threatened with utter extinction." Hemphill and his colleagues sought to preserve and expand this notion of liberty, which included the right of individual settlers to till the soil, engage in commercial pursuits, or hold slaves unfettered by state interference. Hemphill believed that the great purpose of the settlement of Texas was to fight "the tomahawk and scalping knife of the savage" and to fill "the wilderness with a christian, civilized, and laboring population."[26] Only through law, the judges believed, could such "noble" ends be achieved.

Homesteads

One way to plant civilization on the frontier was to make it easier for debtors to acquire and maintain homesteads. Texas had offered a limited degree of assistance for debtors since 1829, when the Mexican state of Coahuila y Texas recodified Spanish exemption principles and extended them to land grants. Large-scale migration of debtors to Texas dictated continued interest in the issue. Although every state in the Union possessed some chattel exemption—which shielded basic items such as furniture, tools, and clothing from the reach of creditors—no state had passed legislation extending the principle of exemption to real estate. In 1839, in addition to providing exemptions for "household and kitchen furniture," "all implements of husbandry," and other items essential to one's trade or livelihood, the republic's Congress exempted "fifty acres of land or one town lot" from the grasp of creditors. This measure, based on the act of 1829, protected the "homestead and improvements not exceeding five hundred dollars in value" from forced sale for payment of debts. By the time of the 1845 constitutional convention, Texans, well versed in concepts of exempt property, incorporated this concept into the new constitution and expanded the size of the homestead thereby exempted.[27] Lipscomb, serving with Hemphill as a delegate to the convention, initially introduced the idea of a homestead-exemption provision to alleviate the "distress I have often seen come upon families, who have been so paralyzed by it as to be incapable of exertion." Owing to the efforts of Lipscomb, Hemphill, and others, the new constitution conferred on the legislature "power to protect by law from forced sale . . . the homestead of a family not to exceed two hundred acres of land not included in a town or city, or any town or city lot or lots in value not to exceed two thousand dollars."[28]

The homestead exemption did not release debtors from their obligations: it simply prevented homesteads from being taken for payment of debts.

Supported by both Spanish tradition and Texas law, in a series of decisions Hemphill and his colleagues broadly interpreted the exemption both to protect debtors and to expand opportunity. Like so many others who struggled to come to grips with the enormous changes wrought by the Market Revolution in antebellum America, Hemphill, who wrote most of the court's opinions in homestead cases, sought to protect families and small property owners from the perils of the marketplace at the same time that he desired his state to reap the benefits of economic expansion.[29] Reared in the southern tradition of Jefferson, Jackson, and Calhoun, Hemphill shared Catron's distrust of powerful banks, monopolies, as well as tariffs, nationally funded internal improvements, and other forms of special privilege. These institutions and policies threatened to concentrate economic power in the hands of a few, undermine the economic opportunities of small property holders and businessmen, and interfere with the autonomy of states. The homestead exemption, in contrast, was a beneficial use of state power, a positive way to promote the public good by facilitating economic independence. Along with the state's constitutional provisions outlawing imprisonment for debt, forbidding monopolies, and requiring legislative approval of corporate charters, the homestead exemption reflected Texans' concern with minimizing economic concentration and maximizing economic liberty.[30]

Over the next several years, Hemphill and his colleagues interpreted the exemption broadly so that it applied to a great number of situations and individuals. In *Sampson and Keene v. Williamson* (1851), for example, Hemphill ruled that the Texas Constitution prohibited not only the forced sale of the homestead but also "any forced disposition of the property," including a foreclosure on a mortgage.[31] Hemphill conceded that the defendants in the case had voluntarily pledged their property as a security for a debt, but, he argued, they could not "waive or renounce the guarantee or immunity with which the Constitution shields the property." With an eye toward protecting debtors, Hemphill criticized the mortgage as a device whereby creditors could circumvent the constitutional protection of homesteads. "The form [of the mortgage] in use is deceptive and fictitious," he wrote. "It conveys the estate, with the right of taking it back on the payment of the money, while its legal effect is to give a mere lien upon the land to secure this payment, with the right of foreclosure on default of the mortgager."[32] Relying on Spanish legal sources, Hemphill broadly defined the notion of a "forced sale" to include a mortgage. "The Constitution obviously intended that the homestead should be exempted from the operation of any species of execution, or from any forced disposition of the property, whether partial or total," he reasoned. Because the framers of the Texas Constitution sought to protect struggling families from the vicissitudes of the marketplace, Hemphill concluded, the exemption protected "the domestic sanctuary from every species of intrusion which, under color of law, would subject the property, by any disposition whatever, to the payment of debts."[33]

Hemphill also argued against limitations on the value that could be exempted. In *Wood v. Wheeler* (1851), the court took up the case of a widowed Mrs. Wheeler, who had assumed ownership of the family's house and town lot appraised at a value of two thousand dollars. Although a probate court had exempted this property from her husband's creditors, a district court later reversed the probate court's ruling and ordered that the house and lot be turned over to a creditor for payment of debts. The widow and her child were to receive five hundred dollars from the proceeds of the sale. The case presented the problem of having to reconcile the state's homestead-exemption statute of 1839 with the state's constitutional provision of 1845. Under the 1839 statute, the value of the homestead exemption was limited to five hundred dollars on improvements on the lot, while the constitution of 1845 placed a two-thousand-dollar limitation on the total value of the lot with improvements. Given the rulings of the probate and the district courts, the supreme court had to decide how much of the widow's property was subject to seizure by creditors.

Because the value of property was constantly changing, according to Hemphill, the constitutional provision limiting the exemption to two thousand dollars failed to offer sufficient protection to individuals. The value of a town lot, without additional improvements, Hemphill reasoned, might increase over time beyond the limits of the exemption, thus falling subject to forced sale for payments of debts. Compelled to relocate, the family might very well find itself in the same situation again, as property values continued to rise. "This round of domiciliation in a home with its endearments, and expulsion with its miseries," Hemphill stated, "may be several times repeated in the course of a few years; and ultimately, the ejection may take place at a time when the price of property is so excessive that the portion of the proceeds of the homestead awarded the owner, may be wholly insufficient to procure a comfortable home suitable for the family."[34] Hemphill thus saw potential danger in the constitutional limit set on the value of the exemption and feared that such limitation undermined the policy's intended purpose. "The object of such exemption," he wrote, "is to confer on the beneficiary a home as an asylum, a refuge which cannot be invaded nor its tranquility or serenity disturbed, and in which may be nurtured and cherished those feelings of individual independence which lie at the foundation and are essential to the permanency of our institutions." Limitations on the exemption, in Hemphill's mind, ran counter to the "wise and beneficial purpose" of the legislation.[35] Bound by the constitution and the homestead-exemption statute, Hemphill could not simply remove all limitations on the exemption. He did, however, overrule the district court and offered the widow a judgment under which she would be able to retain a homestead.[36]

Hemphill even interpreted the exemption to apply potentially to all inhabitants of Texas. Under the 1839 law, the exemption applied to "every citizen or head of family in this Republic." *Cobbs v. Coleman* (1855), presented the question of whether a single man qualified for the exemption in light of his dubious citizenship in the state of Texas as well as the fact that he was not a "head of family." Interpreting the intentions of the authors of both the 1839 act and the 1845 constitutional provision, Hemphill dismissed such queries as irrelevant. "[T]he statute employs the phrase 'every citizen,' yet this is not to be taken in a restricted sense as designating only the native-born or naturalized citizen," he claimed, "but in its general acceptation and meaning as descriptive of the inhabitants of the country. . . . [T]he statute extends as well to single men or individuals as to married men or heads of families." As he had before, Hemphill supported his position with reference to Spanish authorities. Examining the "Institutes of Asso & Manuel," as published in White's *Collection*, Hemphill observed that "nothing is said [in the law] about single men or heads of families." Utilizing Spanish legal principles to sweep aside the literal wording of the statute in question, Hemphill ruled that neither status as a citizen nor a head of family mattered. The homestead exemption applied to all Texas residents.[37]

Further, Hemphill ruled that neither absence from the homestead nor leasing it for a time rendered property subject to forced sale. In *Shepherd v. Cassiday* (1857), the court took up the case of a woman whose lot in the town of Bastrop had been purchased by another in a sheriff's sale six months after she had moved away. Living with her children in Austin but without acquiring a homestead, the woman sued to reacquire the supposedly abandoned piece of property. Hemphill conceded that the questions of what constituted abandonment of a homestead and when one forfeited the right to the homestead exemption were difficult. Yet relying on Story's *Commentaries on the Conflict of Laws* and citing the Massachusetts Supreme Court, Hemphill reasoned that "every man must have a domicile somewhere and . . . that his existing domicile continues until he can acquire another." Hesitating to assert the proposition that "the old homestead remains until a new one is gained," a judicial pronouncement that would, he wrote, "too much embarrass and obscure the condition and rights of property," Hemphill nonetheless held that the woman retained the homestead in question. "The homestead is not to be regarded as a species of prison bounds, which the owner cannot pass over without pains and penalties," he wrote. "His necessities and circumstances may frequently require him to leave his homestead for a greater or less period of time. . . . Let him leave for what purpose he may, or be his intentions what they may, provided they are not those of total relinquishment or abandonment, his right to the exemption cannot be regarded as forfeited."[38] In this way as well, Hemphill broadened the application of the homestead exemption.

Hemphill also held, through a liberal definition of a homestead, that shopkeepers, lawyers, and other independent businessmen could reap the benefits of the exemption. In *Pryor v. Stone* (1857), he ruled that a home and eight lots owned by a family in the city of Dallas were subject to the exemption provisions. The limits of the exemption pertained only to the value, not the number, of the lots, and the properties did not have to be contiguous to each other. The widower head of the family in question resided in a two-room house that also served as his law office, while his children lived with another family. Hemphill held that the man's home was protected from forced sale. "The exemption should not be construed as reserving merely a residence where a family may eat, drink and sleep," he wrote, "but also a place where the head or members may pursue such business or avocation as may be necessary for the support and comfort of the family." He thus held that the exemption applied to the "office of a lawyer or shop of a mechanic," even if it did not serve as part of the residence of the family.[39] Hemphill appeared willing to define the homestead exemption as containing almost no limits or restrictions. In fact, the only stipulation he ever imposed on the exemption was that it actually apply to a home—a physical structure.[40]

The consistently broad interpretation of the state's homestead-exemption provisions demonstrated the ambivalence of the court toward the Market Revolution of the mid-nineteenth century. The court clearly aimed to protect debtors from the perils of the unrestricted marketplace. The design of the exemption, Hemphill once stated, was "to protect citizens and their families from the miseries and dangers of destitution."[41] At the same time, through an expansive reading of the state's homestead law, the court hoped to foster expansion and development by attracting more settlers and new wealth to the state. Almost all the mid-nineteenth-century promotional literature about Texas trumpeted the advantages of the exemption. A booklet entitled *Infor-*

mation about Texas, for example, published in 1857, devoted nearly seven pages solely to the benefits of the state's exemption law. During this period, older southern states, such as Mississippi, Alabama, and Georgia, steadily lost population to Texas because of its leniency toward debtors. Not surprisingly, these states, along with Florida, were the first four to copy Texas's example by passing their own homestead-exemption statutes.[42] More than attracting new settlers, the court's enshrinement of the homestead principle made capital more venturesome by lessening the risk. Like the limited liability associated with corporations, the homestead exemption assured an individual investor that no matter how much money he invested, he still could not lose everything he owned—he would still be assured of retaining his home. In Lipscomb's words, the exemption offered people whose fortunes had plummeted, "a point from which they can start, relieved from any fear of their families being turned out without a home." Such a family could "commence again, Antaeus-like with renewed energy and strength and capacity for business."[43] According to historian James Willard Hurst, by preserving a nucleus of working capital, such debtor exemptions helped foster economic liberty for small enterprisers and reflected nineteenth-century policy's "preference for keeping open the door to change, as against commitments or equities asserted by the past." The homestead exemption, in other words, was characteristic of the "release of energy" principle that distinguished nineteenth-century American legal development.[44]

More important than protecting debtors or promoting development, Hemphill and his colleagues thought that the homestead exemption furthered the values of democracy and citizenship that they believed necessary for the "civilization" of Texas. By guaranteeing the right of struggling families to hold onto their homes, Hemphill believed that the exemption fostered "those feelings of sublime independence which are so essential to the maintenance of free institutions." Lipscomb expressed himself even more directly on this point. Misfortune, he wrote, "should not permit the unfortunate to be treated as animals and hunted down, by the aid of the law, as culprits. Where this is not done, some of the most benevolent hearts are driven, by such omissions and defects in the law, into ultraism, socialism, and Fourierism, and an opposition to all municipal regulations." "It is natural," he reasoned, "for the unfortunate to be grateful to those from whom they received aid in their affliction, and they will love and venerate the laws when they protect misfortune, and not force them into the class of culprits." The homestead exemption thus encouraged respect for law and for democratic institutions. Hemphill and Lipscomb no doubt agreed with Senator Thomas Hart Benton, a famous contemporary advocate of free land, who wrote in his memoirs, "The freeholder . . . is the natural supporter of free government."[45] Their judicial opinions rested on the same principle. Whether agriculturalists or businessmen, Texas debtors could rest assured that the legal system guaranteed protection of their homes and families, a comfort that would, in turn, make them more respectful of the law and more productive as citizens. Offering a liberal interpretation of the homestead exemption was one way the court attempted to "civilize" the frontier.

Hemphill and his colleagues' work in the area of the homestead exemption proved significant for the subsequent legal development of both Texas and the nation. The Texas constitutions of 1861, 1866, and 1876 all included homestead-exemption provisions, and over the next several years the state legislature continued to expand the value of the homestead that could be exempted, in part due to the high inflation after the Civil War. As early as 1850, fourteen states had copied the Texas example and enacted homestead-exemption laws of their own, and by 1870 forty states and territories had adopted exemption laws of some form.[46] The exemption received not only extensive acceptance in state legislatures but also widespread praise from state courts. The California Supreme Court deemed the idea "beneficent," the high court of Iowa called it "liberal and benevolent," and the Vermont Supreme Court referred to it as "of a humane character." Eager to take credit for the increasing popularity of this Texas innovation, a later member of the state supreme court, Judge Alexander S. Walker, hailed the homestead as the "crowning glory of Texas jurisprudence" and the "greatest idea of the age." Judge John F. Dillon of the Iowa Supreme Court similarly credited Texas in his *Laws and Jurisprudence of England and America,* referring to the exemption as "the great gift of the infant Republic of Texas to the world." Moreover, in an 1862 article on the homestead exemption, Dillon repeatedly cited the work of the Texas Supreme Court as foundational for understanding and interpreting the homestead exemption.[47] In Texas the confluence of a large debtor population, an expansive frontier, a traditional southern hostility to concentrated economic power, and the presence of Spanish law created a legal principle that soon spread throughout the nation.

Homicides

Like other antebellum southern state supreme courts, the Texas Supreme Court confronted widespread violence. Debtors, derelicts, and desperadoes of all sorts flocked to Texas during this period, and the oversupply of liquor and guns made the state a dangerous place. Ethnic tensions and southern honor only complicated the mix even further. Skirmishes among Mexicans,

Native Americans, and whites were commonplace, and the Celtic origins of many whites perhaps inclined them to a relatively violent brand of conflict resolution.[48] For whatever reason, Texas earned a particularly notorious reputation as a land of violence and homicide. Profiling the state in his famous postbellum analysis of murder in the North and South, H. V. Redfield concluded that Texas was perhaps the most homicide-ridden state in the nation. Decrying the laxity and ineffectiveness of the criminal justice system there, Redfield contended that "the usual course is to admit to bail, and then acquit on the ground of 'self-defense,' or 'great provocation,' or possibly 'insanity.'" In the absence of a host of quantitative studies of local court records, historians may accept Redfield's assessment of the day-to-day operation of the Texas criminal justice system.[49]

Rarely did such homicide cases make it to the state's highest court. Still, no less than their contemporaries John Catron and Joseph Henry Lumpkin, the members of the Texas Supreme Court proved judicially intolerant of defendants' efforts to excuse homicide. Throughout the antebellum period, the court repeatedly upheld the sufficiency and correctness of indictments and consistently refused to overturn convictions. Many of these appellate cases, of course, involved matters of technical procedure. Unlike Lumpkin, who used every opportunity that arose to condemn violence from the bench, the Texas Supreme Court more often stuck to the narrow legal issues of the case. Even when substantive matters arose on which the justices could speak their minds, their responses were typically more subdued than those of Catron and Lumpkin. Unlike the latter, who combined large doses of moral and biblical arguments with only a smattering of Blackstonian principles, the Texas Supreme Court employed more traditional sources of authority: Francis Wharton's treatises on criminal law and homicide and a variety a state appellate court cases in addition to Blackstone. Nevertheless, their work—if not their words—showed no more toleration of loose interpretations of self-defense than did the decisions of Catron or Lumpkin. Though Hemphill had led the court on the homestead exemption, Judges Wheeler and Lipscomb wrote the opinions in most homicide cases.

Time after time, the Texas Supreme Court held indictments to be sufficient, thus sustaining convictions. *Caldwell v. State* (1849), for example, involved a trial in which it had been discovered after the proceedings had begun that the indictment had not been officially endorsed as filed. The trial judge had thereupon ordered the clerk to make the endorsement. On appeal, counsel for the appellant claimed that this was a significant oversight—that because the document lacked the word *filed,* "the paper was not a record in the court." Writing for the supreme court, Judge Lipscomb ignored this argument, focused his brief opinion on another of the trial court's supposed errors, and affirmed the conviction. In *Givens v. State* (1851), Lipscomb again upheld the sufficiency of an indictment. The appellant had charged that the trial court had erred in rendering a judgment against the appellant for common assault when he was in fact indicted for an assault with an intent to murder. Citing Wharton's *American Criminal Law* as well as several state courts, Lipscomb concluded that it was a "well-settled rule that when an accusation of an offense includes an inferior one the jury may acquit the accused of the most atrocious and convict him of the inferior offense." [50] In *Gehrke v. State* (1855), Lipscomb held that even though the state's penal code distinguished between first-degree murder ("premeditated or deliberate killing") and second-degree murder, the law did not require that the indictment include the words *premeditated or deliberate*. The degree of malice and the nature of the killing, according to Lipscomb, were to be decided at the trial, not stated in the indictment. The conviction stood. The following year, in *White v. State* (1856), Lipscomb reaffirmed the principle in *Gehrke* when he again upheld the sufficiency of a murder indictment that had failed to include the words *premeditated or deliberate*.[51]

Judge Wheeler also regularly upheld the sufficiency of indictments. In one instance he held that there had been no good reason for quashing an indictment that simply failed to state that the defendant had used a deadly weapon in carrying out an assault, and in a similar case he ruled that it was not necessary that the indictment state the manner in which the defendant attempted to use a weapon.[52] Wheeler's most extensive discussion of the sufficiency of an indictment, however, arose in *Wall v. State* (1857), where the court again took up the issue of whether a murder indictment needed to include the degree of the charge. Noting that the court had already settled this issue in *Gehrke* and *White*, Wheeler wrote that "it will not be out of place to refer to a few decisions in our sister states, which show, that what is the settled law of this court is also the well settled doctrine of our courts." Wheeler proceeded to cite opinions and statutes from Tennessee, Pennsylvania, and New York, all of which proved his point: "It would not always appear on the face of the indictment, of what degree the murder was, because the jury are to ascertain the degree by their verdict." He concluded that "an indictment for murder, in the common law form . . . was sufficient to sustain a conviction of murder in the first degree." [53]

The court also upheld convictions when trial judges' charges were at issue. *O'Connell v. State* (1857) involved, from all accounts, an unprovoked attack by O'Connell on an unsuspecting and unarmed victim. Counsel for the defendant argued that because the trial judge's charge failed to outline the distinctions between the various degrees of murder, it was erroneous and misleading. Wheeler affirmed the work of the trial judge and turned the burden back on the defense counsel. "[T]he mere omission to give instruction is not error," he wrote. "The court is not bound in any case to give instructions not asked for by the party. If the charge of the court was not satisfactory, it was the right of the defendant, or his counsel, to ask such instructions as he thought proper." Wheeler went on to conclude that the facts did not warrant a charge regarding the law of justifiable homicide or any other explanation of the degrees of murder. In another case, in which the appellant claimed that the trial judge had not stressed enough in his charge the deliberation and premeditation required for first-degree murder, Wheeler simply concluded that the charge had "implied as plainly as if again expressed that premeditation and deliberation" were necessary for first-degree murder. This implied distinction was sufficient, Wheeler held, and the conviction was affirmed.[54]

Historians of nineteenth-century criminal law claim that the southern criminal-justice system placed such a high premium on procedural exactness that appellate courts often allowed murderers to go free. Edward Ayers, for example, argues that southern judges "wielded the power of the state with great care" and thus proved hesitant to convict criminals, and Lawrence Friedman notes that nineteenth-century appeals courts "often showed an extreme fussiness about procedures and pleadings." The late-nineteenth-century Texas Supreme Court, according to Friedman, was the worst offender. He cites instances in which the court overturned convictions for omitting the word *find* and for misspelling *guilty* as *guity* in jury verdict statements.[55] Yet before the Civil War the Texas Supreme Court certainly did not adhere to this pattern. It overlooked several instances in which the indictment appeared technically inadequate and repeatedly upheld indictments that lacked specific words and phrases. In addition, the court continually supported the work of local trial judges, whose charges to juries frequently came under attack by counsel in appellate cases. While evidence may exist that some trial judges bowed to community opinion and that juries frequently failed to convict their peers for acts of violence, antebellum appellate judges in Texas clearly did not follow the same path. The Old Court placed a higher premium on upholding convictions than on procedural exactness.

Aside from such technical matters, on the substantive issue of the definition of self-defense, Wheeler and Lipscomb sounded much like Catron and Lumpkin. *Lander v. State* (1854) is perhaps the best example of this similarity. The case involved Alfred R. Lander, who had been convicted of the second-degree murder of Eli Ussery. The two men had been long-standing rivals and had exchanged many threats over the years. Ussery, gun in hand, was one day heard to be "hunting" Lander. Advised of these threats by several witnesses, Lander procured a shotgun and secretly observed the movements of his alleged hunter for an afternoon. That evening, Lander concealed himself beside a building and ambushed his enemy, who was heading out of town on horseback with his son. Lander shot Ussery twice and killed him. After being convicted, he appealed his case on the grounds that the trial judge had erroneously outlined to the jury the definition of second-degree murder and of self-defense. Counsel for the appellant also cited Catron's *Grainger* opinion to make the argument that one could kill "for the preservation of his own life from a threatened attack from the deceased." [56]

Wheeler responded by devoting much of his opinion to a richly detailed definition of self-defense. He proceeded to outline the strict criteria that needed to apply to a set of circumstances for a killing to be considered a case of self-defense by turning to a variety of authorities—Wharton, Blackstone, Russell, and Starkie as well as a number of state cases from across the nation. All of these authorities pointed to a few simple truths. A "bare fear" of murder or robbery, "unaccompanied with any overt act," would not constitute self-defense. Or as another authority put it, the threat must not exist "in machination only." One acted in self-defense only when he killed "to avoid death or some severe calamity," and such a response needed to occur "upon a sudden occasion" and could not be premeditated. The principles and rules embedded in all these precedents and authorities, Wheeler concluded, "have their foundation in the law of nature; they are incorporated into and form a component part of the common law; are sanctioned by the wisdom and approved by the experience of ages." The judge warned against abandoning these principles and in doing sounded much like the moralistic Lumpkin. "When they shall be relaxed or departed from, it will impair the estimate of the sanctity of human life," Wheeler argued, "induce a loose estimate of its value, and tend to a state of society in which licentious, wanton violence may go unrestrained, brute force usurp the prerogative of the law, and every man become the avenger of his own wrongs." [57] In the type of society envisioned by the court, the law of personal vengeance would have no place.

After demonstrating his commitment to existing common-law principles regarding self-defense, Wheeler quickly dismissed the appellant's claims. "[T]o denominate this a killing in self-defense would be an abuse of terms," he wrote. "There was, indeed, nothing attending or giving character to the act which the law regards a matter in justification, excuse, or extenuation." Wheeler even challenged the appellant counsel's use of the *Grainger* precedent. Noting the existence of "much apprehension as to what it was intended to decide," the judge deemed the authority of *Grainger* "questionable" and denied its relevance to the case at hand.[58] The conviction stood.

Although they lived and worked in a violent, unruly setting, no evidence suggests that the antebellum appellate judiciary in Texas condoned mayhem or murder by expounding a loose interpretation of self-defense. To the contrary, the members of the pre–Civil War Texas Supreme Court consistently upheld convictions for murder and assault, and they dismissed attempts by defendants to excuse their actions based on self-defense. As Judge Wheeler remarked in an 1856 case, echoing Blackstonian principles and the common law, "the least touching of another's person, willfully and in anger, constitutes in law a battery, and every battery includes an assault."[59] Even in a violence-ridden locale such as Texas, the antebellum southern appellate judiciary apparently went against the tide of popular behavior and arrived at decisions based on higher principles rather than community norms. Only after the Civil War did the judiciary in Texas, as well as in many other states, embrace a more formalistic brand of jurisprudence that worked to the advantage of those who justified their offenses by claiming self-defense. Until then, Texas's appellate judges decried and condemned personal frays, honorable contests, and "street-fight killing" while exalting the ideals of civility and respect for law.[60]

Slaves

The judges of the Texas Supreme Court faced their most formidable task in establishing respect for law when they dealt with slavery. When white settlers carrying slaves from the southern United States first arrived in Mexican Texas, their legal status as masters became ambiguous. As Lipscomb later noted, "The legislation of Mexico had been so fluctuating and unsettled upon this subject as to give rise to great uncertainty as to what might ultimately be adjudged on the subject of their legal titles." As in Florida, where laws regarding race relations under the Spanish had been "mild and flexible," the legal boundaries surrounding slavery in Texas had never been sharply drawn. When Texas gained its independence, however, the republic's new constitution erased all doubts about the legality of slavery and affirmed that immigrants could bring their slave property to the republic without fear of legal interference.[61] Beginning in 1836, slavery in Texas rested on a firm legal foundation.

Because slavery developed later in Texas than in other southern states, lawmakers there had a chance to shape the development of race relations in ways that other states did not. In particular, Texas prevented the growth of a free black population. The constitution of 1836 prohibited free blacks from living in the republic without the specific permission of the Congress, and although an 1837 congressional resolution permitted all free blacks residing in the republic at the time of independence to remain, an 1840 act provided that after two years all "free persons of color" were to leave. Under this law, all those who remained were subject to sale as slaves. The 1840 law also prohibited the immigration of free blacks into the republic. Some received special permission to remain, and others were able to extend their stay another two years after the issuance of a presidential proclamation. Still, Texas lawmakers sent a clear message that free blacks were unwelcome because many white Texans believed free blacks constituted a threat to the institution of slavery. Because of these restrictions as well as a harsh criminal code that made all offenses and punishments apply equally to slaves and free blacks, the number of free persons of color in Texas was always minuscule. In 1850, only 397 free blacks resided in the state, and by 1860 that number had fallen to 355.[62]

Within this social and legal environment, the Texas Supreme Court seemed secure in dealing with the institution of slavery when compared to appellate judges in other southern states. In contrast to most southern judges, who viewed cases involving slaves through the lens of the emerging sectional conflict, ever mindful of the larger implications of every ruling, the Texas Supreme Court focused more on the individual circumstances of the slave and proved more willing to recognize slave humanity. The lack of a perceived threat by a free black population, the geographical distance between Texas slaveholders and abolitionist northerners, and the small number of antebellum insurrectionary scares in the state confirmed the justices' sense of security about the institution of slavery and allowed personal sentiment and legal principles to prevail over politically driven decision making.[63]

Hemphill in particular expressed a belief that undue fear of insurrection or abolition was irrational. Although in 1831 as a young newspaper writer he had decried any open discussion of the slavery issue for fear of revolt, two years later an experience with a supposed insurrectionary plot in South Carolina changed his mind about the plausibility of such threats. Describing the scare as a "ridiculous affair," Hemphill dismissed the paranoia and fear of his fellow whites.[64] After moving to Texas Hemphill lent his name to an 1840 petition requesting permission for a free black man to receive permanent residence in the state, an action that no doubt required personal conviction about the foundations of the peculiar institution. Two decades later, on the eve of the Civil War, Hemphill confidently stated that he viewed slaves as allies in what he saw as the coming war for southern independence. "I was born in the South, have lived long upon the earth, and have never witnessed even an attempt at an insurrection," he observed. "The phantasm that there is no sense of security in the South is utterly groundless and superlatively absurd."[65]

All of the justices implicitly expressed this sense of security about slavery. When dealing with those convicted of violating various police regulations designed to prevent insurrection or to restrict slave liberties, for example, Hemphill and his colleagues consistently chose not to err on the side of severity. In *State v. Wupperman* (1854), Judge Wheeler affirmed a lower court's decision to quash the indictment of a man for buying produce from a slave. State law prohibited such a purchase "without the written consent of [the slave's] master, or mistress, or overseer." Deviating slightly from the wording of the statute, the indictment charged that the defendant had bought the produce of a slave, "the property of one Andrew Herron, without first having the written consent of said Herron, or any one having charge of said slave." Wheeler held that merely substituting the phrase "or any one having charge of said slave" for the words "master, mistress, or overseer" was reason to quash the indictment. In *Rawles v. State* (1855), moreover, Judge Lipscomb overturned a slaveholder's conviction for allowing his slave "to go at large and hire her own time for more than one day in a week." Repeatedly criticizing the sloppy construction of the statute prohibiting such behavior, Lipscomb concluded that it was "unfortunate that, on a subject of so much interest and importance . . . there should be such imperfect legislation." Even more remarkable, in *Allen v. State* (1855) Judge Hemphill reversed the conviction of a man found guilty of selling liquor to slaves. At the man's trial, the only witness testified that he had seen no money traded between the man and the slave and had heard no talk of money or any other consideration rendered in exchange for the alcohol. Nonetheless, the trial judge had charged the jury that whether the defendant had given the slave the liquor or sold it to him was irrelevant—either constituted a violation of the state statute. Hemphill overturned the conviction based on the incorrectness of the charge. In effect, Hemphill ruled that giving liquor to slaves did not violate the law—only selling it to them did. In each of these instances, it would have been very easy for the court to demonstrate a fearful and suspicious commitment to public safety. Instead, the justices, already secure in the legal and social relationships existing between the races, adhered to the strictest conceptions of legality and procedure regardless of the liberties they implicitly granted to slaves.[66]

This approach to decision making proved especially beneficial to slaves in cases involving emancipation. In a series of decisions, the court narrowly interpreted Texas's constitutional provisions regarding emancipation and ruled in favor of those trying to establish free status. The 1836 constitution stated that no slaveholder was "allowed to emancipate his or her slave or slaves without the consent of Congress, unless he or she shall send his or her slave or slaves without the limits of the Republic," and this provision continued to prevail under the 1845 constitution and subsequent statutory law. As the court interpreted it, however, this antimanumission rule did not prevent slaves from attaining freedom, provided their emancipation had occurred previously in another jurisdiction.[67] In *Jones v. Laney* (1847), Lipscomb ruled in favor of former slaves who had been granted their freedom on a Georgia Indian reservation by their Chickasaw owners. The appellees in the case had presented a deed of manumission, thus proving a "prima facie case" for their freedom. As emancipation had occurred in the Chickasaw nation in 1814, Lipscomb concluded, "the laws of Texas did not govern the rights of emancipation in the master." Similarly, in *Guest v. Lubbock* (1851) the court ruled that the constitution's provisions regarding slaves and free blacks did not alter the free status of a black woman who had lived as the wife of a white man in Texas before the republic had won its independence. When the man died without a will, after the establishment of the republic, a dispute arose between his "wife" and his heirs over the legal ownership of some of her property. Lipscomb held that the woman was a free person who exercised the full rights of property ownership. "Although [the husband] may have been at one time her master," Lipscomb wrote, "if he disclaimed that relationship and did not claim to be her master, holding her in bondage when the Constitution was adopted, her status is not affected by it in any way prejudicial to her claim of freedom."[68] Most strikingly, in *Moore v. Minerva* (1856) the court held that a black woman who had been granted her freedom in Ohio but who later returned to Texas with her former master had not forfeited her liberty. Even though the 1840 law prohibited the immigration of free blacks to Texas, Lipscomb held that such measures had no effect on the woman's status. "These enactments do not affect the state of freedom but only provide a mode by which it may be forfeited, and neither the former owner nor his legal representatives can claim such forfeiture."[69] Thus, in all these instances, the court interpreted the constitution's antimanumission provision narrowly and ruled in favor of freedom.

The judges also held that the constitution and the laws of Texas permitted a master to emancipate his slaves outside the state. *Purvis v. Sherrod* (1854), the leading case on the issue, involved a testator who provided in his will that three of his slaves be freed and be settled near his sister, who lived within the state. "If the State of Texas, or any of my relations, should object to their freedom on these conditions," the will stated, "I give my sister full power to send them to a free State, or to Liberia, as she and the negroes may agree." When relatives contested the will, a trial court provided for the emancipation of the slaves outside the state, and the appeal came before the supreme court. There, counsel for the contestants argued that Texas had borrowed its constitutional ban on manumission from the Alabama Constitution and that its adoption brought with it "both the political and judicial construction of the State from which it was borrowed." In Alabama, a series of supreme court decisions had established that "where slaves cannot be freed in a state by will, the executor cannot take them out of the jurisdiction to free them." Therefore, according to counsel, the slaves could not be freed and ought to pass to the heirs.[70]

The court rejected this line of argument. Although he had served as chief justice of the Alabama Supreme Court, Lipscomb dismissed the decision of his former tribunal. He concluded that "although a State by its laws may absolutely prohibit emancipation, or direct the particular mode in which it can only be done, yet a bequest of freedom, not to take effect until the slave is removed beyond the territorial limits of such State, is nevertheless a valid bequest." Lipscomb observed that several southern states allowed emancipation outside their borders. Yet Lipscomb's analysis overlooked an important fact. At the time Lipscomb cited these precedents from other states, all had either been overruled or had received heavy criticism in more recent opinions from state courts.[71] By 1854 only Tennessee's liberal emancipation policy remained unchanged. Thus, instead of relying on Alabama's judicial interpretation of its constitutional provision, Lipscomb chose a Tennessee Supreme Court's ruling by Judge John Haywood as the chief source of authority for his opinion. In other words, though he could easily have chosen to restrict the right of emancipation, Lipscomb went out of his way to justify the court's lenient position. *Purvis* proved to be a powerful precedent. Over the next several years, the court repeatedly permitted emancipation outside the state and invariably cited *Purvis* in the process. Even Wheeler, who made known in other instances his indifferent attitude toward precedent, avoided a lengthy discussion of the issue in an 1859 case by simply resting on *Purvis*. "We do not think it proper to enter upon such an examination," he wrote, "and are content to repose upon the maxim, stare decisis." Only when a testator had not provided for the removal of his slaves outside the state did the judges invalidate an emancipation provision in a will.[72]

In criminal cases as well, the judges focused on the circumstances of the slave rather than the political implications for slavery, and they applied legal principles and personal sentiment to what might otherwise have been politically driven decisions. In *Nels v. State* (1847), for example, the justices ordered a new trial for Nels, a slave convicted of murder, because the jury at his trial had not been sworn, a decision that stood in marked contrast to the court's laxity toward procedural matters in most of its homicide opinions.[73] More significant, the Texas Supreme Court frequently went well beyond legal requirements in punishing white offenders accused of killing or violently assaulting slaves. *Chandler v. State* (1847) was one of the best examples of this judicial response. A jury found David Chandler "guilty of manslaughter" in the death of a slave. Counsel for Chandler argued that the trial judge had erred in charging the jury that it could find Chandler guilty of manslaughter, as no law in Texas provided that a white man could be convicted of manslaughter in the death of a slave. Yet according to the court, common-law rules and definitions applied, which allowed Chandler's conviction to stand. "In the absence of legislation," Wheeler wrote, "the common law is, and since the adoption of the constitution of the late republic ever has been, in criminal cases the rule of decision." To make this argument, Wheeler relied on a similar case that had arisen in Tennessee. Judge Robert Whyte in *Fields v. Tennessee* (1829) had held that the principles of the common law of England could apply in slave cases even though slavery never existed in England itself. Whyte drew a parallel between Norman villenage and American slavery. Because the villein enjoyed the right to sue in common-law courts against all except his lord, the American slave, according to Whyte, ought to receive the same protection.[74]

By relying on *Fields*, Wheeler accepted both the villenage analogy and the idea that slaves could receive the benefits of the common law. Most southern appellate judges emphatically rejected such claims. The Georgia Supreme Court, for example, dismissed the idea that the law pertaining to villenage shed any light on the legal relationships between masters and slaves. "Any analogy drawn from the villeinage of the feudal times," Lumpkin once noted, "is utterly fallacious as to the investigation." In South Carolina, Judge D. L. Wardlaw similarly concluded, "A slave can invoke neither magna carta nor common law. . . . Every endeavour to extend to [a slave] positive rights, is an attempt to reconcile inherent contradictions. In the very nature of things, he is subject to despotism." The Supreme Courts of Tennessee and Texas were the only southern appellate courts to accept the villenage analogy, a concept clearly reflective of a more humanitarian outlook toward the slave. These principles, Wheeler held in *Chandler,* were in perfect accord with the laws of Texas. Examining the state's slave code, he concluded that "the statute makes no difference in respect to this offense, whether it be perpetrated by or upon the person of a slave." Where not otherwise provided in the slave code, Wheeler argued, the general laws providing for the punishment of crimes applied equally to both slaves and whites.[75]

Even at the height of sectionalism in the 1850s, the court applied the principles of the common law to those convicted of harming slaves. *Nix v. State* (1855) involved an assault and battery with a knife "upon a colored woman named Lucy, a slave, the property of one Mrs. McRae." The indictment charged that Nix, the defendant, "did cut, bruise and wound, beat, ill treat" and commit other wrongs against her. After finding Nix guilty, the jury assessed a twenty-five-dollar fine and ten-day imprisonment in the county jail. On appeal, counsel for Nix pointed out at least three serious errors in the trial. First, the indictment did not charge the offense in the correct statutory language. The only applicable statute described the offender as "any person who shall unreasonably treat, or otherwise abuse any slave." The indictment was phrased in different terms. Second, the statute did not provide for a penalty of imprisonment, as had been given to Nix, only a fine. Third, even though the indictment had charged Nix with wounding Mrs. McRae's slave, counsel never presented proof at the trial that Lucy was a slave or that she belonged to Mrs. McRae.[76] Despite these arguably major errors in the indictment, Wheeler affirmed the conviction. Citing *Chandler,* he ruled that "where not otherwise provided . . . crimes committed by violence to the person, apply equally to crimes committed by or upon the person of a slave." Wheeler thus upheld the conviction not under the statute regulating crimes against slaves, which Nix had claimed needed to be adhered to, but under the state's general statute concerning crimes. "The present appears to have been a case of wanton, unprovoked, lawless violence, committed in a fit of drunkenness, upon an unoffending slave, without any pretense of authority, provocation, or excuse," Wheeler concluded. "And we entertain that it was a crime against the law of nature and the laws of society, and equally within the spirit and intention of the statute, as if it had been committed upon a free person."[77] In the years between *Nix* and the outbreak of the Civil War, the Texas Supreme Court continued to hold that whites accused of violent crimes against slaves could be convicted under the state's general criminal code.[78]

The sense of security evident among the members of the Texas Supreme Court allowed personal sentiment and legal principle to prevail in the process of judicial decision making. As the sectional crisis unfolded, many southern state judges articulated concerns about the political implications of rendering judicial decisions that appeared favorable to slaves. In 1848 Judge Thomas Ruffin of North Carolina, fearing the result of reducing the charge against a slave from murder to manslaughter for the killing of a white man, cautioned his colleagues against expressing "rash expositions, not suited to the actual state of things and not calculated to promote the security of persons, the stability of national institutions, and the common welfare." Writing ten years later, Lumpkin voiced his opposition to manumission outside the state in light of the deteriorating national political situation: Free blacks "facilitate the escape of our fugitive slaves. In case of civil war, they would become an element of strength to the enemy, as well as of annoyance to ourselves."[79] In contrast to such overriding concern with the politics of slavery and sectionalism, the members of the Texas Supreme Court never alluded to such national events and instead focused continually on the individual circumstances surrounding the cases at hand.

Personal sentiment on the part of the justices, inferred from both their public statements and private behavior, favored the recognition of slave humanity. Wheeler reportedly "went to some lengths to arrange the sale of a house servant so that she would not be separated from her slave 'husband.'"[80] Hemphill, moreover, especially believed that warm relationships existed between masters and their bondspersons. In early 1861, when assessing the future of slavery should a war ensue, Hemphill described slaves as "constant recipients" of masters' benevolence who "would eagerly sacrifice their lives" in their masters' defense in the event of civil war. "And all of them, regarding their master very justly as their guardians and protectors," he added, "would most willingly encounter danger and render service to secure their triumph." Hemphill's beliefs grew out of his personal experiences. At his death, he owned four slaves—an elderly couple and two young men— all of whom, according to one of Hemphill's relatives, seemed to have been "more expense than profit." Most interestingly, as James Paulsen concludes, Hemphill had a slave mistress named Sabina, with whom he had an "apparently loving relationship" and two children. According to Paulsen, Hemphill cared deeply for his two mulatto daughters and, before the outbreak of the Civil War, placed them both in the care of abolitionists by enrolling them in Wilberforce University in Ohio.[81]

The Texas Supreme Court's recognition of slave humanity through a strict interpretation of the state constitution and a broad application of rights under the common law was the ultimate example of the court's attempt to bring civilization and stability to the frontier. In a land renowned for its lawlessness, Hemphill, Lipscomb, and Wheeler applied personal sentiment and legal reasoning, rather than political extremism, to cases involving slaves. The dictates of law and humanity, they thus demonstrated to their countrymen, applied to all—even those deemed inferior. Of course, in no way did this mean that the members of the Texas Supreme Court opposed slavery, favored abolition, or rose above racism. Obviously they did not. Indeed, during the 1845 constitutional convention, Lipscomb forcefully argued that the state needed to throw more "protection around this species of property," and Hemphill noted that "the institution of slavery ought to be more carefully guarded in this state than in any other in the Union."

Yet Hemphill also introduced the constitutional provision giving the legislature the power to pass laws "to oblige the owners of slaves to treat them with humanity" and in a subsequent supreme court decision eloquently championed humane treatment. "Although slaves are property, yet in many respect they are persons, and are treated as such," he wrote. "The children for years require the care and attention of the mother, and though there is no law preventing the separation of the mother from the child in infancy, yet such separation, unless induced by necessity, is repugnant to the feelings of humanity, and is against the moral sense of the community." [82] As gentlemen who no doubt perceived themselves to be benevolent masters, the members of the Texas Supreme Court sought to civilize and humanize the institution of slavery in Texas.

Secession and War

During the late 1850s the Old Court dissolved. Lipscomb died in 1856, and Wheeler replaced Hemphill as chief justice when Hemphill left to serve in the U.S. Senate. Wheeler's leadership of the court coincided with the traumas of war. Although a Whig throughout his career and the only northern-born justice, Wheeler advocated secession and upheld the power of the Confederate government to prosecute the war effort. In *Ex parte Coupland* (1862), the first southern supreme court case dealing with the constitutionality of the Confederate Conscription Act, Wheeler held that the measure violated neither citizens' liberty nor states' reserved rights.[83] Soon afterward, according to a contemporary political opponent, Wheeler "fell into the morbid belief that, more than any one else, he was responsible for the terrible baptism of blood through which our country was passing." The war drove Wheeler to madness, and in April 1864 he "perished by his own hands." [84]

Hemphill's election to the Senate culminated a successful public career in Texas. While Sam Houston had represented Texas in the U.S. Senate since the state's entrance into the Union, his unwillingness to conform to the orthodoxies that increasingly came to characterize southern politics doomed his chances of reelection in 1858. With civil war looming on the horizon, the Texas legislature sought to elect someone who would take a solidly prosouthern position in the national political arena. Although Hemphill had scarcely played a role in state politics in his nearly two decades of service to the Texas judiciary, his judicial reputation made him the favorite of the legislature, and he resigned his position to accept the Senate post. Hemphill assumed Houston's seat on March 3, 1859.[85]

Hemphill's brief tenure in the Senate reflected the vituperative partisanship that had characterized his early South Carolina career. In his most memorable Senate speech, in January 1861, Hemphill echoed his earlier support for nullification and passionately argued for the right of secession. Drawing on the wisdom of such divergent thinkers as Blackstone, St. George Tucker, Alexander Hamilton, and James Madison, Hemphill offered a legal explanation of secession based on the theory of state sovereignty. Using his home state as an example, Hemphill reaffirmed the power of individual states to decide their own fates. Texas "has not abandoned the powers ceded to the Federal Government; she has only delegated them," he claimed. "She is still a State, a political body, with control over the lives, the liberties, and property of her people. She entered the Confederacy by compact, and the cession of some of her powers does not detract from her sovereignty." Although Hemphill focused on the constitutional and legal principles of secession, believing that they needed to be "clearly understood and conclusively established," his zealous argument made him sound much like the typical southern fire-eater.[86] Thus, despite his and the court's unwillingness to allow the sectional politics to influence their judicial decision making in slave cases for more than a decade and a half, in 1861 Senator Hemphill adhered to southern political orthodoxy. He also supported the Confederate cause by publishing a pamphlet urging Texas planters to buy war bonds. As one contemporary noted, Hemphill was "thoroughly Southern in his sentiments."[87]

Hemphill's advocacy of secession won him favor back home, and when the state legislature met in the spring of 1861 to elect delegates to the Montgomery Convention, the first congress of the Confederate States of America, legislators placed Hemphill's name in nomination. Following his election, he traveled to the first capital of the Confederacy, assisted in writing the new government's constitution, and served on a committee charged with compiling a digest of laws for the Confederate states. At about the same time, Hemphill also received an appointment to the Confederate judgeship for the District of Texas, a post he later declined.[88] Essentially, Hemphill's efforts on behalf of the Confederacy resembled his labors in Texas, for he again assumed the role of the legal architect. But he did not live to witness the fate of the constitutional and legal order he helped to fashion. Hemphill died in January 1862, less than a year after the Civil War began.[89]

Hemphill and the "Taming" of Texas

John Hemphill, later deemed the "John Marshall of Texas," led the Texas judiciary for eighteen years.[90] Although he did not author a majority of the court's opinions, Hemphill nevertheless "exercised a commanding influence in [the judges'] deliberations" in many ways: by mediating between them when disputes arose, through his extensive knowledge of the Spanish legal tradition, by his dedication to legal learning and scholarship, and through the "austere dignity" of his personality.[91] Hemphill's learned and low-key judicial style earned the respect of his colleagues. "He examines every subject very thoroughly," Wheeler once wrote, "and comes very slowly and cautiously to his conclusion—which will rarely be a wrong one." The first of the three members of the court to arrive in Texas, Hemphill had fought Mexicans, done battle with Comanche, helped write the 1845 constitution, and served as chief justice during the rough days of the republic. His leadership qualifications as chief justice were unquestioned, and his standing among the people of Texas nearly impeccable. Hemphill's activities off the bench, in fact, accomplished much in the way of furthering his reputation and authority as a judge. Over and over, Hemphill had proven himself a "staunch friend of Texas."[92]

Hemphill and his colleagues sought to make Texas a haven for sturdy, industrious white homesteaders and planters who would transform the social and cultural landscape into that of a "civilized" American state. Like most public figures in the nineteenth-century United States, Hemphill imbibed and espoused the language of devotion to liberty and respect for law. In his mind, these ideas were the twin pillars of Anglo-American civilization. The liberties of white settlers in Texas, while under Mexican rule, he believed, "were threatened with utter extinction." "The dark masses of the enemy," he wrote of the Texas revolution, "were pouring over the land, with havoc and extermination for their watchword—and desolation marking their path." At the same time, white Texans confronted the possibility of war with Indians, whom he conceived as an equally dangerous threat to liberty.[93] Mexicans and Native Americans obviously existed outside of the social and political order envisioned by Hemphill. Only by encouraging white settlement, adhering to legal principles, and establishing legal institutions, he believed, could Texans' cherished liberties be ensured.

To accomplish this end, Hemphill and the court embraced an innovative style that drew from a multitude of legal sources. In homestead cases, the judges often looked to the Spanish example; on criminal law, the court turned to Wharton and Blackstone; and in slave cases, the justices frequently drew from the decisions of the Tennessee Supreme Court. Hemphill and his colleagues decided cases and wrote opinions in the "grand style" of the antebellum American judiciary. Through the power of law, they hoped to create a new society on the southwestern frontier—a society that assisted struggling debtors, punished dangerous murderers, protected helpless slaves, and excluded "lowly" Mexicans and Native Americans. Such was, in the minds of Hemphill and the Texas Supreme Court, a more civilized social order.

Although the unique environment in Texas in many ways distinguished the history of the state supreme court from that of other southern appellate tribunals, Hemphill and his colleagues remained firmly within the southern judicial tradition. Their commitment to individual economic liberty, the rule of law, and paternalistic race relations mirrored the work of their contemporaries, though obvious variations existed, especially in the substance of their slavery opinions. In the end, however, even the court's innovation in the area of slavery did not prevent Hemphill and Wheeler from becoming ardent champions of southern independence. When faced with the decision to remain in the Union or to embrace secession, Texas judges cast their lot with the South.

CHAPTER FIVE

Thomas Ruffin,
Judicial Pragmatism, and
Southern Constitutionalism

Judges should be . . . cautious against rash expositions, not suited to the actual state of things and not calculated to promote the security of persons, the stability of national institutions, and the common welfare. —THOMAS RUFFIN, 1849

From the perspective of the state's supreme court reports, Thomas Carter Ruffin's North Carolina looked much like the rest of the antebellum South. A contemporary of John Catron, Joseph Lumpkin, and John Hemphill, Ruffin confronted the same legal problems and tensions as his colleagues in other states. Expanding democracy, a growing economy, violent criminal behavior, and the political strains surrounding slavery and sectionalism all converged on Ruffin during his judicial career, which spanned the period 1829–53. Ruffin returned to the state supreme court for a year of service in 1859 and thereafter played an active role in state politics during the secession crisis and wartime. Probably the most well known member of the nineteenth-century southern appellate judiciary, Ruffin received the distinction of being named one of the ten greatest judges in American history by the noted twentieth-century legal scholar Roscoe Pound.[1]

Despite his fame as a jurist, Ruffin devoted nearly as much of his life
to partisan politics—a fact that influenced his judicial decision making. He
stepped in and out of the political arena his entire career—as a state legislator, party leader, presidential elector, peace conference delegate, and secession advocate—and, as a result, conceived of his judicial role in many respects as an extension of his political and policy-making endeavors. Ruffin's
judicial philosophy and substantive record were shaped by an acute awareness of the larger implications of his opinions. Possessing a political shrewd-
ness and pragmatic sensibility, Ruffin displayed a clear understanding of the
political circumstances surrounding legal issues as well as a keen ability to
craft his opinions to resolve social and political tensions. Ruffin's experience
in the legislature and on the bench, moreover, contributed to his adoption
of a dynamic view of the separation of powers that changed depending on
the issue at stake. Thus, while he fought zealously for judicial independence
from the legislature, he also granted extensive authority to the legislative
branch and passively yielded to legislative enactments when he believed the
public interest would benefit. Pragmatism and flexibility were thus hallmarks
of Ruffin's judicial record.

In the same way that his political experiences influenced his judicial philosophy, Ruffin's judicial experience informed his political values. During and
after the Civil War, Ruffin championed the southern constitutional position.
Believing strongly that the Constitution sanctioned slaveholders' rights as
property holders, Ruffin turned away from support for the Union after the
failure of the 1861 peace conference and Lincoln's call for troops and advocated secession as an act of revolution against an oppressive federal government. After the war, Ruffin continued his fight for southern principles in his
rejection of North Carolina's 1866 Reconstruction constitution, which he
believed had been forced on the people of the state without their approval.
Himself the owner of more than a hundred slaves, the interests of slaveholders and—after the war—former planters lay at the center of his constitutional thinking.

Politics, Law, and Democracy in North Carolina

Born in 1787 in King and Queen County, Virginia, the eldest child of Sterling
Ruffin and Alice Roane Ruffin, Thomas Carter Ruffin grew up in the same
Tidewater society known to Spencer Roane, Alice's cousin. After attending
common schools, Thomas left home to attend a classical academy in Warren-
ton, North Carolina, and later enrolled in the College of New Jersey (later

Princeton University). While in college, Ruffin developed an unwavering admiration for Jeffersonian political principles and nearly refused to return to school in the fall of 1804 because of the college president's openly Federalist political bent. Ruffin did go back, though, and celebrated the "mortification of the Feds at Nassau Hall" after Jefferson's reelection in 1804. The next year Ruffin graduated with honors and returned to Virginia, where he planned to read law with his mother's eminent kinsman. When Spencer Roane expressed his inability to take on another law student, however, Ruffin spent a few years studying in Petersburg before deciding to move to North Carolina, where his father had taken the family in 1807.[2]

In the North Carolina Piedmont—specifically Orange County, where he settled in 1809—Thomas Ruffin entered a world far different from that of the Virginia Tidewater. Unlike his conservative agrarian homeland, Orange County was, for its time, a relatively cosmopolitan planter community. Many of its families were recent arrivals who, with connections beyond the local community, tended to be less provincial in their outlook. Linked together by marriage and common economic interests, a number of these planter families figured prominently in promoting railroads, administering local banks, and serving in government. Although they owned plantations throughout the area, they usually lived in Chapel Hill or Hillsboro, the county's two largest towns. During the few decades after he came to Orange County, Ruffin's personal relations and experiences connected him to the interests and ethos of the community's leading families. In 1809 he married Anne Kirkland, a native of Hillsboro and daughter of a prominent merchant. Later, their daughter would marry Paul C. Cameron, the wealthiest planter in antebellum Orange County.[3]

When Ruffin came to study law in North Carolina in 1807, he joined an elite cadre of Piedmont lawyers who were intent on modernizing the state. These attorneys, who hailed from the region including Guilford, Alamance, and Orange Counties, played a key role in the local economy by bridging the economic and cultural gap between agrarian and commercial interests. Among the largest land- and slaveholders in the region, lawyers maintained strong ties with local planters. At the same time, as town dwellers who engaged in a variety of economic pursuits, the lawyers forged strong ties with local businessmen.[4] Family and professional connections, therefore, tied Ruffin to both planters and entrepreneurs.

Ruffin's legal education also linked him to a variety of interests. On arriving in North Carolina, he studied under one of the leaders of the Piedmont legal community, Archibald D. Murphey, a daring, sometimes scheming, intellectual with eclectic interests. Murphey graduated from the University of

North Carolina and later taught ancient languages while he studied law. After gaining admission to the bar, Murphey engaged in a variety of activities. A slaveholding planter, he practiced law in Hillsboro, worked for a few years as a reporter of state court decisions, served in the state senate for six years, owned and operated a country store, and sat for two years as a superior court judge. Above all, however, Murphey made his mark as a social reformer and law teacher. Using both his formal power as a state senator and his informal influence with students, Murphey pushed for educational advancement, internal improvements, and constitutional reform. He was instrumental, for example, in establishing and funding common schools, developing a transportation system linking canals, rivers, and roads, and advocating constitutional changes that gave greater representation and power to the western portion of the state.[5] Murphey imparted to Ruffin some of his passion for reform, but Ruffin proved less the dreamy visionary and more the pragmatic problem solver.

Ruffin's connection to Murphey and some of the state's other up-and-coming lawyers paid dividends during the next few decades. After finishing his studies in 1808, Ruffin gained admission to the bar and found immediate success in both politics and law. In 1813 he won election to the North Carolina House of Commons and, three years later, rose to the position of speaker. Ruffin's accomplishments in state politics led to his growing involvement in the national arena. He served as an elector on James Monroe's presidential ticket in 1816 and later became a member of the Democratic-Republicans' corresponding committee, a select group of party leaders who chose slates of presidential electors. Although during the early 1820s Ruffin considered embarking on a political career, two factors weighed heavily against such a decision. Ruffin's poor financial situation dictated a return to the full-time practice of law, and by 1824 Ruffin displayed a deep displeasure with the Democratic-Republicans and a negative attitude toward the nation's political arena in general. Although Ruffin ardently supported William Crawford in that year's presidential election, after his candidate's defeat and the taking of the election into the House of Representatives, Ruffin was pessimistic. "I have no hope of Crawford," Ruffin wrote in December 1824. "He is too honest and too good for the present day. The Republican party is down—God grant it may not be done!—and he has sunk with it."[6]

While becoming disillusioned with politics, Ruffin was succeeding remarkably in the practice of law. Unlike Lumpkin, Ruffin did not excel at oratory. Instead, Ruffin's reputation rested on his brash yet effective courtroom demeanor. "His manner at the bar towards opposing litigants and opposing witnesses," a contemporary later remarked, "was rough and often offensive, hardly ever courteous and not always respectful and frequently abusive." According to another observer, Ruffin, in the course of zealous interrogation and argumentation, "would sometimes knock the floor instead of the table with his knuckles."[7] While he won few friends for his courtroom antics, Ruffin succeeded in earning the respect of his peers—perhaps through the right combination of intimidation and intelligence. In 1816 he ascended to the superior court, where he served two years before resigning to attend to his finances. After subsequently serving two years as reporter of the North Carolina Supreme Court, Ruffin returned to the superior court in 1825.

Ruffin's renown as a lawyer and a judge spread throughout the state, and during the next few years a considerable number of aspiring lawyers came to Hillsboro to study with him. Many of North Carolina's prominent attorneys took on a few pupils only to find themselves with so many students that they became conductors of law schools. Ruffin never operated his own law school, but he did informally train a large number of students from his office. Ruffin received a steady stream of letters from young men across the state who sought to study with him and wanted to know where they might find boarding in Hillsboro. At times, because Ruffin had more students than he could handle, hopeful lawyers asked simply if they could make a visit to his library either to obtain books or to be examined by the judge.[8]

Ruffin's unimpeachable reputation and Chief Justice John Louis Taylor's death in 1829 portended Ruffin's appointment to the state supreme court. Much of the legal community reacted favorably to the idea. "The members of the Bar whom I have heard speak on that subject . . . express a strong desire that you should be elected a Judge of the Supreme Court," a friend informed Ruffin soon after Taylor's passing, "some of them saying that they did not suppose that there was a lawyer in this Circuit who did not desire it." Ruffin's appointment, however, met with some opposition. Because he had accepted the presidency of the faltering State Bank of North Carolina the previous year, many of the legislature's most zealous Democrats, who despised the bank as a symbol of wealth and aristocracy, viewed Ruffin as one of the defenders of power and privilege. Still, buoyed by strong support among judges, lawyers, and lawmakers, in November 1829 Ruffin won legislative approval.[9] Soon thereafter, he moved to Alamance County, and during the next twenty-four years Ruffin emerged as the leader of the supreme court and a giant in the state's legal community. After the death of Chief Justice Leonard Henderson in 1833, Ruffin's associates elected him chief justice, the capacity in which he served for the next twenty years.

Democratic reformers in the legislature, many of whom had opposed

Ruffin's nomination, presented the judge with his first challenge. Ruffin's ascent to the supreme court occurred in the midst of a fury of democratizing changes—alterations that did not necessarily bode well for the future of the judiciary. The state court system had never enjoyed an easy relationship with the legislative branch. Not until 1818 did the legislature even create a separate supreme court, and lawmakers subsequently continued to assert control over the courts. These critics charged that the supreme court in particular was emblematic of the broader unresponsiveness of government to the interests of the people. The high salaries of the justices as well as the imbalance of political power between the eastern and western parts of the state as reflected in the size of judicial circuits, they claimed, revealed the undemocratic nature of the court system.[10]

During the 1820s, legislators in North Carolina, as throughout the South and the nation, targeted the judiciary with democratic reforms, each year coming closer to success. By the early 1830s it appeared that reformers would have their way. In 1832 the state senate passed a bill reducing the judges' annual salaries by 20 percent. The resignation of one justice in 1832 and the death of Chief Justice Henderson the following year further weakened the institution and led many to believe that the legislature would abolish the court. For his part, Ruffin threatened to resign after the legislature reduced judicial salaries. "I do not covet office for its pay," he wrote, "and can live on my own means and labor, whenever there shall be an attempt to violate the Constitution in any person and destroy the impartial administration of justice." Instead of resigning, Ruffin urged William Gaston, one of the state's most prominent lawyers, to consider accepting an appointment to the supreme bench. When Ruffin again pledged to resign if the legislature failed to offer the position to the esteemed attorney, lawmakers acceded to Ruffin's request. Gaston's selection lent legitimacy and stability to the troubled court, and during the next legislative session the General Assembly defeated both a bill to abolish the court and a bill to reduce judicial salaries further. For the time being, the future of the tribunal appeared safe.[11]

Within the context of this struggle for survival and respectability, Ruffin delivered an opinion with significant ramifications for the growing conflict between judicial independence and democratic reform. In *Hoke v. Henderson* (1833), Ruffin and his colleagues confronted a law providing for the popular election of clerks of the courts—after the sheriffs and justices of the peace, the most powerful officials in local government. With the passage of the act of 1832, all but one of the state's clerks resigned their positions in deference to the law. Lawson Henderson, clerk of a county superior court, refused to comply with the new enactment. After the overwhelming election of his presumed successor, John D. Hoke, the two men laid claim to the same office. After a superior court ruled in favor of Henderson, the case came to the North Carolina Supreme Court.[12]

Ruffin's opinion was a carefully crafted statement that reflected his views not only of the case at hand but also of the separation of powers and the broader movement for democratic government. First, Ruffin argued that judges needed to adhere to the meaning of legislative enactments. "The act as really intended is obligatory upon the mind, the will and the conscience of the Judge, however mischievous the policy, harsh and oppressive in its enactments on individuals, or tyrannous on the citizens generally," he wrote. Because the statute at hand was clear in its intent to remove the sitting clerks, Ruffin believed, the court could not simply dismiss the legislation. "We cannot, under the pretense of interpretation, repeal it and thus usurp a power never confided to us."[13]

Yet after making this nod to the legislature, Ruffin argued for the necessity of judicial review. When legislators exceeded their authority, Ruffin argued, "the preservation of the integrity of the Constitution is confided by the people, as a sacred deposit, to the Judiciary." In such instances, the courts possessed the power and the duty to review legislative acts. Still, Ruffin moved cautiously. "The exercise of [judicial review] is the gravest duty of a judge, and is always, as it ought to be, the result of the most careful, cautious, and anxious deliberation," he wrote. "Nor ought it to be, nor is it ever exercised, unless upon such deliberation, the repugnance between the legislative and constitutional enactments be clear to the Court, and susceptible of being clearly understood by all."[14] Aware of the strained relationship between the two branches of government, Ruffin had no desire to provoke the legislature. To the contrary, he sought to allay fears of judicial interference with democratic reform.

At the same time, Ruffin wanted to carve out a unique role for the judiciary in the state's constitutional order to preserve the courts' power and independence. The linchpin of his opinion—the means by which he challenged legislative authority—was his contention that Henderson's fulfillment of the office of clerk constituted the possession of property. Defining property as "whatever a person can possess and enjoy by right," Ruffin held that "in reference to the person, he who has that right to the exclusion of others, is said to have the property."[15] Having established this definition, the result was clear. The making of decisions concerning titles, whether between individuals or groups, was a judicial rather than a legislative function. Ruffin thus argued that the transfer of offices under the 1832 act providing for election of clerks of the courts was a judicial act, committed unconstitutionally by the legislative branch. The act "is not purely legislative," Ruffin reasoned, "for it leaves the nature of the office as it was, in duties, powers, privileges and emoluments, and confers it on one person as a lucrative place, after taking it from the former possessor, who was before the acknowledged owner." [16] By sharply distinguishing between the powers of the legislature and of the judiciary and by defining the holding of an office as the possession of property, Ruffin effectively thwarted the legislature's attempt to require the election of clerks.

But beyond this issue loomed the larger question of the role of the judiciary in an era of democratic change. Looking past Henderson's claim and fearing for the future of the supreme court, Ruffin made known in dicta his opposition to any attempt by the legislature to limit the courts' independence. Judicial appointments extended for a term of good behavior, he argued, were perfectly appropriate. Such terms of office were established "upon the great public consideration, that he who is to decide controversies between the powerful and poor, and especially between the government and an individual, should be independent in the tenure of his office, of all control and influence which might impair his impartiality." [17] Viewed in this way, lengthy judicial tenures, because they protected the independence of judges, served the public interest. While Ruffin understood that a term of good behavior did not apply to the clerk in this case, he still used this discussion of the nature and property of officeholding to affirm the constitutional validity of judicial tenure and to assert the necessity of judges' independence. [18]

Ruffin's invalidation of the 1832 act proved significant as a response to the political demands of democratic reform. While the long-term doctrinal significance of the decision stemmed from Ruffin's reliance on higher-law constitutionalism, the case had a more immediate impact as a tactful rebuttal to the legislature. The opinion consolidated the court's position within the North Carolina constitutional order and helped prevent further opposition from reformers. Two years after the decision, when the state began a major revision of its constitution, the judiciary remained all but untouched by the new changes. Whereas the new constitution mandated a fundamental restructuring of representation within the legislature and the popular election of the governor, the convention for constitutional reform suggested only three amendments pertaining to the judiciary, none of which proved detrimental. Indeed, one of these provisions offered new protection to the judiciary as the 1835 constitution required that judges' salaries "shall not be diminished during their continuance in office." In sum, the opinion in *Hoke,* coupled with the outstanding reputations of Ruffin and his colleagues, particularly Gaston, helped to silence the critics of the supreme court.[19]

Railroads, Eminent Domain, and the Public Interest

Despite this early battle with the legislature, Ruffin proved willing to expand legislative power when he believed it to be in the public interest. During the mid-1830s, with the infusion of revenue from the federal government's tariff surplus, North Carolina experienced a lengthy and prosperous period of unprecedented growth and development. Spurred by the vision of Archibald D. Murphey, Ruffin's mentor, both Democrats and Whigs, governors and legislators, essentially agreed on the need to devote a considerable portion of state resources to internal improvements and common schools. The legislature chartered North Carolina's first railroad in 1834, and the following year authorized a rival line, the Raleigh and Gaston Railroad. Despite broad support, many residents and legislators from plantation counties, in the eastern part of the state and along the Virginia border, remained opposed to internal improvements. Railroad building presented particularly thorny legal issues, usually pertaining to vested rights of property.[20]

One such dispute arose in *Raleigh and Gaston Railroad Company v. Davis* (1837), an eminent-domain case. The planned Raleigh and Gaston Railroad passed over the land of Richard Davis in Warren County, in the northeastern part of the state. After Davis and the railroad were unable to agree on compensation for the land taken for the railway, Davis appeared before the Court of Pleas and Quarter Sessions. Under the act chartering the railroad, when the company and a landowner could not come to terms, the court was to appoint "five disinterested and impartial free-holders" to assess the damages to the owner from the condemnation of the land. Although Davis objected to this method of resolution and challenged the statute as a violation of the right of private property and as a deprivation of the right to trial by jury, the court proceeded to select the freeholders and later certified their assessment of the property's value. After a series of rulings and appeals, the case came before Ruffin and the supreme court.[21]

Written three years after Massachusetts Chief Justice Lemuel Shaw's famous pronouncement that state appropriation of private property for railroads constituted public use, Ruffin's opinion ranked with Shaw's decision as seminal in the development of American railroad law.[22] In *Wellington, et al., Petitioners* (1834), Shaw and the Supreme Judicial Court of Massachusetts had rejected the contention that such a taking violated the U.S. Constitution's

Contract Clause. In that case, where the construction of a railroad interfered with the operation of a dam, Shaw held that the railway's charter was merely an appropriation of part of the land for another public use. Because the property was taken for a public purpose, the charter did not annul the previously granted franchise of the water-power company and did not impair the obligation of a contract.[23]

Ruffin faced a similar legal issue. Davis claimed that his property was being taken by the legislature and bestowed on private persons in violation of the state constitution. Ironically, Ruffin's decision in *Hoke v. Henderson* stood as Davis's most powerful precedent, for in that case the chief justice had held that the legislature could not take property vested in one individual and bestow it on another. Ruffin conceded that the corporation consisted of private individuals but argued that because the investors effected a "public benefit," the taking of property in this instance was within the legislature's power. In this respect, Ruffin echoed the earlier decisions of Roane and Catron about the scope of legislative power in the public interest. "The land is taken from the defendant for a public purpose, to which it had not been applied while in his hands," Ruffin wrote. "It is taken to be immediately and directly applied to an established public use, under the control and direction of the public authorities, with only such incidental private interests as the legislature has thought proper to admit."[24] The opinions of both Shaw and Ruffin came at a very early point in the history of the concept of eminent domain—as well as the development of broader legislative authority under the police power—and proved significant in the growth of railroad building.[25]

But it was Ruffin's opinion, not Shaw's, that outlined the more expansive view of legislative power to take private property for public use. In *Davis*, Ruffin laid down three important principles for the law of eminent domain in North Carolina, all of which weakened individual rights of property and strengthened the hand of the legislature. First, Ruffin held that compensation need not occur prior to or contemporaneous with the taking of property. "The exigencies of the public may be too urgent to admit of the delay requisite to the simplest mode of previous investigation," he wrote. Ruffin observed that the statute in question authorized the builders of the railroad to "cut, quarry, dig, and carry away wood, stone, gravel, or earth" as necessary for the construction or repair of the railway. An accurate prior appraisal of the value of the lands to be taken or affected by this construction would be very difficult, if not impossible. "Antecedent assessments, in such cases, must be made entirely at a venture, for it is uncertain what quantity of materials will be requisite or can be procured at a particular place, or how many tracks may be broken on the owner's land, and even the weather and season of the year may materially vary the damage," he argued. Attempting both to alleviate restrictions on the legislature's power of eminent domain and to ensure reliable estimates in such instances, Ruffin upheld the law's provisions regarding subsequent compensation.[26]

Second, Ruffin rebuffed the notion that only a twelve-person jury possessed the authority to pass judgment on Davis's case and validated the portion of the law providing for the appointment of five "disinterested and impartial freeholders" to decide on compensation. Davis had claimed that this provision violated his rights to trial by jury under the state constitution. According to the fourteenth section of the Declaration of Rights of North Carolina, "in all controversies at law respecting property, the ancient mode of trial by jury . . . ought to remain sacred and inviolate." Yet Ruffin regarded this clause as inapplicable to the case at hand. "The necessity of a road between different points is a political question, and not a legal controversy," he argued, "and it belongs to the legislature." The only subject that might be appropriate for a jury's consideration, therefore, was the amount of compensation, but even here Ruffin refused to accept Davis's claims. Ruffin interpreted the fourteenth section of the Declaration of Rights as merely a mandate to preserve the trial by jury in its ancient form—not as a guarantee that every dispute over property require a jury trial. "The opinion of the Court is," Ruffin concluded, "that it was competent to the legislature to adopt the mode it did, for the assessment of the damages to the defendant."[27]

Third, Ruffin held that the legislature was not restricted to a mere easement in the property but could take the whole of an individual's lands if public necessity required. "Every beneficial use is included in the easement," he wrote. "[T]he same principle which gives to the public the right to any use, gives the right to the entire use, upon paying adequate compensation of the whole." In Ruffin's view, only the legislature possessed this power to decide what the public interest demanded. "It is for the legislature to judge," he continued, "in cases in which it may be for the public interest to have the use of private property, whether in fact the public good requires the property and to what extent."[28] Such a rule swelled legislative license even more than Ruffin's decisions regarding the time and manner of compensation. Armed with this doctrine, lawmakers proceeded unfettered in their efforts to build railroads and other types of internal improvements.

Ruffin thus fully approved of the legislature's actions restricting vested rights when they clashed with the interests of the public. While the decision in *Davis* seemed inconsistent with Ruffin's view of both property rights and legislative power as expressed in *Hoke,* an inflexible adherence to the earlier decision would have held back railroad building in North Carolina. Ruffin favored development. As a banker and entrepreneur with strong ties to business interests, he looked approvingly on the possibility of creating a network of railroads across the state. "An immense and beneficial revolution has been brought about in modern times," he wrote in *Davis,* "by engaging individual enterprise, industry, and economy, in the execution of public works of internal improvement."[29] Ruffin believed that private individuals engaged in such economic activity, with the guiding hand of the state, were laboring in the public interest. In *Davis* Ruffin elevated this notion of public interest over the rights of property to ensure that individual opposition did not hinder railroad building and internal improvements. Because a broad grant of power to the legislature in this case in no way threatened the position of the court, Ruffin felt free to stretch legislative power to its limits. Although *Davis* seemed diametrically opposed to *Hoke* in terms of both the property and separation-of-powers issues, Ruffin had shrewdly achieved the desired ends. The power and position of the court remained intact, and the legislature became free to embark on an ambitious railroad-building plan.

Ruffin treated these cases not as controversies between individual litigants but as broad social and political conflicts over the future course of democratic reform and internal improvements. Ruffin, in other words, focused less on the personal situation of an individual like Richard Davis, whose property stood to be taken by the state without a jury trial, and more on the implications of the court's decision for the state's railroad-building policy. Elected president of the state railroad convention in 1833, Ruffin actively promoted economic development in his state. An eye for the political forces involved in each situation helped Ruffin to develop flexible legal definitions of property and the separation of powers while he issued decisions that he believed to be in the public interest.[30]

Honor, Violence, and Homicide

This judicial perspective also applied to criminal law, specifically the law of homicide. Ruffin's opinions reveal the various forms that honor and violence assumed in antebellum North Carolina as well as the judiciary's persistent efforts to punish and deter unlawful behavior. Many of the cases coming before the court involved violent encounters arising out of personal insults or long-standing grudges. No less than other southerners, according to court reports, North Carolinians attempted to settle disputes with fists, whips, knives, clubs, and pistols. And no less than other southern appellate judges, Ruffin expressed outrage at such behavior. A civilized society, he believed, required adherence to the rule of law rather than the code of honor.

One such criminal case involved a biting episode. In *State v. Crawford* (1830), the court took up the case of Neil Crawford, who after being hit by Duncan Monroe in the midst of a quarrel, "threw [Monroe] down and bit off his ear." Under a 1791 law prohibiting maiming "on purpose," the trial judge charged the jury with ascertaining whether Crawford voluntarily bit his opponent with an intent to disfigure him. Convicted of this crime, Crawford appealed on the grounds that prosecution under the 1791 law required the state to show "malice aforethought" rather than just prove that such maiming was voluntary.[31]

Relying on a North Carolina Supreme Court precedent, Ruffin rejected this narrow interpretation of the law's applicability. The fact that Crawford's opponent had delivered the initial blow in no way excused the defendant. "The first blow, or a sudden affray, did not palliate the offence under the act; for if it did, the statute would be of little avail," Ruffin wrote. "Almost all such maimings take place, not after lying in wait, and with deliberate intent, but in sudden rencounters." Crawford, therefore, could not claim that prosecution under the law required the state to show premeditation on the part of the defendant. "The very object of the legislature was to suppress this barbarous mode of fighting. If therefore, the maim is perpetrated, the enormity of the act itself and the impossibility almost that it should not be done with the intent to perpetrate it creates the presumption that the offender did the act on purpose and with intent to maim." Ruffin also dismissed the defendant's claim that the state had to prove "malice aforethought" with the simple argument that if the legislature had intended such a requirement, legislators would have written it into the law. Instead, the burden, Ruffin argued, fell on the defendant, "for everything is to be taken against a man who voluntarily maims another." Ruffin thus upheld the conviction.[32]

When convicted murderers appealed on grounds that trial judges improperly instructed juries about the distinction between murder and manslaughter, Ruffin consistently upheld their convictions. In *State v. Martin* (1841), for example, Ruffin and his colleagues dealt with a man who had used a whip to provoke his enemy into drawing his pistol, whereupon the instigator shot and killed his foe. Indicted for murder, Edmund Martin argued that this was a "case of sudden affray or mutual combat in the heat of blood" and that the trial judge should have charged the jury that the circumstances of the killing meant that it could not be murder, only self-defense or manslaughter.[33]

Contrary to the arguments of the defense, Ruffin held, this was not a sudden encounter. Evidence showed that ill will had existed for some time between the two, and the defendant had planned the attack on his enemy. "These facts, if believed by the jury, afford a rational inference that the prisoner . . . designed, upon the exhibition of an attempt on the part of the deceased to resent in that way the indignity of a stroke with a whip, to shoot him before he, the prisoner, could possibly be hurt." "Upon that supposition," Ruffin concluded, "the killing would undoubtedly be murder." The judge showed little regard for the defendant's attempts to excuse his murderous actions by attempting to provoke his opponent: "To follow a person and seek a combat with him for the purpose of killing him, and covering the act with the pretense of a dangerous resistance to a moderate assault, is nothing less than wreaking a diabolical vengeance."[34] Ruffin upheld the conviction.

In two cases involving stabbing homicides, Ruffin also refused to hold in error judicial instructions regarding the degrees of the offenses. *State v. Lane* (1843) involved a conflict between John Bedford and Harry Lane. After Lane began harassing Bedford, who lay drunk on the floor in the house of a third party, the two men exchanged blows and then parted. A few minutes later, once they had left the house, Lane stabbed Bedford to death. Taking issue with Lane's attorney, Ruffin held that the circumstances of the killing showed that the defendant had not acted "under a transport of passion," a legal requirement for mitigation of murder to manslaughter. "It cannot be conceived that a person who . . . when he was giving the other party fatal stabs, to the number of seven, and was receiving no serious hurt himself; who of his own accord separated from his antagonist and had the coolness, instantly after this mortal combat, to call for water to wash his hands and frame the falsehood that he believed the deceased had cut his finger—we say it cannot be conceived that a person thus acting was under a sudden transport of passion." Ruffin again would have nothing of the defendant's claim that his offense was manslaughter rather than murder.[35]

A second stabbing death, at issue in *State v. Scott* (1844), involved two men who met in a street. When one pressed the other for a fight, the man who had been accosted retreated a few steps and allowed his attacker to advance before stabbing him to death with "some sharp instrument." Relying explicitly on common-law authorities, Ruffin held that William Scott's behavior did not constitute self-defense, as he claimed. "The belief that a person designs to kill me, will not permit my killing him from being murder," Ruffin held, "unless he is making some attempt to execute his design, or, at least, is in an apparent situation to do so." Because the victim was unarmed, Ruffin wrote, Scott's self-defense claim could not stand. "There might have been more in it, if the deceased had been found lurking on the way of the prisoner in the dark, when he could not tell whether he was armed or not," Ruffin reasoned. "But it cannot apply to a case where there is light enough for the parties to know each other, and upon a mutual quarrel they begin a fight, in which neither party appears to be armed, and one of them secretly prepares a deadly weapon, with which he assails and kills the other." Ruffin affirmed the trial judge's instructions, which had carefully outlined to the jury the circumstances under which the killing would have been either murder or self-defense, depending on the version of the events the jurors accepted.[36]

Ruffin also upheld a trial judge's instructions in a case involving two neighbors, an extramarital affair, and a beating with a pine branch. The day after learning of his wife's affection for neighbor John Craton, Thomas Harrison and the two lovers were leaving the courthouse after initiating divorce proceedings. Harrison's wife expressed her desire to ride home alone with Craton, but when Harrison objected, she was to ride with Craton and some relatives while Harrison was to catch up to them. When Harrison later overtook the couple on the road, they were riding alone. Angered, Harrison began to threaten Craton with a knife and twice stopped his horse in front of Craton's and implored him to return Mrs. Harrison to him. Craton then dismounted, removed his hat and coat, "broke off a dead old-field pine, and went to Harrison as he sat on his horse and gave him a blow with the billet which fractured his skull and killed him." The trial judge instructed the jury that no legal provocation existed for the killing, and the jury convicted Craton.[37]

Although the defense counsel in *State v. Craton* (1845) argued that Harrison's attempts to stop Craton on the highway constituted an assault or at least false imprisonment, Ruffin disagreed. "Those acts, we think, were not an injurious restraint on the prisoner's liberty, but only a lawful impediment to his carrying away the deceased's wife, to her ruin and the husband's dishonor," Ruffin wrote. "There was, consequently, no provocation to extenuate the killing of Harrison." Harrison's attempt to draw his knife constituted neither an "assault" nor an "attempt to strike" but "a mere threat," according to Ruffin. He concluded that the killing was in fact murder. The instrument that the defendant used—a heavy stick three feet long and three inches thick—"was calculated to do a grievous injury," according to Ruffin, and the fact that the defendant destroyed the weapon to prevent it from appearing in evidence, only further implicated him. "Being established to be a deadly weapon, either because it is to be so held in law or because it has been found by the jury to be so in fact, the legal consequence follows that an intention to kill is established, and that, being without provocation, constitutes the killing murder."[38]

Ruffin also proved unwilling to mitigate a charge from murder to man-slaughter in a case involving insulting "words or gestures." *State v. Barfield* (1848) involved two men who exchanged "angry words" before one, John Barfield, approached the other with a knife. Alfred Flowers responded to the thrusting knife by lifting a chair and "pitched it over the other's head, but without striking or intending to strike him." The act of lifting the chair caused Flowers, who was drunk, to fall to the floor. Barfield then rushed his fallen foe and stabbed him several times. Barfield appealed on the grounds of judicial misdirection regarding the degree of the offense as well as error in refusing to admit testimony pertaining to the character of the deceased.[39]

On neither of these issues was Ruffin willing to grant a new trial. First, he held that the defendant's actions amounted to "murder of a very dark hue, perpetrated in a cruel and diabolical fury." Ruffin saw no grounds for the defense's claim that Flowers had provoked Barfield, and the judge quickly dismissed the idea of reducing the charge to manslaughter. "There could be no provocation to palliate the killing from murder," he wrote, "since, from a reasonable regard for the security of human life, it has been long and per-fectly settled that no words or gestures, nor anything less than the indignity to the person of a battery, or an assault at the least, will extenuate a killing to manslaughter."[40] Second, Ruffin refused to overrule the trial court's un-willingness to admit evidence regarding the character of Flowers, a known "brawler and breaker of peace." Taking a strong stand in support of human life, Ruffin argued, "The law no more allows a man of bad temper and habits of violence to be killed by another, whom he is not assaulting, than it does the most peaceable and quiet of men." As there was no assault on Barfield, a man's "character for turbulence" would certainly not be enough to miti-gate or excuse the killing of another. Such a construction of the law would have opened the door to even more attempts by murderers to extenuate the charges against them.[41] Thus, thinking of what kind of precedent his opinion would establish, Ruffin refused to accept the questionable testimony.

Though his opinions in homicide cases lacked the passionate, condemna-tory rhetoric of those written by Catron and Lumpkin, Ruffin nevertheless resembled his southern colleagues in Tennessee, Georgia, and Texas in accu-mulating a substantive record upholding the convictions of violent criminals. Relying on North Carolina precedent and established common-law authori-ties, Ruffin consistently upheld the instructions of trial judges that involved the distinctions among murder, manslaughter, and excusable homicide. Con-scious of the social implications of the legal rules he was establishing, Ruffin proved unwilling to widen the definitions of manslaughter or self-defense. Before Ruffin's supreme court, as in other appellate courts in the South, convicted murderers had little success in either mitigating the charges against them or excusing their actions.

Slaves, Slavery, and the Public Good

While Ruffin's politically informed, pragmatic brand of decision making presented no difficulty for him in most types of disputes, he experienced an internal tension in criminal cases involving slaves. In some instances, Ruffin personally believed that individual slaves suffered unjustly but felt compelled to rule against them for the sake of the perpetuation of the institution and the public good. Despite whatever moral qualms he may have had, Ruffin expressed a greater sensitivity to the broader social and political implications of his opinions on slavery than on any other issue.

Ruffin's first major decision involving slavery occurred in the context of a stormy racial climate. Beginning in the 1820s, North Carolina lawmakers tightened statutory restrictions on slaves and free blacks in response to the possibility of slave revolt and the emergence of abolitionism. Rumors of a rebellion in the southeastern portion of the state in 1821, the Vesey conspiracy in South Carolina in 1822, and the passage of a resolution by the Vermont legislature describing slavery as "an evil to be deprecated by a free and enlightened people" in 1825 prompted North Carolina legislators to secure greater control over the state's black population. At the request of the governor, in 1826 the legislature made it illegal for free blacks to migrate into North Carolina and deemed "idleness" or "dissipation" among those already in the state a criminal offense carrying up to a three-year sentence of slavery and the loss of all of the offender's children. Moreover, the 1829 publication of David Walker's *Appeal to the Coloured Citizens of the World,* of which Ruffin was probably aware, only heightened white suspicion.[42]

Against this backdrop, Ruffin delivered his opinion in the case of *State v. Mann* (1829). John Mann had been indicted for assault and battery on Lydia, a slave Mann had hired for a year's time. While under the supervision of Mann, the slave committed some small offense, and as Mann attempted to chastise her, Lydia ran off. As she retreated, Mann called for her to stop. She continued to flee, and Mann shot and wounded her. A superior court judge instructed the jury that such punishment constituted an indictable offense, jurors returned a guilty verdict, and Mann appealed his conviction to the supreme court.[43] The case presented the most basic underlying question relating to the institution of slavery: what was the extent of the master's dominion over the slave?

In keeping with the style of reasoning he employed in other types of cases, Ruffin considered the interests of society rather than the welfare of the slave. "The power of the master must be absolute," he wrote, "to render the submission of the slave perfect." Such submission, he argued, was essential "to the value of slaves as property, to the security of the master, and the public tranquility."[44] Because Ruffin focused on slavery as an institution rather than on the slave as an individual, he rejected the application of any category of human relationships to the master-slave relationship. Relations between parent and child, tutor and pupil, or master and apprentice, for example, had no parallel with slavery. "In the one, the end in view is the happiness of the youth, born to equal right with that governor, on whom the duty devolves of training the young to usefulness in a station which he is afterwards to assume among freemen." Slavery, Ruffin observed, was different. "The end is the profit of the master, his security and the public safety; the subject, one doomed in his own person and his posterity, to live without knowledge and without the capacity to make anything his own, and to toil that another may reap the fruits."[45]

Ruffin believed that upholding the absolute dominion of the master was the best public policy for the state at the time, and he ruled accordingly. Yet his conscience pulled him away from adhering to this strict rule in every instance. Despite the holding in the case, Ruffin left the door open for situations in which the master's power would not be absolute. "That there may be particular instances of cruelty and deliberate barbarity where, in conscience, the law might properly interfere, is most probable," he wrote. "The difficulty is to determine where a court may begin."[46] Ruffin knew that instances would arise where masters would undoubtedly exceed their moral and legal authority over slaves. At the same time, however, he feared the consequences of lengthy speculation about the exact nature of such circumstances. Desiring not to foment doubts or questions about the nature of the master-slave relationship, Ruffin simply avoided such conjecture. "We cannot," he wrote, "allow the right of the master to be brought into discussion in the courts of justice. The slave, to remain a slave, must be made sensible that there is no appeal from his master; that his power is in no instance usurped."[47] In the context of white North Carolinians' fears during the 1820s, Ruffin concealed whatever ideas he possessed about possible limits on the master's authority.

Ruffin, therefore, accomplished a dual purpose with his opinion in *Mann*. On the one hand, he signaled that the institution of slavery and the master-slave relationship would remain in accordance with "the established habits and uniform practice of the country."[48] On the other hand, Ruffin left a moral escape hatch for himself and his colleagues by noting that acts of excessive cruelty against slaves would not receive the approbation of the court. The seemingly harsh decision hinged on the necessity of slaves' obedience to their masters; it did not, however, establish that masters' control over slaves would always be absolute. Rather than showing his inflexibility about slavery, Ruffin's decision in *Mann* allowed him both to decide in the public interest and to alleviate his own uncertainty about the harshness of such a rule. If presented with an instance of extremely unwarranted cruelty to a slave, Ruffin could simply use the loophole he created in *Mann* to make an exception.

Ruffin's dilemma in the case also prompted him to urge legislators to deal with such issues in the future. Because of his ambivalent personal feelings about the case, Ruffin announced his reluctance for the court to resolve any disputes regarding the relationship between master and slave. Yet Ruffin knew that the court had to make a decision. "It is useless . . . to complain of things inherent in our political state," he wrote. "And it is criminal in a court to avoid any responsibility which the laws impose. With whatever reluctance, therefore, it is done, the court is compelled to express an opinion." Thus, only after expressing his opposition to judicial intervention did Ruffin deliver the opinion, and even then he revealed his desire for the legislature to address such issues more specifically in the future.[49]

Ten years after *Mann,* Ruffin's moral sensibility prompted him to rule that there were indeed limits to the master's authority. In *State v. Hoover* (1839), Ruffin slipped through the opening he had carved out in *Mann.* Although statutory restrictions surrounding slavery continued to tighten during the 1830s, especially in the aftermath of the Nat Turner Rebellion, other factors pointed toward a more humane decision in *Hoover.*[50] For example, Ruffin built on an 1834 precedent involving a fleeing slave who, wounded by his overseer, still managed to kill the overseer with a knife. In that case, Judge William Gaston held that "the law protects the life of the slave against the violence of his master, and that the homicide of a slave, like that of a freeman, is murder or manslaughter." More pertinent to Ruffin's decision were the peculiar facts in *Hoover.* The court faced the issue of whether to uphold the murder conviction of a master who had inflicted "grievous tortures upon an enfeebled female" for a period of four months. The slave owner had wantonly beat and burned, slowly starved, and mercilessly forced the slave to labor under excruciatingly harsh conditions until she died of her wounds.[51]

Ruffin showed little sympathy for such masters. "The intent, by severe and protracted cruelties and torments, to inflict grievous and dangerous suffering, or, in other words, to do great bodily harm, imports from the means and manner thereof, a disregard of consequences," Ruffin wrote, "and consequently the party is justly answerable for all the harm he did."[52] Refining the rule laid down in *Mann,* Ruffin summed up the opinion of the court: "A master may lawfully punish his slave; and the degree must, in general, be left to his own judgment and humanity, and cannot be judicially questioned. But the master's authority is not altogether unlimited. He must not kill. There is, at the least, this restriction upon his power: he must stop short of taking life." The particularly gruesome nature of the abuse in this case contributed both to Ruffin's recognition of the slave's humanity and his willingness to uphold the conviction of the master. "The acts imputed to this unhappy man do not belong to a state of civilization," he wrote. "They are barbarities which could only be prompted by a heart in which every human feeling had long been stifled; and indeed, there can scarcely be a savage of the wilderness so ferocious as not to shudder at the recital of them." Ruffin's words revealed a measure of moral outrage usually reserved only for white victims.[53]

Ruffin thus employed a pragmatic approach in cases involving violence inflicted on slaves, alternately emphasizing slaves as either property or person depending on the circumstances. In *Mann,* he stressed the master's authority over the slave as property yet left open the possibility that certain circumstances might necessitate restrictions on the slaveholder's dominion. When such a situation arose in *Hoover,* Ruffin showed respect for the life of the slave as a human being and sided against absolute authority for the master.

If *Mann* defined slaves as property and *Hoover* granted them protection similar to white citizens, *State v. Caesar* (1849) revealed a third aspect of the slave's judicially constructed legal personality. *Caesar* involved a violent, late-night confrontation between three slaves and a pair of intoxicated white men. The two men came across two of the slaves lying in a field, and after falsely identifying themselves as patrollers, each of the white men grabbed a piece of board and inflicted a few minor blows on the slaves. After the beating, the third slave arrived on the scene, whereupon the white men seized him and ordered one of the other two slaves to find a whip with which to beat him. When the slave refused to aid the white men in the beating, both the whites grabbed and battered him. The second slave, Caesar, in a burst of anger, took hold of a fence rail and inflicted a single blow on each of the white men before the three slaves fled together. One of the men eventually died from the injury, and Caesar was indicted for murder.[54]

In seriatim opinions, Ruffin's two colleagues on the court reduced the charge against Caesar to manslaughter. Because of the nature of the provocation by the white men and the type of blow inflicted by the slave, Judges

Richmond M. Pearson and Frederick Nash concluded that the injurious act was attributable not to malice but to the honorable desire to come to a friend's aid. Imparting to slaves a sense of reason and heroism not often found in the opinions of southern courts, Pearson attempted to describe the situation from the perspective of the accused: "He was present from the beginning; saw the wanton injury and suffering inflicted upon his helpless, unoffending and unresisting associate; he must either run away and leave him at the mercy of two drunken ruffians, . . . or he must yield to a generous impulse and come to the rescue. He used force enough to release his associate and they made their escape, without a repetition of the blow. Does this show he has the heart of a murderer? On the contrary, are we not forced, in spite of stern policy, to admire, even in a slave, the generosity which incurs danger to save a friend?" Pearson's and Nash's admiration for the accused in this instance caused them to downgrade the conviction to manslaughter.[55]

Ruffin sharply disagreed. In a vigorous dissent, he displayed yet another dimension of his view of slaves. Ruffin conceded that if all the persons involved in the incident had been white men, the charge against the accused would have been manslaughter. To Ruffin, therefore, the case turned on the race and status of those involved. "[I]t has been repeatedly declared by the highest judicial authorities," he contended, "that the rule for determining what is a mitigating provocation cannot, in the nature of things, be the same between persons who . . . stand in the very great disparity of free whites and black slaves."[56] Because the accused was a slave, the common law of manslaughter did not apply.

In his analysis of the incident, Ruffin interpreted the slave's distinct legal status. The behavior of the slave who was being beaten at the time of the fatal injury provided Ruffin with ample evidence for his argument. Because the slave did not resist the beating, Ruffin denied that provocation existed for Caesar to come to his aid. "Did [the white men] make his blood boil and transport him," Ruffin asked, "so that, being wrought into a tempest of passion, he attempted in retaliation to slay his assailant, or even to join battle with him with their natural weapons?"[57] Because the beleaguered slave did not resist his captors—as a white man could and perhaps should have—Ruffin argued that Caesar's violent reaction constituted murder, not manslaughter.

Ruffin's opinion imparted to slaves human qualities, but they were unquestionably the qualities of the Sambo.[58] The slave being held and beaten in this instance, Ruffin contended, responded as a slave ordinarily would. "He sought no assistance, but submitted without a struggle, and begged; and, when freed from forcible detention, he made no effort to be revenged, nor showed any resentment, but merely escaped quietly." The fact that the slave had acted this way not only meant that no provocation for his friend's retaliation existed but also provided confirmation of Ruffin's perception of the slave. "Negroes—at least, the great mass of them—born with deference to the white man, take the most contumelious language without answering again, and generally submit tamely to his buffet, though unlawful and unmerited. Such are the habits of the country." [59] In other words, such were the norms of slave behavior. The actions of the persecuted slave in this instance only offered further support for Ruffin's view. When Caesar failed to yield submissively like his companion, he violated Ruffin's definition of acceptable slave behavior. By interpreting the slave and his actions in this manner, Ruffin imbued slaves with human qualities yet held them to a higher standard of responsibility than whites. In essence, Ruffin expected slaves to behave obsequiously, despite whatever transgressions against their person or dignity, and any violation of this code of conduct would meet with swift legal resistance.

In Ruffin's view, therefore, the opinions of his fellow justices rested on a false assumption—that slaves possessed a legal status similar to that of white citizens. Only by the acceptance of such an idea could the common law of manslaughter apply to slaves. Ruffin took issue with this proposition. "The dissimilarity in the condition of slaves from anything known at the common law cannot be denied," he reasoned. "[T]herefore as it appears to me, the rules upon this, as upon all other kinds of intercourse between white men and slaves, must vary from those applied by the common law between persons so essentially differing in their relations, education, rights, principles of action, habits and motives for resentment." Because his fellow justices ignored these differences in deciding the case, Ruffin regarded the opinions of his brethren as extremist judicial pronouncements, based on fanciful ideals rather than the reality of the social order. "Judges should be . . . cautious against rash expositions," he proclaimed, "not suited to the actual state of things and not calculated to promote the security of persons, the stability of national institutions, and the common welfare." [60]

Ruffin's pronouncement succinctly captured the essence of his decisions in criminal cases involving slaves. Writing in 1849, as the nationwide conflict over slavery and sectionalism worsened in the aftermath of the Wilmot Proviso and the Mexican War, Ruffin viewed the public-policy implications of any decision as prevailing over the legal rights of individual slaves. The application of the common law of manslaughter to an impudent slave might only add to the arguments of abolitionists and antislavery advocates at a time when slavery as a national institution seemed threatened.[61] For this reason,

by the late antebellum period Ruffin expressed no reluctance whatsoever
about rendering judicial opinions relating to the master-slave relationship.
The gravity of the larger political situation dictated a gradual abandonment
of the hesitancy expressed in *Mann* to use the judicial office to establish legal
rules regarding masters and slaves.

Ruffin's decisions in *Mann, Hoover,* and *Caesar* all point to a cautious
flexibility on his part—a preoccupation with weighing the social and political outcome of any decision involving slavery. In cases where slaves were victims of violent crimes, Ruffin demonstrated a willingness to decide whether
the action was justified based on the particular facts of the case and in light
of new precedents. Conversely, in instances where whites were the victims
of alleged slave violence, Ruffin simply refused to extend the rights of free
people to bondspeople. Ruffin thus maneuvered easily among defining slaves
as property at the master's disposal, as persons deserving of legal protection,
or as Sambos with a degraded legal personality. Nevertheless, in each of these
cases, Ruffin sought to deliver an opinion with the larger social and political
implications in mind.

By the 1850s, as he became increasingly sensitive to the national political
debate over sectionalism and slavery, Ruffin used his power and influence to
speak out on such issues. He devoted a large portion of a speech to the state
agricultural society in 1855, just after his retirement, to challenging explicitly
the arguments of northern Free-Soilers and abolitionists. A planter all his life,
Ruffin dismissed the idea that "slavery degrades free labor, and consequently
that our population are too proud or too lazy to work." Instead, Ruffin argued, the South's system of "mixed labor"—free whites and black slaves—
was especially suited to the region's agricultural demands.[62] Slavery, did not,
as Free-Soil advocates claimed, cause whites to view labor as beneath their
dignity because of its association with black slaves. "Why, there is not a
country on earth in which honest labor and diligence in business in all classes
and conditions, is considered more respectable or more respected," he argued. If slavery had any effect on white work habits, Ruffin asserted, it made
whites even more industrious and productive.[63] In this way, Ruffin responded
to the critics of slavery as an economic system.

Ruffin also took issue with those who viewed the peculiar institution as
a moral evil. A faithful, lifetime member of the Episcopal Church, Ruffin
shared Lumpkin's and other judicial contemporaries' belief in the Christian
paternalistic benevolence of slavery. When masters treated their slaves with
Christian concern and responsibility, slaves responded with "devoted obedience and fidelity of service." "The comfort, cheerfulness, and happiness of
the slave should be, and generally is, the study of the master," Ruffin wrote,

"and every Christian master rejoices over the soul of his slave saved, as of a brother, and allows of his attendance on the ministry of God's word and sacraments, in any church of his choice in his vicinity." Reality, of course, rarely equaled Ruffin's righteous rhetoric. Still, he did not hesitate to make assertions regarding slavery's transformative powers that rivaled even Lumpkin's lofty claims. "Slavery in America has not only done more for the civilization and enjoyments of the African race than all other causes," Ruffin contended, "but it has brought more of them into the Christian fold than all the missions to that benighted continent from the Advent to this day have, or, probably, those for centuries to come would, excepting only the recent Colonies of blacks on the western coast of Africa, by which one may hope and believe that under divine direction the lights of civilization and the knowledge of the true God may be reflected back on that whole land." He concluded with unconscious arrogance, "Such are some of the beneficial effects on that race of their connexion with us." [64]

By the middle of the 1850s, Ruffin believed that paternalistic slavery was the highest ideal to which southern society could aspire. In simplest terms, slavery served the public good—the interest of whites and blacks. "There is an unanimous conviction of our people that slavery as it exists here, is neither unprofitable, nor impolitic, nor unwholesome," he wrote. Ruffin believed that a consensus existed among all classes of whites in North Carolina in favor of the perpetuation of slavery. Those northerners who criticized the institution and its supposed ill societal and moral effects knew nothing of what they spoke. "It is a great error in those who do not know our slavery, to confound authority in the private relations, though it be that of a slaveowner, with the absolute power of a prince on a throne. A political despot is separated from his subjects. He knows them not, nor loves them." In contrast, relations between masters and slaves were like those of a family. "Authority in domestic life, though not necessarily," he reasoned, "is naturally considerate, mild, easy to be entreated, and tends to an elevation in sentiment in the superior which generates a humane tenderness for those in his power, and renders him regardful alike of the duty and dignity of his position." In Ruffin's words, slavery was not "a blot upon our laws, nor a stain on our morals, nor a blight upon our land." Rather, according to Ruffin, paternalistic slavery served the public good. [65]

Judicial Pragmatism and Southern Constitutionalism

In 1852, after twenty-three years on the North Carolina Supreme Court, Ruffin retired to his plantation, Haw River, in Alamance County. "Discharge me from professional toils and official solicitudes and responsibilities," he wrote to a friend late that year, "and allow me to turn to the congenial pursuits of agriculture, and the tranquil amusements and occupation of domestic rural life."[66] Although he was later mentioned as a possible U.S. Supreme Court nominee and asked to help revise the North Carolina statutes in 1853, Ruffin declined the opportunity to continue in public service.[67] Instead, he devoted much of the remainder of the decade to his two plantations and to his duties as president of the state agricultural society, a post he held until 1860.[68] Having done his utmost as a jurist to create the kind of polity and society he thought best for the state, Ruffin sought to enjoy the comfortable life of a gentleman planter.

Ruffin's retirement met with praise for his performance mixed with concern for his departure. "No one of all the Judges, who have ever sat on the Bench," extolled the *Raleigh Register*, "has left so many judicial opinions — and such is the variety of the subjects, and the ability with which he has treated them, that his opinions constitute, of themselves, almost a code of law." Others expressed more alarm than adulation. A lawyer and friend of Ruffin's described himself as "deeply pained" on hearing of the resignation. "I have no idea what the Legislature will now do with the Judiciary System of our State," he wrote, "but am satisfied that the fact of your being Chief Justice has heretofore been a check upon innovation. I am fearful that your resignation will open up the door to all kinds of mischief."[69] Such fears were not unfounded. In 1850 the state Democratic Party had specifically come out in favor of the election of judges, while the Whig Party included the idea among those proposals to be considered in future constitutional revision. As news of Ruffin's retirement spread, many reform-minded lawmakers sensed the perfect opportunity to enact legislation mandating judicial election.

Ruffin solemnly warned against a return to the partisan battles over the court that had marked its earlier history. "I cannot refrain from expressing the most earnest wish and prayer," he wrote, "that North Carolina and the Union may religiously preserve the independence of the Judiciary, and thereby have one both sound and able, and, in the mercy of Providence, be saved from dependent, and by consequence, flexible, cringing, time-serving, weak, bad men for Judges. All experience and all just reasoning concur in proving a dependent Judiciary to be, practically, the heaviest and most enduring curse that can befall a deluded depraved, and gain-saying people."[70] Ruffin believed that the existence of a strong, independent judiciary had allowed him to evaluate cases in light of their societal impact without fear of reprisal from either the legislature or the public. In this way, the court could work to pursue the public good without pressure from individual competing interests that stood to be harmed. Ruffin's two main concerns as a judge—maintaining institutional independence and taking social implications into account in decision making—came together. He advocated judicial independence because it strengthened the court's position as a institutional body in the service of the public interest. Despite Ruffin's concerns that his conception of the court might be undercut, North Carolina did not embark on the path of judicial election chosen by so many states during the antebellum period.[71]

When the secession crisis erupted, the retired chief justice reemerged as a leading figure in North Carolina politics. Initially, Ruffin's was a moderate voice in support of compromise and conciliation. Throughout his career, he had devoted himself to the Union. In his 1855 speech to the agricultural society, for example, Ruffin expressed "a deep conviction of the inestimable value of the Union, and a profound reverence for the Constitution which created it." With the election of Lincoln and the subsequent secession of seven southern states in early February 1861, Ruffin attended the peace conference in Washington, D.C., as one of five delegates from North Carolina. At age seventy-three, Ruffin was one of the most senior in attendance. He made known early in the proceedings his reason for participating. "I came here for a purpose which I openly and distinctly avow. I proclaim it here and everywhere. I will labor to carry it into execution with all the strength and ability which my advanced years and enfeebled health have left me," he stated, his voice rising. "I came to maintain and preserve this glorious Government! I came here for Union and peace!" His words ringing throughout the hall, applause erupted among the delegates. Ruffin continued by reminding his audience of his age, experience, and devotion to the Constitution. "As for me, I am an old man. My heart is very full when I look upon the present unhappy and distracted condition of our affairs. I was born before the Constitution was adopted. May God grant that I do not outlive it."[72]

Ruffin's initial Unionist fervor waned during the remaining days of the conference. Although he arrived as a hopeful ambassador of "Union and peace," Ruffin became dejected and frustrated at others' unwillingness to compromise. Northern antislavery radicals and southern proslavery secessionists alike made it difficult for moderate delegates like Ruffin to craft an acceptable and workable agreement. The end product of the convention's contentious labors was a proposed constitutional amendment that, among other things, would have extended the old Missouri Compromise line (which had since been held unconstitutional in the Dred Scott case) through the western territories, prohibiting slavery north of that line and preventing any change in the status of slaves to the south. When the House of Representatives refused even to receive the results of the peace conference and the Senate rejected the amendment by a wide margin, the compromise proposal died.[73]

The acrimonious nature of the convention combined with the amendment's defeat destroyed Ruffin's unionist beliefs. The judge's famous cousin, the fire-eating secessionist Edmund Ruffin of Virginia, described the impact of the convention's failure on his kinsman: "When I was here before, in last October, Judge Ruffin was still strongly opposed to secession. . . . [H]is late stay in Washington, as a member of the 'Peace Conference' & his necessary communication in that body with noted abolitionists, & his then opportunity of observing their conduct in the government, have excited his indignation & contempt so that he speaks of them as harshly as I would."[74]

Over the next few months, the outbreak of hostilities at Fort Sumter followed by Lincoln's call for troops pushed the judge toward secession and southern constitutionalism. At a public meeting in Hillsboro in April, Ruffin publicly abandoned his well-known Unionist position by urging his fellow citizens to "Fight! Fight! Fight!" The following month, while attending a state convention, Ruffin proposed an ordinance of secession that explained North Carolina's actions. "By reason of various illegal, unconstitutional, oppressive and tyrannical acts of the Government of the United States of America, and of unjust and injurious acts of divers of the Northern non-slaveholding states, it is the settled sense of the people of this state that they cannot longer live in peace and security in the Union heretofore existing under the Constitution of the United States."[75]

Ruffin believed that the Constitution sanctioned slaveholding and that a series of aggressive acts by the North had destroyed constitutional government in the United States. "[T]he Constitution clearly recognizes our slavery, sustains the rights of ownership, and enforces the duty of service," Ruffin proclaimed in 1855, "and I am persuaded, that the obligation of those provisions and their execution will be ultimately pronounced and carried out by those on whom the Constitution itself confers the authority." Ruffin proved correct in predicting the Supreme Court's decision in *Dred Scott v. Sandford* (1857), which upheld the rights of slaveholders. But by 1861, with the election of an administration apparently unwilling to recognize these constitutional rights, Ruffin rejected the Union. He later described this position as a belief in the "sacred right of revolution"—"the right of a whole people to change their form of Government by annulling one Constitution and forming another for themselves." Thus he endorsed secession not because he believed in a constitutional right to separate from the Union but only as a revolutionary act against an oppressive federal government that he believed had already destroyed the existing Constitution.[76]

Defeat apparently changed Ruffin's outlook. After the war, in August 1865, Ruffin wrote to President Andrew Johnson seeking a pardon. Attempting to explain his actions during wartime, Ruffin underscored his lengthy record of public service, his opposition to nullification, his longtime support for the Union, and his participation in the peace conference. Moreover, he expressed his hope for a "general amnesty [to] bring back a conciliated People with such small means of livelihood as a protracted and most wasting war has left them, with renewed citizenship in this great country, with a patient submission to the losses they have incurred and quiet acquiescence in the laws under which they may have to live." For his part, Ruffin stated, he planned to live "in unbroken retirement and certainly without any resistance in any form to the National authorities."[77] Supported by a letter of reference from noted North Carolina Unionist Bartholomew F. Moore, a friend of Ruffin's, as well as the recommendation of provisional Governor William W. Holden, Ruffin eventually received a full pardon for his participation in the rebellion.[78]

But Ruffin's commitment to traditional southern values proved stronger than his pledge to support "the National authorities." Less than a year after his contrite letter to the chief executive, Ruffin again entered the political arena, this time to express his opposition to North Carolina's proposed 1866 constitution. The state constitutional convention, following the guidelines Johnson established, annulled the ordinance of secession, proclaimed freedom for the slaves, and eventually repudiated the state's war debts. After implementing these specific measures, the convention reassembled a few months later, in May 1866, and proceeded to write a new constitution for the state. The new document explicitly forbade slavery, changed the basis for representation in the House of Commons to the white population (previously, under the "federal basis," ⅗ of the slave population had been counted for purposes of representation), and provided that only whites could vote and hold office.[79]

In a letter to a friend later published in a newspaper, Ruffin attacked the new constitution on two grounds. First, he criticized the basis of representation because it stripped power from wealthy whites who lived in areas with large concentrations of former slaves. Although he explicitly denied that blacks should have any voting rights, Ruffin argued that the former slaves should be counted for reasons of representation. "[S]urely those, who live where the Negroes are most numerous, who know their means, their willingness and their ability to pay this or that tax," Ruffin argued, "are best qualified to judge, what revenue can be raised from them or what they cannot or will not willingly pay or cannot be expected without grievous distress and oppression." In this way, Ruffin believed, paternalistic whites could look out for the interests of improvident blacks. "[T]he representation from the County ought to embrace as many, in proportion to others, as will bring the largest share of the required knowledge, guard the rights of these people, keep open the way for their advancement, and make them contented and as happy as their subordinate and dependent condition will allow." By extending the basis of representation to all persons—while maintaining racial restrictions on voting—Ruffin hoped to keep power in the plantation belt and out of the hands of the state's poorer areas, where slaveholders had never predominated.[80]

In addition to his opposition to the changes regarding representation, Ruffin assailed the legitimacy of the new constitution. Called by President Johnson, the convention had assembled without the consent of the people of North Carolina. Although delegates were elected by citizens of the state, Ruffin believed that the suffrage restrictions put in place after the war prevented many people—Ruffin called them "the best portion of our qualified citizens"—from voting for delegates. Thus, according to the former judge, the convention lacked the true authority of the people. "The whole proceeding arose out of arbitrary assumption," he wrote, "over-throwing all just notions of popular and free government and destructive of the very first principles of Republican Freedom." Ruffin thus urged fellow North Carolinians to join him in opposing the ratification of the new constitution. "Let every citizen of North Carolina, say 'No! too: I scorn and reject an instrument tendered to me under the name of a Constitution of North Carolina, which the People of North Carolina did not make and which was made for them by men in the guise of our representatives, who were not our representatives, but those of a power exercising at the time the authority of a Conqueror in military possession of our territory and arrogating to itself the rights of superseding all our Civil officers and the abrogation our laws.'" Such opposition initiated intense public debate over constitutional ratification, and the people of the state ultimately rejected the new constitution in a referendum.[81]

Ruffin's actions in this, the last political battle of his life, demonstrated his devotion to southern constitutional principles. His belief in the constitutionality of slavery, his acceptance of secession as a revolutionary act, his commitment to maintaining the antebellum power structure, and his attempt to prevent the national government from imposing its will on the state through a new constitution were all emblematic of his faith in southern constitutional ideals. However, Ruffin's commitment to racial control and defiance in the face of national interference did not manifest themselves in an acceptance of extralegal activity. In fact, in a letter written just before his death in 1870, even after Reconstruction had entered its more radical phase, Ruffin strongly urged his son, John, to avoid joining the Ku Klux Klan, because the judge believed "the whole proceeding is against law and the civil power of government and assumes to supersede by taking the power of trying, condemning, and punishing in their own hands."[82] As a jurist and a legalist, Ruffin did not merely advocate southern values or the preservation of the southern way of life—he believed deeply in a set of legal and constitutional principles that he identified with the South he had always known.

That the last public act of Ruffin's life was a political one was not surprising for a judge who had always understood the interconnectedness of law and politics. Throughout his career, Ruffin had demonstrated a keen awareness of the broad implications of all of his judicial opinions, whether they concerned judicial independence, railroads, homicide, or slavery. In his classic examination of antebellum legal history, Roscoe Pound made a distinction between the "deciding and the declaring function" of the judge.[83] Ruffin knew that every decision was also a declaration—a potential precedent with far-reaching policy implications. His roles as judge and a politician—as a judicial pragmatist and a southern constitutionalist—were mutually reinforcing.

CHAPTER SIX

George W. Stone,
Political Sectionalism, and
Legal Nationalism

By the memory and insults and indignities we have suffered, by the bitter memories of Reconstruction; by all the accumulated wrongs which have been heaped upon us in the last twenty-five years; and above all by the brighter recollection of the happier days during the earlier and better years of the republic, let us make one united, grand, heroic effort to elect a Democratic President. — GEORGE W. STONE, 1892

The life of Alabamian George Washington Stone, unlike those of other leading southern jurists, spanned nearly the whole nineteenth century. Born while James Madison occupied the White House, Stone lived through the decades of sectional antagonism that followed, experienced the fiery trials of the Civil War and Reconstruction, and welcomed the post-Reconstruction promise of a New South. He twice served on Alabama's highest court: from 1856 to 1865 and from 1876 to 1894, the last ten years as chief justice. Because of his lengthy tenure, Stone confronted a wide variety of issues, including the constitutional consequences of southern independence, the impact of Reconstruction on postwar race relations, the scope of economic regulation in an industrial age, and the need for reform of Alabama's late-nineteenth-century homicide law.

Stone's service at century's end demonstrated the convergence of sectionalism and nationalism within the southern judicial tradition. In his commitment to the Confederacy, his post-Reconstruction suppression of civil-rights protections, and his devotion to the Democratic Party in the midst of the Populist challenge, Stone stood firm in his faithfulness to southern principles. At the same time, his acceptance of Marshall Court precedents when upholding Confederate power, his interpretation of police powers and economic regulation, and his general ideas about the inferiority of African Americans fit with larger late-nineteenth-century American trends. Thus, though Stone always perceived himself as a southerner, his career, more than that of any other nineteenth-century southern jurist, demonstrates the convergence of southern distinctiveness with national legal ideals. Though a sectional consciousness among the southern judiciary remained intact, by the end of the century the national legal culture that had been developing for decades began to reach maturity.

Alabama Origins

A native of Bedford County, Virginia, George Washington Stone was born in 1811, one of ten children of Micajah Stone and Sarah Leftwich Stone. As the nation expanded, the Stones migrated westward in search of fresh land and new opportunities, and in 1818 they settled in Lincoln County, Tennessee, along the Alabama border.[1] There Micajah Stone established himself as a "planter in comfortable circumstances," while George Stone received his early education in the area's common schools and its village academy. After the death of his father in 1827, George engaged briefly in "some mercantile pursuit" before entering the law office of James Fulton, a respected member of the Fayetteville, Tennessee, bar. Like John Catron, another product of the old Southwest, Stone never attended college. Yet after exhaustive self-study, in 1834 Stone earned his license to practice law, and the same year he married Mary Gillespie.[2]

The newlyweds immediately headed south to Alabama, a state that offered many opportunities for aspiring lawyers. After teaching school for a few months in Coosa County, in the central part of the state, Stone set up his law practice in the village of Syllacauga in neighboring Talladega County. In 1836 Stone and the small but talented cadre of lawyers who had settled in the area assembled for the first meeting of the county's bar association, where they established a set of guidelines for practice in the local court. Of the eleven members of this group, three—including Stone—later went on to serve as chief justices of the state.[5]

Stone soon became a popular figure in this community of young, ambitious lawyers. Although never considered a great orator, he distinguished himself by the sharpness of his mind and the thoroughness of his arguments. "With painstaking exactness he would con over a minute point for hours," a later contemporary observed, "in order to bring it into exact adjustment. His arguments were perfectly mortised, no matter how much time was necessary to effect this end." Stone thought the practice of law required the highest degree of professional responsibility and rectitude. In an opinion he later rendered as a judge, he held attorneys accountable when they blatantly disregarded well-established legal rules or practices when arguing a case. Lawyers did not constitute a "privileged class," Stone wrote in the opinion, and negligent behavior was inexcusable for the legal profession. Lawyers, "like all other professional men and artizans, impliedly stipulate that they will bring to the service of their clients ordinary and reasonable skill and diligence," he wrote, "and, if they violate this implied stipulation, they are accountable to their clients for an injury traceable to such want of skill and diligence."[4] Judge Stone expected such high professional standards from the bar because, as a young lawyer, his Talladega County cohorts impressed on him the significance and the seriousness of the practice of law.

Stone's contact with such an able contingent of attorneys also paid handsome dividends when it came to career advancement, and during the next few years the ambitious Stone made every effort to further his professional status. In 1839 he traveled to the state capital at Tuscaloosa for the June term of the Alabama Supreme Court, where he gained admission to the bar of the court and argued two cases. Although he lost both, Stone used the opportunity to meet many of the state's leading lawyers and politicians and to position himself to run for judicial office in a few years. Later in 1839, after Stone's return to Talladega County, W. P. Chilton, the most respected member of the county bar and among the most prominent lawyers in the state, asked Stone to move to Talladega, the county seat, and become his partner.[5]

The association with Chilton, along with subsequent trips to Tuscaloosa to gain political support among state legislators, continued to elevate Stone's reputation. While he lost his initial bid for a circuit judgeship in 1843, Stone impressed a number of the state's leaders, and six months later, when the veteran circuit judge who had defeated him died, Governor Benjamin Fitzpatrick appointed Stone as an interim replacement. In December 1843 he won a close election to the position, but he served only a single six-year term as circuit judge. He decided against a bid for reelection because of the heavy workload and slight compensation that accompanied the judgeship. In addition, his wife had died in 1848. In 1849 he resigned from the bench and moved to Hayneville, in Lowndes County, to return to the practice of law. Late that year, he married Emily Moor, the daughter of a wealthy and influential Lowndes County planter.[6]

Despite his resignation, Stone maintained a presence in Alabama politics. An "Andrew Jackson Democrat," he was considered by his party as a candidate for governor in 1849, though he preferred a state supreme court judgeship.[7] Political circumstances prevented him from gaining judicial office for the next few years, a brief period of dominance by the state's Union Party. But the Democrats returned to power in Alabama in 1853, and the court's personnel underwent a series of changes. Legislators reduced the supreme court's membership from five to three, as it had been before the outgoing party expanded it, and several judges resigned during the next few years. Stone lost a bid for election to the court in 1853. Two years later, his political future seemed in doubt when he accepted a challenge to a duel from lawyer George W. Gayle. The dispute involved "some court business," although the details are unknown. "Upset and humiliated because he despised the practice," Stone nevertheless named pistols as the weapons and practiced firing with the help of friends in preparation for the showdown. Associates helped resolve the dispute before the duel occurred, but Stone's acceptance of the challenge made him ineligible for public office under Alabama law. A lifelong Presbyterian, Stone dutifully submitted to the church's discipline for his involvement in the affair. The incident with Gayle, however, did not hinder Stone's political ambitions, and he finally attained a seat on the state supreme court when one became vacant in 1856. After narrowly defeating Robert C. Brickell, sixty-one to fifty-nine, on the twenty-third ballot, the legislature made a special exception to the antidueling oath sworn by public officials to permit Stone to hold office again.[8]

Stone's dogged persistence had paid off. Although he displayed "no personal magnetism" and lacked "the fire, variety, and eloquence necessary for the pioneer jury," Stone nevertheless found success in the legal profession. By 1856 he had become, in the words of a leading Alabama newspaper, "well known as a gentleman of highly estimable character" who enjoyed "a fair and deserved reputation as a first class lawyer."[9]

State Sovereignty and the Confederacy

Because his elevation to the bench coincided with the Civil War era, Stone had to confront the question of the relationship between the states and the national government during the sectional crisis. Although early in his career he identified with the Unionism of Andrew Jackson, when Alabama chose the path of secession in 1861 Stone speedily embraced the state-sovereignty theory as a rationale for separation from the Union. Like many southerners, however, Stone seemed to overlook this doctrine of minority power when it conflicted with the cause of a united Confederate nation.

Stone first dealt with the issue of state sovereignty versus national exigency when the Confederate Congress enacted the first conscription law in American history. With some exceptions, the 1862 statute mandated three years' military service for all able-bodied white male citizens between ages eighteen and thirty-five.[10] Although the new constitution called for the establishment of a supreme court, the Confederate Congress never created one, thus leaving state courts as the final arbiters of all national legal and constitutional questions. *Ex parte Hill, in re Willis v. Confederate States* (1863), the first of several conscription cases to come before the Alabama Supreme Court, involved a challenge to the law brought by three men, all of whom petitioned a probate court for a writ of habeas corpus. Each believed that physical incapacity rendered him ineligible for military duty and claimed he was being unlawfully held for service in the Confederate army. In a long and confusing opinion, Stone attempted to reconcile his simultaneous devotion to both state sovereignty and the Confederate war effort.[11]

Stone upheld the conscription act and argued that it was an "unquestioned right" of the national government to call young men into military service. Citing the Confederate Constitution's various grants of power to Congress—to "declare war," "raise and support armies," "to provide and maintain a navy," and "to make rules for the government and regulation of the land naval forces"—Stone took a broad view of the Confederacy's ability to wage war. Moreover, Stone described Congress as the "sole arbiter" of the means of executing such express powers. Here he drew upon the Necessary and Proper Clause, which, although long the source of southerners' objections to encroaching federal power, remained in the Confederate Constitution. In addition to these textual sources of authority, Stone argued that the crisis of wartime augmented the scope of national power. For these reasons, he sanctioned Confederate power to conscript.[12]

Even more, Stone imparted seemingly unlimited authority to the legislature while he diminished judicial power over such matters. He denied to the probate court—or any state court—the jurisdiction to inquire into a soldier's physical fitness for military service. "Wherever, as in the present case, the privilege of exemption is granted on conditions, the adjudication of which is expressly reserved to certain officers named or provided for," he reasoned, "state courts have no authority to supervise the action of such officers, thus provided for and exercised, or to retry any question thus exclusively conferred on an officer of the Confederate government." [13] This right to review the eligibility of individual draftees, he believed, belonged solely to the Congress and whatever agencies it might create for such purposes, not to the judicial tribunals of the various states. On this point Stone cited such nationalistic Marshall Court decisions as *Sturges v. Crowninshield* (1819) and *Martin v. Hunter's Lessee* (1816), long the bane of some southerners who opposed the growth of federal power. Stone thus found himself empowering the Confederate Congress at the expense of states, particularly state courts. Aware of the incongruity of this position, he nevertheless conceived of no alternative. "To entertain jurisdiction in such cases," Stone concluded, "would lead to the most embarrassing and disastrous collisions between the authorities of the two governments." [14] Stone sought to avoid strife within the Confederacy not only by upholding the conscription acts but also by suppressing whatever opposition might arise from within the states.

At the same time, Stone used the latter half of his opinion in *Ex parte Hill, in re Willis* to reaffirm his belief in state sovereignty and restricted national power. "I am of that school who believe," he wrote, "that the Confederate government is one of limited and defined powers, and that great care should at all times be exercised to prevent it from enlarging its powers by construction." Reviewing early-nineteenth-century constitutional history, Stone argued that the U.S. Supreme Court had exceeded its constitutional authority and fostered "the too great subordination of the state to the federal government." The Confederacy, he believed, would not repeat such mistakes. Stone expressed confidence that the new constitution of the slaveholding republic, along with the future organization of the Confederate court system, would guarantee that the federal and state governments remained within their proper spheres. Sounding a reassuring note, Stone stated that upholding conscription would not adversely affect state power. "This will neither destroy nor impair the sovereignty of the several states," he avowed. [15] Despite Stone's best efforts to display devotion to both state sovereignty and national supremacy, his opinion in *Ex parte Hill, in re Willis* decisively established the dominance of the central government. In effect, Stone mouthed state sovereignty rhetoric at the same time that he granted a virtually unlimited degree of power to the Confederate Congress and rendered state courts impotent to challenge national legislation.

Moreover, Stone reaffirmed this position in subsequent cases. *State, ex rel. Dawson, in re Strawbridge and Mays* (1864), for example, involved a clash between two laws relating to the draft status of agriculturalists, one enacted by the Alabama legislature, the other by the Confederate Congress.[16] By the time this case came before the court, during its June 1864 term, Confederate Alabama teetered on the edge of collapse. More than two thousand Union troops occupied the heart of the state and began the destruction of the Montgomery and West Point Railroad, Alabama's lifeline to Atlanta and the rest of the Confederacy. With this military-induced mayhem undermining the already flagging political support for the Confederate nation, Stone's colleagues on the court ruled in favor of the Alabama—as opposed to the Confederate—law. When faced with this stark choice between loyalty to the state or to the nation, Stone dissented in favor of the Confederacy. Under the Supremacy Clause of the Confederate Constitution, he stubbornly argued, the state law had to "yield the precedence to this supreme [national] law." [17]

The contradictions presented by such cases were obvious, and Stone's ambivalent attitude toward U.S. Supreme Court precedents in *Ex parte Hill, in re Willis* typified the dilemma facing members of southern state supreme courts. Although Stone cited some of the most nationalistic opinions of the Marshall Court to assert Confederate power, he also blamed the Marshall Court for creating many of the constitutional and legal problems that led to the creation of the Confederacy. Stone struggled to explain this discrepancy but had little success, for he referred to the "heresies" of the Supreme Court in one sentence only to affirm its "distinguished ability" and "long and brilliant history" in the next.[18] Civil war and the establishment of the Confederacy brought the tension between sectional identity and the development of a national legal culture into sharp relief. A southerner through and through, Stone wanted to maximize the authority of the Confederate government during wartime, but the only precedents on which he could draw were those of the early-nineteenth-century U.S. Supreme Court.

Of course, Stone was not alone in confronting this difficulty. During the war, the constitutionality of the conscription acts directly came before the supreme courts of Texas, Georgia, North Carolina, and Virginia, and all except North Carolina rendered similarly forceful opinions in favor of the Confederacy's power to conduct a military draft. Many of these opinions, as well as those in cases regarding other laws enacted by the Confederate government, drew heavily on Marshall's nationalism and the American legal tradition.[19] The Texas Supreme Court, for example, in *Ex parte Mayer* (1864), a case involving congressional repeal of the substitute provision of the conscription act, summarized its position in particularly Marshallian terms: "The government of the Confederate States, like the government of a state, is derived from the same source, the people, and founded on their authority; that the constitution and laws of the Confederate States are the supreme law of the land, and not in any sense dependent on the constitution of a state for their authority; and that we must look to the instrument which confers the power to ascertain whether a law of Congress, in a given case, is constitutional or not." Judge William Sharkey of Mississippi, moreover, revealed the inability of southern jurists to disconnect themselves from U.S. legal culture. In an essay on martial law written during the war, Sharkey sought the wisdom of two quintessential northern jurists: "Judge Story and Chancellor Kent, *our ablest commentators*," he wrote with unconscious irony, "have both failed to give us any light on the subject." Conscription and the waging of war in general thus forced Stone and other southern judges to confront difficult issues about the nature of the Confederate constitutional order as well as the practice of judging within a nation created by secession.[20]

When southern jurists left the Union, they did not relinquish their early training and the decades of subsequent experience that connected them to the nation's constitutional and legal heritage. Though obviously affected by the southern political order that had led to the establishment of the Confederacy, southern judges nevertheless revealed their attachment to a broader set of values associated with American legal culture, including the decisions of the U.S. Supreme Court and the ideas of northern commentators. Even secession could not sever this link.

Reconstruction, Redemption, and Race

The end of the war and the beginning of Reconstruction dramatically altered Alabama's political landscape. Antebellum Unionists and other opponents of the Confederacy—mostly from the northern portion of the state—came to power, while Alabama's Confederate supporters felt the stinging consequences of defeat. Reconstruction lawmakers especially disliked Stone's opinions in the conscription cases, which they believed had simply prolonged the war. While the members of the state supreme court had displayed varying degrees of loyalty to the Confederacy during wartime, Stone's dissent in the *Strawbridge* case marked him as particularly committed to the Confederate cause. In 1865 Alabama's provisional governor issued a proclamation to the state's newly elected legislators in which he claimed that the members of the supreme court, because they had been installed in office during Alabama's period of separation from the Union, held their positions illegally. The legislature hastily reelected Chief Justice A. J. Walker but chose two new justices to take the places of Stone and John D. Pelham.[21]

Stone's removal from the court reflected more the temper of Alabama politics than his reputation as a judge. The establishment of the provisional government and its later supplanting by a radical Republican regime meant the banishment of devoted Confederates from key government positions. Stone's loyalty to the Confederacy discredited him as a jurist, but it apparently did not diminish his reputation—even among Unionists—as a competent legal professional. In 1865 the same legislature that had denied him reelection asked him to prepare a revised penal code for the state; Stone's interest and expertise in criminal law made him ideally suited for such a task.[22]

When the political climate in Alabama changed over the next decade, Stone rode the rising tide of southern conservatism back onto the supreme court. The 1874 election of a Democratic governor and legislature initiated the process of "redemption," which ultimately concluded in 1877 with the withdrawal of the last three companies of federal troops from the state. In 1876 Alabama's Redeemer Democratic governor, George Houston, reappointed Stone to the bench.[23]

For the next decade or so, Stone cooperated with other white Alabamians in attempting to suppress black civil rights. In 1865 the legislature had enacted the Black Code, some of the provisions of which attempted to coerce the black labor force into the service of whites. While Alabama's code superficially ranked among the mildest in the South, magistrates engaged in such vigorous enforcement of these enactments that local jails were soon filled to capacity with freedmen.[24] Such wholesale violations of civil rights in the South prompted congressional Republicans to advocate changes in the U.S. Constitution. In 1868 they succeeded in gaining ratification of the Fourteenth Amendment, which bestowed citizenship on freed slaves and ensured legal protection of their civil rights against discriminatory state action. The amendment took on real meaning during the reign of radical Republicans in Congress, but with the return of white rule to state and local governments in the South during the mid-1870s, many state and federal courts began to circumvent the new constitutional guarantees.

Stone shared the racist and paternalistic assumptions of other southern judges, viewing African Americans as inferior and ill prepared for freedom. In the handful of antebellum slave cases Stone heard, he almost always, unlike Lumpkin and Ruffin, refrained from making extraneous statements about the nature of slavery or slaves apart from the narrow legal issues at hand. Nevertheless, he held masters to a high level of responsibility and described whites as "morally bound to furnish to this dependent and subject class . . . moral and religious instruction."[25] After emancipation, Stone joined other white southern officials in rendering the Fourteenth Amendment ineffectual to solidify white control. Only a few cases relating to the amendment came before the Alabama Supreme Court, but the justices did make significant statements about the amendment in at least two important areas: the state's prohibition of interracial marriage and discrimination in jury selection.

In a series of cases, the court assessed the impact of the Fourteenth Amendment on the state's antimiscegenation law. After the war, a new state constitution directed lawmakers to make interracial marriages null and void and to "make the parties to any such marriage subject to criminal prosecutions." The legislature speedily complied with this charge by establishing "a penalty of two to seven years imprisonment for both members of any interracial couple." In 1872, while the Reconstruction government held power in Alabama, a Republican-dominated supreme court overturned this antimiscegenation law. Viewing marriage as a civil contract, the court held that citizenship for African Americans encompassed all contractual rights, including marriage.[26]

When Stone and other Redeemers returned, however, the court reversed its position. In an 1877 case Judge Amos Manning held that neither the federal Civil Rights Act of 1866 nor the Fourteenth Amendment impaired the ability of states to regulate marital relationships. Contending that marriage was more than a mere civil contract, he denied that the Civil Rights Act gave freedpeople the right to marry whites based on the right to contract. Manning also argued that the framers did not intend to eradicate such social distinctions between the races because at the time of the passage of the act similar antimiscegenation statutes existed in several northern states. Moreover, Manning dismissed the constitutional question by citing the opinions of state courts across the country, most notably that of Pennsylvania, which held that "natural law" prohibited such "amalgamation" and "corruption of the races." In sum, Manning held that the Reconstruction amendments "were evidently designed to secure to citizens, without distinction of race, rights of a civil or political kind only."[27]

In a similar case, Stone fully concurred with Manning's interpretation of the Fourteenth Amendment and the antimiscegenation law. *Hoover v. State* (1877) involved the fate of Robert Hoover, a black man, and Betsey Litsey, a white woman, who "lived together openly 'in a house containing only one room'" just outside Talladega. Stating his satisfaction with Manning's arguments, Stone relied on his colleague's reasoning to dismiss any questions about the antimiscegenation statute's constitutionality. "The marriage being absolutely void," he summarized, "the offending parties must be treated as unmarried persons, and their sexual cohabitation as fornication within the statute."[28] Aside from the constitutional question, the only other important matter to be decided in the case was whether the couple's marriage constituted a criminal act. "It is very true that to constitute a crime, there must be both an act and an intent," Stone wrote. In this case, he reasoned, "the act being intentionally done, the criminality necessarily follows." Stone, who believed any interracial union to be a "very gross offense against morals and decorum," clung to the ideas of the established order on the issue of race. Like his colleague Judge Manning, Stone rendered the Fourteenth Amendment irrelevant when it came to laws prohibiting miscegenation.[29]

The amendment also did not affect discrimination in jury selection. In *Green v. State* (1882), involving the murder trial of Bill Green, "a Negro of full blood," the court took up the issue of whether local governmental officials' efforts to select a grand jury composed entirely of white citizens violated the amendment. Green was tried and convicted of second-degree murder and sentenced to twelve years' imprisonment. At trial, Green filed both a motion to quash the indictment and a plea in abatement. He charged that Macon County, the site of the alleged crime, contained a total of seventeen thousand residents, twelve thousand of whom were of African descent, and that two thousand of these people were qualified voters. Moreover, Green claimed that for more than eight years no African American had been summoned or had served on a jury in the county. The officials involved—the judge of probate, the sheriff, and the clerk of the court—argued that there was no person of African descent in the county who possessed the "requisite qualifications of a grand juror." The circuit judge presiding in the original case found in favor of these officials; thus, the indictment, trial, and conviction were upheld. When the case came to the Alabama Supreme Court, Stone and his colleagues faced the matter of whether to uphold or overturn the ruling of the circuit judge in light of the Fourteenth Amendment's civil-rights guarantees.[30]

Stone held that the behavior of the officials in question did not abridge the Fourteenth Amendment. Reviewing the language of the amendment, Stone reasoned that its prohibition of "state action" in violation of civil rights did not apply to the conduct of the probate judge, sheriff, or clerk of the court. Rather, Stone equated state action with legislation. "The first thought which presents itself on reading this amendment is," Stone reasoned, "that it is a limitation on the powers of the states. No state shall commit these abuses. It erects no barrier against the wrongs individuals may commit against life, liberty, or property." Not only was this the "plain, unmistakable language of the amendment," he argued, it was also the interpretation offered by the U.S. Supreme Court.[31]

Much of Stone's opinion, in fact, consisted of his reading of various recent Supreme Court decisions on similar issues. He criticized, for example, the ambiguous definitions of state action offered by Justices William Strong and John Marshall Harlan. Strong's explanations of the concept in various cases seemed to contradict one another, while Harlan's expansive notion of state action in *Neal v. Delaware* (1880) ran counter to Stone's intent to define the concept as narrowly as possible.[32] Conversely, Stone praised the "ponderous logic" of the Court's opinions in the *Slaughterhouse Cases* (1873) and *United States v. Cruikshank* (1876), both of which interpreted the ideas of citizenship and state action in such a way as to weaken the national government's ability to protect the civil rights of freedpeople. After this extensive review of Supreme Court precedents, Stone concluded that a violation of the Fourteenth Amendment was only "complete" when expressed in a statute or "shown in an official act" of "final determination." "But, if the alleged violation be an act, or failure to act by a subordinate or inferior officer, in a matter not final in its character," he continued, "then it is not the act of the state, and does not violate the Fourteenth Amendment, unless it be a matter cognizable before, and brought to the knowledge of the courts, and its redress is denied by that department of the government." Drawing from various Supreme Court opinions, Stone decided that the conduct of the officials in *Green* did not constitute state action and, therefore, did not violate the Fourteenth Amendment. In such an instance, he concluded, the courts were "powerless to redress the abuse."[33]

In discussing U.S. Supreme Court precedents in *Green*, Stone explicitly recognized the authority of the nation's highest court. He noted that on federal questions the Alabama Supreme Court had conformed its rulings to those issued by the U.S. Supreme Court. "This we have done," he wrote, "because, on all questions arising under the Constitution of the United States, and the acts of Congress thereunder, the rulings of that court are final, to which all State tribunals must yield."[34] In contrast to early-nineteenth-century southern jurists—Spencer Roane, John Catron, and Henry Benning among them—who overtly challenged the high court's authority, by the end of the century Judge Stone and his colleagues had no difficulty in upholding the Supreme Court's authoritative voice.[35] The Court, after all, agreed with most southerners in its narrow interpretation of the Constitution's civil-rights guarantees. Convergence between state courts and the U.S. Supreme Court on the issue of race therefore prompted the disappearance of the oppositional tone that had characterized many early-nineteenth-century southern state court opinions.

Stone shared the U.S. Supreme Court's view that the Reconstruction

amendments had been intended neither to revolutionize the federal-state relationship nor to remake the South in the North's image. He believed, like
Justice Samuel Miller, that a zealous interpretation of the Fourteenth Amendment would transform the Supreme Court into, as Miller wrote in *Slaughterhouse,* a "perpetual censor" of state legislation. As a loyal southerner who
desired to preserve his region's traditions, Stone chafed at the prospect of a
victorious North forever reigning over a defeated South.[36]

While Stone's resistance to civil rights for freedmen on one level constituted an attempt to preserve the racial order of the Old South, the fact that
southern jurists could turn to the U.S. Supreme Court and northern state
courts for support on such matters demonstrated the national character of
post-Reconstruction hostility to African-American civil rights. Stone and his
fellow Alabama justices were scarcely alone in circumventing the equalitarian
language of the Reconstruction amendments. Even the existence of state anti-
discrimination statutes in the mid-Atlantic states, as one historian notes, did
not prevent state appellate courts in that region from restricting the applicability of such laws to preserve racist ideals. Throughout the nation, late-
nineteenth-century judges began to utilize the Fourteenth Amendment more
as a means of protecting entrepreneurial interests from state regulation than
of guarding the civil-rights guarantees made to African Americans.[37]

Police Powers and Railroads

In the area of economic regulation, Stone built on the work of his southern
predecessors in developing a "police powers jurisprudence." Through much
of the nineteenth century, American state judges struggled to define the idea
of "public purpose" by distinguishing between legitimate regulatory measures that worked to the public's benefit and discriminatory laws that imposed special burdens on a specific class or interest. These issues became
most apparent for Stone in railroad cases. There the judge had to decide
whether state interference in the marketplace constituted a legitimate exercise of the police power or what late-nineteenth-century jurists regarded as
unjust "class legislation."[38]

Stone's earliest and most complete statement on police power came in
Perry v. New Orleans, Mobile, and Chattanooga Railroad Co. (1876). The
case involved property owners in Mobile who sought to enjoin the laying of
railroad track along a city street as authorized by a Mobile ordinance. These
businessmen argued that Commerce Street, "the most important commercial
street in the city," had been opened by "the owners of lands over and through

which it passes for their own convenience." Although the street had become a "public highway," the businessmen claimed that they continued to own the lands in front of their buildings and that the city had never established legal possession of any part of the thoroughfare. According to these property owners, the "construction and use of the railroad" would obstruct and devastate the street and its businesses, thus proving injurious to their rights. Stone used this conflict between private property and public purpose to engage in a lengthy discussion of economic development and the police power.[39]

The judge spoke glowingly of the wonders of modern technology and economic progress, and he believed that law needed to accommodate societal change. Having witnessed throughout his lifetime the appearance of steamboats, railroads, telegraphs, telephones, and electric lights, Stone appreciated the role of capital and corporations in initiating and facilitating progress. For this reason, he believed, ancient rules at times needed to undergo modification. "Inventions new and useful, and new industries and new enterprises consequent thereon, necessarily impose the duty of making new applications of legal principles," he wrote. "The world, in its industries and commerce, is making giant strides; and judicial science must struggle to keep pace with the necessities which are the fruits of such wonderful progress."[40]

Stone believed that the preservation of highways and streets, "necessities in every civilized community," clearly fell within the purview of the state's police power.[41] Citing notable authorities such as Massachusetts Chief Justice Lemuel Shaw, Pennsylvania Chief Justice John Bannister Gibson, and Michigan jurist and treatise writer Thomas Cooley in addition to precedents from various state courts, Stone contended that legislatures had every power to close a public highway to establish a railroad line for public use. "Long and connecting lines of railroad greatly facilitate and cheapen transportation," Stone pragmatically observed. "To construct and operate such long and connecting lines, it is necessary that cities, towns, and navigable watercourses shall be traversed by them. The city is traversed, necessarily, by and through its street; and in laying a railroad track along a public street, the use and comfort of the latter, as a highway or thoroughfare, must necessarily be somewhat impaired."[42] Even when the property holders along the street retained title to the land except for an easement, as in this instance, the legislature possessed the authority to grant rights to construct a railroad track over the street.

Having established the legitimacy of legislative action on behalf of railways serving the public interest, in this case Stone ruled against construction of the railroad. As the land belonged to the business owners and the city charter lacked any mention of the authority to grant rights to railroad companies, Stone ruled that "such power cannot be exercised by the city government, unless it is conferred upon it by the legislature."[43] In other words, though the state legislature could authorize the building of the railway under its police powers, the city of Mobile lacked this authority. Despite the holding in *Perry*, Stone's opinion was a powerful expression linking the police power to the public interest.

If legislative acts promotive of the public good fell within the scope of the state's police powers, laws that specifically discriminated against corporations—or specific types of corporations—did not meet constitutional standards. Like most late-nineteenth-century American jurists, Stone conferred on corporations all the rights of persons. As such, railroad companies could not be singled out by the legislature in a discriminatory manner. In *Zeigler v. South and North Alabama Railroad* (1877), for example, the court considered the constitutionality of an act that fixed liability on railroad companies "for all damages to livestock, or cattle of any kind, caused by locomotives or railroad cars." The law required companies to make compensation for any damage to livestock unless the person who owned the animal contributed to the injury, but allowing stock to roam at will was not considered negligence on the part of the owner. The statute made no reference to the skill or diligence of the locomotive operator, and under the law the railroad company had no chance to exculpate itself. In this case, a train had killed a "yearling calf," whose owner brought suit for $50.06.[44]

Stone struck down the law as a violation of the state constitutional guarantee of due process of law. Citing Thomas Cooley's *Constitutional Limitations* and Thomas Ruffin's opinion in *Hoke v. Henderson* (1833), Stone explained that all acts of the legislature were not necessarily the "law of the land." Because it failed to protect private individuals from the arbitrary exercise of state power, the statute in question violated the higher principle of due process. "Due process of law implies the right of the person affected thereby to be present before the tribunal which pronounces judgment upon the question of life, liberty, or property . . . to be heard, by testimony or otherwise, and to have the rights of controverting, by proof, every material fact which bears on the question of right in the matter involved," Stone wrote. "If any question of fact or liability be conclusively presumed against him, this is not due process of law." Concluding his opinion, Stone thought it unfair that corporations be held to higher standards of accountability "than would be exacted from natural persons for injuries which result from unavoidable accidents."[45]

In another case, this time involving the death of a child, Stone similarly struck down such "class legislation." *Smith v. Louisville and Nashville Railroad* (1883) involved an Alabama law providing that when the death of a minor child was caused by "an incorporated company, or private association of persons," the father of the deceased could recover damages determined by a jury. Stone attacked the statute as unfair because it discriminated against corporations as opposed to individual business owners. "If the employer, being a single individual, be not responsible for the wrongful act or omission of the agent he employs, how can the same act by the same agent, employed under the same circumstances, impose a penalty on the innocent employer, merely because two or more owned the business, and united in employing the agent?" Stone succinctly captured the essence of the law's deficiency: "Is individual enterprise less amenable to legislative surveillance than associated capital?"[46] Because corporations were "persons," Stone reasoned, no laws could discriminate between individual business owners and corporations. Here he cited the circuit opinion of Justice Stephen Field in *County of San Mateo v. Southern Pennsylvania Railroad* (1882), the decision of a U.S. circuit judge in the same case, as well as the Alabama Constitution. "No burden can be imposed on one class of person, natural or artificial," Stone concluded, "which is not, in like conditions, imposed on all other classes." The law, in his view, was unconstitutional.[47]

Stone again invalidated a law discriminating against railroad corporations in *Brown v. Alabama Great Southern Railroad Co.* (1888). The case involved a statute allowing a justice of the peace to have jurisdiction in cases involving "injury to or destruction of stock, by the locomotive cars of a railroad, if the sum in controversy does not exceed one hundred dollars." Under established statutes and precedent, the jurisdiction of justices of the peace in tort cases was limited to fifty dollars. "We have thus the naked inquiry," Stone wrote, "whether the constitutions, Federal and State, permit the legislature to discriminate between railroad corporations and other persons, natural or artificial, in the matter of the jurisdiction of an inferior tribunal." Holding that state law could not limit the justices' jurisdiction to fifty dollars in general but one hundred dollars in suits involving railroads, Stone invalidated the statute.[48]

Stone's opinions regarding economic regulation reflected the rhetoric of New South boosters as well as that of typical late-nineteenth-century government and business leaders. Like many of these contemporaries, Stone paid homage to the tremendous economic growth and technological advancement that accompanied the consolidation of capital during the late nineteenth century. "During the present century human progress has been wonderful," he exulted in an 1889 speech. "Wonderful in the industrial arts, and their appliances. Wonderful in scientific discovery. Most wonderful in the facilities for travel, and means of intercommunication." Stone exuded the optimism of many leaders of his day who believed that because of the efforts of America's great capitalists, the United States was entering an unprecedented era of progress and prosperity.[49]

In addition, Stone's values regarding economic regulation represented the late-nineteenth-century American judiciary's concern with promoting economic liberty in the public interest. Michigan jurist Thomas Cooley, the most notable contemporary advocate of this way of thinking, believed that the scope of the police power was defined by the government's powers to promote the public good. As Howard Gillman notes, "'public purpose' as a limit on the powers of government did not mean 'laissez-faire'; it meant, by and large, class-neutral legislation—legislation that did not impose special burdens or benefits on certain market competitors." To Stone, as to most judges of his day, only class-free legislation would satisfy constitutional requirements. Legislation favoring one class or interest over another violated the ideas of due process of law and vested rights. Here, like other jurists, Stone drew on Ruffin's opinion in *Hoke v. Henderson* (1833), which, although it had involved a clerk's right to hold office, influenced the development of higher-law constitutionalism in America. Ruffin's opinion, along with other mid-nineteenth-century precedents, helped judges develop the idea that legislatures lacked the power "arbitrarily to transfer property rights from one citizen to another." As guardians of constitutional rights, judges believed that only courts—rather than legislatures—could make such decisions. Despite its roots in the Jacksonian era's antimonopoly and antiprivilege rhetoric, by the late nineteenth century this mode of constitutional thought in many instances served to invalidate regulations and benefit corporations. In Stone's Alabama Supreme Court, as in many other state courts during that time, special legislation that regulated corporations often failed to win judicial approval.[50]

Violence and Homicide

Like his southern judicial counterparts, Stone faced difficult legal questions involving violence and homicide. Toward the end of the nineteenth century, the American judiciary's commitment to common-law principles in the adjudication of homicide cases began to wane. Although throughout the antebellum period southern judges joined their northern counterparts in holding defendants to strict standards regarding the definition of self-defense and in overlooking technical inadequacies at trial in hopes of preventing rampant homicide, after the war northern state courts began to take an approach more sympathetic to defendants. In particular, the American interpretation of self-defense underwent a transformation. For centuries, the common-law understanding was that an individual, when pursued by an attacker, was required to "retreat to the wall" before retaliating. Only after attempting to escape could an individual justify acting in self-defense. Perhaps Blackstone best captured the justification for this centuries-old presumption that all killing was felonious when he revealed his concern that "the right to defend may be mistaken as the right to kill." [51]

After the Civil War, a pair of rulings from the Midwest began to undermine this common-law notion of the "duty to retreat." *Erwin v. State* (1876), heard by the Ohio Supreme Court, involved Erwin's slaying of his son-in-law. A long-standing dispute between the men culminated one day when the son-in-law approached Erwin in a threatening manner with an axe. Erwin warned his foe not to advance, but when the angry relative closed in, Erwin stood his ground and killed his daughter's husband with a pistol. Convicted of second-degree murder, Erwin appealed on the grounds that the trial judge had incorrectly charged the jury that he had a duty to retreat. On appeal, Judge George W. McIlvaine viewed Erwin as blameless and not required to flee from his angry son-in-law: "The law, out of tenderness for human life and the frailties of human nature, will not permit the taking of it to repel a mere trespass, or even to save life, where the assault is provoked; but a true man, who is without fault, is not obliged to fly from an assailant, who, by violence or surprise, maliciously seeks to take his life or do him enormous bodily harm." The judge struck down the duty-to-retreat doctrine in Ohio and ordered a new trial. In Indiana, meanwhile, the state supreme court similarly overturned a murder conviction in *Runyan v. State* (1877). During a dispute, a man tried to strike Runyan two or three times with his fists, but Runyan warded off the blows and pushed his attacker away. Runyan then grabbed for the revolver in his coat pocket, fired at the man's chest, and mortally wounded him. During Runyan's trial for murder, the judge instructed the jury that Runyan had a duty to retreat before killing in self-defense. On appeal, Judge William E. Niblack of the Indiana Supreme Court rejected the charge. After citing Bishop on criminal law and Wharton's criminal law as authorities, Niblack concluded that "the tendency of the American mind seems to be very strongly against the enforcement of any rule which requires a person to flee when assailed." [52] Over the next thirty years, the high courts of several other states followed Ohio and Indiana in explicitly abandoning the duty-to-retreat doctrine. [53]

Texas became most famous for discarding the rule. There both the penal code and the state supreme court upheld the idea that an individual could act in self-defense without fleeing from an assailant. In *Bell v. State* (1885), one of a series of Texas cases establishing this principle, Judge Samuel A. Willson held a trial judge's charge erroneous because of his failure to inform the jury of the "Texas rule" of self-defense. "This is a very material part of the law of self-defense, and is a statutory innovation upon the common law, and upon the common view of what constitutes self-defense," Willson wrote. "The common law required the assailed party to 'retreat to the wall,' and this requirement, while it no longer exists as to the law of this state, is still believed by many. . . . In all cases, therefore, where the issue of self-defense arises from the evidence, the jury should be instructed that the assailed party is not bound to retreat in order to make pertinent his right of self-defense." This and other late-nineteenth-century Texas Supreme Court rulings on the subject clearly stood in contrast to the decisions rendered by the antebellum members of that court, who went to great lengths to uphold murder convictions.[54] After the Civil War, the Texas Supreme Court proved less willing to convict murderers and more tolerant of personal combat resulting in death.

Though these increasingly national trends favored defendants, in a series of opinions Judge Stone opposed this loose definition of self-defense and the social attitudes that lay behind it. Stone's opinion in *McManus v. State* (1860) set the tone for the next thirty years of decisions by the Alabama Supreme Court in the area of manslaughter, homicide, and self-defense. The case involved a dispute between two drunken men that eventually erupted into a fight. During the course of the struggle, McManus threw a piece of brick, "large as one-fourth or one-half of a brick," at his opponent's head, and the resulting injury proved fatal. Stone and his colleagues heard the case on appeal from a lower court, which had convicted the brick thrower of voluntary manslaughter. Although counsel for the appellant argued for a reduced charge of involuntary manslaughter, Stone was unyielding. "It is a perversion of language," he wrote, "to say that a force which is direct and unlawful, and which is intentionally aimed at a particular person, and causes his death, or that the homicide thus brought about, is involuntary."[55]

In *McManus* Stone not only proved unwilling to lessen the offense but also articulated two important themes that would characterize his opinions in homicide cases for the remainder of his career. First, Stone denounced an honorific code that promoted violence. "A false opinion, has, we fear, obtained extensive credence," he lamented, "that notions of chivalry or personal prowess, can lawfully enter into individual quarrels and combats." No verbal affront to manhood or honor, in his view, justified retaliation to the point of mayhem or homicide. "An insult, or an assault, or an assault and battery, which does not endanger life or member, furnishes no excuse for taking life," he firmly stated.[56] Second, in addition to his opposition to the prevailing ethic of honor, Stone invoked the spirit of the common law as the basis for the type of civilized society that he envisioned. The common law, which clearly distinguished between defense and revenge, required that an individual who acted in self-defense first attempt to retreat to avoid a dangerous encounter and then make a reasonable determination of the necessity of violent action in self-defense.[57] The duty to retreat was essential to Stone's understanding of homicide and self-defense. "The humane doctrine of the common law, which, for the protection of human life, required the citizen to decline a combat, and to abstain from the shedding of blood, whenever he could do so, without endangering his person in the one case, and his life in the other, seems, in a great degree, to have been lost sight of," he remarked. Stone sought to elevate the principles of the common law over the ethic of honor.[58]

Stone subsequently reaffirmed the superiority of the common law. In *Ex parte Nettles* (1877), a case involving a personal dispute that resulted in murder, he refused to grant a writ of habeas corpus for the killer. In the opinion, Stone discussed a similar case from Mississippi, where Judge Ephraim Foster had held that the statements of a man made while he obtained weapons in preparation for an anticipated confrontation did not reveal express malice to kill. Defining malice in such a way as to require proof that the alleged murderer actually informed others of his plans to harm his rival, the Mississippi Supreme Court held that the charge of murder could not be sustained. The court ordered the slayer released from jail.[59] Presented with a similar set of issues in *Nettles,* Stone not only refused the writ of habeas corpus but also openly rejected the Mississippi precedent. The relative ease with which the Mississippi court dismissed all charges against the accused in the case, Stone argued, was further evidence of the "popular fallacy" that was "annually rushing scores, if not hundreds of our citizens into eternity, red with their own blood causelessly shed."[60] Echoing the earlier concerns of Catron and Lumpkin, Stone linked the Mississippi decision with a culture of violence and lawlessness, and he chastised nearly every component of the justice system for failure to take seriously the rule of law: "Until courts and juries learn to place a proper estimate on the sacredness and inestimable value of human life; learn that life is not to be taken to avenge an insult, even though gross; learn that felonious homicide, even willful and deliberate murder, may be committed during a personal, nay, mutual rencontre; until juries learn that the crime of murder is not expunged from our statute book, nor retained only for the friendless or humble, we may expect the carnival of the manslayer to be prolonged if not intensified." Stone again held up the common law as the solution to the characteristic leniency of the justice system and as the guide for judges to follow in homicide cases. Every murder as defined by the common law, he affirmed in *Nettles,* constituted murder under the statutes of Alabama.[61]

When Alabama's lower courts followed common-law principles and repudiated the code of honor, Stone eagerly upheld their work. In *Judge v. State* (1877), for example, a case involving a trial judge's charge to a jury in a homicide case, Stone carefully scrutinized the judge's instructions. Because of errors in the charge, he ordered the trial decision reversed and the case remanded. Nevertheless, Stone expressed his approval on learning that the trial judge had instructed the jury about an individual's duty to retreat when confronted with danger. "We are pleased to observe that in this case, the old, sound, and much disregarded doctrine, that no man stands excused for taking human life, if, with safety to his own person, he could have avoided or retired from the combat, has been given in charge and must have been acted on by the jury," he wrote. "It is to be regretted that this salutary rule is not universally observed by juries, without reference to the social standing of the prisoner." Simple adherence to this common-law rule, Stone believed, would restrain "unbridled passions and lawlessness" and would save "many valuable lives."[62]

Having given a clear indication that common-law principles would stand at the center of his rulings regarding excusable homicide, Stone proposed specific guidelines regarding self-defense. In a pair of important decisions, *Mitchell v. State* (1877) and *Bain v. State* (1881), Stone held that the slayer had to establish three criteria to justify killing another person in self-defense: "that the difficulty should not have been provoked or encouraged by the defendant; that he was at the time so menaced, or appeared to be so menaced, as to create a reasonable apprehension of the loss of his life, or that he would suffer grievous bodily harm; and that there was no other reasonable mode of escape from such present impending peril."[63] Stone essentially drew these rules, although more precise in their wording, from Blackstonian concepts. In his *Commentaries on the Laws of England,* the venerable English jurist argued that self-defense did not "imply a right of attacking," that it was only justified in the face of "certain and immediate suffering" and when an individual had "no other possible means of escaping from his assailant."[64]

Over the next several years, Stone confirmed and strengthened these rules. In *Myers v. State* (1878), for example, Stone reiterated that the defendant could not provoke or encourage a confrontation and still claim self-defense.

Testimony in the case revealed that, after quarreling the day before, two men met the following morning and resumed their argument—the defendant armed with a knife, the deceased with a hickory stick. Because the defendant made the first offensive remarks, made the first effort to start a fight, and "by his movements, made the first hostile demonstration," Stone ruled that he could not claim self-defense. "A man may not bring on or provoke a difficulty, and then justify the use of deadly weapons, under the plea of self-defense," he concluded.[65] Further, Stone emphasized that the burden fell to the defendant to prove that the circumstances necessitated killing in self-defense. In *Cleveland v. State* (1888), a case involving a late-night murder on a Mobile sidewalk, Stone rejected the defendant's claims that the state had to prove that the slayer had a reasonable means of escaping the danger posed by the attacker. Instead, Stone upheld the lower court's conviction and affirmed that "the duty and burden were on the defendant to show the excuse and necessity for taking life."[66]

Despite waging this "principled courtroom campaign" against rampant killing, by the end of the nineteenth century Stone stood outside the American mainstream. Few voices in the nation's legal community seemed willing to condemn the evolution of the common-law understanding of homicide that was occurring in the United States.[67] After issuing a few ambiguous rulings on the duty to retreat in 1895–96, the U.S. Supreme Court followed the emerging trend among state courts by definitively adopting the no-duty-to-retreat rule in *Brown v. United States* (1921). Justice Oliver Wendell Holmes, writing for the Court, held that a man who had been previously threatened by another was not required to retreat from his knife-wielding assailant. The defendant, Brown, was thus justified in shooting his foe with a pistol concealed in his coat. Holmes contended that the common-law duty to retreat had evolved into new rules more "consistent with human nature." "Many respectable writers agree," Holmes wrote, "that if a man reasonably believes that he is in immediate danger of death or grievous bodily harm from his assailant, he may stand his ground, and that if he kills him, he has not exceeded the bounds of lawful self-defense." In typical fashion, Holmes concluded with a memorable phrase: "Detached reflection cannot be demanded in the presence of an uplifted knife."[68] Although the southern judiciary had demonstrated a firm commitment to the rule of law and a strict definition of self-defense throughout much of the nineteenth century, by the turn of the century the "stand one's ground" principle became the rule in the United States. Of southern supreme courts, Texas had proven more influential than Alabama. Most southern, central, and western states, along with the U.S. Supreme Court, rejected the duty-to-retreat doctrine. Only a handful of northeastern states as well as Alabama, South Carolina, and Florida retained the traditional common-law rule.[69]

Stone's decisions in homicide cases reflected his larger concern with curtailing rampant violence in Alabama. He consistently worked to change the state's law of concealed weapons, both by narrowing the legal loopholes that allowed gun toters to carry their arms and by encouraging the legislature to remove all such exceptions to the prohibition on carrying concealed weapons.[70] In another line of decisions, moreover, Stone carefully scrutinized the insanity defense and other forms of legal excuse and sought to increase the burden placed on defendants to prove their insanity. Stone's devotion to criminal-justice reform reflected more than a commitment to the fair administration of justice or even common-law principles. Throughout his life, this genteel lawyer expressed little sympathy or understanding for the raw culture of honor that governed the lives of so many in his home state and region. A devotee of arts and letters, Stone treasured flowers, violin music, and poetry; he was hardly typical of the roughneck culture of rural Alabama.[71] His unpretentious personal piety and even-tempered judicial professionalism set him apart from many of those whose fates he so often decided.

In the deepest sense, Stone desired his fellow Alabamians to endeavor to live by the same disciplined code of civility he believed he had so diligently attempted to follow all his life. To him, criminal-law reform was really about personal attitudes and individual behavior. Like other southern jurists, Stone conceived of appellate opinions as transcending the two parties involved in the dispute; he hoped to use his position as a forum to promote right behavior and the reformation of society.

Political Sectionalism and Legal Nationalism

Stone spent his last years busily engaged, "dividing the time between law and politics."[72] In 1889 and 1890, he delivered important addresses at the Alabama State Bar Association meeting on the necessity of judicial reform. Stone promoted the combination of common-law and equity jurisdiction into a single court system, advocated the simplification of pleading in civil suits, recommended that circuit judges hold monthly terms for probate court business in each of the state's counties, and urged an increase in the size of the supreme court. All of these changes, he felt, would assist in the fair and efficient administration of justice, particularly the merging of law and equity, which he believed would aid the "helpless" in securing their legal rights. Sounding the theme of progress, Stone observed the "wonderful" advances in industry, science, travel, and communication that had marked the nineteenth century. "It cannot be supposed," he said in 1889, "that judicial administration can or will stand still amid this stirring activity." Stone was right. Many of his ideas later became law.[73]

Stone's political involvement during these years consisted of strong partisan support for the Democratic ticket. With the party facing a serious challenge in 1892 from the Populists, leading Democrats in Alabama called on Stone and other prominent leaders to provide active support for the party at both the local and national levels. Although he had avoided active partisanship for much of his career, Stone wrote a series of essays in the state's newspapers pleading the Democratic cause. "By the memory and insults and indignities we have suffered, by the bitter memories of Reconstruction," he wrote, "by all the accumulated wrongs which have been heaped upon us in the last twenty-five years; and above all by the brighter recollection of the happier days during the earlier and better years of the republic, let us make one united, grand, heroic effort to elect a Democratic President."[74]

Stone's impassioned appeal demonstrated the importance that he and many Democrats attached to the campaign. To many white Democrats of his day, in Alabama and throughout the South, the 1892 election represented a renewed battle in the continuing contest over sectionalism and race. A political contest characterized by rumors and personal invective in Alabama, the election pitted agrarian Populists and Democrats against the state's "regular Democrats." These regular Democrats supported Grover Cleveland's presidential candidacy and linked their opponents to the Republican Party, the defeated "Force Bill," and the reimposition of Reconstruction. Stone's ardent support of Cleveland represented the Alabamian's enduring commitment to the southern way of life. His references to the "bitter memories of Reconstruction" and the "happier days" of the republic conjured up the ghosts of the Old South and sectional warfare. At a time when race relations were in flux in Alabama and the number of lynchings reached an all-time high, the state's voters overwhelmingly cast their ballots for Cleveland and the Democratic Party.[75]

Stone's political activism in the 1892 election constituted one of the "final public acts" of a member of the "Southern Civil War generation." The elder statesman hoped to instill in young southerners the desire to preserve the heritage of their fathers. Throughout his life and career, Stone identified with the traditions of the southern past. He exhibited political loyalty to the region through his strong support of secession and the Confederate nation, while his racial views and interpretation of the Fourteenth Amendment reflected established assumptions about the innate inferiority of blacks and the need for whites to treat their inferiors with paternalistic care and concern. Born early in the century, Stone possessed a link to the history of the South that many in the 1890s did not share. Through his life and judicial work, Stone sought to impart a sense of these values and traditions to his compatriots. Stone thus participated in the creation of the myth of the Lost Cause, whereby white southerners institutionalized then ritualized the remembrance of the war and the Confederate nation.[76]

At the same time, Stone's judicial service converged with the forging of an American legal culture at the end of the century. The first great American legal treatises appeared during the 1820s and 1830s—Chancellor Kent's *Commentaries* and Joseph Story's *Commentaries on the Conflict of Laws,* to name two of the most significant—but not until after the Civil War did the number of such works explode. Numerous treatises on railroad law, the law of negligence, corporate law, and constitutional law appeared, including two classics, Cooley's *Constitutional Limitations* and John F. Dillon's *Municipal Corporations.* The creation of the American Bar Association and other smaller professional organizations, as well as the proliferation of law journals, magazines, and published reports and the appearance of the *Index to Legal Periodicals,* all contributed to an increasingly integrated and professionalized bench and bar during the late nineteenth century. Perhaps most significant in this regard was the revolution in American legal education. From 1865 to 1900, the number of law schools in the United States increased sixfold, and the institutionalization of Christopher Columbus Langdell's case method of legal instruction ensured that aspiring lawyers throughout the country would receive in some sense similar preparation. By 1900 a maturing national legal culture was developing in the United States.[77]

Unlike his early-nineteenth-century counterparts, who often did their best with a copy of Blackstone and a few state reports, Stone operated within a legal environment that offered numerous sources of authority to an appellate judge. In his years on the Alabama Supreme Court, Stone was able to cite and to address the opinions of the U.S. Supreme Court and lower federal courts, state courts from all over the country, American treatise writers like Story and Cooley, and traditional sources like Blackstone. Stone's willingness to turn to the U.S. Supreme Court in civil-rights-related cases, moreover, especially given the South's rocky relationship with the Court throughout the century, certainly attests to at least some degree of national convergence regarding legal norms and institutional authority. His reliance on the principles established by Lemuel Shaw and elaborated by Cooley in the area of economic regulation further undermines the notion that late-nineteenth-century southern appellate judges were narrow provincialists.

By the close of his life, none of Stone's contemporaries doubted that he had attained the rank of a great jurist. In 1893, a year before his death, the Alabama Bar Association gathered in honor of the fiftieth anniversary of his initial appointment to the bench. From all over the state and from the entire country, members of the legal community assembled to pay homage to the aging chief justice of the Alabama Supreme Court. After reading a resolution commending Stone for his half century of service, members of the association presented the judge with an engraved silver cup. Stone then delivered a "brief, untheatrical" response in which he graciously thanked his colleagues and affirmed his basic belief in the necessity of honesty and moral uprightness.[78] In the days after this assembly, Stone received dozens of letters from members of the Alabama bar, all of them praising his judicial and personal achievements. "Your name honors Alabama, the South, and our general country," wrote one admirer. "Your decisions make our Reports valuable, and your personal character will shape and form for good the life of many a young man."[79]

Judge George Washington Stone had indeed made an indelible mark upon the law of his state. At his death in 1894, the *Birmingham Age Herald* wrote that "he impressed himself on the judicial jurisprudence of the State as no other Justice has. Of the fifteen Chief Justices he stands pre-eminent."[80] Perhaps the greatest testament to his impact as a judge was the extraordinary number of opinions he wrote—2,449, according to a leading authority.[81] Stone's incisive and voluminous writings helped make the Alabama Supreme Court, in the words of New York's *Albany Law Journal,* "one of the ablest in this country" and helped repair the tarnished reputation of southern state courts in general after the Civil War. Once described as a "patient, plodding lawyer," Stone's career demonstrated his ability to accomplish with efficiency and skill nearly any task laid before him. Although he did not possess the personal charisma of Lumpkin, the innovative spirit of Hemphill, or the political savvy of Ruffin, Stone displayed a persistence and professional competence in all of his judicial efforts. Most important, like those southern jurists of the previous generation, Stone hoped that his numerous opinions would ultimately help reshape the society in which he lived.[82]

Southern Judges and American Legal Culture

Legal nationalism and political sectionalism defined the lives and work of nineteenth-century state judges in the American South. National unity and integration increasingly characterized American legal culture by century's end: southern judges read the same case reports, law treatises, magazines, and journals as their northern colleagues, while southern jurists conceived of the judicial role and created a body of substantive judicial opinions in many ways comparable to their counterparts. Sectionalism manifested itself in southern judges' commitment to secession before the war, redemption during the Reconstruction period, and the Democratic Party and Lost Cause ideology during the late nineteenth century. Although conformity to national standards characterized much of their judicial work, jurists in the states of the Confederacy continually expressed loyalty to the South through their political activities and cultural identification.

Southern judges' conception of the judicial role in many respects mirrored national trends. Throughout the nineteenth century, southern state judges viewed themselves as essential actors in the process of lawmaking. As the social and cultural ties that the revolutionary generation had held to the English began to fade, southern judges, especially in the new states carved out of the frontier, paid less attention to precedent and more to the demands of society. John Catron thus criticized the citation of a "parade of authorities" in his judicial opinions as he sought to distribute state lands to squatters rather than to speculators. Joseph Henry Lumpkin gushed about dismantling ancient doctrines, even if they had been built by "the trowel of Blackstone and the masonic genius of a hundred Chief Justiciaries," while he ruled in favor of new bridges in the public interest. John Hemphill and his colleagues, often operating without any law books except a copy of Joseph White's *New Collection of Laws,* expanded Mexican homestead-exemption principles in Texas practically by judicial fiat. None of these judges, of course, ever expressed a desire to completely discard precedent. Especially when it came to the law of homicide, southern jurists in general proceeded cautiously and ruled in accordance with Blackstonian tradition. Yet in many cases involving property, contracts, corporations, and slaves, southern judges interpreted statutes and common law in such a way as to fit the changing needs of their society. In this way, their behavior followed the innovative style of judging evident nationally during the antebellum era.[1]

In his study of nineteenth-century American judging, legal historian Peter Karsten distinguishes between the jurisprudence of the "heart" and of the "head" by describing formalistic tendencies as driven by the head's devotion to precedent and innovation as based on the heart's willingness to change ancient doctrines to assist the weak. Yet the experiences of southern jurists show that Karsten draws his lines too sharply. In general, nineteenth-century southern judges saw themselves as ruled by their hearts—by protecting life, opposing special interests, and advancing paternalism—yet in so doing they at times clung to established common-law principles. For example, southern judges' devotion to Blackstonian ideals regarding the law of homicide issued from concerns both of precedent and humanitarianism. Southern judges, at least when it came to homicide, believed that precedent—rather than the values of their society—was right, just, and beneficent. Southern judges innovated when they believed American society required new legal prescriptions—in the distribution of lands and homesteads and in the building of new bridges and railroads. But these jurists clung to tradition in homicide cases when they believed contemporary society undermined their deeply held beliefs about the value of human life. In this sense, as Karsten concludes, the story of nineteenth-century judging was one both of reverence for ancient doctrines and of the creation of new ones.[2]

In deciding either to adhere to or to discard precedent, southern judges always considered society's interest as paramount. William Wiethoff, a professor of communication, describes this as southern jurists' "judicial sense of civic humanism"—their conceptions of "themselves as trustworthy guardians because of their moral tendencies."[3] Whatever the terminology, southern judges saw themselves as playing a significant role in their society as both makers of law and models of gentility. Despite continued popular threats to the existence of their tribunals, because of their high social standing southern state judges saw it as their duty and obligation to create the good society. Even with the gradual proliferation of case reports and law treatises, and even as southern judges cited more of these authorities in their judicial opinions, late-nineteenth-century southern jurists did not cease to conceive of judging as occurring within a social context. George W. Stone, for example, viewed the law as a "living" part of American society. "Law pervades every human transaction, every question of status, every inquiry of right and wrong, as vital force pervades every fibre, every corpuscle of the living animal," he wrote in 1887. Contrary to the formalistic mode of judicial decision making described by many legal historians as characteristic of this period, Stone viewed many of the cases before him as "resolution[s] of competing social issues" rather than conflicts between individual litigants. This willingness to employ judicial review, make policy, and set a social example helped quell the popular opposition to judicial authority that characterized early-nineteenth-century southern judicial history.[4]

If southern judges in many respects followed national patterns in terms of their conception of the judicial role, as the century wore on the substance of their opinions also increasingly mirrored American judicial thinking. By the 1890s the United States became a more united nation than it had been in nearly half a century. When northerners and southerners went off to fight the Spanish in 1898, the rise of corporations, the growth of trade and professional organizations, and the appearance of an increasingly urban mass culture all helped wipe away the "island communities" that had characterized nineteenth-century American life. As economic conflict and ethnocultural tensions replaced sectionalism as the dominant features of American politics, sectional distinctions faded from constitutional and legal debates.[5] In the four areas of substantive law discussed in this book—homicide, economic development, federalism, and race—the North and South began to resemble each other more closely than they had since the revolutionary era.

By the end of the century, northern and southern judges deciding homicide cases agreed in rejecting the Blackstonian principle of the "duty to retreat." Rulings in Indiana, Ohio, and Texas—eventually supported by the U.S. Supreme Court—all announced that an individual could "stand his ground" and kill his attacker in self-defense. Judge George W. Stone's efforts notwithstanding, the nation moved away from the common-law heritage and toward this new American view. Violence, an American way of life according to historian Richard M. Brown, thus received official judicial approbation by century's end. Judge William E. Niblack of the Indiana Supreme Court perhaps best captured the national consensus among judges and commentators on this issue when he asserted in *Runyan v. State*, "The tendency of the American mind seems to be very strongly against the enforcement of any rule which requires a person to flee when assailed, to avoid chastisement or even to save human life."[6] Americans, Niblack implied, valued courage, honor, and physical prowess more than the preservation of life itself. Such a view prevailed in

American law, even though Stone and handful of others, particularly Harvard Law Professor Joseph H. Beale Jr., warned of the consequences. In a pair of law-review articles at the turn of the century, Beale condemned the idea of "no duty to retreat" as a retrograde symbol of the problems besetting the nation's criminal-justice system. "The duel, war, and lynching show the unnecessary failure of law; so does the doctrine of *Runyan v. State*," Beale boldly pronounced.[7] Indeed, in such a changed legal environment—where courts degraded the value of human life—lynching could thrive. By the 1890s neither northern nor southern state judges seemed particularly alarmed by this steady move toward lawlessness.

During the 1890s the "police powers jurisprudence" that emerged in the early-nineteenth-century South came to dominate American constitutional and legal thinking. Throughout the century, southern judges elevated community interest over special privilege and, in cases where regulatory statutes were at issue, upheld only those measures that, in their view, legitimately served the public good. Upholding legislative power to alter corporate charters, distributing lands to frontier settlers, and granting wide legislative discretion to exercise power of eminent domain all served the public interest according to southern jurists, while implied monopolies did not. Eventually, this opposition to "class legislation" merged with higher-law constitutionalism. Thus, John Catron's 1831 pronouncement in *Wally's Heirs v. Kennedy* that "the rights of every individual must stand or fall by the same rule of law, that governs every other member of the body politic" combined with Thomas Ruffin's concern in *Hoke v. Henderson* with upholding "the law of the land." The result became enshrined in American legal and constitutional thought through the subsequent decisions of state judges and the writings of Thomas Cooley.[8] A series of famous cases in northern states, including *In re Jacobs* (1885), in which the high court of New York struck down a statute prohibiting the making of cigars in tenement dwellings, and *Ritchie v. People* (1895) in which the Supreme Court of Illinois invalidated a maximum-hours law for women working in the garment industry, exhibited the opposition to such regulations. The southern judiciary's emphasis on the public good, therefore, became part of a general consensus within the national legal community that emphasized the distinction between beneficial public-purpose legislation and unfair "class legislation." Although Cooley's *Constitutional Limitations* best captured the constitutional and legal values of the late-nineteenth-century American judiciary on this matter, southern judges operating in the Jacksonian tradition—especially Catron and Ruffin—made an important contribution to this strand of American legal thought.[9]

By century's end, debates over federalism had little relevance to sectional differences. The advocates of state sovereignty and secession during the nineteenth century had often looked to this constitutional theory to promote sectional or regional agendas, particularly white supremacy. Spencer Roane's long-standing commitment to the principles of state sovereignty became even deeper in the midst of the Missouri Crisis, when he feared that "our slaves are incited to insurrection." Similarly, John Catron, Andrew Jackson's judicial agent in Tennessee during the Cherokee removal, embraced the theory of state sovereignty, despite his earlier opposition to nullification, to expunge any Cherokee claims to sovereignty in Tennessee.[10] Both Roane and Catron specifically criticized U.S. Supreme Court rulings: Roane attacked the Court's decisions in *Martin v. Hunter's Lessee* (1816), *McCulloch v. Maryland* (1819), and *Cohens v. Virginia* (1821); Catron assailed *Worcester v. Georgia* (1832). But the national government's flagging commitment to the enforcement of civil rights after Reconstruction marked the end of sectionally based debate over the position of the states relative to that of the nation, particularly the states' need to adhere to opinions of the U.S. Supreme Court. Southern state courts embraced the U.S. Supreme Court's initial interpretation of the Reconstruction amendments—that the amendments had not revolutionized the relationship between the national government and the states. Judge Stone thus approvingly cited U.S. Supreme Court rulings in the *Slaughterhouse Cases* (1873) and *U.S. v. Cruikshank* (1876), which fitted with southerners' belief in local autonomy over matters of civil rights. When new debates over economic regulation came to dominate constitutional discourse about federalism after Reconstruction, the issue did not polarize the judiciary along sectional lines. The preservation of state power mattered most to southern jurists—and to most white southerners—when it involved the issues of race and civil rights.[11]

During the last decade of the nineteenth century, a national consensus arose in America on the issue of race. While the southern judiciary's record in the area of slavery and race relations had been its most distinctive characteristic throughout the century, American culture—North and South— reverberated with racism during the 1890s. White America's relative silence on the subject of lynching, the U.S. Supreme Court's sanctioning of legal segregation in *Plessy v. Ferguson* (1896), the scientific and social scientific communities' espousal of new theories of white supremacy, and the U.S. policy of racial imperialism beginning with the Spanish-American War all revealed the degree to which white Americans North and South could agree that they reigned superior over blacks and other darker-skinned peoples, both domestic and foreign. Though clear differences had characterized northern and southern judicial records on racial issues before the Civil War, by the end of the century the constitutional and legal guarantees of civil rights of African Americans lay dormant and unenforced. Judicial interpretation of state constitutions and the U.S. Constitution rendered these documents, for the time being, impotent and unimportant as statements of rights.[12]

The nationalism and sectionalism evident in the southern judicial tradition converged in the constitutional and legal establishment of white supremacy at the turn of the century. Questions surrounding slavery, race, and civil rights had lain at the heart of southern judicial distinctiveness throughout the century, and when northern jurists abandoned the legal commitment to African Americans that they had exhibited in antebellum cases involving fugitives, differences between the judiciaries of the sections ceased to be significant or relevant. The vast majority of northern and southern state judges could agree on white supremacy and black inferiority. Such judicial racism reflected the broader outlines of American culture at the turn of the century, for in literature, music, and art as well as in law, the sectionalism of the Lost Cause combined with the nationalism surrounding the war with Spain.[13]

Decades later, in the middle of the twentieth century, when activists renewed the call for racial justice and civil rights, southern state judges would reassert the spirit of nineteenth-century racism. As the national legal order initiated a revolution in civil rights, southern state appellate courts, as Michael Meltsner wrote in the 1960s, would become a "dead end" in the pursuit of equality under law.[14] Sectionalism—though it had existed alongside nationalizing tendencies in nineteenth-century America—would again emerge within the southern judiciary.

NOTES

INTRODUCTION: SOUTHERNERS, JUDGES, AND SOUTHERN JUDGES

1. Hall, "Route to Hell," 244–50; Hall, "Promises and Perils." The few African Americans who served briefly on state benches during Reconstruction were not typical of the nineteenth-century southern judicial experience and consequently are not included here.

For the purposes of this study, the term *American* does not include the states and territories of the Far West, as nearly all of my comparisons are to the judiciaries of the northeastern and midwestern United States.

2. *Commonwealth v. Caton,* 8 Va. 5 (1782); *Bayard v. Singleton,* 1 N.C. 42 (1787); Clinton, *Marbury v. Madison,* 43–55; G. Edward White, *American Judicial Tradition,* 7–63.

3. Pound, *Formative Era;* Haar, *Golden Age;* Gilmore, *Ages,* 19–40.

4. For this debate, see Horwitz, *Transformation, 1780–1860,* 1–30, 253–66; Horwitz, *Transformation, 1870–1960,* 9–31; William Nelson, "Impact"; Scheiber, "Instrumentalism." Karsten, *Heart versus Head,* has recently challenged this dominant view. My conclusion takes fuller account of Karsten's findings.

5. On the question of southern attitudes toward formal law, see Sydnor, "Southerner"; Ayers, *Vengeance,* 31–33; Cash, *Mind,* 31–34; *Chisholm v. Georgia,* 2 Dallas (2 U.S.) 419 (1793); *Martin v. Hunter's Lessee,* 1 Wheaton (14 U.S.) 304 (1816); *Cohens v. Virginia,* 6 Wheaton (19 U.S.) 264 (1821); *Cherokee Nation v. Georgia,* 5 Peters (30 U.S.) 1 (1831); *Worcester v. Georgia,* 6 Peters (31 U.S.) 515 (1832).

6. "Speech of Mr. Allen of Smith, in Committee of the Whole House, upon the Following Preamble and Resolution," in Robert H. White, ed., *Messages,* 2:365; Saye, *Constitutional History,* 185–86; Manley, Brown, and Rise, *Supreme Court,* 154–70; Hall, "Route to Hell," 229; Ely and Bodenhamer, "Regionalism and the Legal History," 16–17.

7. Title XVIII, no. 62, *Acts of the General Assembly of the State of Georgia.*

8. Wiethoff, *Peculiar Humanism,* 14–34; *Birmingham Age Herald,* March 13, 1894.

9. On southern distinctiveness in general, see Smiley, "Quest"; Carl N. Degler, *Place over Time,* 1–25; Faust, "Peculiar South."

10. Franklin, *Militant South;* Wyatt-Brown, *Southern Honor;* Ayers, *Vengeance;* Bruce, *Violence and Culture.*

11. Redfield, *Homicide,* 120, 18.

12. Richard Maxwell Brown, "Southern Violence," 233; Finkelman, "Exploring," 105.

13. Genovese, *Political Economy,* 180–208.

14. Hurst, *Law;* Horwitz, *Transformation, 1780–1860;* G. Edward White, *American Judicial Tradition;* Ely and Bodenhamer, "Regionalism and American Legal History," 549–55; Ely and Bodenhamer, "Regionalism and the Legal History," 7.

15. *Currie's Administrators v. Mutual Assurance Society,* 14 Va. 315, 347–48 (1809). Although invariably protecting and promoting the interests of slaveholders, in most instances southern state judges did not perceive masters as a "special interest" harmful to the public good.

16. Gillman, *Constitution Besieged;* Benedict, "Laissez-Faire"; Novak, *People's Welfare.*

17. Gillman, *Constitution Besieged,* 101–93.

18. Schlesinger, "State Rights Fetish," 234–56; Bestor, "State Sovereignty"; Finkelman, "States' Rights," 128–29.

19. Finkelman, *Imperfect Union;* Finkelman, "States' Rights," 125. On O'Neall, see Nash, "Negro Rights."

20. See, e.g., Tushnet, *American Law;* Nash, "Fairness"; Fede, *People;* Thomas D. Morris, *Southern Slavery.*

21. William W. Fisher III, "Ideology"; Wiethoff, *Peculiar Humanism,* 35–74; Wahl, "Legal Constraints." On slavery and southern political culture, see Greenberg, *Masters;* Cooper, *Liberty;* Cooper, *South.*

22. On northern courts and the U.S. Supreme Court, see McBride, "Mid-Atlantic State Courts"; Nieman, *Promises,* 78–113; Ely, *Chief Justiceship,* 155–60.

23. Finkelman, "Prelude," 415–82.

24. Potter, "Historian's Use of Nationalism," 75.

25. I accept Kermit L. Hall's definition of legal culture: "the matrix of values, attitudes, and assumptions that have shaped both the operation and the perception of the law" (*Magic Mirror,* 6).

CHAPTER ONE: SPENCER ROANE, VIRGINIA LEGAL CULTURE, AND THE RISE OF A SOUTHERN JUDICIARY

1. Horsnell, *Spencer Roane,* 2–3; "Roane Family," 199; Mays, "Judge Spencer Roane," 446; Edwin J. Smith, "Spencer Roane," 4–5; Breen, *Tobacco Culture.*

2. Slaughter, *Settlers,* 114; Breen, *Tobacco Culture,* 31–32; Evans, "Private Indebtedness."

3. "Biographical Sketch of Spencer Roane, Esq.," *Richmond Enquirer,* September 17, 1822.

4. Gelbach, "Spencer Roane," 6–7; Alan M. Smith, "Virginia Lawyers," 77–81.

5. Adams, *Circulars,* 38–39; Roeber, *Faithful Magistrates,* 167. See also Devitt, "William and Mary"; Hughes, "William and Mary," 40–43.

6. Ellis, *Jeffersonian Crisis,* 119–21; Shepard, "George Wythe," 90–91; Bryson, *Legal Education,* 21.

7. Bryson, *Legal Education,* 22–23.

8. "Biographical Sketch of Spencer Roane, Esq."; "Judge Spencer Roane," 1242; Horsnell, *Spencer Roane*, 6–7; Gelbach, "Spencer Roane," 8.

9. *Calendar*, 3:361, 411–12. On Virginia lawyers and their penchant for political pursuits, see Shepard, "Lawyers."

10. "Judge Spencer Roane," 1242–43.

11. Slaughter, *Settlers*, 73–74; Gelbach, "Spencer Roane," 14.

12. Slaughter, *Settlers*, 74; "Judge Spencer Roane's Memorandum," in George Morgan, *True Patrick Henry*, 441.

13. Smith, "Spencer Roane," 6; *Calendar*, 4:31; Horsnell, *Spencer Roane*, 17.

14. Henry to daughter Anne in Henry, ed., *Patrick Henry*, 2:305; "Judge Spencer Roane's Memorandum," in George Morgan, *True Patrick Henry*, 441. Roane once wrote of Henry's oratorical abilities, "I have myself heard some touches of eloquence from him which would almost disgrace Cicero or Demosthenes" (Roane to Philip Aylett, June 26, 1788, in "Letters of Spencer Roane," 167).

15. Slaughter, *Settlers*, 74; Roane to governor of Virginia, September 3, 1787, in *Calendar*, 4:338–39.

16. Newman Brockenbrough, William Latane, John Brockenbrough, John Beale, Henry Garnett, William Waring and Robert L. Waring, justices, to Governor Randolph, March 27, 1788, in *Calendar*, 4:417; Slaughter, *Settlers*, 75.

17. "Letter of a Plain Dealer, accredited to Spencer Roane, and printed in the *Virginia Independent Chronicle*, February, 1788," in Ford, ed., *Essays*, 389–92; Roane to Philip Aylett, June 26, 1788, in "Letters of Spencer Roane," 167. The later adoption of the Bill of Rights dispelled many of Roane's fears about the Constitution ("Judge Spencer Roane," 1243–44).

18. "Judge Spencer Roane," 1244; *Hylton v. United States*, 3 Dallas (3 U.S.) 171 (1796).

19. Gelbach, "Spencer Roane," 26–30.

20. Mays, "Judge Spencer Roane," 449; "Judge Spencer Roane," 1243–44; Mays, *Edmund Pendleton*, 2:299.

21. On these changing conceptions of the judicial role, see Horwitz, *Transformation, 1780–1860*, 1–30.

22. *Commonwealth v. Caton*, 8 Va. 5, 8 (1782); Kirtland, *George Wythe*, 216–19. See also Mays, *Edmund Pendleton*, 2:187–202. Mays notes that Judge James Mercer moved beyond Wythe and actually declared the law unconstitutional. Because the reporter's record did not contain the opinion (Mays discovered it in Pendleton's notes), Wythe has received most of the credit for originating judicial review in Virginia.

23. *Cases of the Judges of the Court of Appeals*, 8 Va. 135 (1788). In the *Cases of the Judges*, the Court of Appeals challenged a legislatively enacted reorganization of the court system by arguing that the legislature could not impose new duties on the judiciary without its consent. While not declaring the act unconstitutional, the judges collectively issued a remonstrance urging that the judiciary remain indepen-

dent of legislative control. Judicial review also emerged in *Turner v. Turner's Executor* (1792), where Judge Edmund Pendleton held unconstitutional the legislature's enactment of an ex post facto law as "oppressive and contrary to the spirit of the Constitution" (8 Va. 234, 237). See also Thomas R. Morris, *Virginia Supreme Court*, 11–12; Horsnell, *Spencer Roane*, 22.

24. *Bayard v. Singleton*, 1 N.C. 42 (N.C. 1787); *Ham v. M'Claws*, 1 Bay 93 (S.C. 1789); William Nelson, "Changing Conceptions," 1167; Clinton, *Marbury v. Madison*, 76–77; Hall, *Magic Mirror*, 64; Haines, *American Doctrine*; Goebel, *History*, 1:125–42; Meigs, "Relation," 175.

25. *Kamper v. Hawkins*, 3 Va. 20, 22 (1793); Cullen, *St. George Tucker*, 85.

26. 3 Va. 20, 79, 81; Cullen, *St. George Tucker*; John Randolph Tucker, "St. George Tucker." Unlike any of his colleagues in *Kamper*, Tucker also contended that one of the fundamental principles behind the Constitution was the absolute separation of law and equity jurisdiction. In this sense, Tucker's opinion went farther than Roane's; however, by imbuing the Constitution with this particular principle, Tucker did not necessarily advocate a more forceful implementation of judicial review than did Roane.

27. 3 Va. 20, 35–36.

28. 3 Va. 20, 40, 87.

29. 3 Va. 20, 36–38.

30. 3 Va. 20, 38–39.

31. 3 Va. 20, 39–42.

32. The constitutionality of a law was at issue in only thirty-five cases in the Virginia courts before the Civil War. Of these cases, laws were declared unconstitutional in only two (Margaret Nelson, *Study*, 32). The U.S. Supreme Court, of course, declared only two laws of Congress unconstitutional—in *Marbury v. Madison* (1803) and in *Dred Scott v. Sandford* (1857).

33. *Jones v. Commonwealth*, 5 Va. 555, 556–57 (1799).

34. *Currie's Administrators v. Mutual Assurance Society*, 14 Va. 315, 347, 348–49 (1809). On the Virginia Court of Appeals's reliance on unwritten natural law, see Sherry, "Early Virginia Tradition."

35. See Smith, "Spencer Roane," 8–9; Radabaugh, "Spencer Roane"; Margaret Nelson, *Study*, 31–38. Nelson writes, "Judge Roane, more than any other person, helped to establish the practice of judicial review in Virginia" (*Study*, 32).

36. Mays, "Judge Spencer Roane," 451; "Roane, Spencer"; "Biographical Sketch," *Richmond Enquirer*, September 17, 1822; Mays, *Edmund Pendleton*, 2:300.

37. Thomas R. Morris, *Virginia Supreme Court*, 65–67; Miller, *Juries and Judges*, 69–73.

38. Order Book, Supreme Court of Appeals, VI, 161f., Friday, December 2, 1808, as quoted in Beach, "Spencer Roane," 11–12, and paraphrased in Gelbach, "Spencer Roane," 43. Roane probably did not act from personal motives in introducing the resolutions, as the nature of the resolutions, particularly the one regarding wit-

ness testimony, was such that Roane would necessarily have benefited little from their implementation.

39. Miller, *Judges and Juries*, 71; St. George Tucker to Judge William Fleming, May 10, 1809, Wooldridge-Fleming-Stanard Papers.

40. "Opinion on the Question of the Rights of the Judges, Propounded in Open Court, by Judge Roane, May 11th 1809," St. George Tucker to Judge William Fleming, May 11, 1809, and Judge Creed Taylor to Judge William Fleming, April 20, 1810, all in Wooldridge-Fleming-Stanard Papers; Miller, *Judges and Juries*, 71–72.

41. Judge St. George Tucker to the governor, April 2, 1811, in 16 Va. 289–91; Miller, *Judges and Juries*, 72. Roane was probably not the impetus behind the judicial reorganization act because most people figured that he stood to lose some of his power with the new appointments of Francis T. Brooke, William H. Cabell, and John Coalter. Cabell was a friend of Tucker's, and Coalter was Tucker's son-in-law.

42. Mays, *Edmund Pendleton*, 2:300.

43. These figures are derived from all reported cases between April 3, 1811, and September 4, 1822. Not all cases appeared in print.

44. *Ballard v. Leavell & al.*, 9 Va. 531, 533 (1805); *Young v. Gregorie and Another*, 7 Va. 446, 451 (1803); *Johnson and Others v. Johnson's Widow and Heirs*, 15 Va. 549 (1810).

45. *Baring v. Reeder*, 11 Va. 154, 158 (1806).

46. Kirtland, *George Wythe*, 232; Mays, *Edmund Pendleton*, 2:300–301; Horton, *James Kent*, 193–96, 269–74; Newmyer, *Supreme Court Justice Joseph Story*, 243–48; *Baring v. Reeder*, 11 Va. 154, 162–63.

47. *Claiborne and Wife v. Henderson and Others, and Henderson and Others v. Claiborne and Wife*, 13 Va. 322, 375–76 (1809). In other instances as well, Roane overlooked Virginia precedents and turned instead to English authorities. See, e.g., *Commonwealth v. Martin's Executors and Devisees*, 19 Va. 117 (1816), *Harrison Dance's Case*, 19 Va. 349 (1817).

48. 11 Va. 154, 163.

49. Thomas R. Morris, *Virginia Supreme Court*, 68.

50. *Richmond Enquirer*, August 13, 1811, June 28, 1815; Agreement between Spencer Roane and Oliver Brand for sale of corn, September 15, 1809, Brand Papers.

51. Wiecek, *Sources*, 142–43; *Hudgins v. Wrights*, 11 Va. 134 (1806); *Rankin v. Lydia*, 9 Ken. 467 (1820); *Lunsford v. Coquillon*, 2 Martin (N.S.) 401 (La. 1824). See also Finkelman, *Imperfect Union*, 404–8.

52. *Pleasants v. Pleasants*, 6 Va. 319 (1800). For discussions of this famous case, see Cover, *Justice Accused*, 69–72; Horsnell, *Spencer Roane*, 82–84; Thomas D. Morris, *Southern Slavery*, 404–8.

53. Cover, *Justice Accused*, 67–70; 6 Va. 319. The 1782 law stated "that it shall hereafter be lawful for any person by his or her last will and testament, or by any other instrument in writing, under his or her hand and seal attested and proved in the county court by two witnesses, or acknowledged by the party in the court of the

county where he or she resides, to emancipate and set free his or her slaves, or any of them."

54. 6 Va. 319, 339.

55. 6 Va. 319, 346–57; Thomas D. Morris, *Southern Slavery,* 405.

56. 6 Va. 319, 335–36.

57. 6 Va. 319. 340, 344.

58. *Charles v. Hunnicutt,* 9 Va. 311 (1804).

59. Cover, *Justice Accused,* 72; 9 Va. 311, 324, 326.

60. *Wilson v. Isbell,* 9 Va. 425 (1805).

61. *Woodley v. Abby,* 9 Va. 336, 342, 343 (1805).

62. *Patty v. Colin,* 11 Va. 519 (1807); 9 Va. 336, 343. After Roane's death, the Virginia Court of Appeals moved increasingly away from the liberty-oriented stance it had taken in the late 1790s, as evidenced by the much-discussed case of *Maria v. Surbaugh* (23 Va. 228 [1824]). See Cover, *Justice Accused,* 74; Thomas D. Morris, *Southern Slavery,* 406–9.

63. St. George Tucker, *Dissertation;* Edmund Morgan, *American Slavery,* 385; Winthrop D. Jordan, *White over Black,* 555–60.

64. *Hudgins v. Wright,* 11 Va. 134, 141 (1806).

65. Bruce A. Campbell, "John Marshall," 45–46.

66. *Turner v. Turner's Executrix,* 8 Va. 234, 237 (1792); Bruce A. Campbell, "John Marshall," 47.

67. *Elliott's Executor v. Lyell,* 7 Va. 268, 279, 280 (1802).

68. *Turpin v. Locket,* 10 Va. 113, 169 (1804).

69. *Currie's Administrators v. Mutual Assurance Society,* 14 Va. 315 (1809); Horsnell, *Spencer Roane,* 97–98.

70. 14 Va. 315, 347–48.

71. *Dartmouth College v. Woodward,* 4 Wheaton (17 U.S.) 518 (1819); 14 Va. 315, 352.

72. 14 Va. 315, 352; Horsnell, *Spencer Roane,* 102.

73. Roane to James Barbar, December 29, 1819, in "Missouri Compromise," 8; G. Edward White, *American Judicial Tradition,* 50; Horton, *James Kent,* 165–66; *Emans v. Turnbull,* 2 Johns. (N.Y.) 318, 322 (1807).

74. G. Edward White, *American Judicial Tradition,* 61.

75. 6 Va. 319, 344.

76. See, e.g., Olken, "John Marshall."

77. Miller, "Richmond Junto," 67.

78. Miller, "Richmond Junto," 67. In 1822, some Virginians considered Roane to be a serious presidential candidate for the election of 1824. Roane died, however, later in 1822 (F. W. Gilmer to John Randolph, January 27, 1822, in "Letters of Francis Walker Gilmer," 190–91).

79. Channing, *History,* 5 : 406–7; Kerr, "If Spencer Roane Had Been Appointed," 172. Channing wrote, "One can trace the [secession] movement directly from him to Ft. Sumter."

80. Roane to James Monroe, December 6, 1817, Monroe Papers.

81. *Hunter v. Martin,* 18 Va. 1 (1814), reprinted in *Richmond Enquirer,* February 1, 1816; *Fairfax's Devisee v. Hunter's Lessee,* 7 Cranch (11 U.S.) 603 (1813). The Supreme Court, of course, eventually challenged the Virginia Court of Appeals's refusal to adhere to *Fairfax* by issuing a second decision in *Martin v. Hunter's Lessee* (1816). This case presented, through the clash of two important judicial tribunals, the larger question of sovereignty in the new nation. See Miller, "John Marshall."

82. 18 Va. 1, 33.

83. 18 Va. 1, 34.

84. *Commonwealth v. Cobbett,* 3 Dallas 467 (1799).

85. 18 Va. 1, 31–32, 52–53.

86. Historians now agree that there is no evidence to support the claim that as president, Jefferson would have appointed Roane as Chief Justice of the United States had Adams not selected John Marshall just prior to leaving office in 1801. Jefferson and Roane probably did not have any contact with each other until about 1808, well after Adams's appointment of Marshall. Beach, "Judge Spencer Roane," 41; Gelbach, "Spencer Roane," 105; and Horsnell, *Spencer Roane,* 33–34, all concur on this issue.

87. Jefferson to Roane, October 12, 1815, Roane to Jefferson, October 22, 1815, Jefferson Papers, ser. 1; Patterson, *Constitutional Principles,* 151–54; Mayer, *Constitutional Thought,* 185–208.

88. Roane to James Barbour, January 4, 1815, in "Letters of Spencer Roane," 169.

89. *McCulloch v. Maryland,* 4 Wheaton (17 U.S.) 316 (1819); *Richmond Enquirer,* June 11, 15, 18, 22, 1819. These essays, published under the pseudonym "Hampden," are reprinted in Gunther, ed., *John Marshall's Defense,* 106–54.

90. Roane to James Barbour, January 4, 1815, February 16, 1819, in "Letters of Spencer Roane," 168–69, 172; Roane to William H. Roane, February 16, 1819, in "Roane Correspondence," 136.

91. Gunther, *John Marshall's Defense,* 138–39.

92. Gunther, *John Marshall's Defense,* 124.

93. Gunther, *John Marshall's Defense,* 121.

94. Gunther, *John Marshall's Defense,* 135.

95. Gunther, *John Marshall's Defense,* 111, 151–52.

96. Jefferson to Roane, September 6, 1819, in Ford, ed., *Writings,* 10:140–43; Roane to James Barbour, January 30, 1819, in "Letters of Spencer Roane," 171–72.

97. Harry L. Watson, *Liberty,* 70–72; Fehrenbacher, *Constitutions,* 45–50; Roane to James Barbour, December 29, 1819, in "Missouri Compromise," 7–8.

98. Roane to James Monroe, February 16, 1820, in "Letters of Spencer Roane," 174–75. See also Roane to James Barbour, February 19, 1820, in "Missouri Compromise," 17–18.

99. See Wiecek, *Sources,* 126–49, for a discussion of the significance of the Missouri Crisis for American constitutional history.

100. *Cohens v. Virginia,* 6 Wheaton (19 U.S.) 264 (1821); Newmyer, *Supreme Court under Marshall and Taney,* 47–48; G. Edward White, *Marshall Court,* 504–24.

101. Roane essay in *Richmond Enquirer,* in Kutler, *John Marshall,* 108.

102. Roane essay in *Richmond Enquirer,* in Kutler, *John Marshall,* 112, 111; Roane to Archibald Thweatt, December 11, 1821, in "Roane Correspondence," 140–41.

103. G. Edward White, *Marshall Court,* 523; Roane to Archibald Thweatt, December 24, 1821, in "Roane Correspondence," 141–42.

104. Sutton, "Nostalgia"; Jefferson to John Holmes, April 22, 1820, in Ford, ed., *Writings,* 10:157.

CHAPTER TWO: JOHN CATRON, JACKSONIAN JURISPRUDENCE, AND THE EXPANSION OF THE SOUTH

1. On Catron the U.S. Supreme Court justice, see Chandler, "Centenary"; Gass, "Constitutional Opinions"; Gatell, "John Catron"; Nash, "John Catron"; Swisher, *History.*

2. Dunlap, "Judge John Catron," 171–72.

3. Guild, *Old Times,* 459; Ingersoll, "John Catron," 4:247; Catron, "Biographical Letter," 2:805–7.

4. Hale and Merritt, *History,* 3:835; Chandler, "Centenary," 32–33; "Biographical Letter," 2:807.

5. Ingersoll, "John Catron," 248; Chandler, "Centenary," 33–34; Catron, "Biographical Letter," 2:807.

6. Clayton, *History,* 364, 257; Chandler, "Centenary," 50; Foote, *Bench and Bar,* 145; Ingersoll, "John Catron," 251; Catron, "Biographical Letter," 2:809.

7. Laughlin, "Sketches," 76–77; Chandler, "Centenary," 34. On Laughlin, see Frank B. Williams Jr., "Samuel Hervey Laughlin."

8. Samuel C. Williams, *Phases,* 75; Marks, "Supreme Court," 120; Frierson, "Some Incidents," 148–49.

9. Samuel C. Williams, *Phases,* 29–45; Marks, "Supreme Court," 123–25; Caldwell, *Sketches,* 33.

10. "Report to the Judiciary Committee of the House of Representatives, in Relation to the Supreme Court of Errors and Appeals," in Robert H. White, ed., *Messages,* 2:353–55.

11. *Public Acts Passed at the Stated Session,* chap. 52; Robert H. White, ed., *Messages,* 2:416. The chief justice became the fourth member of the court. Tennessee frequently altered the number of judges on its high court. When Catron arrived in 1824, the court consisted of four members. Although later increased to five and then decreased again to four, the number of justices stood at three before the passage of the 1831 measure (see Frierson, "Some Incidents," 148–49). For a discussion of the larger debate during this period over judicial accountability and independence, see Hall, "Route to Hell."

12. "Speech of Mr. Allen of Smith, in Committee of the Whole House, upon the

Following Preamble and Resolution," in Robert H. White, ed., *Messages,* 2:365; *Journal of the House,* December 19, 1831.

13. Catron, "Biographical Letter," 2:810–11.

14. On southern violence in general and dueling in particular, see Franklin, *Militant South,* 44–58; Ayers, *Vengeance,* 9–33; Wyatt-Brown, *Southern Honor,* 349–61. On the rituals surrounding the duel, see Steven Stowe, *Intimacy,* 5–49.

15. Catron, "Biographical Letter," 2:808.

16. Franklin, *Militant South,* 58–62; *Public Acts Passed at the General Assembly* (1801), chap. 32, sec. 3; *Public Acts Passed at the General Assembly* (1809), chap. 5, sec. 1; *Smith v. State,* 9 Tenn. 228, 230 (1829).

17. 9 Tenn. 228.

18. 9 Tenn. 229, 233. On Jackson's famous duel with Charles Dickinson, see Bassett, *Life,* 1:61–64; Remini, *Life,* 42–54;

19. 9 Tenn. 228, 233.

20. 9 Tenn. 228, 234.

21. 9 Tenn. 228, 235–37.

22. Catron, "Biographical Letter," 2:809; Caldwell, *Sketches,* 90.

23. *Grainger v. State,* 13 Tenn. 459, 460 (1830).

24. 13 Tenn. 459, 461–62; Ingersoll, "John Catron," 260.

25. 13 Tenn. 459, 462; Ingersoll, "John Catron," 262.

26. *Copeland v. State,* 26 Tenn. 477 (1846); *Morgan v. State,* 35 Tenn. 474, 480 (1856).

27. *Shorter v. People,* 2 N.Y. 193 (1849); Francis Wharton, *Treatise,* 216; Ingersoll, "John Catron," 260.

28. *Rippy v. State,* 39 Tenn. 219 (1858).

29. Finkelman, "Exploring," 104. See also Richard Maxwell Brown, "Southern Violence," 232–33.

30. Corlew, *Tennessee,* 199, 231; Phelps and Willett, "Iron Works," 311–13. On economic development in Tennessee, see Folmsbee, *Sectionalism.*

31. Hofstadter, *American Political Tradition,* 74.

32. Arda S. Walker, "Andrew Jackson," 78–79; Sioussat, "Some Phases," 64–66; *Knoxville Register,* July 8, 1829.

33. On Jacksonian beliefs regarding the relationship between political liberty and economic privilege, see Ashworth, *"Agrarians";* *Knoxville Register,* July 8, 1829.

34. Catron to Andrew Jackson Donelson, December 31, 1829, Donelson Papers; *Knoxville Register,* July 8, 15, 1829; James, *Life,* 558.

35. "Jackson's Veto of the Bank Bill," in Commager, *Documents,* 270–74; Harry L. Watson, *Liberty,* 144; Catron to Donelson, December 31, 1829, Donelson Papers; Spencer Roane to James Monroe, February 16, 1820, in "Letters of Spencer Roane," 174. One observer writes that Catron's essays on the bank "were extensively copied" and "not without their effect in Jackson's 'war on Biddle's Bank'" (Phelan, *History,* 379).

36. Catron to James K. Polk, September 10, 1837, in Weaver and Cutler, eds., *Correspondence*, 4:231. On the bank war, see Remini, *Andrew Jackson*.

37. Guild, *Old Times*, 460–61; Thomas B. Jones, "Public Lands," 21; Marks, "Supreme Court," 126; Chandler, "Centenary," 35; Fancher, *Sparta Bar*, 13.

38. *Hickman's Lessee v. Gaither and Frost*, 10 Tenn. 199, 202–3 (1828).

39. 10 Tenn. 199, 201.

40. *Love v. Love's Lessee*, 10 Tenn. 288, 289 (1829).

41. 10 Tenn. 288, 290.

42. *Guion's Lessee v. Bradley Academy*, 12 Tenn. 231, 252 (1833). For an example of a similar ruling in favor of settlers while Catron was a U.S. Supreme Court justice, see *Moore v. Brown*, 52 U.S. (11 Howard) 414 (1850).

43. Catron to Hugh Lawson White, May 1, 1831, in Scott, ed., *Memoir*, 249; Green, *Lives*, 83; Guild, *Old Times*, 461.

44. *Currie's Administrators v. Mutual Assurance Society*, 14 Va. 315, 347–48 (1809); Carrington, "Law," 509; *Vanzant v. Waddel*, 10 Tenn. 260 (1829). See also *Wally's Heirs v. Kennedy*, 10 Tenn. 554 (1831); Gillman, *Constitution Besieged*, 53–54.

45. Corlew, *Tennessee*, 147–52; Norgren, *Cherokee Cases*, 38; Sioussat, "Tennessee," 340.

46. *Cornet v. Winton's Lessee*, 10 Tenn. 143, 144 (1826).

47. 10 Tenn. 143, 146–47, 150.

48. Norgren, *Cherokee Cases*, 80–86.

49. *Blair and Johnson v. Pathkiller's Lessee*, 10 Tenn. 407, 410, 415 (1830).

50. 10 Tenn. 407, 416, 421.

51. *M'Connell and Mayfield v. Mousepaine's Lessee*, 10 Tenn. 438, 440 (1830).

52. *Cherokee Nation v. Georgia*, 5 Peters (30 U.S.) 1 (1831); *Worcester v. Georgia*, 6 Peters (31 U.S.) 515 (1832); Norgren, *Cherokee Cases*, 84; Bergeron, "Tennessee's Response"; Catron to Andrew Jackson, January 2, 1833, July 5, 1838, Catron Papers.

53. *State v. Foreman*, 16 Tenn. 256 (1835). Catron also privately endorsed Cherokee removal: "The Indian disturbances will afford the occasion for the removal of this population beyond the M'pi, including the Cherokees I hope" (Catron to Andrew Jackson, June 8, 1836, in Bassett, ed., *Correspondence*, 5:401).

54. Catron to Martin Van Buren, December 12, 1835, Catron Papers; Norgren, *Cherokee Cases*, 57, 87–95.

55. 16 Tenn. 256, 262–63, 277.

56. 16 Tenn. 256, 332–33. See also on *State v. Foreman*, Colyar, *Life*, 2:780–85. Catron indicated in letters in 1835 that Foreman's case was to be argued before the U.S. Supreme Court, but the Court apparently never did hear the case (Catron to Martin Van Buren, December 12, 1835, Catron Papers). Also, in a letter to the governor, Catron reiterated the holding in Foreman (Catron to Governor Newton Cannon, November 2, 1835, in Robert H. White, ed., *Messages*, 3:94–98).

57. *Fields v. State,* 9 Tenn. 156 (1829); England, "Free Negro," 41–42, 49–50; Patterson, *Negro,* 153–57.

58. *Fisher's Negroes v. Dabbs,* 14 Tenn. 119, 126, 129–30 (1834).

59. 14 Tenn. 119, 131; *Loftin v. Espy,* 12 Tenn. 84, 92 (1833). Catron's paternalism did allow him to look past the societal impact of his decision making in at least one major instance. Although he had openly declared his opposition to emancipation within the state in *Dabbs,* in *Harris v. Clarissa* (1834), the chief justice endorsed emancipation of children whose mother had gained her freedom through her master's will. Clarissa had been freed by her master in Maryland by last will and testament, and Catron affirmed her free status in Tennessee. Further, the chief justice held that the status of Clarissa's three children, born before their mother attained freedom at age twenty-five, followed that of their mother and that they gained their freedom when she did. They did not have to wait until they themselves reached the age of twenty-five. The combination of a will executed in Maryland, the authority of various states' precedents, and the paternal idea of children remaining in every way attached to their parents pushed Catron toward a more humane position in this instance (*Harris v. Clarissa,* 14 Tenn. 227 [1834]).

60. Catron's personal servant, Henry, was to receive five thousand dollars of stock in the Nashville Gas Light Company, along with $150 annual rent on a house in Nashville ("The Will of John Catron," recorded June 29, 1865, sec. 2, Catron Papers).

Catron might have had a mulatto son. James P. Thomas claimed that Catron was his father, although no available evidence corroborates this claim. Thomas wrote in his autobiography that his father "presided over the supreme court ten years but he had no time to give me a thought. He gave me 25 cents once. If I was correctly informed, that is all he ever did for me" (Schweninger, *From Tennessee Slave,* 60).

61. 16 Tenn. 256, 336.

62. 14 Tenn. 119, 129–30; Cooper, *South.* In subsequent years, the Tennessee Supreme Court generally returned to a more humanitarian policy toward slaves. See Howington, "Property"; Howington, "Not in the Condition."

63. Catron, "Biographical Letter," 2:808, 810; Marks, "Supreme Court," 128.

64. This group of supporters became known as the Committee. See Fancher, *Sparta Bar,* 13–14; Parton, *Life,* 3:142–43; Remini, *Election,* 63–64.

65. Powell Moore, "Revolt"; Atkins, *Parties,* 45–47; Bergeron, *Antebellum Politics,* 54–63; Catron to James K. Polk, January 8, 1836, in Weaver and Hall, eds., *Correspondence,* 3:428; Gresham, "Public Career"; *Tennessee,* 2:88.

66. Greene and Avery, *Government,* 15; Tennessee Constitution (1834), art. 6, sec. 2, 3.

67. Phelan, *History,* 378; *Journal of the House,* October 16, December 4, 1835.

68. Powell Moore, "Revolt," 350; Catron to James K. Polk, April 22, 1837, in Weaver and Cutler, eds., *Correspondence,* 5:96–97.

69. James Polk to Andrew Jackson, March 3, 1837, in Weaver and Cutler, eds.,

Correspondence, 4:73; Hallum, *Diary,* 106–8; *Nashville Union,* March 21, 1837; Abraham, *Justices,* 102–3.

70. Catron to Polk, May 8, 1837, Weaver and Cutler, eds., *Correspondence,* 5: 115–16; Roger B. Taney to Andrew Jackson, September 12, 1838, as quoted in biographical sketch of Catron, Catron Papers.

71. *License Cases,* 5 Howard (46 U.S.) 504 (1847); *Cooley v. Board of Wardens of the Port of Philadelphia,* 12 Howard (53 U.S.) 299 (1852); *Ohio Life Insurance Company v. Debolt,* 16 Howard (57 U.S.) 416, 426 (1854); *Rundle v. Delaware and Raritan Canal Company,* 14 Howard (55 U.S.) 80 (1853); *Marshall v. Baltimore and Ohio Railroad Company,* 16 Howard (57 U.S.) 314 (1854).

72. *Dred Scott v. Sandford,* 19 How. (60 U.S.) 393 (1857). Catron engaged in extensive correspondence with President James Buchanan regarding the Dred Scott decision. See Auchampaugh, "James Buchanan."

73. Fehrenbacher, "Roger B. Taney," 565; Schmidhauser, "Judicial Behavior."

74. Foote, *Bench and Bar,* 153; "Memoranda," 3 Wall. (70 U.S.) 1866, xi–xii.

75. "Memoranda," 3 Wall. (70 U.S.) 1866, xi–xii; Swisher, *History,* 858–59.

76. "Memoranda," 3 Wall. (70 U.S.) 1866, xii; Gatell, "John Catron," 748; Temple, *East Tennessee,* 562.

77. *History of Tennessee,* 382.

78. "Memoranda," 3 Wall. (70 U.S.), xiii; *Prize Cases,* 2 Black (67 U.S.) 635 (1863); Swisher, *History,* 886–92; *United States v. Republican Banner Officers,* 27 Fed. Cas. 781, no. 16,148 (1863); Chandler, "Centenary," 49.

79. Perhaps most revealing of this contrast was Catron's reaction to the Richmond aristocracy's excessive emphasis on origins. In 1850, Catron toured the city with Justice Peter V. Daniel, himself a native of the Old Dominion. Daniel's extensive pride in and knowledge about the pedigree of each of the city's prominent families amused Catron. Noticing that usually the women had claims to high ancestry, Catron wondered about the effect on aristocracy of "downward breeding" (Swisher, *History,* 728–29).

80. Van Deusen, *Jacksonian Era,* 179; Cole, *Presidency,* 256–57; Latner, *Presidency,* 198–200.

CHAPTER THREE: JOSEPH HENRY LUMPKIN AND THE VISION OF AN INDEPENDENT SOUTH

1. *Studstill v. State,* 7 Ga. 2, 19 (1849).

2. On Lumpkin's family background, see Ben Gray Lumpkin and Martha Neville Lumpkin, eds., *Lumpkin Family,* 30. Lumpkin refers to his father as a "skillful planter" in a letter to his wife, Callendar C. Grieve, February 4, 1821, Lumpkin Papers, Law Library, University of Georgia. Wilson Lumpkin, Joseph Henry's older brother, discusses his parents in *Removal,* 1:9–10. On Lumpkin's early life, see also Cody, *Lumpkin Family,* 4–5; Northen, ed., *Men,* 2:301–4; "Lumpkin, Joseph

Henry"; "Joseph Henry Lumpkin, The First Chief Justice of Georgia, Died June 4th, 1867, In Memoriam," 36 Ga. 20 (1867); Brantly, *Life,* 5–50.

3. "In Memoriam," 36 Ga. 20, 22; Johnston, *Autobiography,* 104; Brantly, *Life,* 16.

4. Grice, *Georgia Bench and Bar,* 261–62; Wilson Lumpkin to William Schley, John A. Cuthbert, Joseph Henry Lumpkin, January 22, 1833, in Wilson Lumpkin, *Removal,* 1:213, 135; *Southern Banner,* December 7, 1833.

5. Grice, *Georgia Bench and Bar,* 263–66; Saye, *Constitutional History,* 185–86; Coulter, *Georgia,* 294–95; *Southern Banner,* November 12, 1835; Andrews, *Reminiscences,* 19–20. See also Cleveland, "Establishment"; Almand, "Supreme Court."

6. Cleveland, "Establishment," 423.

7. "In Memoriam," 36 Ga. 20, 30; Grice, *Georgia Bench and Bar,* 267; *Southern Banner,* December 23, 1845.

8. Brantly, *Life,* 43–44.

9. Charles C. Jones Jr. to Rev. and Mrs. C. C. Jones, in Robert Manson Myers, ed., *Children,* 148.

10. Hargrett, "Student Life," 55; Thos. W. Rogers to Lumpkin, August 16, 1842, Lumpkin Papers, Hargrett Rare Book and Manuscripts Library, University of Georgia (hereafter cited as JHL Papers); Knight, *Reminiscences,* 363; Coulter, *College Life,* 197.

11. Ayers, *Vengeance,* 14; Rorabaugh, *Alcoholic Republic;* Tyrrell, *Sobering Up,* 16–32; Lender and Martin, *Drinking,* 41–86. For a more extensive discussion of Lumpkin's temperance activities, see Huebner, "Joseph Henry Lumpkin," 258–65.

12. Brantly, *Life,* 37; Charles S. Dod to Lumpkin, October 26, 1846, JHL Papers; Committee of State Temperance Society to Lumpkin, June 19, 1844, JHL Papers; Scomp, *King Alcohol,* 492, 261; Cory, "Temperance," 21.

13. Howe, *Political Culture;* Howe, "Religion."

14. Joseph Henry Lumpkin, *Address;* Joseph Henry Lumpkin, "Industrial Regeneration"; L. Andrews to Lumpkin, January 27, 1857, JHL Papers.

15. Joseph Henry Lumpkin, *Address,* 21, 14.

16. Joseph Henry Lumpkin, "Industrial Regeneration," 49; Howe, *Political Culture,* 101. On Lumpkin and economic development, see Huebner, "Joseph Henry Lumpkin," 269–73.

17. *Southern Banner,* July 13, 1833; *Milledgeville Federal Union,* July 18, 1833. See also Scomp, *King Alcohol,* 300–301; *American Colonization Society v. Gartrell,* 23 Ga. 448, 464, 465 (1857).

18. Mathews, *Religion,* 152; Raboteau, *Slave Religion,* 174; *Southern Banner,* August 3, 1833; Donald, "Proslavery Argument," 8. See also Sparks, "Mississippi's Apostle," 95–100, for an insightful discussion of evangelical attitudes toward slavery.

19. J. C. Brigham to Lumpkin, October 20, 1852, JHL Papers; Thomas Smyth to Thomas Chalmers, April 27, 1845, in Shepperson, ed., "Thomas Chalmers," 526.

20. Joseph Henry Lumpkin, "Law Reform," 384–85. This is a condensed version

of Lumpkin's report to the Georgia legislature, published in a contemporary legal journal. All quotations are taken from this version.

21. Hindus, *Prison*, 185; Joseph Henry Lumpkin, "Law Reform," 391.

22. "Extract from the Minutes of the Board of Trustees of the University of Georgia, in Session at Milledgeville, the 13th of Nov. 1843," JHL Papers; McCash, *Thomas R. R. Cobb*, 125.

23. McCash, *Thomas R. R. Cobb*, 125–26; prospectus entitled "University of Georgia, Law Department," June 1, 1859, 1, quoted in McCash, *Thomas R. R. Cobb*, 125, 126; Sylvanus Morris, "Lumpkin Law School," 3; Huebner, "Joseph Henry Lumpkin," 266–68. See also *Athens Banner*, October 11, 1959, on the hundredth anniversary of the school.

24. Sam Miller to Rev. Dr. Chalmers, May 9, 1845, Lumpkin Papers, Law Library, University of Georgia; Brantly, *Life*, 16.

25. "In Memoriam," 33 Ga. 199, 201 (1864).

26. A number of individuals have noted the connections among honor, violence, and vengeance in the Old South. See, e.g., Redfield, *Homicide*; Sydnor, "Southerner"; Wyatt-Brown, *Southern Honor*; Ayers, *Vengeance*, 9–33; Richard Maxwell Brown, "Southern Violence." On Georgia, see Almand, "Code Duello."

27. Wyatt-Brown, "Religion and the 'Civilizing Process.'" For a discussion of the changing role of evangelical religion in southern culture, see Boles, "Evangelical Protestantism."

28. Richard Maxwell Brown, "Southern Violence"; Finkelman, "Exploring," 101–8.

29. *Hudgins v. State*, 2 Ga. 173, 186, 188 (1847).

30. 2 Ga. 173, 189.

31. *Hawkins v. State*, 25 Ga. 207, 209, 210 (1858)

32. 25 Ga. 207, 211.

33. *Revel v. State*, 26 Ga. 275, 280–81 (1858).

34. 26 Ga. 275, 281.

35. *Teal v. State*, 22 Ga. 81, 85 (1857).

36. Baum and Baum, *Law*, 6; Richard Maxwell Brown, "Southern Violence," 233.

37. *Mitchell v. State*, 22 Ga. 211, 234 (1857).

38. 22 Ga. 211, 234–35.

39. *Choice v. State*, 31 Ga. 424, 427 (1860). See also *Golden v. State*, 25 Ga. 527 (1858).

40. 31 Ga. 424, 472–73.

41. On moral insanity, see Tighe, "Francis Wharton"; Friedman, *History*, 592.

42. *Biggs v. State*, 29 Ga. 723 (1860); *Haynes v. State*, 17 Ga. 465 (1855).

43. 17 Ga. 465, 484.

44. Joseph Henry Lumpkin, "Industrial Regeneration," 43.

45. *Georgia Railroad and Banking Company v. Anderson*, 33 Ga. 110, 113 (1861). Because many legal historians place a strong emphasis on contractual ques-

tions in their analyses of the nation's economic growth, such cases provide the best evidence for an assessment of Lumpkin's judicial behavior on economic matters. See esp. Horwitz, *Transformation, 1780–1860*, 160–211; Hurst, *Law*, 3–32. For a more extensive discussion of Lumpkin and contracts, see Huebner, "Encouraging Economic Development."

46. *Robinson v. Schley and Cooper*, 6 Ga. 515, 524 (1849).

47. *Bryant v. Hambrick*, 9 Ga. 133 (1850), 134.

48. *Harrison and Another v. Young and Another*, 9 Ga. 359 (1851), 364.

49. *Shorter and Others v. Smith and the Justices of the Inferior Court of Floyd County*, 9 Ga. 517 (1851).

50. *Shorter v. Smith and Justices of the Inferior Court of Floyd County*, 9 Ga. 517, 521; *Charles River Bridge Company v. Warren Bridge Company*, 11 Peters (36 U.S.) 420 (1837). On the Charles River Bridge case, see Kutler, *Privilege;* Horwitz, *Transformation, 1780–1860*, 130–39; Newmyer, *Supreme Court under Marshall and Taney*, 89–97; Mensel, "Privilege."

51. Kent quoted in Newmyer, *Supreme Court Justice Joseph Story*, 232.

52. 9 Ga. 517, 524, 526.

53. 9 Ga. 517, 526, 527.

54. 9 Ga. 517, 524, 526.

55. 9 Ga. 517, 532.

56. 9 Ga. 517, 528–29.

57. *Blair v. Carmichael*, 2 Yerger 306, 309 (1829).

58. *Tuckahoe Canal Company v. Tuckahoe and James River Railroad Company*, Leigh 11 (Va. 38), 43 (1840); Kutler, *Privilege*, 137–38.

59. Ely and Bodenhamer, "Regionalism and American Legal History," 554; Wiecek, "Old Times," 182. Both authors make this contention but do so without post-1837 evidence. Wiecek's claims are worded even more strongly than Bodenhamer and Ely's, yet he relies only on their footnotes.

60. For Kent's defense of monopoly rights, see *Livingston v. Van Ingen*, 9 Johns. 507 (N.Y. Court for Trial of Impeachments and Corrections of Errors, 1812), and *Croton Turnpike Road Co. v. Ryder*, 1 Johns. Ch. 611 (N.Y. Chancery, 1815). On Story, see Newmyer, *Supreme Court Justice Joseph Story*, 226–35. A few months before Lumpkin's opinion in *Shorter*, his Georgia colleague Judge Eugenius Nisbet rendered a similar decision in another bridge case, stating that "any ambiguity in the terms of the contract, must operate against the adventurers and in favor of the public" (*McLeod v. Burroughs*, 9 Ga. 213 [1851]).

61. On northerners' views about slavery and the economy, see Foner, *Free Soil*, 11–39. For Lumpkin's views on slavery, see Stephenson and Stephenson, "To Protect and Defend." See also William W. Fisher III, "Ideology."

62. Quoted from Foner, *Free Soil*, 59. On abolitionism, see Filler, *Crusade;* Stewart, *Holy Warriors;* Wyatt-Brown, *Lewis Tappan*.

63. Scomp, *King Alcohol*, 278–79; J. C. Brigham to Lumpkin, October 20, 1852, JHL Papers.

64. Lumpkin to Howell Cobb, January 21, 1848, in Phillips, ed., *Correspondence,* 2:94–95.

65. Joseph Henry Lumpkin, "Judge Lumpkin's Report on Law Reform," 68, 77–78, as quoted in Reid, "Lessons of Lumpkin," 590–91.

66. The myth of Ham and Japheth originated from the biblical account in Genesis, chapters 9 and 10, which states that after the flood, Ham looked upon his father's nakedness while Noah lay drunk in his tent. Noah's other two sons, Shem and Japheth, had covered their father without looking upon him. When Noah awoke, he cursed Canaan, Ham's son, declaring that he was to be a "servant of servants" to his brothers. Although the passage makes no reference to race, it was clear to white southerners that blacks were the descendants of Ham and were therefore cursed with perpetual bondage. See Peterson, *Ham;* Winthrop D. Jordan, *White over Black,* 17–20.

67. Lumpkin to daughter Callie, October 13, 1853, Lumpkin Papers, Law Library, University of Georgia. Lumpkin referred to Priest, *Slavery.* According to Peterson, Priest, a New York harness maker, wrote a number of popular works interpreting the American experience in religious terms. *Slavery,* for example, was reprinted five times in eight years (Peterson, *Ham,* 42, 60). In *Bryan v. Walton,* where the court took up the issue of whether a free black had the right to "dispose of slaves by deed of gift," Lumpkin used the myth of Ham as justification for denying such rights. "The act of manumission confers no other right but that of freedom from the dominion of the master," he wrote, "and limited liberty of locomotion; that it does not and cannot confer citizenship, nor any powers, civil or political, incident to citizenship; that the social and civil degradation, resulting from the taint of blood, adheres to the descendants of Ham in this country" (*Bryan v. Walton,* 14 Ga. 185, 197, 198 [1853]).

68. Thomas R. R. Cobb, *Inquiry,* 64; Maddex, "Proslavery Millennialism."

69. "Ex-Slave Interview: Anna Parkes," in Rawick, ed., *American Slave,* 13:155, 157. Parkes insightfully notes that Lumpkin's reputation as a judge contributed to his humanity: "Dey sho' wuz good white folkses, but den dey had to be good white folkses, kaze Old Marster, he wuz Jedge Lumpkin, and de Jedge wuz bound to make evvybody do right, and he gwine do right his own self 'fore he try to make udder folkses behave deyselvs" (155). Russell and Thornberry, "William Finch," 309–10. Lumpkin was the owner of a moderate number of slaves, thirteen in 1848 (*Georgia Tax Digests,* Clarke County, 1848).

70. *Ingram and Ingram v. Fraley,* 29 Ga. 553, 561 (1859).

71. Mathews, "Charles Colcock Jones"; *Southern Banner,* August 3, 1833; *Cleland v. Waters,* 19 Ga. 35, 41 (1855).

72. Joseph Henry Lumpkin, *Address,* 13; *American Colonization Society v. Gartrell,* 23 Ga. 448, 464 (1857); Genovese, *Roll, Jordan, Roll,* 76.

73. Stephenson and Stephenson, "To Protect and Defend," 582.

74. *Farwell v. Boston and Worcester Railroad Corporation,* 45 Mass. 49 (1842); Levy, *Law,* 166–82; Hall, *Magic Mirror,* 125.

75. *Scudder v. Woodbridge,* 1 Ga. 195, 199 (1846); Finkelman, "Slaves," 290–91.

76. 1 Ga. 195, 199–200; *Gorman v. Campbell,* 14 Ga. 137 (1853); Finkelman, "Slaves," 293.

77. *Lennard v. Boynton,* 11 Ga. 109, 110, 113 (1852); *Latimer v. Alexander,* 14 Ga. 261, 266 (1853).

78. 14 Ga. 261, 262. See also Langum, "Role." Langum perceptively observes that Lumpkin's opinions in slave hiring cases were not representative of judicial sympathy for planters at the expense of an emerging industrial class. There was no unity to the interest of slave hirers, Langum shows, and it would make no sense, moreover, for a proindustrial reformer like Lumpkin to deliberately try to hinder economic development. Lumpkin's ideology of paternalism is a more reasonable explanation for his behavior than is an ulterior economic motive.

79. *Brooks v. Smith,* 21 Ga. 261, 265 (1857).

80. 11 Ga. 109, 113.

81. Cover, *Justice Accused;* Nash, "Fairness," 90.

82. During his first years on the Court, Lumpkin exhibited a less restrictive view of manumission than he would later espouse. In a case involving the legality of a will directing the freeing of the testator's slaves, Lumpkin distinguished between foreign and domestic emancipation and permitted the emancipation of three of the testator's slaves in Liberia. However, in accordance with an 1818 act regarding emancipation, the chief justice would not tolerate domestic manumission. See *Vance v. Crawford,* 4 Ga. 445, 458–59, 460 (1848).

83. *Adams v. Bass,* 18 Ga. 130, 134–35 (1855).

84. 18 Ga. 130, 135–36.

85. 18 Ga. 130, 138–39.

86. *American Colonization Society v. Gartrell,* 23 Ga. 448, 451 (1857).

87. 23 Ga. 448, 464–65.

88. *Cleland v. Waters,* 19 Ga. 35, 36 (1855).

89. 19 Ga. 35, 47, 43.

90. 19 Ga. 35, 47.

91. *Sanders v. Ward,* 25 Ga. 109, 119 (1858).

92. 25 Ga. 109, 124 (1858).

93. Nash, "Reason," 118.

94. For this debate, see Tushnet, *American Law;* Fede, "Toward a Solution"; Finkelman, "Peculiar Laws," 358.

95. Pound, *Formative Era;* Gilmore, *Ages,* 19–40.

96. Coulter, *College Life,* 237; Joseph Henry Lumpkin, "Industrial Regeneration," 48.

97. *Padelford, Fay and Co. v. Mayor of Savannah,* 14 Ga. 438, 506 (1854); James C. Cobb, "Making"; "Henry L. Benning's Secessionist Speech, Monday Evening, November 19," in Freehling and Simpson, eds., *Secession Debated,* 115–44.

98. *Edmondson v. Union Bank of Tennessee,* 33 Ga. 91, 93 (1861); *Cox and Hill v. Cummings,* 33 Ga. 549, 554–55 (1863).

99. "Tribute of Respect, to the Memory of General Thomas R. R. Cobb," 33 Ga.

389 (1863); "In Memoriam," 33 Ga. 199, 201 (1864). On Cobb, see McCash, *Thomas R. R. Cobb;* Michael Johnson, *Toward a Patriarchal Republic.*

100. 33 Ga. 549; 33 Ga. 91; *Jenkins v. Mayor,* 35 Ga. 146 (1866).

101. Robert E. Martin to Lumpkin, March 13, 18, 1855; E. A. Nisbet to Lumpkin, March 28, 1858; JHL Papers. See also Hiram Warner to Lumpkin, March 27, 1855. Warner urged Lumpkin to take the federal judgeship.

102. Title XVIII, no. 62, *Acts of the General Assembly of the State of Georgia.*

CHAPTER FOUR: JOHN HEMPHILL, THE TEXAS SUPREME COURT, AND THE "TAMING" OF THE FRONTIER

1. Curtis, *John Hemphill,* 1–8. On Rev. John Hemphill, see Lathan, *History,* 22–29.

2. Curtis, *John Hemphill,* 11–14; Gaines, "John Hemphill," 4:4; Gregg, *Eulogy,* 4–5.

3. "Copy of the Valedictory Oration of John Hemphill at Commencement of Jefferson College, Pennsylvania, 1825," Hemphill Papers; John Hemphill to William Hemphill, December 29, 1833, John Hemphill to Robert R. Hemphill, December 23, 1859, McCord-Hemphill Copartnership Agreement, December 13, 1829, all in Hemphill Family Papers.

4. Stubbs, "Fourth Estate," 186.

5. *Sumter Gazette,* April 28, 1832, as quoted in Freehling, *Prelude,* 83.

6. James Hemphill to William Hemphill, August 22, 1832, Hemphill Family Papers; Freehling, *Prelude,* 84–85; Gregorie, *History,* 151. Curtis, *John Hemphill,* 16–18, offers a different, less credible account of this incident. On Richardson as a political writer, see *Remains,* xxix–xxxii, 3–70.

7. Hemphill, *Oration,* 13.

8. Stubbs, "Fourth Estate," 186; nullification oath, in Hemphill Papers. For more clues about Hemphill's politics, see his statements about President John Tyler and the Whig Party, in Weeks, *Debates,* 139.

9. Gregorie, *History,* 152–53; Curtis, *John Hemphill,* 18–19; certificate from Rev. John L. Preply, December 15, 1826, Hemphill Papers. Hemphill's seemingly violent proclivities prompted one observer to describe him as "an expert skullbuster in a streetfight" (Farber, *Texas,* 10). On the resolution of the nullification crisis, see Freehling, *Prelude,* 260–97.

10. James Hemphill to William R. Hemphill, March 17, 1836, Certification of Honorable Discharge, April 12, 1836, both in Hemphill Family Papers; Curtis, *John Hemphill,* 20–21. On the formation of these southern volunteer companies for military service, see Mahon, *History,* 135–37.

11. King, *Louis T. Wigfall,* 46–47; Curtis, *John Hemphill,* 23. Perhaps Hemphill simply believed that Texas offered a climate more conducive to recovery from the bouts of malaria he occasionally suffered after his service in Florida.

12. Siegel, *Political History,* 5–7; Hogan, *Texas Republic,* 10–11. Randolph B. Campbell, *Empire,* 2, notes that "77 percent of household heads in Texas in 1860 were southern-born." Terry G. Jordan, "Imprint."

13. Quoted in Hogan, *Texas Republic,* 247. See also Bloomfield, "Texas Bar."

14. Curtis, *John Hemphill,* 25–26; Gaines, "John Hemphill," 4:5; Gregg, *Eulogy,* 5; commission to practice law in the Republic of Texas, September 10, 1838, Hemphill Papers; James Hemphill, undated biographical sketch of John Hemphill, Hemphill Family Papers; Paulsen, "Short History," 241; *Telegraph and Texas Register,* December 16, 1840, as quoted in Hart, "John Hemphill," 398. In 1839 Lamar offered Hemphill an appointment as the republic's secretary of the treasury, but Hemphill declined (Hemphill to Lamar, March 3, 1839, in Gulick and Elliot, eds., *Papers,* 2:480–81).

15. John Henry Brown, *Indian Wars,* 78; Curtis, *John Hemphill,* 29–35; Gaines, "John Hemphill," 4:6–8; Mayhall, *Indian Wars.* On Texas's military-oriented political culture, see Nackman, "Making."

16. Paulsen, "Short History"; Hart, "John Hemphill," 400–402; Gaines, "John Hemphill," 4:8–10; Curtis, *John Hemphill,* 37–53. Hemphill apparently had not always favored annexation. See John Hemphill to James Hemphill, February 13, 1845, in *Southwestern Historical Quarterly* 57 (1953): 222–24. The president of the constitutional convention, Thomas J. Rusk, appointed Hemphill chairman of the convention's judiciary committee (Middleton, "Texas Convention," 31, 37–41). On Rusk's work as president of the convention, see Clarke, *Thomas J. Rusk,* 49–58; Huston, *Towering Texan,* 113–20.

17. Lynch, *Bench,* 86; Davenport, *History,* 30–31.

18. 28 Tex. vi; "Hon. Royall T. Wheeler," 27 Tex. v–vii; Lynch, *Bench,* 91–96; Davenport, *History,* 22–25.

19. Paulsen, "Uncommon Law"; *Northern Standard* (Clarksville), November 22, 1856, quoted in Paulsen, "Uncommon Law," 4.

20. Preface, 28 Tex. vii; Paulsen, "Uncommon Law," 6–7, table A, 31; "Presentation of Portrait of Justice Hemphill," 59 Tex. viii.

21. "Presentation of Portrait of Justice Hemphill," 59 Tex. viii; Royall T. Wheeler to Oran M. Roberts, September 20, 1849, Roberts Papers; Paulsen, "Uncommon Law," 6. Again, Paulsen's figures refer to reported opinions.

22. Hogan, *Texas Republic,* 245–66; Hart, "John Hemphill," 400–401; Bloomfield, "Texas Bar," 275.

23. Paulsen, "Short History," 270; Charles Richard Williams, ed., *Diary,* 1:260.

24. McKnight, "Law Books," 76, 79; Joseph M. White, ed., *New Collection.*

25. Texas Constitution (1836), art. 4, sec. 13; Butte, "Early Development," 700; Clarence Wharton, "Early Judicial History," 323; Gilmer, "Early Courts," 438–39; *Fowler v. Stoneum,* 11 Tex. 478, 500 (1854).

26. Hemphill, *Eulogy,* 13–14; *Heirs of Holliman v. Peebles,* 1 Tex. 673, 690 (1847).

27. London, "Initial Homestead Exemption," 435–42; McKnight, "Century," 1054; Homestead Act, quoted in Raines, "Enduring Laws," 101; Ashford, "Jacksonian Liberalism," 8–10; McKnight, "Protection"; McKnight, "Mexican Roots."

28. Weeks, *Debates,* 423; Texas Constitution (1845), art. 7, sec. 22.

29. Sellers, *Market Revolution;* Goodman, "Emergence."

30. Texas Constitution (1845), art. 1, sec. 15, 18; art. 7, sec. 31.

31. *Sampson and Keene v. Williamson,* 6 Tex. 102, 117 (1851).

32. 6 Tex. 102, 115.

33. 6 Tex. 102, 117; White, ed., *New Collection,* 1:139.

34. *Wood v. Wheeler,* 7 Tex. 14, 22 (1851).

35. 7 Tex. 14, 22.

36. 7 Tex. 14, 25–26. The chief justice offered the widow two options, both of which were more favorable than the district court's ruling. Either the widow could pay the excess of the value of the improvements over five hundred dollars and retain the homestead, or the lot and improvements could be sold and out of the proceeds she would receive the value of the lot (not the improvements) plus five hundred dollars. The remaining sum, under this second option, became subject to her husband's debts. Regardless of the widow's choice, under Hemphill's order she would still have a homestead—either the one she possessed or one purchased with the money from the sale of the first. As a practical matter, however, the widow faced a sale of her home because of her inability to raise the cash value of improvements in excess of five hundred dollars.

37. *Cobbs v. Coleman,* 14 Tex. 594, 597–98 (1855); Raines, "Enduring Laws," 101; White, ed., *New Collection,* 1:322–23. In the same case, moreover, Hemphill broadly defined the exemption of other articles of property listed under the 1839 statute. In this instance, the court had to decide whether the exemption of a horse under the law extended to the saddle and bridle. Hemphill entertained no doubts on the matter. "A horse was not reserved because he was horse, but because of his useful qualities and his almost indispensable services," Hemphill observed. "But what would be the benefit of a horse without shoes, or without saddle and bridle, or without gears, if employed for purposes of agriculture?" In Hemphill's view, debtors needed all of those ancillary articles that might be necessary for the enjoyment and use of the exempted article. Under Spanish law, those items necessary for the practice of one's trade were exempt from creditors, and Hemphill rendered a similarly expansive interpretation of the law: "It would seem that by fair construction the grants in the statute must include not only the subject itself but everything absolutely essential to its beneficial enjoyment." By extending the state's debtor exemption statutes to include more than just the specific items listed under law, Hemphill again demonstrated his prodebtor position (14 Tex. 594, 598–99; White, ed., *New Collection,* 1:322–23).

38. *Shepherd v. Cassiday,* 20 Tex. 24 (1857). Hemphill reiterated this decision later that term in *Gouhenant v. Cockrell,* 20 Tex. 96 (1857). In a previous case, *Trawick v. Harris* (1852), the court held that a married woman who had left Texas and "domiciliated in another state" could not claim the exemption (8 Tex. 312).

39. *Pryor v. Stone,* 19 Tex. 371, 373 (1857). See also *Hancock v. Morgan,* 17 Tex. 582 (1856). Justice James Bell later apparently overturned, or at least ignored, *Pryor* in *Philleo v. Smalley* (1859), where he ruled that the home of a man in a similar situation did not constitute a homestead.

40. *Franklin v. Coffee,* 18 Tex. 413, 417 (1857). Hemphill's opinion in this case apparently simply made explicit what the court had already decided in *Methery v. Walker* (17 Tex. 593 [1856]).

41. 18 Tex. 413, 415–16.

42. Prather, "Economic Effects," 24; Georgia (1841), Mississippi (1841), Alabama (1843), and Florida (1845) all passed exemption laws soon after Texas (Goodman, "Emergence," 472 [table 1], 477).

43. Prather, "Economic Effects," 25–26; *Franklin v. Coffee,* 18 Tex. 413, 415–16 (1857); *Trawick v. Harris,* 8 Tex. 312, 316 (1852).

44. 18 Tex. 413, 416 (1857); Hurst, *Law,* 66; Goodman, "Emergence," 478, 497.

45. 18 Tex. 413, 416; 8 Tex. 316; Benton, *Thirty Years' View,* 104.

46. Goodman, "Emergence," 472 (table 1). Delaware, Rhode Island, and Maryland did not enact homestead exemption laws during the nineteenth century. Connecticut and South Carolina repealed their exemption laws in 1848 and 1858, respectively.

47. *Cook v. McChristian,* 4 Cal. 23, 26 (1854); *Charless and Blow v. Lamberson,* 1 Iowa, 435, 441 (1855); *True, Sprague, and Spear v. Morrill,* 28 Verm. 674 (1856); Prather, "Economic Effects," 21; Dillon, *Laws,* 360; Dillon, "Homestead Exemption." Dillon cites Texas decisions forty-six times in the article, more than any other state court except for California, which he cites forty-nine times.

After the Civil War, southern states in particular expanded their homestead provisions as they sought to alleviate their disastrous economic situation. Most of these measures remained in place until the late nineteenth century, when legislatures, envisioning a New South built on credit, began to scale the value of the exemption back to antebellum levels. See Goodman, "Emergence," 491–96, esp. 493 (table 2). For a contemporary criticism of these Reconstruction-era homestead laws, see Thomas, "Homestead Exemption Laws."

48. Hogan, *Texas Republic,* 267–90; Hollon, *Frontier Violence,* 36–55; Fischer, *Albion's Seed,* 759–76.

49. Redfield, *Homicide,* 79.

50. *Caldwell v. State,* 5 Tex. 18, 19 (1849); *Givens v. State,* 6 Tex. 344, 346 (1851).

51. *Gehrke v. State,* 13 Tex. 568 (1855); *White v. State,* 16 Tex. 206 (1856).

52. *State v. Rutherford,* 13 Tex. 23 (1854); *State v. Croft,* 15 Tex. 575 (1855).

53. *Wall v. State,* 18 Tex. 683, 693 (1857).

54. *O'Connell v. State,* 18 Tex. 343, 363, 365 (1857); *Jordan v. State,* 10 Tex. 480, 497 (1853).

55. Ayers, *Vengeance,* 32; Friedman, *Crime,* 256.

56. *Lander v. State,* 13 Tex. 462, 467–68 (1854).

57. 13 Tex. 462, 476–77.

58. 13 Tex. 462, 480, 484–85.

59. *Johnson v. State,* 17 Tex. 515 (1856).

60. Richard Maxwell Brown, "Southern Violence," 233.

61. *Guess v. Lubbock,* 5 Tex. 535, 547 (1851); Schafer, "Class," 587; Texas Constitution (1836), general provisions, sec. 9; Randolph B. Campbell, *Empire,* 1–3, 96–114.

62. Texas Constitution (1836), general provisions, sec. 9; Randolph B. Campbell, *Empire,* 112–13; Smallwood, "Blacks," 462–63.

63. Contrary to the attitudes of the supreme court, most white Texans apparently shared the insurrectionary fears of other white southerners. See Randolph B. Campbell, *Empire,* 219–30.

64. Hemphill, *Oration;* John Hemphill to William Hemphill, July 26, 1833, Hemphill Family Papers.

65. Paulsen, "Uncommon Law," 23; Hemphill speech in U.S. Senate, January 28, 1861, *Congressional Globe,* 36th Cong., 2d sess., pt. 1, 595.

66. *State v. Wupperman,* 13 Tex. 33 (1854); *Rawles v. State,* 15 Tex. 581 (1855); *Allen v. State,* 14 Tex. 633 (1855). See also *Cain v. State,* 18 Tex. 387 (1857) and *Carter v. State,* 20 Tex. 339 (1857), both decided by Wheeler. Judge Hemphill's successor, Judge James H. Bell, continued this trend in *Greer v. State* (22 Tex. 588 [1858]) and *Kingston v. State* (25 Supp. Tex. 166 [1860]), where he overturned the convictions of a slave for possessing firearms and of a white man for buying chickens from a slave. Also, Justice Oran Roberts, Lipscomb's successor, held insufficient an indictment against a master for allowing a slave to hire his own time (*Anderson v. State,* 20 Tex. 5 [1857]) and overturned a conviction for selling liquor to a slave because of a faulty charge from the trial judge (*Smith v. State,* 24 Tex. 547 [1859]).

67. Texas Constitution (1836), general provisions, sec. 9; John E. Fisher, "Legal Status," 351–52.

68. *Jones v. Laney,* 2 Tex. 342, 349–50 (1847); *Guest v. Lubbock,* 5 Tex. 535, 544, 548 (1851).

69. *Moore v. Minerva,* 17 Tex. 20, 25 (1856).

70. Alabama Constitution (1819), slaves, sec. 1; *Purvis v. Sherrod,* 13 Tex. 140, 141, 146 (1854); *Trotter v. Blocker,* 6 Porter 269 (1838). The constitutions of Alabama and Texas were by no means identical on the subject of slavery. Alabama's constitution stated, "The General Assembly shall have no power to pass laws for the emancipation of slaves, without the consent of their owners, or without paying their owners, previous to such emancipation, a full equivalent in money of the slaves so emancipated." Nowhere did the Alabama constitution prohibit slaveholders from emancipating their slaves without legislative consent, as the Texas constitution did. On its face, the appellant counsel's argument is difficult to accept.

71. *Purvis v. Sherrod,* 13 Tex. 140, 171 (1854); Nash, "Texas Supreme Court," 632–33.

72. *Armstrong v. Jowell,* 24 Tex. 58, 61 (1859). See also *Hillard v. Frantz,* 21 Tex. 192 (1858). In *Philleo v. Holliday* (1859), the court invalidated the will.

73. *Nels v. State,* 2 Tex. 280 (1847). See also *Calvin v. State,* 25 Tex. 789 (1860).

74. *Chandler v. State,* 2 Tex. 305, 309 (1847); *Fields v. State,* 1 Yerger 156 (1829); Nash, "Texas Supreme Court," 625–26.

75. *Neal v. Farmer,* 9 Ga. 555 (1851); *Bryan v. Walton,* 14 Ga. 185 (1853); *Ex parte Boylston,* 2 Strob. 41 (1846); Thomas D. Morris, *Southern Slavery,* 52–53; 2 Tex. 305, 309.

76. *Nix v. State,* 13 Tex. 575, 576 (1855).

77. 13 Tex. 575, 578–79.

78. *State v. Stephenson,* 20 Tex. 151 (1857); *Bumpus v. Fisher,* 21 Tex. 561 (1858); *Callihan v. Johnson,* 22 Tex. 596 (1858). See also *Brady v. Price,* 19 Tex. 285 (1857), where Wheeler noted in dicta that an overseer was not justified in shooting one of his employer's slaves who had refused to submit to chastisement.

79. *State v. Caesar,* 31 N.C. 391, 415 (1849); *Sanders v. Ward,* 25 Ga. 109, 124 (1858).

80. Paulsen, "Uncommon Law," 24.

81. *Congressional Globe,* 36th Cong., 2d sess., pt. 1, 595; Paulsen, "Uncommon Law," 25–27. Paulsen has unearthed mounds of evidence on this matter, which he fully documents, but see esp. Andrew Forest Muir, "John Hemphill, Miscegenist," unpublished typescript in Rice University Library; *Theodora Hemphill v. C. S. West et al.,* case #3074, vol. J, p. 624, June 7, 1871, District Court, Travis County, Texas; *Catalogue,* 9. I extend special thanks to Professor Paulsen for sharing this material with me.

82. Weeks, *Debates,* 217, 476, 535; *Cartwright v. Cartwright,* 18 Tex. 626, 635 (1857).

83. 28 Tex. vi; *Ex parte Coupland,* 26 Tex. 386 (1862); Hamilton, "State Courts," 435.

84. 28 Tex. vii.

85. Cooper, *South;* Curtis, *John Hemphill,* 73; U.S. Congress, *Biographical Directory,* 1038, 1080.

86. *Congressional Globe,* 36th Cong., 2d sess., pt. 1, 592, 593.

87. Lynch, *Bench,* 72; Hemphill, "To the Planters of Texas," Hemphill Papers.

88. Winkler, ed., *Journal,* 78–80; William M. Robinson Jr., *Justice,* 124, 573–74; *Journal of the Congress,* 1:153, 204.

89. "Death of Judge Hemphill," *Richmond Enquirer,* January 10, 1862.

90. "Presentation of Portrait of Justice Hemphill," 59 Tex. viii; Gregg, *Eulogy,* 7; Royall T. Wheeler to O. M. Roberts, November 21, 1845, quoted in Hogan, *Texas Republic,* 254; Townes, "Sketch, II," 145; Gaines, "John Hemphill," 4:10.

91. Gregg, *Eulogy,* 8; 59 Tex. viii.

92. Royall Wheeler to O. M. Roberts, May 29, 1847, Roberts Papers; William M. Walton to Thomas A. Watkins, February 4, 1862, in Dimond and Hattaway, eds., *Letters,* 268.

93. Hemphill, "Eulogy," 14.

CHAPTER FIVE: THOMAS RUFFIN, JUDICIAL PRAGMATISM,
AND SOUTHERN CONSTITUTIONALISM

1. Pound, *Formative Era*, 4.

2. Graham, *Life*, as reprinted in Hamilton, ed., *Papers*, 1:21; Walter Clark, "Thomas Ruffin," 4:279–81; Walter Clark, *Addresses*, 7–10; Blackwell Pierce Robinson, "Thomas Ruffin," 12; Spencer Roane to Ruffin, July 28, 1806, in Hamilton, ed., *Papers*, 1:101.

3. Kenzer, *Kinship*, 42–46; Escott, *Many Excellent People*, 4–7; Billings, *Planters*, 87.

4. O'Brien, *Legal Fraternity*, 79–92. Other members of this community were Bartlett Yancy, Joseph Caldwell, Charles Fisher, John Gilmer, and D. Frank Caldwell. See Powell, *North Carolina*, 253–66.

5. Turner, *Dreamer*; Powell, *North Carolina*, 253–66.

6. Ruffin to Kemp Plummer and others, August 20, 1816, Ruffin to Bartlett Yancey, December 3, 1824, both in Hamilton, ed., *Papers*, 1:176, 320–21; Robinson, "Thomas Ruffin," 78.

7. Judge Jesse Turner to Judge Archibald Murphey Aiken, n.d., in Hoyt, ed., *Papers*, 2:427; Chroust, *Rise*, 2:104; Farmer, "Legal Practice," 339.

8. Farmer, "Legal Education." John Louis Taylor, Leonard Henderson, Archibald D. Murphey, and John L. Bailey were some of the prominent attorneys who operated law schools.

9. Patrick Henry Winston to Ruffin, February 10, 1829, in Hamilton, ed., *Papers*, 1:469. See also for further details and correspondence concerning support for and opposition to Ruffin's appointment, Hamilton, ed., *Papers*, 1:467–502; Carpenter, "Influence," 36–39.

10. Pratt, "Struggle," 133–39. See also Hoffman, *Andrew Jackson*.

11. Pratt, "Struggle," 133–39; Connor, *North Carolina*, 2:65–67; Ruffin to William Gaston, August 21, 1833, Gaston Papers; Schauinger, "William Gaston." On the national movement for judicial reform and election, see Hall, "Judiciary on Trial."

12. *Hoke v. Henderson*, 15 N.C. 1 (1833); Pratt, "Struggle," 139–44.

13. 15 N.C. 1, 8–9.

14. 15 N.C. 1, 10, 8.

15. 15 N.C. 1, 17.

16. 15 N.C. 1, 13–14.

17. 15 N.C. 1, 23.

18. In a subsequent case, *Williams v. Somers* (18 N.C. 61 [1834]), Ruffin refused to extend the holding in *Hoke* to allow a clerk who had surrendered his office and records to a new clerk under the same act to return to his position. The clerk's behavior, Ruffin held, constituted a surrender of the office.

19. North Carolina Constitution, amendments, art. 3; Pratt, "Struggle," 129–59, esp. 131–32; Counihan, "North Carolina," 360. See also Powell, *North Carolina*,

267–81. The opinion in *Hoke* fitted with the early-nineteenth-century development of judicial power to review legislative enactments when such laws violated the law of the land. Ruffin, like many antebellum state judges, sought to use the judiciary to restrain an uncontrolled legislature through advocating higher-law constitutionalism. "Those terms 'law of the land' do not mean merely an act of the General Assembly," Ruffin contended. "If they did, every restriction upon the legislative authority would be at once abrogated." Instead, Ruffin viewed the judiciary as the guarantor of constitutional government. With these arguments, Ruffin and the North Carolina Supreme Court contributed to the development of the ideas of higher law and due process of law during the first half of the nineteenth century (15 N.C. 1, 15–16; Hyman and Wiecek, *Equal Justice*, 22–23; Corwine, "Doctrine," 383–84).

20. Boyd, *History*, 343–53; Powell, *North Carolina*, 253–66, 285–88; Jeffrey, "Internal Improvements"; Alan D. Watson, "North Carolina"; Harry L. Watson, "Squire Oldway"; Trelease, "Passive Voice."

21. *Raleigh and Gaston Railroad Company v. Davis*, 19 N.C. 451, 454 (1837). See also Carlson, "Iron Horse."

22. The contemporary significance of Ruffin's opinion was much greater than subsequent legal scholars ascribed to it. See, e.g., citations to the case in the following nineteenth-century treatises on railroad law: Pierce, *Treatise*, 144, 147, 164, 165, 173; Elliott and Elliott, *Treatise*, 3:1333–35; Lacey, *Digest*, 214, 264, 267; Wood, *Treatise*, 1:641, 650, 660, 2:765, 819, 824.

23. *Wellington, et al., Petitioners*, 16 Pick. 87, 102–3 (1834). See also Levy, *Law*, 120.

24. 19 N.C. 451, 470 (1837). In a variation on *Davis*, Ruffin held in *State v. Rives* that "railroads, although publicis juris in some respects, are the subjects of private property, and it is in the latter character that they are liable to be sold, unless forbidden by the legislature: not the franchise, but the estate of the corporation in the land, which is a distinct thing from the franchise" (27 N.C. 297, 310–11 [1844]). In that case, Ruffin thus upheld the sale of a railroad.

25. *Wellington, et al, Petitioners*, 16 Pick. 87 (1834); Levy, *Law*, 120. Lenhoff, "Development," 598–99, notes that the term *eminent domain* was first used as early as 1796 in *Lindsay v. Commissioners* (2 Bay 38, 46. 53 [S.C.]) by the South Carolina attorney general. The first decision to use the term was *Beekman v. Saratoga and Schenectady R.R.* (3 Paige 45, 73 [1831]), a New York Chancery Court case.

26. 19 N.C. 451, 462.

27. *Declaration of Rights Made by the Representatives of the Freemen of North Carolina*, sec. 14; 19 N.C. 451, 464–66.

28. 19 N.C. 451, 466–67.

29. 19 N.C. 451, 469.

30. *Raleigh Register*, September 24, 1833; G. Edward White, *American Judicial Tradition*, 127–28.

31. *State v. Crawford*, 13 N.C. 425 (1830).

32. 13 N.C. 425, 426.

33. *State v. Martin,* 24 N.C. 101, 115 (1841).

34. 24 N.C. 101, 116–17.

35. *State v. Lane,* 26 N.C. 113, 120–21 (1843).

36. *State v. Scott,* 26 N.C. 409, 415, 416 (1844).

37. *State v. Craton,* 28 N.C. 165, 171 (1845).

38. 28 N.C. 165, 176, 179, 181–82.

39. *State v. Barfield,* 30 N.C. 344, 347–48 (1848).

40. 30 N.C. 344, 348–49.

41. 30 N.C. 344, 349–50.

42. Powell, *North Carolina,* 297; Lefler and Newsome, *History,* 372; Sowle, "North Carolina," 64; Yanuck, "Thomas Ruffin," 457; Franklin, *Free Negro,* 62–63; Hadden, "Worldview."

43. *State v. Mann,* 13 N.C. 263 (1829).

44. 13 N.C. 263, 265, 268. Cf. Mark Tushnet, *American Law,* 61–63, which argues that *Mann* actually represents the recognition of slave humanity.

45. 13 N.C. 263, 266.

46. 13 N.C. 263, 267.

47. 13 N.C. 263, 267.

48. 13 N.C. 263, 265.

49. 13 N.C. 263, 264.

50. *State v. Hoover,* 20 N.C. 500 (1839); Africa, "Slaveholding," 298. On the Nat Turner Rebellion as it related to North Carolina, see Elliott, "Nat Turner."

51. *State v. Will,* 18 N.C. 121, 171 (1834); *State v. Hoover,* 20 N.C. 500, 504.

52. 20 N.C. 500, 502–5 (1839).

53. 20 N.C. 500, 503.

54. *State v. Caesar,* 31 N.C. 391 (1849).

55. 31 N.C. 391, 405–6.

56. 31 N.C. 391, 413.

57. 31 N.C. 391, 420.

58. By making this argument, I do not intend—like Stanley Elkins—to claim that slaves internalized the perceptions of their masters, only that slaveholders did indeed think of their bondsmen in this way. See Elkins, *Slavery.*

59. 31 N.C. 391, 421.

60. 31 N.C. 391, 415.

61. Potter, *Impending Crisis,* 63–89.

62. "Address of Thomas Ruffin, Delivered before the State Agricultural Society of North Carolina, October 18th, 1855," in Hamilton, ed., *Papers,* 4:331, 329.

63. Hamilton, ed., *Papers,* 4:331.

64. Hamilton, ed., *Papers,* 4:333.

65. Hamilton, ed., *Papers,* 4:331, 333–34.

66. Ruffin to B. F. Moore, November 10, 1852, in Hamilton, ed., *Papers,* 2:346–47.

67. President Millard Fillmore considered Ruffin as a possible nominee when the nominations of Edward A. Bradford, George E. Badger, and William C. Micou ran into Senate opposition (Frederick Nash to Ruffin, December 27, 1852, Ruffin to J. B. G. Roulhac, February 7, 1853, Abram W. Venable to J. B. G. Roulhac, February 15, 1853, Edward Stanley to B. F. Moore, February 28, 1853, all in Hamilton, ed., *Papers,* 2:370–71, 386–88, 389). For Ruffin's refusal to revise the North Carolina statutes, see Ruffin to David S. Reid, July 11, 1853, in Hamilton, ed., *Papers,* 2: 401.

68. *Cyclopedia,* 2:43.

69. *Raleigh Register,* November 20, 1852, reprinted in Hamilton, ed., *Papers,* 2: 348; "Proceedings in the State Senate upon the Occasion of Judge Ruffin's Resignation, November 17, 1852," reprinted in Hamilton, ed., *Papers,* 2:350; James R. Dodge to Ruffin, November 17, 1852, in Hamilton, ed., *Papers,* 2:351. On Ruffin's retirement, see Connor, *North Carolina,* 2:65–70.

70. Connor, *North Carolina,* 2:68; Ruffin to B. F. Moore, November 10, 1852, in Hamilton, ed., *Papers,* 2:346–47.

71. On judicial election, see Hall, "Judiciary on Trial." Ruffin accepted the legislature's unanimous nomination to return to the supreme court in 1859 to lend legitimacy to a still struggling tribunal, though he resigned after less than a year's service for health reasons. See "Proceedings in the House of Commons, December 11, 1858: Election of Judge Ruffin," in Hamilton, ed., *Papers,* 2:618–19; Ruffin to Governor John W. Ellis, November 5, 1859, in Hamilton, ed., *Papers,* 3:49.

72. Hamilton, ed., *Papers,* 4:329; Chittenden, *Report,* 126–28.

73. Chittenden, *Report,* 126; Gunderson, *Old Gentlemen's Convention,* 94–95, 107–9; Andrew, "Judge Thomas Ruffin," 4–7.

74. Ruffin, *Diary,* 572.

75. Francis Nash, "Chief Justice Thomas Ruffin," in Hamilton, ed., *Papers,* 1: 42; "Thomas Ruffin's Substitute Ordinance of Separation from the Union, 1861," in Hamilton, ed., *Papers,* 4:337.

76. Hamilton, ed., *Papers,* 4:330; Ruffin to Andrew Johnson, August 19, 1865, in Hamilton, ed., *Papers,* 4:19; Andrew, "Judge Thomas Ruffin," 7–8. See also "Synopsis of a Speech by Thomas Ruffin in the Convention of 1861–1862," in Hamilton, ed., *Papers,* 4:337–38.

77. Ruffin to Andrew Johnson, August 19, 1865, in Hamilton, ed., *Papers,* 4:18–19, 20.

78. B. F. Moore to Ruffin, August 19, 1865, in Hamilton, ed., *Papers,* 4:21–23.

79. Hamilton, *Reconstruction,* 171–75.

80. Ruffin to Edward Conigland, July 2, 1866, in Hamilton, ed., *Papers,* 4:64–65.

81. Foner, *Reconstruction,* 181–84; Ruffin to Conigland, July 2, 1866, in Hamilton, ed., *Papers,* 4:66; Hamilton, *Reconstruction,* 171–76.

82. Ruffin to John K. Ruffin, July 8, 1869, in Hamilton, ed., *Papers,* 4:226.

83. Pound, *Formative Era,* 121.

CHAPTER SIX: GEORGE W. STONE, POLITICAL SECTIONALISM,
AND LEGAL NATIONALISM

1. "George W. Stone," 613; "Chief Justice George W. Stone"; "Stone, George Washington." Other useful sketches of Stone's life include Caffey, "George Washington Stone"; Owen, *Story*, 2:338–39.

2. Caffey, "George Washington Stone," 167. On legal education during this period, see Friedman, *History*, 318–22.

3. Brantley, *Chief Justice Stone*, 32–39; Vandiver, "Pioneer Talladega," 67. Brantley's book actually contains very little about Stone's life or work, although it does offer extensive quotations from Stone's poetry and much about Alabama politics. Its perspective, however, is quite outdated. The other two members of this group to become chief justice were W. P. Chilton and Samuel Rice.

4. Riley, *Makers*, 168–69; *Goodman and Mitchell v. Walker*, 30 Ala. 482, 495–96 (1857). On Alabama law, courts, and legal culture, see Brantley, "Law and Courts"; Brannon, "More"; Gardner, "Circuit Judges"; Brantley, "Our Law Books."

5. Brantley, *Chief Justice Stone*, 53–55.

6. Brantley, *Chief Justice Stone*, 55–58, 70–71; Vandiver, "Talladega County History," 235.

7. Brantley, *Chief Justice Stone*, 73; Albert Burton Moore, *History*, 205.

8. Brantley, *Chief Justice Stone*, 85–86, 93–97; *Memorial Record*, 2:149; Anderson, "Centennial," 147; Garrett, *Reminiscences*, 620–21.

9. Vandiver, "Pioneer Talladega," 110; *Mobile Daily Register*, January 22, 1856.

10. McPherson, *Battle Cry*, 430; Albert Burton Moore, *Conscription*, 12–26.

11. Confederate States of America Constitution, art. 3, sec. 1; *Ex parte Hill, in re Willis, Johnson, and Reynolds v. Confederate States*, 38 Ala. 429 (1863).

12. 38 Ala. 429, 445–47.

13. 38 Ala. 429, 454.

14. 38 Ala. 429, 450, 454.

15. 38 Ala. 429, 454–56.

16. *Ex parte Stringer*, 38 Ala. 457 (1863); *Ex parte Hill, in re Armistead v. Confederate States*, 38 Ala. 458 (1863); *State, ex rel. Dawson, in re Strawbridge and Mays*, 39 Ala. 367 (1864).

17. Gray and Starr, *Alabama*, 151; 39 Ala. 367, 400.

18. 38 Ala. 429, 455. On Stone and the conscription cases, see Caffey, "George Washington Stone," 174–79; DeBray, "Two Judicial Giants," 4–11.

19. *Ex parte Walton*, 60 N. C. 350 (1864); *Ex parte Coupland*, 26 Tex. 397; *Jeffers v. Fair*, 33 Ga. 347; *Burroughs v. Payton, Abrahams v. Same*, 16 Grattan, Va. 470; Hamilton, "State Courts"; Brummer, "Judicial Interpretation"; Van Zant, "Confederate Conscription." See also Manley, *Supreme Court*, on Florida's experience with conscription.

20. *Ex parte Mayer*, 27 Tex. 715 (1864); Sharkey, "Essay," 79 (emphasis added); Albert Burton Moore, *Conscription*, 162–63.

21. Bailey, "Disloyalty"; McMillan, *Constitutional Development*, 92–93; Brantley, *Chief Justice Stone*, 181–82.

22. *Penal Code*. Stone also married again in 1866, four years after his second wife's death.

23. Riley, *Makers*, 168; Gray and Starr, *Alabama*, 175–76; McMillan, *Constitutional Development*, 175–88; Going, *Bourbon Democracy*, 9–26; Brantley, *Chief Justice Stone*, 256–59; *Mobile Daily Register*, March 9, 1876.

24. John B. Myers, "Freedman," 61–64. See also Bethel, "Freedmen's Bureau," 65–67.

25. *Pickens' Adminstrator v. Pickens' Distributees*, 35 Ala. 442 (1860).

26. Bardaglio, *Reconstructing*, 182–83; Wallenstein, "Race," 375; *Burns v. State*, 48 Ala. 195 (1872).

27. *Green v. State*, 58 Ala. 190, 191, 194, 196 (1877).

28. *Hoover v. State*, 59 Ala. 57, 58, 60 (1877).

29. 59 Ala. 57, 60 (1877). In a later case, *Pace and Cox v. State*, 69 Ala. 231 (1881), Judge Henderson Sommerville again upheld the constitutionality of the anti-miscegenation statute and cited the previous opinions of both Manning and Stone.

30. *Green v. State*, 73 Ala. 26, 29–31 (1882).

31. 73 Ala. 26, 31–32.

32. 73 Ala. 26, 34–38; *Virginia v. Rives*, 100 U.S. 313 (1880); *Ex parte Virginia*, 100 U.S. 339 (1880); *Neal v. Delaware*, 103 U.S. 370 (1880).

33. 73 Ala. 26, 37, 41; *Slaughterhouse Cases*, 83 U.S. 36 (1873); *United States v. Cruikshank*, 92 U.S. 542 (1876).

34. 73 Ala. 26, 31. Judge Henderson Sommerville later affirmed this position in *State v. Agee*, 83 Ala. 110 (1887).

35. See, e.g., *Hunter v. Martin*, 4 Munford 1 (1814); *State v. Foreman*, 8 Yerger 256 (1835); *Padelford v. Savannah*, 14 Ga. 438 (1854).

36. *Slaughterhouse Cases*, 16 Wallace (83 U.S.), 36, 78 (1873); *Green v. State*, 73 Ala. 26, 32. Of Miller's interpretation of the amendment, Stone wrote, "Human sagacity cannot predict the clash of jurisdictions, the endless contentions, the usurpations and oppression which would ensue from the construction he was combatting so eloquently."

37. McBride, "Mid-Atlantic State Courts"; Nieman, *Promises*, 78–113; Woodward, *Strange Career*, 69–74.

38. Gillman, *Constitution Besieged*, 54–55.

39. *Perry v. New Orleans, Mobile and Chattanooga Railroad*, 55 Ala. 413, 425 (1876).

40. 55 Ala. 413, 420 (1876).

41. 55 Ala. 413, 420.

42. 55 Ala. 413, 418–24.

43. 55 Ala. 413, 426.

44. *Zeigler v. South and North Alabama Railroad*, 58 Ala. 594, 595–96 (1877).

45. 58 Ala. 594, 599.

46. *Smith v. Louisville and Nashville Railroad,* 75 Ala. 449, 450–51 (1883).

47. 75 Ala. 449, 451; *County of San Mateo v. Southern Pennsylvania Railroad,* 13 Fed. 145 (C.C. Cal. 1882).

48. *Brown v. Alabama Great Southern Railroad,* 87 Ala. 370, 371–72 (1888).

49. Stone, "Address," 112; Trachtenberg, *Incorporation,* 80–81.

50. Gillman, *Constitution Besieged,* 55, 57; Carrington, "Law"; Hyman and Wiecek, *Equal Justice,* 22–23; Corwine, "Doctrine," 383–84; Benedict, "Laissez-Faire," 323; Ely, *Guardian,* 87–88.

51. Richard Maxwell Brown, *No Duty,* 3.

52. Richard Maxwell Brown, *No Duty,* 8–17; *Erwin v. State,* 29 Ohio St. 186 (1876); *Runyan v. State,* 57 Ind. 80, 84 (1877). Neither of these decisions cited John Catron's infamous opinion in *Grainger v. State* (1829).

53. Richard Maxwell Brown, *No Duty,* 17–29; *State v. Gardner* 104 N.W. Rep. (1st ser.) 971 (1905); *State v. Barlett* 71 S.W. Rep (1st ser.) 148 (1902); *State v. Meyer,* 164 Pac. 926 (1917); *Miller v. State* and *Bromley v. State,* 110 N.W. 850 (1909).

54. *Bell v. State,* 17 Tex. Ct. App. 538 (1885).

55. *McManus v. State,* 36 Ala. 285, 286, 291 (1860).

56. 36 Ala. 285, 293–94.

57. Baum and Baum, *Law,* 6–8.

58. 36 Ala. 285, 293. On Stone's use of common-law principles in homicide cases, see also Adkinson, "George Washington Stone," 20–34.

59. *Ex parte Wray,* 30 Miss. 673 (1856). *Wray* seems typical of Mississippi's insistence on the highest degree of procedural and substantive exactness in the trying of criminal cases. Meredith D. Lang approvingly notes that "criminal justice in antebellum Mississippi developed into a precociously liberal phenomenon as it was molded by a high court which evinced a rather pronounced belief that the Mississippi courts should tolerate no unfair prosecution" (*Defender,* 122). Lang reads these Mississippi decisions through a contemporary lens, apparently unaware of the South's penchant for violence and of some courts' willingness to bend to community opinion (*Defender,* 94–122).

60. *Ex parte Nettles,* 58 Ala. 268, 274 (1877).

61. 58 Ala. 268, 274–75.

62. *Judge v. State,* 58 Ala. 406, 413–14 (1877).

63. *Mitchell v. State,* 60 Ala. 26, 32 (1877); *Bain v. State,* 70 Ala. 4, 7 (1881), quotation from *Bain.*

64. Blackstone, *Commentaries,* 4:184.

65. *Myers v. State,* 62 Ala. 599, 603 (1878). See also *Johnson v. State,* 102 Ala. 1, 19 (1893)

66. *Cleveland v. State,* 86 Ala. 1, 10 (1888). Stone's colleagues seconded his tough stance on the duty to retreat. See *Springfield v. State,* 96 Ala. 81 (1892).

67. Richard Maxwell Brown, "Southern Violence," 236. Professor Joseph H. Beale Jr. of Harvard Law School was one of the few to condemn this development. See Richard Maxwell Brown, *No Duty,* 24–26; Beale, "Retreat"; Beale, "Homicide."

68. *Alberty v. United States,* 162 U.S. 499 (1895); *Allen v. United States,* 164 U.S. 492 (1896); *Brown v. United States,* 256 U.S. 335, 343 (1921).

69. Richard Maxwell Brown, *No Duty,* 23–24.

70. *Polk v. State,* 62 Ala. 237 (1878); *Shorter v. State,* 63 Ala. 129 (1879); Adkinson, "George Washington Stone," 38–47.

71. "Memorial," 100 Ala. ix, xvi.

72. Stone to Mrs. David Clopton, September 29, 1888, Clay Papers.

73. Stone, "Address," 112, 119; Merchant, "Historical Background," 286; *Albany Law Journal* 41 (May 3, 1890), 360; Brantley, *Chief Justice Stone,* 281–82.

74. Brantley, *Chief Justice Stone,* 284.

75. Rodabaugh, "Turbulent Nineties," 140–41, 171–79; John B. Clark, *Populism,* 121, 145–46; Hackney, *Populism,* 43.

76. Donald, "Generation"; Foster, *Ghosts.*

77. Hall, *Magic Mirror,* 211–21; Chase, "Birth"; Surrency, "Law Reports"; Warren, *History,* 542–57.

78. "Fifty Years on the Bench," *American Law Review* 28 (March–April 1894): 263–64.

79. Quoted from John H. Miller to Stone, August 4, 1893, Stone Papers. See also *Birmingham Age Herald,* August 5, 1893; Sam Will John to Stone, n.d., H. Austill to Stone, August 4, 1893, J. Q. Cohen to Stone, August 4, 1893, William C. Ward to Stone, August 4, 1893, Thomas R. Rhoulhac to Stone, August 5, 1893, J. A. Bilbro to Stone, August 5, 1893, N. H. R. Dawson to Stone, August 12, 1893, all in Stone Papers. Stone undoubtedly received many more such letters.

80. See, e.g., *American Law Review* 228 (May–June 1894): 415; "Judge George W. Stone," extract from an unidentified newspaper, Stone Papers; "Memorial," 100 Ala. ix–xx; *Birmingham Age Herald,* March 13, 1894.

81. Francis G. Caffey to Mrs. James H. Hardaway, March 5, 1906, Stone Papers. Caffey did extensive research on Stone for *Great American Lawyers.* Caffey claimed that this figure was authoritative, unlike previous estimates.

82. *Albany Law Journal* 35 (June 11, 1887): 462; Vandiver, "Pioneer Talladega," 110.

CONCLUSION: SOUTHERN JUDGES AND AMERICAN LEGAL CULTURE

1. Catron, "Biographical Letter," 2:811; *Studstill v. State,* 7 Ga. 19 (1849); Horwitz, *Transformation, 1780–1860.*

2. Karsten, *Heart versus Head.*

3. Wiethoff, *Peculiar Humanism,* 6–7.

4. *Parsons v. State,* 81 Ala. 577 (1887); G. Edward White, *American Judicial Tradition,* 127. For a good example of a late-nineteenth-century judge who does not fit within this "formalistic" paradigm, see John Phillip Reid, *Chief Justice.*

5. Wiebe, *Search.*

6. Richard Maxwell Brown, *No Duty; Runyan v. State,* 57 Ind. 80, 84 (1877).

7. Beale, "Retreat," 582. See also Beale, "Homicide."

8. *Wally's Heirs v. Kennedy,* 10 Tenn. 554, 555–56 (1831); *Hoke v. Henderson,* 15 N.C. 1, 15 (1833).

9. *In re Jacobs,* 98 N.Y. 98 (1885); *Ritchie v. People,* 155 Ill. 98 (1895); Cooley, *Treatise;* Gillman, *Constitution Besieged,* 86–99.

10. Roane to James Monroe, February 16, 1820, in "Letters of Spencer Roane," 174; *State v Foreman,* 16 Tenn. 256 (1835).

11. Nieman, *Promises,* 78–113; *Slaughterhouse Cases,* 83 U.S. 36 (1873); *United States v. Cruikshank,* 92 U.S. 542 (1876).

12. *Plessy v. Ferguson,* 163 U.S. 537 (1896); Nieman, *Promises,* 78–113.

13. Foster, *Ghosts,* 145–59; Silber, *Romance,* 159–96.

14. Meltsner, "Southern Appellate Courts."

BIBLIOGRAPHY

MANUSCRIPT COLLECTIONS

Brand, Benjamin. Papers, 1779–1863. Virginia Historical Society, Richmond.

Catron, John. Papers. Tennessee State Library and Archives, Nashville.

Clay, Clement C. Papers. Special Collections Library, Duke University, Durham, N.C.

Donelson, Andrew Jackson. Papers. Tennessee State Library and Archives, Nashville.

Gaston, William. Papers. Southern Historical Collection, University of North Carolina, Chapel Hill.

Hemphill Family Papers. Special Collections Library, Duke University, Durham, N.C.

Hemphill, John. Papers. South Caroliniana Library, University of South Carolina, Columbia.

Jefferson, Thomas. Papers. Library of Congress.

Lumpkin, Joseph Henry. Papers. Hargrett Rare Book and Manuscripts Library, University of Georgia, Athens.

Lumpkin, Joseph Henry. Papers. Law Library, University of Georgia, Athens.

Monroe, James. Papers. Earl Greg Swem Library, College of William and Mary, Williamsburg, Va.

Roberts, Oran. Papers. Eugene C. Barker Texas History Collection, University of Texas, Austin.

Ruffin, Thomas. Papers. Southern Historical Collection, University of North Carolina, Chapel Hill.

Stone, George Washington. Papers. Alabama Department of Archives and History, Montgomery.

Wooldridge-Fleming-Stanard Papers. Virginia Historical Society, Richmond.

NEWSPAPERS AND CONTEMPORARY PERIODICALS

Albany Law Journal, Albany, N.Y.

American Law Register, Philadelphia, Pa.

American Law Review, Boston, Mass.

Birmingham Age Herald, Birmingham, Ala.

Knoxville Register, Knoxville, Tenn.

Milledgeville Federal Union, Milledgeville, Ga.

Mobile Daily Register, Mobile, Ala.

Nashville Union, Nashville, Tenn.

Raleigh Register, Raleigh, N.C.

Richmond Enquirer, Richmond, Va.

Southern Banner, Athens, Ga.

PUBLISHED DECISIONS, STATUTES, DEBATES, AND LEGISLATIVE JOURNALS

Acts of the General Assembly of the State of Georgia, Passed at Milledgeville at an Annual Session in November and December, 1858. Columbus, Ga.: Tenant Lomax State Printer, 1859.

Cases Argued and Decided in the Supreme Court of Mississippi. Chicago: T. H. Flood, 1910–65.

Cases Argued and Determined in the Supreme Court of North Carolina. Raleigh: State of North Carolina, 1903.

Chittenden, L. E. *A Report of the Debates and Proceedings in the Secret Sessions of the Conference Convention, for proposing Amendments to the Constitution of the United States, Held at Washington, D.C. in February, A.D. 1861.* New York: Appleton, 1864.

Journal of the Congress of the Confederate States of America, 1861–1865. Washington, D.C.: U.S. Government Printing Office, 1904.

Journal of the Convention, Assembled at the City of Austin on the Fourth of July, 1845, for the Purpose of Framing a Constitution of the State of Texas. Austin: Miner and Cruger, 1845.

Journal of the House of Representatives of the State of Tennessee. Knoxville: Ramsey and Craighead, 1831–36.

Laws Passed by the Second Legislature of the State of Texas. Houston: *Telegraph,* 1848.

Massachusetts Reports (includes *Pickering's Reports*). Boston: H. O. Houghton, 1900.

Official Reports of the Supreme Court. Washington, D.C.: U.S. Supreme Court.

Opinions of the Supreme Court of Texas, from 1840 to 1844. St. Paul, Minn.: West Publishing, 1883.

Penal Code of Alabama, Prepared by Geo. W. Stone and J. W. Shepherd and Adopted by the General Assembly at the Session of 1865–1866; Together with Other Criminal Laws Now in Force. Montgomery, Ala.: Reid and Screws, 1866.

Public Acts Passed at the General Assembly of the State of Tennessee. Nashville: Hall and Heiskell, 1801–9.

Public Acts Passed at the Stated Session of the Nineteenth General Assembly of the State of Tennessee, 1831. Nashville: Hall and Heiskell, 1832.

Reports of Cases Argued and Determined in the Court of Chancery of the State of New York, 1820–1845 (includes *Paige's Reports*). New York: Gould and Banks, 1830–48.

Reports of Cases Argued and Determined in the Supreme Court of Alabama. 2d ed. St. Paul, Minn: West Publishing Co., 1904–11.

Reports of Cases Argued and Determined in the Supreme Court of Judicature and in the Court for the Trial of Impeachments and the Correction of Errors in the State of New York. New York: I. Riley, 1814.

Reports of Cases Argued and Determined in the Supreme Court of Ohio. Cincinnati: Robert Clark, 1873–1982.

Reports of Cases Argued and Determined in the Supreme Court of South Carolina (includes *Bay's Reports*). St. Paul, Minn.: West Publishing, 1916–22.

Reports of Cases Argued and Determined in the Supreme Court of Tennessee. Nashville: State Printer, 1913–71.

Reports of Cases Decided in the Supreme Court of Indiana. Indianapolis: Bookwalter-Ball-Greathouse Printing, 1864–1981.

Reports of Cases in Law and Equity, Argued and Determined in the Supreme Court of the State of Georgia. Atlanta: State of Georgia, 1900–1907.

The Texas Reports: Cases Argued and Decided in the Supreme Court of the State of Texas. Austin: State of Texas, 1876–1963.

Virginia Reports, Jefferson—33 Grattan, 1730–1880, Annotated under the Supervision of Thomas Johnson Michie (includes *Call's Reports, Hening and Munford's Reports, Munford's Reports, Virginia Cases*). Charlottesville, Va.: Michie, 1900–1904.

Weeks, William. *Debates of the Texas Convention.* Houston: J. W. Cruger, 1846.

White, Joseph M., ed. *A New Collection of Laws, Charters, and Local Ordinances of the Governments of Great Britain, France, and Spain, Relating to the Concessions of Land in Their Respective Colonies; Together with the Laws of Mexico and Texas on the Same Subject.* 2 vols. Philadelphia: T. and J. W. Johnson, 1839.

OTHER SOURCES

Abraham, Henry J. *Justices and Presidents: A Political History of Appointments to the Supreme Court.* 3d ed. New York: Oxford University Press, 1992.

Adams, Herbert B. *Circulars of Information of the Bureau of Education, No. 1–1887, The College of William and Mary: A Contribution to the History of Higher Education, with Suggestions for Its National Promotion.* Washington, D.C.: U.S. Government Printing Office, 1887.

Adkinson, Janis Faye. "George Washington Stone and Alabama Criminal Law: A Battle against the Southern Legal Tradition," Master's thesis, University of Florida, 1991.

Africa, Philip. "Slaveholding in the Salem Community, 1777–1851." *North Carolina Historical Review* 54 (July 1977): 271–307.

Almand, Bond. "Code Duello in Georgia, 1740–1889." *Georgia Bar Journal* 13 (November 1950): 160–70.

———. "The Supreme Court of Georgia: An Account of Its Delayed Birth." In *A History of the Georgia Supreme Court,* ed. John B. Harris, 1–18. Savannah: Georgia Bar Association, 1948.

Ammon, Harry. "The Richmond Junto, 1800–1824." *Virginia Magazine of History and Biography* 61 (October 1953): 395–18.

Anderson, John C. "Centennial of the Supreme Court of Alabama." *Alabama Law Journal* 2 (May 1927): 143–60.

Andrew, Michael W., Jr. "Judge Thomas Ruffin and the Crisis of the Union: Ideology, Interest, and Secession." Bachelor's thesis, University of Florida, 1992.

Andrews, Garnett. *Reminiscences of an Old Georgia Lawyer.* Atlanta: Franklin, 1870.

Ashford, Gerald. "Jacksonian Liberalism and Spanish Law in Early Texas." *Southwestern Historical Quarterly* 57 (1953): 1–37.

Ashworth, John. *"Agrarians" and "Aristocrats": Party Political Ideology in the United States, 1837–1846.* Atlantic Highlands, N.J.: Humanities Press, 1983.

Atkins, Jonathan M. *Parties, Politics, and the Sectional Conflict in Tennessee, 1832–1861.* Knoxville: University of Tennessee Press, 1997.

Auchampaugh, Phillip. "James Buchanan, the Court and the Dred Scott Case." *Tennessee Historical Magazine* 9 (1926): 234–38.

Ayers, Edward. *The Promise of the New South: Life after Reconstruction.* New York: Oxford University Press, 1992.

———. *Vengeance and Justice: Crime and Punishment in the Nineteenth-Century American South.* New York: Oxford University Press, 1984.

Bailey, Hugh C. "Disloyalty in Early Confederate Alabama." *Journal of Southern History* 23 (November 1957): 522–28.

Baker, Leonard. *John Marshall: A Life in Law.* New York: Macmillan, 1974.

Baldwin, Joseph. *The Flush Times of Alabama and Mississippi: A Series of Sketches.* Reprint, New York: Hill and Wang, 1957.

Bardaglio, Peter. *Reconstructing the Household: Families, Sex, and the Law in the Nineteenth-Century South.* Chapel Hill: University of North Carolina Press, 1995.

Basch, Norma. *In the Eyes of the Law: Women, Marriage, and Property in Nineteenth-Century New York.* Ithaca: Cornell University Press, 1982.

Bassett, John Spencer, ed. *Correspondence of Andrew Jackson.* Vol. 5. Washington, D.C.: Carnegie Institution of Washington, 1931.

———. *The Life of Andrew Jackson.* Vol. 1. New York: Doubleday, Page, 1911.

Baum, Frederic S., and Joan Baum. *Law of Self-Defense.* Dobbs Ferry, N.Y.: Oceana Publications, 1970.

Beach, Rex. "Judge Spencer Roane." Master's thesis, University of Virginia, 1941.

———. "Spencer Roane and the Richmond Junto." *William and Mary Quarterly,* 2d ser., 22 (January 1942): 1–17.

Beale, Joseph H., Jr. "Homicide in Self-Defence." *Columbia Law Review* 3 (1903): 526–45.

———. "Retreat from Murderous Assault." *Harvard Law Review* 16 (1902–3): 567–82.

Benedict, Michael Les. "Laissez-Faire and Liberty: A Re-Evaluation of the Meaning and Origins of Laissez-Faire Constitutionalism." *Law and History Review* 3 (1985): 293–331.

Bergeron, Paul H. *Antebellum Politics in Tennessee.* Lexington: University Press of Kentucky, 1982.

———. "Tennessee's Response to the Nullification Crisis." *Journal of Southern History* 39 (1973): 23–44.

Bestor, Arthur, Jr. "State Sovereignty and Slavery: A Reinterpretation of Pro-Slavery Constitutional Doctrine, 1846–1860." *Journal of the Illinois State Historical Society* 54 (summer 1961): 117–80.

Bethel, Elizabeth. "The Freedmen's Bureau in Alabama." *Journal of Southern History* 14 (February 1948): 49–92.

Beveridge, Albert J. *Life of John Marshall.* 4 vols. Boston: Houghton Mifflin, 1919.

Billings, Dwight B., Jr. *Planters and the Making of a "New South": Class, Politics, and Development in North Carolina, 1865–1900.* Chapel Hill: University of North Carolina Press, 1979.

Bishop, Joel Prentiss. *Commentaries on the Criminal Law.* Boston: Little, Brown, 1856–58.

Blackstone, William. *Commentaries on the Laws of England.* New York: Oceana Publications, 1967.

Bloomfield, Maxwell. *American Lawyers in a Changing Society.* Cambridge: Harvard University Press, 1976.

———. "The Texas Bar in the Nineteenth Century." *Vanderbilt Law Review* 32 (January 1979): 261–76.

Bodenhamer, David J. "The Efficiency of Criminal Justice in the Antebellum South." *Criminal Justice History* 3 (1982): 81–95.

Boles, John B. "Evangelical Protestantism in the Old South: From Religious Dissent to Cultural Dominance." In *Religion in the South,* ed. Charles Reagan Wilson, 13–34. Jackson: University Press of Mississippi, 1985.

Boyd, William K. *History of North Carolina: The Federal Period, 1783–1860.* Chicago: Lewis Publishing, 1919.

Brannon, Peter A. "More about Early Alabama Lawyers." *Alabama Lawyer* 6 (April 1945): 123–69.

Brantley, William H., Jr. *Chief Justice Stone of Alabama.* Birmingham, Ala.: Birmingham Publishing, 1943.

———. "Law and Courts in Pioneer Alabama." *Alabama Lawyer* 6 (October 1945): 390–400.

———. "Our Law Books, 1819–1865." *Alabama Lawyer* 3 (October 1942): 363–82.

Brantly, W. T. *Life and Character of Joseph Henry Lumpkin: An Oration Delivered in Athens, Georgia before the Phi Kappa Society, August 5, 1867.* Savannah, Ga.: News and Herald, 1867.

Breen, T. H. *Tobacco Culture: The Mentality of the Great Tidewater Planters on the Eve of the Revolution.* Princeton: Princeton University Press, 1985.

Brisbin, Richard A., Jr. "John Marshall and the Nature of Law in the Early Republic." *Virginia Magazine of History and Biography* 98 (January 1990): 57–80.

Brown, John Henry. *Indian Wars and Pioneers of Texas.* Austin, Tex.: L. E. Daniell, n.d.

Brown, Richard Maxwell. *No Duty to Retreat: Violence and Values in American History and Society.* New York: Oxford University Press, 1991.

———. "Southern Violence—Regional Problem or National Nemesis? Legal Attitudes toward Southern Homicide in Historical Perspective." *Vanderbilt Law Review* 32 (January 1979): 225–50.

Bruce, Dickson, Jr. *Violence and Culture in the Antebellum South.* Austin: University of Texas Press, 1979.

Brummer, S. D. "The Judicial Interpretation of the Confederate Constitution." In *Studies in Southern History,* 107–33. New York: Columbia University Press, 1914.

Bryson, W. Hamilton. *Legal Education in Virginia, 1779–1979: A Biographical Approach.* Charlottesville: University Press of Virginia, 1982.

Butte, George C. "Early Development of Law and Equity in Texas." *Yale Law Journal* 26 (June 1917): 699–708.

Caffey, Gordon. "George Washington Stone, 1811–1894." In *Great American Lawyers: The Lives and Influence of Judges and Lawyers Who Have Acquired Permanent National Reputation, and Have Developed the Jurisprudence of the United States: A History of the Legal Profession in America,* ed. William Draper Lewis, 6:165–93. Philadelphia: John C. Winston, 1907–9.

Caldwell, Joshua W. *Sketches of the Bench and Bar of Tennessee.* Knoxville: Ogden Brothers, 1898.

Calendar of Virginia State Papers and Other Manuscripts. Vols. 3–7. Richmond: Library Committee, Virginia Legislature, 1883–88.

Calhoon, Robert M. *Evangelicals and Conservatives in the Early South, 1740–1861.* Columbia: University of South Carolina Press, 1990.

Campbell, Bruce A. "John Marshall, the Virginia Political Economy, and the Dartmouth College Decision." *American Journal of Legal History* 19 (1975): 40–65.

Campbell, Randolph. *An Empire for Slavery: The Peculiar Institution in Texas, 1821–1865.* Baton Rouge: Louisiana State University Press, 1989.

———. "Planters and Plain Folks: The Social Structure of the Antebellum South." In *Interpreting Southern History: Historiographical Essays in Honor of Sanford W. Higginbotham,* ed. John B. Boles and Evelyn Thomas Nolen, 48–77. Baton Rouge: Louisiana State University Press, 1987.

Carlson, James A. "The Iron Horse in Court: Thomas Ruffin and the Development of North Carolina Railroad Law." Master's thesis, University of North Carolina—Chapel Hill, 1972.

Carpenter, Channing C. "The Influence of Justice Thomas Ruffin on American Constitutional Law." Ph.D. diss., University of Nebraska, 1972.

Carrington, Paul D. "Law as 'The Common Thoughts of Men': The Law-Teaching and Judging of Thomas McIntyre Cooley." *Stanford Law Review* 49 (1997): 495–546.

Cash, W. J. *The Mind of the South.* New York: Vintage, 1991.

Catalogue of Wilberforce University, 1859–1860. Cincinnati: R. P. Thompson, 1860.

Catron, John. "Biographical Letter from Justice Catron." In *Portraits of Eminent Americans Now Living, with Biographical and Historical Memoirs of Their Lives and Actions,* ed. John Livingston, 2:805–12. New York: Cornish, Lamport, 1853.

Chandler, Walter. "The Centenary of Associate Justice John Catron of the United States Supreme Court." *Tennessee Law Review* 15 (1937): 32–51.

Channing, Edward. *A History of the United States.* New York: Macmillan, 1927–30.

Chase, Anthony. "The Birth of the Modern Law School." *American Journal of Legal History* 23 (1979): 329–48.

"Chief Justice George W. Stone." *Alabama Lawyer* 31 (January 1970): 165.

Chroust, Anton-Hermann. *The Rise of the Legal Profession in America.* Vol. 2. Norman: University of Oklahoma Press, 1965.

Clark, John B. *Populism in Alabama.* Auburn, Ala.: Auburn Printing, 1927.

Clark, Walter. *Addresses at the Unveiling and Presentation to the State of the Statue of Thomas Ruffin, by the North Carolina Bar Association, Delivered in the Hall of the House of Representatives, 1 February, 1915.* Raleigh, N.C.: Edwards and Broughton, 1915.

———. "Thomas Ruffin, 1787–1870." In *Great American Lawyers: The Lives and Influence of Judges and Lawyers Who Have Acquired Permanent National Reputation, and Have Developed the Jurisprudence of the United States: A History of the Legal Profession in America,* ed. William Draper Lewis, 4:279–97. Philadelphia: John C. Winston, 1907–9.

Clarke, Mary Whatley. *Thomas J. Rusk: Soldier, Statesman, Jurist.* Austin, Tex.: Jenkins Publishing, 1971.

Clayton, W. W. *History of Davidson County, Tennessee.* Philadelphia: J. W. Lewis, 1880.

Cleveland, Len G. "The Establishment of the Georgia Supreme Court." *Georgia State Bar Journal* 9 (May 1973): 417–23.

Clinton, Robert Lowry. *Marbury v. Madison and Judicial Review.* Lawrence: University Press of Kansas, 1989.

Cobb, James C. "The Making of a Secessionist: Henry L. Benning and the Coming of the Civil War." *Georgia Historical Quarterly* 60 (1976): 313–23.

Cobb, Thomas R. R. *An Inquiry into the Law of Negro Slavery in the United States of America, to Which Is Prefixed an Historical Sketch of Slavery.* Vol. 1. Philadelphia: T. and J. W. Johnson, 1858.

Cody, L. L. *The Lumpkin Family of Georgia.* Macon, Ga.: n.p., 1928.

Cole, Donald B. *The Presidency of Andrew Jackson.* Lawrence: University Press of Kansas, 1993.

Colyar, A. S. *Life and Times of Andrew Jackson: Soldier, Statesman, President.* Vol. 2. Nashville, Tenn.: Marshall and Bruce, 1904.

Commager, Henry S. *Documents of American History*. 7th ed. New York: Appleton-Century-Crofts, 1963.

Connor, R. D. W. *North Carolina: Rebuilding an Ancient Commonwealth, 1584–1925*. Vol. 2. Chicago: American Historical Society, 1929.

Cooley, Thomas. *A Treatise upon the Constitutional Limitations Which Rest upon the Legislative Power of the States of the American Union*. Boston: Little, Brown, 1927.

Cooper, William J., Jr. *Liberty and Slavery: Southern Politics to 1860*. New York: McGraw-Hill, 1983.

———. *The South and the Politics of Slavery, 1828–1856*. Baton Rouge: Louisiana State University Press, 1978.

Corlew, Robert E. *Tennessee: A Short History*. Knoxville: University of Tennessee Press, 1990.

Corwine, Edward S. "The Doctrine of Due Process of Law before the Civil War." *Harvard Law Review* 24 (March 1911): 366–85.

Cory, Earl Wallace. "Temperance and Prohibition in Ante-Bellum Georgia." Master's thesis, University of Georgia, 1961.

Coulter, E. Merton. *College Life in the Old South, as Seen at the University of Georgia*. Athens: University of Georgia Press, 1928.

———. *Georgia: A Short History*. Chapel Hill: University of North Carolina Press, 1947.

Counihan, Harold J. "The North Carolina Constitutional Convention of 1835: A Study in Jacksonian Democracy." *North Carolina Historical Review* 46 (October 1969): 335–64.

Cover, Robert. *Justice Accused: Antislavery and the Judicial Process*. New Haven: Yale University Press, 1975.

Cullen, Charles T. *St. George Tucker and the Law in Virginia*. New York: Garland Publishing, 1987.

Curtis, Rosalee Morris. *John Hemphill: First Chief Justice of the State of Texas*. Austin, Tex.: Jenkins Publishing, 1971.

Cyclopedia of Eminent and Representative Men of the Carolinas of the Nineteenth Century. 2 vols. Madison, Wis.: Brant and Fuller, 1892.

Davenport, J. H. *The History of the Supreme Court of the State of Texas*. Austin, Tex.: Southern Law Book Publishers, 1917.

DeBray, Thomas R. "Two Judicial Giants of the Alabama Supreme Court." Bachelor's thesis, University of Alabama, 1977.

Degler, Carl N. *Place over Time: The Continuity of Southern Distinctiveness*. Baton Rouge: Louisiana State University Press, 1977.

Devitt, Fred, Jr. "William and Mary: America's First Law School." *William and Mary Law Review* 2 (1960): 424–36.

Dillon, John F. *Commentaries on the Law of Municipal Corporations*. 3d ed. Boston: Little, Brown, 1881.

———. "The Homestead Exemption." *American Law Register* 10 (1862): 641–717.

————. *The Laws and Jurisprudence of England and America, Being a Series of Lectures Delivered before Yale University.* Boston: Little, Brown, 1895.

Dimond, E. Grey, and Herman Hattaway, eds. *Letters from Forest Place: A Plantation Family's Correspondence, 1846–1881.* Jackson: University Press of Mississippi, 1993.

Dodd, William E. "Chief Justice Marshall and Virginia, 1813–1821." *American Historical Review* 12 (July 1907): 776–87.

Donald, David. "A Generation of Defeat." In *From the Old South to the New: Essays on the Transitional South,* ed. Walter J. Fraser Jr. and Winfred B. Moore Jr., 3–20. Westport, Conn.: Greenwood, 1981.

————. "The Proslavery Argument Reconsidered." *Journal of Southern History* 37 (February 1971): 3–18.

Dumbauld, Edward. *Thomas Jefferson and the Law.* Norman: University of Oklahoma Press, 1978.

Dunlap, Boutwell. "Judge John Catron of the United States Supreme Court." *Virginia Magazine of History and Biography* 28 (1920): 171–74.

Elkins, Stanley. *Slavery: A Problem in American Institutional and Intellectual Life.* Chicago: University of Chicago Press, 1959.

Elliott, Robert N. "The Nat Turner Insurrection as Reported in the North Carolina Press." *North Carolina Historical Review* 38 (January 1961): 1–18.

Elliott, Byron K., and William F. Elliott. *A Treatise on the Law of Railroads, Containing a Consideration of the Organization, Status, and Powers of Railroad Corporation, and of the Rights and Liabilities Incident to the Location, Construction, and Operation of Railroads, and also the Duties, Rights, and Liabilities of Railroad Companies as Carriers, under the Rules of the Common Law and the Interstate Commerce Act.* Indianapolis: Bowen-Merrill, 1897.

Ellis, Richard E. *The Jeffersonian Crisis: Courts and Politics in the Young Republic.* New York: Norton, 1971.

Ely, James W., Jr. *The Chief Justiceship of Melville W. Fuller, 1888–1910.* Columbia: University of South Carolina Press, 1995.

————. *The Guardian of Every Other Right.* New York: Oxford University Press, 1992.

Ely, James W., Jr. and David J. Bodenhamer. "Regionalism and American Legal History: The Southern Experience." *Vanderbilt Law Review* 39 (1986): 539–67.

————. "Regionalism and the Legal History of the South." In *Ambivalent Legacy: A Legal History of the South,* ed. David J. Bodenhamer and James W. Ely Jr., 3–29. Jackson: University Press of Mississippi, 1984.

England, J. Merton. "The Free Negro in Antebellum Tennessee." *Journal of Southern History* 9 (1943): 37–58.

Escott, Paul. *Many Excellent People: Power and Privilege in North Carolina, 1850–1900.* Chapel Hill: University of North Carolina Press, 1985.

Evans, Emory G. "Private Indebtedness and the Revolution in Virginia, 1776–1796." *William and Mary Quarterly,* 3d ser., 28 (1971): 349–74.

Fancher, Frank Trigg. *The Sparta Bar*. Milford, N.H.: Cabinet Press, 1950.

Farber, James. *Texas, C.S.A.. A Spotlight on Disaster*. New York: Jackson, 1947.

Farmer, Fannie Memory. "Legal Education in North Carolina, 1820–1860." *North Carolina Historical Review* 28 (July 1951): 271–97.

———. "Legal Practice and Ethics in North Carolina, 1820–1860." *North Carolina Historical Review* 30 (July 1953): 329–53.

Faulkner, Robert Kenneth. *The Jurisprudence of John Marshall*. Princeton: Princeton University Press, 1968.

Faust, Drew G. "The Peculiar South Revisited: White Society, Culture, and Politics in the Antebellum Period, 1800–1860." In *Interpreting Southern History: Historiographical Essays in Honor of Sanford W. Higginbotham*, ed. John B. Boles and Evelyn Thomas Nolen, 78–119. Baton Rouge: Louisiana State University Press, 1987.

Fede, Andrew. *People without Rights: An Interpretation of the Fundamentals of the Law of Slavery in the U.S. South*. New York: Garland Publishing, 1992.

———. "Toward a Solution of the Slave Law Dilemma: A Critique of Tushnet's *The American Law of Slavery*." *Law and History Review* 2 (fall 1984): 301–20.

Fehrenbacher, Don E. *Constitutions and Constitutionalism in the Slaveholding South*. Athens: University of Georgia Press, 1989.

———. *The Dred Scott Case: Its Significance in American Law and Politics*. New York: Oxford University Press, 1978.

———. "Roger B. Taney and the Sectional Crisis." *Journal of Southern History* 43 (November 1977): 555–66.

Fielder, Herbert. *A Sketch of the Life and Times and Speeches of Joseph E. Brown*. Springfield, Mass.: Press of Springfield Printing Company, 1883.

Filler, Louis. *The Crusade against Slavery*. New York: Harper and Row, 1960.

Finkelman, Paul. "Exploring Southern Legal History." *North Carolina Law Review* 64 (November 1985): 77–116.

———. *An Imperfect Union: Slavery, Federalism, and Comity*. Chapel Hill: University of North Carolina Press, 1981.

———. "The Peculiar Laws of the Peculiar Institution." *Reviews in American History* 10 (September 1982): 358–63.

———. "Prelude to the Fourteenth Amendment: Black Legal Rights in the Antebellum North." *Rutgers Law Journal* 17 (1986): 415–586.

———. "Slaves as Fellow Servants: Ideology, Law, and Industrialization." *American Journal of Legal History* 31 (1987): 269–305.

———. "States' Rights North and South in Antebellum America." In *An Uncertain Tradition: Constitutionalism and the History of the South*, ed. Kermit L. Hall and James W. Ely, Jr., 125–58. Athens: University of Georgia Press, 1989.

Fischer, David Hackett. *Albion's Seed: Four British Folkways in America*. New York: Oxford University Press, 1989.

Fisher, John E. "The Legal Status of Free Blacks in Texas, 1836–1861." *Texas Southern Law Review* 4 (1976): 342–62.

Fisher, William W., III. "Ideology and Imagery in the Law of Slavery." In *Slavery and the Law,* ed. Paul Finkelman, 43–85. Madison, Wis.: Madison House, 1997.

Flanigan, Daniel. "Criminal Procedure in Slave Trials in the Antebellum South." *Journal of Southern History* 40 (November 1974): 537–64.

Folmsbee, Stanley J. *Sectionalism and Internal Improvements in Tennessee, 1796–1845.* Knoxville: University of Tennessee Press, 1939.

Foner, Eric. *Free Soil, Free Labor, Free Men: The Ideology of the Republican Party on the Eve of the Civil War.* New York: Oxford University Press, 1970.

———. *Reconstruction: America's Unfinished Revolution, 1863–1877.* New York: Oxford University Press, 1988.

Foote, Henry S. *The Bench and the Bar of the South and Southwest.* St. Louis, Mo.: Soule, Thomas and Wentworth, 1876.

Ford, Paul L., ed. *Essays on the Constitution of the United States.* Brooklyn, N.Y.: Historical Printers Club, 1892.

———, ed. *The Writings of Thomas Jefferson.* 12 vols. New York: G. P. Putnam's Sons, 1904–5.

Foster, Gaines M. *Ghosts of the Confederacy: Defeat, the Lost Cause, and the Emergence of the New South.* New York: Oxford University Press, 1987.

Franklin, John Hope. *The Free Negro in North Carolina, 1790–1860.* Chapel Hill: University of North Carolina Press, 1943.

———. *The Militant South, 1800–1861.* Cambridge: Harvard University Press, 1956.

Freehling, William W. *Prelude to Civil War: The Nullification Controversy in South Carolina, 1816–1836.* New York: Harper and Row, 1965.

Freehling, William W., and Craig M. Simpson, eds. *Secession Debated: Georgia's Showdown in 1860.* New York: Oxford University Press, 1992.

Friedman, Lawrence. *Crime and Punishment in American History.* New York: Basic Books, 1993.

———. *A History of American Law.* 2d ed. New York: Simon and Schuster, 1985.

Frierson, William L. "Some Incidents in the History of Tennessee's Court of Last Resort." *Proceedings of the Twenty-Third Annual Meeting of the Bar Association of Tennessee* (1904): 148–62.

Gaines, Reuben Reid. "John Hemphill, 1803–1862." In *Great American Lawyers: The Lives and Influence of Judges and Lawyers Who Have Acquired Permanent National Reputation, and Have Developed the Jurisprudence of the United States: A History of the Legal Profession in America,* ed. William Draper Lewis, 4:3–26. Philadelphia: John C. Winston, 1907–9.

Gardner, Lucien D. "The Circuit Judges of Alabama." *Alabama Lawyer* 1 (October 1940): 280–92.

Garrett, William. *Reminiscences of Public Men in Alabama, for Thirty Years.* Atlanta: Plantation, 1872.

Gass, Edmund C. "The Constitutional Opinions of Justice John Catron." *East Tennessee Historical Society's Publications* 8 (1936): 54–73.

Gatell, Frank Otto. "John Catron." In *The Justices of the United States Supreme Court, 1789–1978,* ed. Leon Friedman and Fred L. Israel, 1:737–49. New York: Chelsea House, 1969.

Gelbach, Clyde Christian. "Spencer Roane of Virginia, 1762–1822: A Judicial Advocate of States' Rights." Ph.D. diss., University of Pittsburgh, 1955.

Genovese, Eugene D. *The Political Economy of Slavery.* New York: Vintage, 1965.

———. *Roll, Jordan, Roll: The World the Slaves Made.* New York: Random House, 1972.

"George W. Stone." In *Northern Alabama: Historical and Biographical,* 613. Birmingham, Ala.: Smith and DeLand, 1888.

Gillman, Howard. *The Constitution Besieged: The Rise and Demise of Lochner Era Police Powers Jurisprudence.* Durham, N.C.: Duke University Press, 1993.

Gilmer, Daffan. "Early Courts and Lawyers of Texas." *Texas Law Review* 12 (June 1934): 435–52.

Gilmore, Grant. *The Ages of American Law.* New Haven: Yale University Press, 1977.

Goebel, Julius, Jr. "The Common Law and the Constitution." In *Chief Justice Marshall: A Reappraisal,* ed. W. Melville Jones, 101–23. Ithaca: Cornell University Press, 1956.

———. *History of the Supreme Court of the United States.* Vol. 1, *Antecedents and Beginnings to 1801.* New York: Macmillan, 1971.

Going, Allen Johnston. *Bourbon Democracy in Alabama, 1874–1890.* University: University of Alabama Press, 1951.

Goodman, Paul. "The Emergence of Homestead Exemption in the United States: Accommodation and Resistance to the Market Revolution, 1840–1880." *Journal of American History* 80 (September 1993): 470–98.

Graham, William A. *Life and Character of the Hon. Thomas Ruffin, Late Chief Justice of North Carolina: A Memorial Oration by William A. Graham, Delivered before the Agricultural Society of the State, by Its Request, at the Annual Fair in Raleigh, Oct. 21st, 1870.* Raleigh: Nichols and Gorman, 1871.

Gray, Daniel Savage, and J. Barton Starr. *Alabama: A Place, a People, a Point of View.* Dubuque, Iowa: Kendall/Hunt Publishing, 1977.

Green, John W. *Lives of the Judges of the Supreme Court of Tennessee, 1796–1947.* Knoxville, Tenn.: Archer and Smith, 1947.

Greenberg, Kenneth. *Masters and Statesmen: The Political Culture of American Slavery.* Baltimore: Johns Hopkins University Press, 1985.

Greene, Lee Seifert, and Robert Sterling Avery. *Government in Tennessee.* 2d ed. Knoxville: University of Tennessee Press, 1982.

Gregg, Alexander. *Eulogy on the Hon. John Hemphill and Gen. Hugh McLeod, Delivered in the Capitol, Austin, February 1st, 1862.* Houston: Telegraph, 1862.

Gregorie, Anne King. *History of Sumter County, South Carolina.* Sumter, S.C.: Library Board of Sumter County, 1954.

Gresham, L. Paul. "The Public Career of Hugh Lawson White." *Tennessee Historical Quarterly* 3 (1944): 291–318.

Grice, Warren. *The Georgia Bench and Bar: The Development of Georgia's Judicial System.* Macon, Ga.: J. W. Burke, 1931.

Guild, J. C. *Old Times in Tennessee with Historical, Personal, and Political Scraps and Sketches.* Nashville: Tavel, Eastman, and Howell, 1878.

Gulick, C. A., and K. Elliot, eds. *The Papers of Mirabeau Buonaparte Lamar.* 6 vols. New York: AMS Press, 1973.

Gunderson, Robert Gray. *The Old Gentlemen's Convention: The Washington Peace Conference of 1861.* Madison: University of Wisconsin Press, 1961.

Gunther, Gerald, ed. *John Marshall's Defense of McCulloch v. Maryland.* Stanford, Calif.: Stanford University Press, 1969.

Haar, Charles M. *The Golden Age of American Law.* New York: George Braziller, 1965.

Hackney, Sheldon. *Populism to Progressivism in Alabama.* Princeton: Princeton University Press, 1969.

Hadden, Sally. "The Worldview of Thomas Ruffin: Before *State v. Mann.*" Paper presented at the annual meeting of the American Society for Legal History, Minneapolis, Minn., October 18, 1997.

Haines, Charles Grove. *The American Doctrine of Judicial Supremacy.* New York: Macmillan, 1914.

Hale, Will T., and Dixon L. Merritt. *A History of Tennessee and Tennesseeans.* Vol. 3. Chicago: Lewis Publishing, 1913.

Hall, Kermit L. "The Judiciary on Trial: State Constitutional Reform and the Rise of an Elected Judiciary, 1846–1860." *Historian* 46 (May 1983): 337–54.

———. *The Magic Mirror: Law in American History.* New York: Oxford University Press, 1989.

———. "The Promises and Perils of Prosopography—Southern Style." *Vanderbilt Law Review* 32 (1979): 331–39.

———. "The 'Route to Hell' Retraced: The Impact of Popular Election on the Southern Appellate Judiciary, 1832–1920." In *Ambivalent Legacy: A Legal History of the South,* ed. David J. Bodenhamer and James W. Ely Jr., 229–55. Jackson: University Press of Mississippi, 1984.

Hallum, John. *The Diary of an Old Lawyer.* Nashville, Tenn.: Southwestern Publishing, 1895.

Hamilton, J. G. de Roulhac, ed. *The Papers of Thomas Ruffin.* 4 vols. Raleigh, N.C.: Edwards and Broughton, 1918.

———. *Reconstruction in North Carolina.* New York: Longmans, Green, 1914.

———. "The State Courts and the Confederate Constitution." *Journal of Southern History* 4 (November 1938): 425–48.

Hargrett, Lester. "Student Life at the University of Georgia in the 1840s." *Georgia Historical Quarterly* 8 (March 1924): 49–59.

Harris, John B., ed. *A History of the Georgia Supreme Court*. Savannah: Georgia Bar Association, 1948.

Harrison, Joseph H. "Oligarchs and Democrats: The Richmond Junto." *Virginia Magazine of History and Biography* 78 (April 1970): 184–98.

Hart, James P. "John Hemphill—Chief Justice of Texas." *Southwestern Law Journal* 3 (fall 1949): 395–415.

Haskins, George L. "Homestead Exemptions." *Harvard Law Review* 63 (June 1950): 1289–1320.

Hemphill, John. *Eulogy on the Life and Character of the Hon. Thomas J. Rusk, Late U.S. Senator from Texas*. Austin, Tex.: John Marshall, 1857.

———. *An Oration Delivered on the Fourth of July, 1832, at Sumter Court House*. Sumterville, S.C.: *Gazette*, 1832.

Henry, William Wirt, ed. *Patrick Henry: Life, Correspondence, and Speeches*. New York: Charles Scribner's Sons, 1891.

Hill, Samuel S., Jr. *The South and the North in American Religion*. Athens: University of Georgia Press, 1980.

Hindus, Michael. *Prison and Plantation: Crime, Justice, and Authority in Massachusetts and South Carolina, 1767–1878*. Chapel Hill: University of North Carolina Press, 1980.

History of Tennessee, from the Earliest Time to the Present. Nashville: Goodspeed, 1887.

Hoffman, William S. *Andrew Jackson and North Carolina Politics*. Chapel Hill: University of North Carolina Press, 1958.

Hofstadter, Richard. *The American Political Tradition*. New York: Vintage, 1948.

Hogan, William Ransom. *The Texas Republic: A Social and Economic History*. Norman: University of Oklahoma Press, 1946.

Hollon, W. Eugene. *Frontier Violence: Another Look*. New York: Oxford University Press, 1974.

Horsnell, Margaret E. *Spencer Roane: Judicial Advocate of Jeffersonian Principles*. New York: Garland Publishing, 1986.

Horton, John. *James Kent: A Study in Conservatism, 1763–1847*. Reprint, New York: Da Capo Press, 1969.

Horwitz, Morton J. *The Transformation of American Law, 1780–1860*. Cambridge: Harvard University Press, 1977.

———. *The Transformation of American Law, 1870–1960: The Crisis of Legal Orthodoxy*. New York: Oxford University Press, 1992.

Howe, Daniel Walker. *The Political Culture of the American Whigs*. Chicago: University of Chicago Press, 1979.

———. "Religion and Politics in the Antebellum North." In *Religion and American Politics: From the Colonial Period to the 1980s*, ed. Mark Noll, 121–45. New York: Oxford University Press, 1990.

Howington, Arthur F. "'Not in the Condition of a Horse or an Ox': *Ford v. Ford*, the Law of Testamentary Manumission and the Tennessee Court's Recognition of Slave Humanity." *Tennessee Historical Quarterly* 34 (1975): 249–63.

———. "'A Property of Special and Peculiar Value': The Tennessee Supreme Court and the Law of Manumission." *Tennessee Historical Quarterly* 44 (1985): 302–17.

Hoyt, William Henry, ed. *The Papers of Archibald D. Murphey.* 2 vols. Raleigh, N.C.: E. M. Uzzell, 1914.

Huebner, Timothy S. "Consolidation of State Judicial Power: Spencer Roane, Virginia Legal Culture, and the Southern Judicial Tradition." *Virginia Magazine of History and Biography* 102 (1994): 47–72.

———. "Encouraging Economic Development: Joseph Henry Lumpkin and the Law of Contract, 1846–1860." *Georgia Journal of Southern Legal History* 1 (1991): 357–75.

———. "Joseph Henry Lumpkin and Evangelical Reform in Georgia: Temperance, Education, and Industrialization, 1830–1860." *Georgia Historical Quarterly* 75 (1991): 254–74.

Hughes, Robert M. "William and Mary, the First American Law School." *William and Mary Quarterly,* 2d ser., 2 (January 1922): 40–48.

Hurst, James Willard. *Law and the Conditions of Freedom in the Nineteenth Century United States.* Madison: University of Wisconsin Press, 1956.

Huston, Cleburne. *Towering Texan: A Biography of Thomas J. Rusk.* Waco, Tex.: Texian Press, 1971.

Hyman, Harold, and William M. Wiecek. *Equal Justice under Law: Constitutional Development, 1835–1875.* New York: Harper and Row, 1982.

Ingersoll, Henry Hulbert. "John Catron, 1781–1865." In *Great American Lawyers: The Lives and Influence of Judges and Lawyers Who Have Acquired Permanent National Reputation, and Have Developed the Jurisprudence of the United States: A History of the Legal Profession in America,* ed. William Draper Lewis, 4:241–76. Philadelphia: John C. Winston, 1907–9.

James, Marquis. *The Life of Andrew Jackson.* New York: Bobbs-Merrill, 1933.

Jeffrey, Thomas E. "Internal Improvements and Political Parties in Antebellum North Carolina, 1836–1860." *North Carolina Historical Review* 55 (April 1978): 111–56.

Johnson, Herbert A. "The Palmetto and the Oak: Law and Constitution in Early South Carolina, 1670–1800." In *An Uncertain Tradition: Constitutionalism and the History of the South,* ed. Kermit L. Hall and James W. Ely Jr., 83–101. Athens: University of Georgia Press, 1989.

Johnson, Michael. *Toward a Patriarchal Republic: The Secession of Georgia.* Baton Rouge: Louisiana State University Press, 1977.

Johnston, Richard Malcolm. *Autobiography of Col. Richard Malcolm Johnston.* Washington, D.C.: Neale, 1900.

Jones, Alan Robert. "The Constitutional Conservatism of Thomas McIntyre Cooley: A Study in the History of Ideas." Ph.D. diss., University of Michigan, 1960.

Jones, Thomas B. "The Public Lands of Tennessee." *Tennessee Historical Quarterly* 27 (1968): 13–36.

Jordan, Terry G. "The Imprint of the Upper and Lower South of Mid–Nineteenth Century Texas." *Annals of the Association of American Geographers* 57 (1967): 667–90.

Jordan, Winthrop D. *White over Black: American Attitudes toward the Negro, 1550–1812*. Chapel Hill: University of North Carolina Press, 1968.

Journal of the House of Representatives of the State of Tennessee. Knoxville: Ramsey and Craighead, 1831–36.

"Judge Spencer Roane of Virginia: Champion of States' Rights—Foe of John Marshall." *Harvard Law Review* 66 (1953): 1242–59.

Karsten, Peter. *Heart versus Head: Judge-Made Law in Nineteenth-Century America*. Chapel Hill: University of North Carolina Press, 1997.

Kent, James. *Commentaries on American Law*. New York: O. Halsted, 1826–30.

Kenzer, Robert. *Kinship and Neighborhood in a Southern Community: Orange County, North Carolina, 1849–1881*. Knoxville: University of Tennessee Press, 1987.

Kerr, Charles. "If Spencer Roane Had Been Appointed Chief Justice Instead of John Marshall." *American Bar Association Journal* 20 (1934): 167–72.

King, Alvy L. *Louis T. Wigfall: Southern Fire-Eater*. Baton Rouge: Louisiana State University Press, 1970.

Kirtland, Charles. *George Wythe: Lawyer, Revolutionary, Judge*. New York: Garland Publishing, 1986.

Knight, Lucien Lamar. *Reminiscences of Famous Georgians*. Atlanta: Franklin-Turner, 1908.

Kutler, Stanley I. *John Marshall: Great Lives Observed*. Englewood Cliffs, N.J.: Prentice-Hall, 1972.

———. *Judicial Power and Reconstruction Politics*. Chicago: University of Chicago Press, 1968.

———. *Privilege and Creative Destruction: The Charles River Bridge Case*. Baltimore: Johns Hopkins University Press, 1990.

Lacey, John F. *A Digest of Railway Decisions*. Chicago: Callaghan, 1875.

Lang, Meredith D. *Defender of the Faith: The High Court of Mississippi, 1817–1875*. Jackson: University Press of Mississippi, 1977.

Langum, David J. "The Role of Intellect and Fortuity in Legal Change: An Incident from the Law of Slavery." *American Journal of Legal History* 28 (1984): 1–16.

Lathan, Robert. *History of Hopewell Associate Reformed Presbyterian Church, Chester County, South Carolina, Together with Biographical Sketches of Its Former Pastors*. Yorkville, S.C.: Yorkville Enquirer, 1879.

Latner, Richard B. *The Presidency of Andrew Jackson: White House Politics, 1829–1837*. Athens: University of Georgia Press, 1979.

Laughlin, S. H. "Sketches of Notable Men: Judge John Catron." *Tennessee Historical Magazine* 4 (1918): 76–77.

Lefler, Hugh Talmage, and Albert Ray Newsome. *The History of a Southern State: North Carolina*. Chapel Hill: University of North Carolina Press, 1973.

Lender, Mark Edward, and James Kirby Martin. *Drinking in America: A History*. New York: Free Press, 1992.

Lenhoff, Arthur. "Development of the Concept of Eminent Domain." *Columbia Law Review* 42 (March 1942): 596–638.

"Letters of Francis Walker Gilmer to John Randolph." *Tyler's Quarterly Historical and Genealogical Magazine* 6 (January 1925): 190–91.

"Letters of Spencer Roane, 1788–1822." *Bulletin of the New York Public Library* 10 (March 1906): 167–80.

Levy, Leonard. *The Law of the Commonwealth and Chief Justice Shaw*. New York: Oxford University Press, 1957.

London, Lena. "The Initial Homestead Exemption in Texas." *Southwestern Historical Quarterly* 57 (April 1954): 432–53.

Lumpkin, Ben Gray, and Martha Neville Lumpkin, eds. *The Lumpkin Family of Virginia, Georgia, and Mississippi*. Clarksville, Tenn.: n.p., 1973.

"Lumpkin, Joseph Henry." In *Dictionary of American Biography*, 2:502–3. New York: Scribner's, 1964.

Lumpkin, Joseph Henry. *An Address Delivered before the South Carolina Institute at Its Second Annual Fair on 19th November, 1850*. Charleston, S.C.: Walker and James, 1851.

———. "Industrial Regeneration of the South." *DeBow's Review* 12 (1852): 41–50.

———. "Law Reform in Georgia—Judge Lumpkin's Report." *Western Law Journal* 2 (May 1850): 383–91.

Lumpkin, Wilson. *The Removal of the Cherokee Indians from Georgia, 1827–1841*. 2 vols. New York: Dodd, Mead, 1907.

Lynch, James D. *The Bench and Bar of Texas*. St. Louis, Mo.: Nixon-Jones, 1885.

Maddex, Jack. "Proslavery Millennialism: Social Eschatology in Antebellum Southern Calvinism." *American Quarterly* 31 (spring 1979): 46–62.

Maestro, Marcello. *Cesare Beccaria and the Origins of Penal Reform*. Philadelphia: Temple University Press, 1973.

Mahon, John K. *History of the Second Seminole War, 1835–1842*. Rev. ed. Gainesville: University Press of Florida, 1985.

Main, Jackson Turner. *The Anti-Federalists: Critics of the Constitution, 1781–1788*. New York: Norton, 1961.

Manley, Walter W., E. Canter Brown, and Eric W. Rise. *The Supreme Court of Florida and Its Predecessor Courts, 1821–1917*. Gainesville: University Press of Florida, 1997.

Marks, Albert T. "The Supreme Court of Tennessee." *Green Bag* 5 (1893): 120–28.

Mathews, Donald. "Charles Colcock Jones and the Southern Evangelical Crusade to Form a Biracial Community." *Journal of Southern History* 41 (August 1975): 299–320.

———. *Religion in the Old South*. Chicago: University of Chicago Press, 1977.

Mayer, David. *The Constitutional Thought of Thomas Jefferson.* Charlottesville: University of Virginia Press, 1994.

Mayhall, Mildred P. *Indian Wars of Texas.* Waco, Tex.: Texian Press, 1965.

Mays, David J. *Edmund Pendleton, 1721–1803: A Biography.* Cambridge: Harvard University Press, 1950.

———. "Judge Spencer Roane." *Virginia State Bar Association Proceedings* 40 (1928): 446–63.

McBride, David. "Mid-Atlantic State Courts and the Struggle with the 'Separate but Equal' Doctrine: 1880–1939." *Rutgers Law Journal* 17 (1986): 569–89.

McCash, William B. *Thomas R. R. Cobb: The Making of a Southern Nationalist.* Macon, Ga.: Mercer University Press, 1983.

McKnight, Joseph W. "A Century of Development in Texas Law." *Texas Bar Journal* 36 (November 1973): 1051–61.

———. "Law Books on the Hispanic Frontier." *Journal of the West* 27 (1988): 74–84.

———. "Mexican Roots of the Homestead Law." In *Estudios Jurídicos en Homenaje al Maestro Guillermo Floris Margadant,* 291–304. Mexico: Universidad Nacional Autónoma de México, 1988.

———. "Protection of the Family Home from Seizure by Creditors: The Sources and Evolution of a Legal Principle." *Southwestern Historical Quarterly* 86 (January 1983): 392–99.

———. "The Spanish Legacy to Texas Law." *American Journal of Legal History* 3 (1959): 222–41.

McMillan, Malcolm Cook. *Constitutional Development in Alabama, 1798–1901: A Study in Politics, the Negro, and Sectionalism.* Reprint, Spartanburg, S.C.: Reprint Company, 1978.

McPherson, James M. *Battle Cry of Freedom: The Civil War Era.* New York: Oxford University Press, 1988.

Meigs, William M. "The Relation of the Judiciary to the Constitution." *American Law Review* 19 (1885): 175–203.

Meltsner, Michael. "Southern Appellate Courts: A Dead End." In *Southern Justice,* ed. Leon Friedman, 136–54. New York: Pantheon, 1965.

Memorial Record of Alabama: A Concise Account of the State's Political, Military, Professional, and Industrial Progress, Together with the Personal Memoirs of Many of Its People. Madison, Wis.: Brant and Fuller, 1893.

Mensel, Robert E. "'Privilege against Public Right': A Reappraisal of the Charles River Bridge Case." *Duquesne Law Review* 33 (1994): 1–38.

Merchant, Alice. "The Historical Background of the Procedural Reform Movement in Alabama." *Alabama Law Review* 9 (spring 1957): 284–97.

Merriwether, Robert L., ed. *The Papers of John C. Calhoun, 1825–1829.* Columbia: University of South Carolina Press, 1959–86.

Middleton, Annie. "The Texas Convention of 1845." *Southwestern Historical Quarterly* 25 (July 1921): 26–60.

Miller, Frederick Thornton. "John Marshall v. Spencer Roane: A Reevaluation of *Martin v. Hunter's Lessee.*" *Virginia Magazine of History and Biography* 96 (July 1988): 297–314.

———. *Juries and Judges versus the Law: Virginia's Provincial Legal Perspective, 1783–1828.* Charlottesville: University Press of Virginia, 1994.

———. "The Richmond Junto: The Secret All-Powerful Club—or Myth." *Virginia Magazine of History and Biography* 99 (January 1991): 63–80.

"Missouri Compromise: Letters to James Barbour, Senator of Virginia in the Congress of the United States." *William and Mary Quarterly,* 1st ser., 10 (July 1901): 5–24.

Moore, Albert Burton. *Conscription and Conflict in the Confederacy.* New York: Macmillan, 1924.

———. *History of Alabama.* University, Ala.: University Supply Store, 1934.

Moore, Powell. "The Revolt against Jackson in Tennessee, 1835–1836." *Journal of Southern History* 2 (1936): 335–59.

Morgan, Edmund. *American Slavery, American Freedom: The Ordeal of Colonial Virginia.* New York: Norton, 1975.

Morgan, George. *The True Patrick Henry.* Philadelphia: J. B. Lippincott, 1907.

Morris, Sylvanus. "The Lumpkin Law School." *Georgia Law Review* 1 (1927): 3–7.

Morris, Thomas D. *Southern Slavery and the Law, 1619–1860.* Chapel Hill: University of North Carolina Press, 1996.

Morris, Thomas R. *The Virginia Supreme Court: An Institutional and Political Analysis.* Charlottesville: University Press of Virginia, 1975.

Muir, Andrew Forest. "John Hemphill, Miscegenist." Unpublished typescript.

Myers, John B. "The Freedman and the Law in Post-Bellum Alabama, 1865–1867." *Alabama Review* 23 (January 1970): 56–69.

Myers, Robert Manson, ed. *The Children of Pride: A True Story of Georgia and the Civil War.* New Haven: Yale University Press, 1972.

Nackman, Mark E. "The Making of the Texas Citizen-Soldier, 1835–1860." *Southwestern Historical Quarterly* 78 (January 1975): 231–53.

Nash, A. E. Keir. "Fairness and Formalism in the Trials of Blacks in the State Supreme Courts of the Old South." *Virginia Law Review* 56 (February 1970): 64–100.

———. "John Catron." In *The Supreme Court Justices: A Biographical Dictionary,* ed. Melvin I. Urofsky, 95–99. New York: Garland Publishing, 1994.

———. "A More Equitable Past? Southern Supreme Courts and the Protection of the Antebellum Negro." *North Carolina Law Review* 48 (February 1970): 197–242.

———. "Negro Rights, Unionism, and Greatness on the South Carolina Court of Appeals: The Extraordinary Chief Justice John Belton O'Neall." *South Carolina Law Review* 21 (1969): 141–90.

———. "Reason of Slavery: Understanding the Judicial Role in the Peculiar Institution." *Vanderbilt Law Review* 78 (January 1979): 7–218.

———. "The Texas Supreme Court and the Trial Rights of Blacks, 1845–1860." *Journal of American History* 58 (December 1971): 622–42.

Nelson, Margaret. *A Study of Judicial Review in Virginia, 1789–1828*. New York: AMS Press, 1967.

Nelson, William. "Changing Conceptions of Judicial Review: The Evolution of Constitutional Theory in the States, 1790–1860." *University of Pennsylvania Law Review* 120 (June 1972): 1166–85.

———. "The Impact of the Antislavery Movement upon Styles of Judicial Reasoning in Nineteenth Century America." *Harvard Law Review* 87 (1974): 513–66.

Newmyer, R. Kent. "John Marshall and the Southern Constitutional Tradition." In *An Uncertain Tradition: Constitutionalism and the History of the South*, ed. Kermit L. Hall and James W. Ely Jr., 105–24. Athens: University of Georgia Press, 1989.

———. *Supreme Court Justice Joseph Story: Statesman of the Old Republic*. Chapel Hill: University of North Carolina Press, 1985.

———. *The Supreme Court under Marshall and Taney*. Arlington Heights, Ill.: Harlan Davidson, 1968.

Nieman, Donald G. *Promises to Keep: African-Americans and the Constitutional Order*. New York: Oxford University Press, 1991.

Nolan, Dennis R. "Comment: Southern Violence—Regional Problem or National Nemesis? Legal Attitudes toward Southern Homicide in Historical Perspective." *Vanderbilt Law Review* 32 (January 1979): 251–59.

Norgren, Jill. *The Cherokee Cases: The Confrontation of Law and Politics*. New York: McGraw-Hill, 1996.

Northen, William J., ed. *Men of Mark in Georgia*. Spartanburg, S.C.: Reprint Company, 1974.

Novak, William J. *The People's Welfare: Law and Regulation in Nineteenth-Century America*. Chapel Hill: University of North Carolina Press, 1996.

O'Brien, Gail Williams. *The Legal Fraternity and the Making of a New South Community, 1848–1882*. Athens: University of Georgia Press, 1986.

Olken, Samuel R. "John Marshall and Spencer Roane: An Historical Analysis of Their Conflict over U.S. Supreme Court Appellate Jurisdiction." *Journal of Supreme Court History* (1990): 125–41.

Owen, Marie Bankhead. *The Story of Alabama: A History of the State*. 2 vols. New York: Lewis Historical Publishing, 1949.

Parton, James. *Life of Andrew Jackson*. New York: Mason Brothers, 1861.

Patterson, Caleb P. *The Constitutional Principles of Thomas Jefferson*. Austin: University of Texas Press, 1953.

———. *The Negro in Tennessee, 1790–1865*. New York: Negro Universities Press, 1968.

Paulsen, James. "A Short History of the Supreme Court of the Republic of Texas." *Texas Law Review* 65 (1986): 237–303.

———. "The Uncommon Law of Slavery in the Texas Supreme Court." Paper presented at the annual meeting of the Law and Society Association, Phoenix, Ariz., June 16, 1994.

Peterson, Thomas Virgil. *Ham and Japheth: The Mythic World of Whites in the Antebellum South.* Metuchen, N.J.: Scarecrow Press, 1978.

Phelan, James. *History of Tennessee: The Making of a State.* Boston: Houghton Mifflin, 1888.

Phelps, Dawson A., and John T. Willett. "Iron Works, on the Natchez Trace." *Tennessee Historical Quarterly* 12 (1953): 309–22.

Phillips, U. B., ed. *The Correspondence of Robert Toombs, Alexander H. Stephens, and Howell Cobb.* 2 vols. Washington, D.C.: American Historical Association, 1913.

Pierce, Edward L. *A Treatise on the Law of Railroads.* Boston: Little, Brown, 1881.

Potter, David M. "The Historian's Use of Nationalism and Vice Versa." In *The South and the Sectional Conflict,* 34–83. Baton Rouge: Louisiana State University Press, 1968.

———. *The Impending Crisis, 1848–1861.* New York: Harper and Row, 1976.

Pound, Roscoe. *The Formative Era of American Law.* Gloucester, Mass.: Peter Smith, 1938.

Powell, William S. *North Carolina through Four Centuries.* Chapel Hill: University of North Carolina Press, 1989.

Prather, William. "The Economic Effects of the Homestead Exemption Laws, with Special Reference to the Development of the Homestead and Exemption Laws in Texas." Master's thesis, University of Texas, 1903.

Pratt, Walter F., Jr. "The Struggle for Judicial Independence in Antebellum North Carolina: The Story of Two Judges." *Law and History Review* 4 (spring 1986): 129–59.

Priest, Josiah. *Slavery, as It Relates to the Negro, or African Race, Examined in the Light of Circumstances, History and the Holy Scriptures; with an Account of the Origin of the Black Man's Color, Cause of His State of Servitude and Traces of His Character in Ancient as in Modern Times.* Albany, N.Y.: C. Van Benthuysen, 1843.

Raboteau, Albert J. *Slave Religion.* New York: Oxford University Press, 1978.

Radabaugh, John. "Spencer Roane and the Genesis of Virginia Judicial Review." *American Journal of Legal History* 6 (1962): 63–70.

Raines, C. W. "Enduring Laws of the Republic of Texas." *Quarterly of the Texas State Historical Association* 1 (July 1897): 96–107.

Rawick, George P., ed. *The American Slave: A Composite Autobiography.* Vol. 13, *Georgia Narratives,* pts. 3–4. Westport, Conn.: Greenwood, 1971.

Redfield, H. V. *Homicide, North and South: Being a Comparative View of Crime against the Person in Several Parts of the United States.* Philadelphia: J. B. Lippincott, 1880.

Reid, John Phillip. *Chief Justice: The Judicial World of Charles Doe.* Cambridge: Harvard University Press, 1967.

———. "Lessons of Lumpkin: A Review of Recent Literature on Law, Comity, and the Impending Crisis." *William and Mary Law Review* 23 (summer 1982): 571–624.

The Remains of Maynard Davis Richardson, with a Memoir of His Life, by His Friend. Charleston, S.C.: O. A. Roorback, 1833.

Remini, Robert. *Andrew Jackson and the Bank War: A Study in the Growth of Presidential Power.* New York: Norton, 1967.

———. *The Election of Andrew Jackson.* Philadelphia: J. B. Lippincott, 1963.

———. *The Life of Andrew Jackson.* New York: Harper and Row, 1988.

Riley, B. F. *Makers and Romance of Alabama History.* N.p., 1915.

"Roane Correspondence." *John P. Branch Historical Papers* 2 (June 1905): 123–42.

"Roane Family." *William and Mary Quarterly,* 1st ser., 18 (January 1910): 194–200.

"Roane, Spencer." In *Dictionary of American Biography,* 7:417–18. New York: Scribner's, 1964.

Robinson, Blackwell Pierce. "Thomas Ruffin, 1787–1870." Unpublished manuscript in the North Carolina Collection, Wilson Library, University of North Carolina, Chapel Hill.

Robinson, William M., Jr. *Justice in Grey: A History of the Judicial System of the Confederate States of America.* Cambridge: Harvard University Press, 1941.

Rodabaugh, Karl L. "The Turbulent Nineties: The Agrarian Revolt and Alabama Politics, 1887–1901." Ph.D. diss., University of North Carolina—Chapel Hill, 1991.

Roeber, A. G. *Faithful Magistrates and Republican Lawyers: Creators of Virginia Legal Culture, 1680–1810.* Chapel Hill: University of North Carolina Press, 1981.

Rorabaugh, W. J. *The Alcoholic Republic: An American Tradition.* New York: Oxford University Press, 1979.

Ruffin, Edmund. *The Diary of Edmund Ruffin.* Baton Rouge: Louisiana State University Press, 1972.

Russell, James M., and Jerry Thornberry. "William Finch of Atlanta: The Black Politician as Civic Leader." In *Southern Black Leaders of the Reconstruction Era,* ed. Howard N. Rabinowitz, 309–34. Urbana: University of Illinois Press, 1982.

Russell, William Oldnall. *A Treatise on Crimes and Misdemeanors.* 9th American ed. Philadelphia: T. and J. W. Johnson, 1877.

Saye, Albert. *Constitutional History of Georgia, 1732–1945.* Athens: University of Georgia Press, 1948.

Schafer, Daniel L. "'A Class of People neither Freemen nor Slaves': From Spanish to American Race Relations in Florida, 1821–1861." *Journal of Social History* 26 (1993): 587–609.

Schauinger, Joseph Herman. "William Gaston and the Supreme Court of North Carolina." *North Carolina Historical Review* 21 (April 1944): 97–117.

Scheiber, Harry. "Instrumentalism and Property Rights: A Reconsideration of American 'Styles of Reasoning' in the Nineteenth Century." *Wisconsin Law Review* (1975): 1–18.

————. "The Road to *Munn:* Eminent Domain and the Concept of Public Purpose in the State Courts." *Perspectives in American History* 5 (1971): 329–402.

Schiller, Reuel E. "Conflicting Obligations: Slave Law and the Late Antebellum North Carolina Supreme Court." *Virginia Law Review* 78 (August 1992): 1207–51.

Schlesinger, Arthur. "The State Rights Fetish." In *New Viewpoints in American History,* ed. Arthur Schlesinger, 234–56. New York: Macmillan, 1925.

Schmidhauser, John R. "Judicial Behavior and the Sectional Crisis of 1837–1860." *Journal of Politics* 23 (November 1961): 615–40.

Schweniger, Loren. "A Slave Family in the Antebellum South." *Journal of Negro History* 60 (1975): 29–44.

————, ed. *From Tennessee Slave to St. Louis Entrepreneur: The Autobiography of James Thomas.* Columbia: University of Missouri Press, 1984.

Scomp, Henry A. *King Alcohol in the Realm of King Cotton: A History of the Liquor Traffic and of the Temperance Movement in Georgia from 1733–1887.* Chicago: Blakely Press, 1888.

Scott, Nancy N., ed. *A Memoir of Hugh Lawson White.* Philadelphia: J. B. Lippincott, 1856.

Sellers, Charles. *The Market Revolution: Jacksonian America, 1815–1846.* New York: Oxford University Press, 1991.

Sharkey, William. "An Essay on the Power to Proclaim and Enforce Martial Law." *Mississippi Valley Historical Review* 20 (1933): 75–90.

Shepard, E. Lee. "George Wythe." In *The Virginia Law Reporters before 1880,* ed. W. Hamilton Bryson, 90–95. Charlottesville: University Press of Virginia, 1977.

————. "Lawyers Look at Themselves: Professional Consciousness and the Virginia Bar, 1770–1850." *American Journal of Legal History* 25 (January 1981): 1–23.

Shepperson, George, ed. "Thomas Chalmers, the Free Church of Scotland, and the South." *Journal of Southern History* 17 (November 1951): 517–37.

Sherry, Suzanna. "The Early Virginia Tradition of Extratextual Interpretation." In *Toward a Usable Past: Liberty under State Constitutions,* ed. Paul Finkelman and Stephen E. Gottlieb, 157–88. Athens: University of Georgia Press, 1991.

Siegel, Stanley. *A Political History of the Texas Republic, 1836–1845.* Austin: University of Texas Press, 1956.

Silber, Nina. *The Romance of Reunion: Northerners and the South, 1865–1900.* Chapel Hill: University of North Carolina Press, 1993.

Sioussat, St. George Leakin. "Some Phases of Tennessee Politics in the Jackson Period." *American Historical Review* 14 (1908): 51–69.

————. "Tennessee and the Removal of the Cherokees." *Sewanee Review* 16 (1908): 337–44.

Slaughter, James B. *Settlers, Southerners, Americans: The History of Essex County, Virginia, 1608–1984.* Salem, W.Va.: Walsworth Press, 1985.

Smallwood, James. "Blacks in Antebellum Texas: A Reappraisal." *Red River Valley Historical Review* 2 (1975): 443–66.

Smiley, David L. "The Quest for a Central Theme in Southern History." *South Atlantic Quarterly* 7 (1972): 307–25.

Smith, Alan M. "Virginia Lawyers, 1680–1776: The Birth of an American Profession." Ph.D. diss., Johns Hopkins University, 1967.

Smith, Edwin J. "Spencer Roane." *John P. Branch Historical Papers* 2 (June 1905): 4–33.

Sowle, Patrick. "The North Carolina Manumission Society, 1816–1834." *North Carolina Historical Review* 42 (winter 1965): 47–69.

Sparks, Randy J. "Mississippi's Apostle of Slavery: James Smylie and the Biblical Defense of Slavery." *Journal of Mississippi History* 51 (May 1989): 89–106.

Starkie, Thomas. *A Practical Treatise on the Law of Evidence.* 9th American ed. Philadelphia: T. and J. W. Johnson, 1869.

Stephenson, Mason W., and D. Grier Stephenson Jr. "'To Protect and Defend': Joseph Henry Lumpkin, the Supreme Court of Georgia, and Slavery." *Emory Law Journal* 25 (summer 1976): 579–608.

Stewart, James B. *Holy Warriors: The Abolitionists and American Slavery.* New York: Hill and Wang, 1976.

"Stone, George Washington." *Dictionary of American Biography,* 9:74–75. New York: Scribner's, 1964.

Stone, George Washington. "Address by Chief Justice George Washington Stone." *Proceedings of the Annual Meeting of the Alabama State Bar Association* (1889): 108–21.

Story, Joseph. *Commentaries on the Conflict of Laws, Foreign and Domestic, in Regard to Contracts, Rights, and Remedies, and Especially in Regard to Marriages, Divorces, Wills, Successions, and Judgments.* 2d ed. Boston: Little, Brown, 1841.

Stowe, Harriet Beecher. *A Key to Uncle Tom's Cabin, Presenting the Original Facts and Documents upon Which the Story Is Founded, Together with Corroborative Statements Verifying the Truth of the Work.* Reprint, New York: Arno Press, 1968.

Stowe, Steven. *Intimacy and Power in the Old South: Ritual in the Lives of the Planters.* Baltimore: Johns Hopkins University Press, 1987.

Stubbs, Thomas McAlphin. "The Fourth Estate of Sumter, South Carolina." *South Carolina Historical Magazine* 54 (January 1953): 185–200.

Surrency, Erwin C. "Law Reports in the United States." *American Journal of Legal History* 25 (1981): 48–66.

Sutton, Robert P. "Nostalgia, Pessimism, and Malaise: The Doomed Aristocrat in Late-Jeffersonian Virginia." *Virginia Magazine of History and Biography* 76 (January 1968): 41–55.

Swisher, Carl B. *History of the Supreme Court of the United States: The Taney Period, 1836–1864.* New York: Macmillan, 1974.

Sydnor, Charles. "The Southerner and the Laws." *Journal of Southern History* 6 (February 1940): 3–23.

Taylor, Joe Gray. "The White South from Secession to Redemption." In *Interpret-

ing Southern History: Historiographical Essays in Honor of Sanford W. Higginbotham, ed. John B. Boles and Evelyn Thomas Nolen, 162–98. Baton Rouge: Louisiana State University Press, 1987.

Temple, Oliver P. *East Tennessee and the Civil War.* Cincinnati: R. Clarke, 1899.

Tennessee: The Volunteer State, 1769–1923. Vol. 2. Chicago: S. J. Clarke Publishing, 1923.

Thomas, J. H. "Homestead Exemption Laws of the Southern States." *American Law Register* 19 (1871): 1–17, 137–50.

Tighe, Janet A. "Francis Wharton and the Nineteenth Century Insanity Defense: The Origins of a Reform Tradition." *American Journal of Legal History* 27 (1983): 223–53.

Townes, John C. "Sketch of the Development of the Judicial System of Texas, I." *Texas State Historical Association Journal* 2 (July 1898): 29–53.

———. "Sketch of the Development of the Judicial System of Texas, II." *Texas State Historical Association Journal* 2 (October 1898): 134–51.

Trachtenberg, Alan. *The Incorporation of America: Culture and Society in the Gilded Age.* New York: Hill and Wang, 1982.

Trelease, Allen W. "The Passive Voice: The State and the North Carolina Railroad, 1849–1871." *North Carolina Historical Review* 61 (April 1984): 174–204.

Tucker, John Randolph. "St. George Tucker, LL.D." *Virginia State Bar Association Proceedings* 40 (1928): 465–73.

Tucker, St. George. *A Dissertation on Slavery with a Proposal for the Gradual Abolition of It, in the State of Virginia.* Philadelphia: M. Carey, 1796.

Turner, Herbert Snipes. *The Dreamer: Archibald DeBow Murphey, 1777–1832.* Verona, Va.: McClure Press, 1971.

Tushnet, Mark V. *The American Law of Slavery, 1810–1860: Considerations of Humanity and Interest.* Princeton: Princeton University Press, 1981.

Tyrrell, Ian. *Sobering Up: From Temperance to Prohibition in Antebellum America, 1800–1860.* Westport, Conn.: Greenwood, 1979.

U.S. Congress, *Biographical Directory of the American Congress, 1774–1961.* Washington, D.C.: U.S. Government Printing Office, 1961.

Van Deusen, Glyndon G. *The Jacksonian Era, 1828–1848.* New York: Harper, 1959.

Vandiver, Wellington. "Pioneer Talladega, Its Minutes and Memories." *Alabama Historical Quarterly* 16 (spring 1954): 61–117.

———. "Talladega County History." In *Sketches of Talladega County, Alabama: A Collection,* 116–343. Birmingham, Ala.: Birmingham Library Board, 1938.

Van Zant, Jennifer. "Confederate Conscription and the North Carolina Supreme Court." *North Carolina Historical Review* 72 (1995): 54–75.

Wahl, Jenny Bourne. "Legal Constraints on Slave Masters: The Problem of Social Cost." *American Journal of Legal History* 41 (1997): 1–24.

Walker, Arda S. "Andrew Jackson: Frontier Democrat." *East Tennessee Historical Society Publications* 18 (1946): 78–79.

Walker, David. *David Walker's Appeal, in Four Articles, Together with a Preamble, to the Coloured Citizens of the World, but in Particular, and Very Expressly, to Those of the United States of America*. New York: Hill and Wang, 1965.

Wallenstein, Peter. "Race, Marriage, and the Law of Freedom: Alabama and Virginia, 1860s–1960s." *Chicago-Kent Law Review* 70 (1994): 371–437.

Warren, Charles. *A History of the American Bar*. Boston: Little, Brown, 1913.

———. *The Supreme Court in United States History*. Rev. ed. 2 vols. Boston: Little, Brown, 1922.

Watson, Alan D. "North Carolina and Internal Improvements, 1783–1861: The Case of Inland Navigation." *North Carolina Historical Review* 74 (1997): 38–73.

Watson, Harry L. *Liberty and Power: The Politics of Jacksonian America*. New York: Oxford University Press, 1990.

———. "Squire Oldway and His Friends: Opposition to Internal Improvements in Antebellum North Carolina." *North Carolina Historical Review* 54 (April 1977): 105–19.

Weaver, Herbert, and Wayne Cutler, eds. *Correspondence of James K. Polk*. Vols. 4–5. Nashville, Tenn.: Vanderbilt University Press, 1977–79.

Weaver, Herbert, and Kermit Hall, eds. *Correspondence of James K. Polk*. Vol. 3. Nashville, Tenn.: Vanderbilt University Press, 1975.

Wharton, Clarence. "Early Judicial History of Texas." *Texas Law Review* 12 (April 1934): 311–25.

Wharton, Francis. *A Treatise on Criminal Law*. 8th ed. Philadelphia: Kay and Brother, 1880.

———. *A Treatise on the Law of Homicide in the United States*. Philadelphia: Kay and Brother, 1855.

White, G. Edward. *The American Judicial Tradition: Profiles of Leading American Judges*. New York: Oxford University Press, 1988.

———. *The Marshall Court and Cultural Change, 1815–1835*. New York: Macmillan, 1988.

White, Robert H., ed. *Messages of the Governors of Tennessee, 1821–1835*. Vols. 2–3. Nashville: Tennessee Historical Commission, 1952–54.

Wiebe, Robert. *The Search for Order, 1877–1920*. New York: Hill and Wang, 1967.

Wiecek, William M. "'Old Times There Are Not Forgotten': The Distinctiveness of the Southern Constitutional Experience." In *An Uncertain Tradition: Constitutionalism and the History of the South*, ed. Kermit L. Hall and James W. Ely Jr., 159–97. Athens: University of Georgia Press, 1989.

———. *The Sources of Antislavery Constitutionalism in America, 1760–1848*. Ithaca: Cornell University Press, 1977.

Wiethoff, William. *A Peculiar Humanism: The Judicial Advocacy of Slavery in High Courts of Old South, 1820–1850*. Athens: University of Georgia Press, 1996.

Williams, Charles Richard, ed. *Diary and Letters of Rutherford Birchard Hayes, Nineteenth President of the United States*. Columbus: Ohio State Archaeological and Historical Society, 1922.

Williams, Frank B., Jr. "Samuel Hervey Laughlin, Polk's Political Handyman." *Tennessee Historical Quarterly* 24 (1965): 356–77.

Williams, Jack K. "Crime and Punishment in Alabama, 1819–1840." *Alabama Review* 6 (January 1953): 14–30.

Williams, Samuel C. *Phases of the History of the Supreme Court of Tennessee.* Johnson City, Tenn.: Watauga Press, 1944.

Winkler, Ernest William, ed. *Journal of the Secession Convention of Texas, 1861.* Austin, Tex.: Austin Printing, 1912.

Wood, H. G. *A Treatise on the Law of Railroads.* Boston: Charles C. Soule, 1885.

Woodward, C. Vann. *Origins of the New South.* Baton Rouge: Louisiana State University Press, 1951.

———. *The Strange Career of Jim Crow.* 3d rev. ed. New York: Oxford University Press, 1974.

Wren, John Thomas. "Republican Jurisprudence: Virginia Law and the New Order, 1776–1830." Ph.D. diss., College of William and Mary, 1988.

Wyatt-Brown, Bertram. *Lewis Tappan and the Evangelical War against Slavery.* Cleveland: Case Western Reserve University Press, 1969.

———. "Religion and the 'Civilizing Process' in the Early American South, 1800–1860." In *Religion and American Politics: From the Colonial Era to the 1980s,* ed. Mark Noll, 172–95. New York: Oxford University Press, 1990.

———. *Southern Honor: Ethics and Behavior in the Old South.* New York: Oxford University Press, 1982.

Yanuck, Julius. "Thomas Ruffin and North Carolina Slave Law." *Journal of Southern History* 21 (November 1955): 456–75.